T0337394

Growth and Human Development
in North-East India

Growth and Human Development in North-East India

Edited by

P. NAYAK

OXFORD
UNIVERSITY PRESS

OXFORD
UNIVERSITY PRESS

Oxford University Press is a department of the University of Oxford.
It furthers the University's objective of excellence in research, scholarship,
and education by publishing worldwide. Oxford is a registered trademark of
Oxford University Press in the UK and in certain other countries

Published in India by
Oxford University Press
2/11 Ground Floor, Ansari Road, Daryaganj, New Delhi 110 002, India

ISBN-13: 978-0-19-806363-6
ISBN-10: 0-19-806363-6

Typeset in ITC Legacy Serif Std 10/12.6
by Sai Graphic Design, New Delhi 110 055
Printed in India by Replika Press Pvt. Ltd

Contents

Tables

Figures

Acknowledgements

This book would not have been possible without the encouragement and support of many individuals and institutions. I, along with the contributors of the volume, owe a debt of gratitude to the Ministry of Tribal Affairs, Government of India; Indian Council of Social Science Research, New Delhi and Shillong; and the North-Eastern Hill University (NEHU), Shillong, for providing all sorts of help and logistical support to carry out this work. I would like to express my sincere appreciation and thanks to the authors of each chapter and to colleagues, administrative staff, and students of the Department of Economics, NEHU, for their keen interest and sustained support. I am deeply grateful to the anonymous referee(s) who made valuable comments and suggestions for improving the book. I am thankful to Professor Sudhanshu K. Mishra for taking special interest in the book, for going through the preface and suggesting necessary changes. Professor Arindam Banik, International Management Institute, New Delhi, deserves special thanks for his encouragement and cooperation. Thanks are also due to the Academic Publishing team at Oxford University Press, New Delhi, for their all-round cooperation and help, and for their excellent work. I am most deeply indebted to my wife Sanghamitra, son Swadesh, and daughter Swati for their encouragement, help, and sacrifice. Last but not the least, all those who were directly or indirectly involved in carrying out the work deserve special thanks.

Preface

It took centuries to realize that people are the real wealth of a nation. They produce goods and services for their own welfare. The development and growth of a nation depends upon the proper utilization of natural and cultural endowments available to it. To utilize these endowments, human participation is required. Human participation, on a sustained and autonomous basis, cannot be expected without enhancement in the capability of the population. Thus, self-sustained growth cannot be ensured without human development. Further, since the basic objective of development of a nation is to improve the well-being of the people, every nation strives hard, not only to increase her wealth and productive resources, but also to ensure a better standard of living for its citizens by providing them with adequate food, clothing, housing, medical facilities, education, etc. In fact, governments of various nations, at different levels, take the initiative to create an enabling environment for their people to enjoy healthy, long, and creative lives. However, technical considerations of the means to achieve human development and the use of statistical aggregates to measure national income and its growth have, at times, obscured the fact that the primary objective of development is to benefit the people. Of course, people want higher incomes as one of their options, but income is not the aggregate of human life and, hence, not an end in itself.

The human development approach of looking at development differs from conventional approaches to economic growth, human capital formation, human resource development, human welfare, and basic human needs. Gross National Product (GNP) growth is treated as being necessary but not sufficient for human development. Human progress may be lacking in some societies despite rapid GNP growth unless some additional steps are undertaken to improve the same. Human welfare approaches look at human beings more as beneficiaries of development processes than as participants in it. They emphasize only the distributive policies rather than production structures. Recent development experience has once again underlined the need for paying close attention to the link between economic growth and human development for a variety of reasons. Many fast-growing developing countries are discovering that their high GNP growth rates have failed to reduce the socio-economic deprivation of substantial sections of their population. Even industrial nations are realizing that high income is no protection against the rapid spread of such problems as drugs, alcoholism, AIDS, homelessness, violence, and the breakdown of family relations. At the same time, some low-income countries have demonstrated that it is possible to achieve high levels of human development if they skillfully use available means to expand basic human capabilities.

Human development also encompasses elements that constitute the critical issues of gender and development. There are four major elements in the concept of human development—productivity, equity, sustainability, and empowerment. People must be enabled to increase their productivity and to participate fully in the process of income generation and remunerative employment to achieve higher economic growth, which is a subset of human development models. Productivity is not the only means to achieve welfare in a society. People must have access to equal opportunities. All barriers to economic and political opportunities must be eliminated so that people can participate in and benefit from these opportunities. These benefits also need to be distributed over generations. Access to opportunities must be ensured, not only for the present generation but for future generations as well. All forms of capital such as physical, human, and environmental should be replenished. Besides, empowerment is a necessity. People must participate fully in the decision-making process that can shape their lives. Human development is impossible without gender equality. As long as women are excluded from the development process, development will remain weak and lopsided (UNDP 1995).

Development should increase peoples' choices. While enhancing the choices of one individual or a section of a society, it should not restrict the choices of another. It calls for equity in human relationships. It should not mortgage the choices of future generations while improving the lives of the present generation (UNDP 1991). In other words, the development process must be sustainable.

Literature in this regard is vast and varied. It reveals that a large number of studies have been undertaken in India and abroad on various aspects of human development. While some literature dealt with concepts of human development, some have dealt with methods of measurement, construction of Human Development Index (HDI) for various states and sub-states, and for different sections of society. There have been numerous efforts over time to remedy the defects of traditional measures of development, and to create composite indicators that could serve either as complements or alternatives to this. There are studies relating to debates on the selection of variables to be included in HDI and weights to be assigned to different variables under consideration. While some studies dealt with disparities in human development between rural and urban areas and between males and females, some others concentrated on trends of human development. There are some studies that concentrated on finding the two-way relation between human development and economic growth of nations. Available evidence reveals interesting insights relating to the impact of economic growth on human development, and vice versa, with different time lags. Some scholars have also tried to examine the link between poverty and human development. The factors responsible for low levels of human development are also identified in some studies. While some authors prescribed increased allocation of resources on social sectors for improving human development, some others put emphasis on the aspects of implementation of programmes relating to social sector development. There are some authors who believe that high growth could lead to high human development, while some others opine for achieving high growth through the achievement of high human development. There are also some studies that argue in favour of a balanced path of development that combines the strategies of growth and human development with appropriate weights.

Since 1990, United Nations Development Programme (UNDP) has been publishing *Human Development Reports* (*HDRs*) at the global level for various nations and every year a report is published to this effect with emphasis on a different theme. The Planning Commission of India has also undertaken a similar exercise and has published the *National Human Development Report* (*NHDR*) for the years 1981, 1991, and 2001. The reports for the years 1981 and 1991 include data on HDI for all the states and union territories of India. But in the 2001 report, the index has been constructed only for fifteen major states due to non-availability of required data for smaller states, including the states in the North-East.

If we take a look at the *NHDR 2002*, we get some idea on the status of human development in the North-East, though data is somewhat dated. The report reveals that the region comprising the eight states of Arunachal Pradesh, Assam, Manipur, Meghalaya, Mizoram, Nagaland, Sikkim (the last to be included in the region), and Tripura constitutes a land surface of 262,230 square kilometers with a population of 38.9 million belonging to different ethnic and cultural groups. Topographically, the region is a mixture of hills and plains. While Arunachal Pradesh, Meghalaya, Mizoram, Nagaland, and Sikkim are almost entirely hilly, about four-fifths of Assam is plains. Manipur and Tripura have both plains and hilly tracts. The hills account for about 70 per cent of the area and accommodate about 30 per cent of the population of the region while the plains, constituting the remaining 30 per cent area, hold about 70 per cent of its population. A wide variation in altitude coupled with abundance of rainfall has given rise to a wide variation in climatic conditions within the region, which in turn has endowed the region with rich biodiversity. The richness of biodiversity of the region is almost matched by its ethnic diversity. The region is a meeting place of large number of races, creeds, cultures, and languages. The impingement of the diversity of physical and cultural environment is naturally found in the organization of economic life of the people of the region.

Keeping all this in view, it was thought to bring out a volume on growth and human development for the region by inviting papers from academicians from within and outside the region. The present book is an outcome towards achieving that end. While every effort has been made to bring analysis and discussion on the issues of human development, touching upon various states in the region, the study is constrained due to non-inclusion of the newly included state, Sikkim. It must be borne in mind that although Sikkim has been included in the north-eastern region for administrative and developmental considerations, it is geographically non-contiguous to the rest of the states in the region. Its cultural background is much different from the other states. This sociological, cultural, and geographical difference gives a different character to Sikkim.

The book has been broadly divided into three sections on three different themes:

1. Concept and measurement issues;
2. The national scenario; and
3. The issues at the level of the north-eastern region.

The first section deals with the concept and measurement, and has three chapters. The first chapter titled 'Human Development: Concept and Measurement' contributed by the editor discusses in detail not only the evolution of the concept of human development but also its measurement. The author provides an account of change in the methods of measurement of human development proposed by UNDP, the Government of India, and individual academics.

The second chapter 'Concept of Human Development: A Critique' contributed by P.K. Chaubey, critically examines the literature on the concept of human development and its measurement. He points out that the motivation for UNDP, under the advice of Mahbub-ul-Haq, to bring out a report on human outcomes of economic, social, development, and welfare activities in the public, private, and other spheres in different countries emanated from the fact that wide failures were noticed in terms of reduction in poverty and infant mortality, enhancement in longevity, education, improvement in health, and the like. Contributions from economists like Amartya Sen, on capability approach as against the commodity approach, provided the right kind of theoretical support to define 'human development' in terms of enlarging people's choice through enhancement of capabilities. However, everything is not hunky dory with the idea of human development as it is too individualistic in approach, and shorn of communitarian ethos. Again, when it comes to measuring human development, it is not in terms of capabilities but in terms of attainment and performance, which is possible only when capability space interacts with commodity space. The author, in this connection, tries to delineate the history of evolution of the idea of human development and its contribution in shifting the focus of the development debate, and the weakness it inheres.

The third chapter 'Construction of an Index: A New Method' has been contributed by Sudhanshu K. Mishra. In this paper the author argues that composite indices are often constructed by a linear combination or weighted sum of indicator variables. While constructing indices, weights are either subjectively determined on the basis of expert opinion, or mathematically determined by the Principal

Components Analysis (PCA). By its very logic, such composite indices are elitist—assigning large weights to highly correlated variables and negligible weights to poorly correlated variables. The author proposes to construct a composite index by maximizing the sum of absolute correlation between the composite index and the indicator variables. In the first part of this chapter, the author shows that such a composite index is inclusive—duly weighting the poorly correlated variables. Thus, composite index does not undermine the importance of an indicator variable merely because it is not well correlated with others. In the later part of the paper, the author, by adopting the proposed method, has constructed HDI with equality in income distribution for 125 countries. The study reveals that while the traditional PCA assigns poor weight to the measure of income inequality, the proposed method ameliorates its position by assigning reasonable weight to it.

The second section of the book which deals with growth, human development, and other related issues at the all India level, has seven chapters. In this section, Saundarjya Borbora in the chapter titled 'Economic Growth and Human Development: Chain Relationship' discusses the relationship between economic growth and human development, and opines that they reinforce each other. He argues that development of social sectors, such as education, health, and good governance, is a major precondition for achieving economic growth with the help of effective government policy and appropriate public expenditure. This in turn would help the states to move above the threshold level in human development. He also admits that it is necessary to identify the weak links between growth and human development, and that appropriate policies are required to be formulated and implemented to strengthen the links; and that such policies must be dynamic in nature with changes in the development process. He suggests that in the early stages, priorities might be given to education and health, and at a later stage higher education, technology, and better health facilities might assume a greater role. He concludes by reiterating that the view of *grow first and worry about human development later* is not supported by evidence and, hence, focus on human development must be targeted at the beginning of the growth process.

Santanu Ray, in his chapter 'Transformation of Economic Growth to Human Development: A Long-Run Study of Indian States' states that the role of income growth in determining the level of human well-being has become a topical issue in recent literature. Indian performance in this regard has been far from satisfactory. Using disaggregated data for the country over a long period of time, Ray examines the relationship between growth and human development. He also addresses the question whether the economic growth achieved by Indian states in the last three decades has any significant influence in determining the level of human development. Using the latest formulation of UNDP, he not only computes HDI for each of the major states of India, but also makes an analysis of HDI over time and across states. His study reveals that per capita income levels of Indian states play a positive role in determining the non-income component of human development in the long-run. He expresses his concern over huge regional variation in income levels and disparity in human development indicators across states.

The chapter titled 'Effect of Structural and Conditional Rigidities: A Case Study of a Poverty Reduction Programme' has been contributed jointly by Arindam Banik and Pradip K. Bhaumik. In their paper, the authors are very critical about the previous studies conducted on poverty reduction programmes, most of which concentrated on evaluation of the effectiveness of government interventions in meeting the stated programme objectives and targets, gaps between desired and actual targeting of beneficiaries, and adherence to programme guidelines. In their paper the authors have made an attempt to analyse the effect of structural and conditional rigidities, on moving a beneficiary of poverty reduction programme from passive to active state, with the help of micro-level field data comprising a fairly large sample of poor beneficiary artisans collected under SITRA programme. Using ordered logistic analysis, they have provided an analytical characterization of the beneficiaries in a situation of structural and conditional rigidity, where all beneficiaries do not move from a passive state to an active state and are able to take advantage of the government intervention despite their having access to the benefit. The authors view that identification of ageing artisans as beneficiaries of the programme might not bear much fruit as they are unlikely to become economically active due to their conditional rigidities. Therefore, they opine that a thorough understanding of the conditional and structural rigidities and their impact on economic behaviour of beneficiary artisans is required, which perhaps would go a long way in helping to design and implement poverty reduction programmes.

The chapter titled 'Public Distribution System: An Instrument for Improving Human Development' has been contributed by R. Gopinath. The author states that the PDS is a major component of public delivery system in India that started functioning during the 1930s and, subsequently, was replaced by the Targeted Public Distribution System (TPDS) in the 1990s. The programmes were mainly designed to play an important role in improving human development, particularly among the rural masses and the poor people. The paper revolves around the discussion on the loopholes in operational mechanism of both PDS and TPDS, and strongly argues for addressing the problems associated with their implementation.

Taking a careful look at the HDI estimates for the various districts in Orissa, P.K. Tripathy and Bhabagrahi Mishra, in the chapter 'Status of Human Development in Orissa', make a few intriguing observations. They point out that the districts of Kalahandi and Deogarh, two of the least developed districts by conventional yardsticks, turn out to be ranked as high HDI districts in the *HDR* of Orissa. Keeping this paradoxical result in mind, they raise some important questions on the suitability of the concept of HDI while assessing the economic status of a region. They observe that the implication of high literacy in developed economies is not the same as that in backward economies. In backward economies, mere literacy without employment opportunities neither turns out meaningful educational attainment nor estimated higher life expectancy, and that lower infant mortality reflects sound health conditions of the majority of the population in general, and agricultural labourers, marginal and small farmers, and poor artisans, in particular. In the light of the above observations, they argue that there is a need for inclusion of alternative variables for health, education, and standard of living in the index that can lead to a more realistic ranking of a region based on such indices. For example, a composite index of property ownership (land and other resources), per capita income obtained on the basis of income accrual method, and the average man days employed for the working population shall capture the standard of living index more accurately than mere per capita income. Similarly, education index could be a composite index of literacy as well as its linkage with employment opportunities and the health index as a composite index of anthropometric measurements and pattern of mortality.

The chapter 'Good Governance: The Force behind Human Development', contributed jointly by Ashutosh Dash and Paohulen

Kipgen, reveals that human development cannot just automatically happen without economic development. The authors argue that growth oriented economic progress alone cannot bring progressive human development without good governance which demands greater transparency. That is why social activists are increasingly paying attention to governance, both at the macro and micro level. The authors conclude by laying stress on the importance of governance in the process of human development.

The last chapter in the section, titled 'Politics of Human Development', has been contributed by Apurba K. Baruah. The author brings out the politics involved in the issues concerning human development. Citing the example of poverty, he explains that in Contemporary Development Theory, poverty has been basically reduced to an issue of measurement, and the important issue of the mechanism of its generation is often overlooked. He also pleads that the economic efficiency is in its top gear only when the state takes control. Whether the state controls or leaves the market in private hands is a matter of politics to which the nature of human development is inalienably connected.

The third section deals with the issues of human development in the context of North-East India and has fifteen chapters. M.P. Bezbaruah, in his chapter 'Socio-political Transition, Growth Trends, and Development Attainment in the North-East in the Post-Independence Period', reviews the development experience of the region in the context of its political–administrative transformation in the post-Independence period. He points out that development experience in the region has been mixed and uneven. While there are periods of high growth for individual states, the region as a whole has been increasingly lagging behind the country in terms of per capita income. He believes that the rapid post-liberalization growth of the country is a far cry for the region. While the recent service sector led growth of the country is propelled by expansion of frontier areas like information technology, pubic administration and other services are the faster growing services in the region. He argues for enhancement of the rate of economic growth in the region based on its inherent strength and endowed resource base. Though funds required for building up the necessary infrastructure to activate the inherent growth potential of the region are no longer a constraint, disruptions caused by insurgency and the *bundh* culture make deployment of such investments difficult and add to the cost of any business venture, reducing the competitiveness and economic viability. However, he is optimistic about the future of the region in the globalized era.

The editor of the book, in the chapter titled 'Human Development in North-East India' highlights that India, in spite of pursuing the policy of liberalization and globalization since the early eighties and witnessing higher growth rates, has not been able to achieve much on account of human development and welfare in comparison to many countries at the global level. Human Development Index in the country was as low as 0.56 in 2001. While some states in the region have performed better than the national level, some others have lagged behind. Rural–urban disparity, gender disparity, and uneven human development across the states in the region are quite significant. The disturbing trend of increasing gender disparity in Nagaland and the escalating rural–urban gap, particularly in the states of Assam and Meghalaya, is a matter of concern. The author, while highlighting some of these issues, stresses on the urgent need for taking appropriate action in this regard.

Nirankar Srivastav analyses the poverty status in the region using three conventional measures of poverty in the chapter titled 'Severity of Poverty and Status of Public Services in North-Eastern States'. His study reveals that poverty, in most of the states in the region, has declined. It has declined more in the hill states and in urban areas. The access to public services is observed to be very poor in the poverty-stricken states. The author states that there is a positive and strong relationship between poverty levels and access to public services in the region and recommends a target-oriented and region-specific poverty reduction programme.

Bhagirathi Panda, in the chapter 'Economic Growth, Exclusion, and Human Development', studies the mismatch between economic growth and human development in the region using empirical data. He observes and apprehends that the region, which is witnessing continuous low economic growth accompanied by relatively high human development, is susceptible to social tension. This has to be overcome by promoting a policy of high economic growth by taking some concrete measures. He prescribes accelerating industrialization and putting emphasis on greater value addition. The author also identifies some of the obstacles to indus-trialization, such as poor physical infrastructure, lack of culture of genuine entrepreneurship, security deficit, and poor governance. He suggests that in order to overcome these hurdles the governments in the region should play a proactive role along with developmental Non-Governmental Organizations (NGOs) and promote Self Help Groups (SHGs), their movement, and effective participation in development programmes. He also emphasizes the role of civil society, academia, and peer groups towards reorientation in the value-systems for inculcating a culture of entrepreneurship.

Biswambhar Panda, in the chapter 'Non-Governmental Organizations and Participatory Development' analyses the approaches of the grassroot NGOs and their role in contributing towards participatory development in addressing issues relating to human development, with special reference to the North-East. The author argues that participatory development can ensure integrated development, where all sections of society would be involved and benefited. This would not only bring about economic growth but would also dissipate social inequality. The micro approaches along with people-centred development objectives can bring considerable dividend by resolving conflicts, avoiding programme uncertainties, and evolving synergy among the key actors of society. He further argues that though participatory development may not ensure development for all the people but it certainly creates confidence among them, and most importantly provides them opportunities to share their ideas and knowledge. He believes that a development plan, armed with indigenous practices and native wisdom, can accelerate the developmental process at the grassroots level. Though NGOs are not the only force within the civil society to work towards inclusive growth, they are certainly a force to reckon with in the development domain. They can inch towards this objective through (various) people-centred approaches and strategies despite so much of apprehensions on their accountability and sustainability.

The chapter 'Inter-District Disparities in Meghalaya: A Human Development Approach' contributed jointly by Purusottam Nayak and Santanu Ray highlights widespread variations in the magnitude of human development across all the seven districts and three hills regions representing three different ethnic tribal groups in the state, between rural and urban areas, and between male and female groups of population. The authors also show that there exists a significant level of disparity, both in income consumption and in non-income attainments, among these districts. The inequality in economic attainment (income, as well as consumption expenditure) happens to be very high. However, both measures of variation and inequality indices suggest that few non-income indicators, namely intensity of formal education and infant mortality rates, have disparities over economic indicators, which, according to the authors, are indeed a cause of considerable concern. In addition, they observe that economic inequality is much higher than inequality in overall HDI. Keeping in view a huge shortfall in HDI, accompanied by the existing level of variation and disabilities, the authors feel the need for a redesign of public policies that directly affect the welfare of the people. The study also reveals that the improvement of human development in Meghalaya, on account of better performance in respect of some socio-economic indicators, has been neutralized because of its laggardness in respect of some other indicators over time.

The next chapter titled 'Does Micro Finance Bring Human Development?' contributed by A.P. Pati, explains the success stories of micro-finance through SHGs in different parts of the country and abroad. The author suggests ways for economic empowerment of women through micro finance in the region. However, he concludes by stating that micro finance endeavour in Meghalaya is still at the nascent stage to make any visible impact at the macro level, so as to measure its contribution in attaining higher human development.

P.S. Suresh and Biswambhara Mishra, in their chapter 'Public Expenditure and Human Development in North-East India: A Case Study of Meghalaya', point out that Meghalaya, in the last few decades, has been witnessing a paradoxical and explosive economic growth because of the mismatch between growth rates of state domestic product and public expenditure. Disproportionate growth of the social sector over the years has not only eaten up most of the public investment in the state, but also given rise to a weaker linkage among different sectors. The study explores the nature, extent, and the degree of interdependence between the level of public expenditure and human development with the aim of understanding the cause and effect relationship and the extent to which the public expenditure on social services gets transformed to the end result of a better level of human development. The study reveals that at the regional level there is a positive functional relationship between public expenditure on social sectors and human development. The authors conclude that per capita spending on education and health has a relatively stronger impact on human development than per capita income growth.

Kishor Singh Rajput in the chapter 'Antenatal Care, Institutional Delivery, and Human Development in Meghalaya' highlights some of the facts and figures on mothers' health with special reference to institutional deliveries of the child. Further, using logistic regression, he examines the role of certain background variables of women like her education and the spouse, work status, place of residence, etc., along with the role of antenatal care on institutional delivery.

E. Bijoykumar Singh in 'Human Development in Manipur' states that in spite of having a low per capita income, the HDI of Manipur for 1981 and 1991 has been higher than most of the major Indian states. In his chapter, he makes an attempt to examine the change in HDI for the state in the post (economic) reform period with available indicators of development like Infant Mortality Rate (IMR), sex ratio, life expectancy at birth, and literacy rate. He also examines the quality of development through an analysis of data on structural change, occupational distribution of work force, employment, and productivity of workers. He argues that though performance of Manipur in terms of IMR, sex ratio, literacy rate, and life expectancy at birth has been positive, low per capita income and continued dominance of low productivity activities in the occupational structure has weakened the link between employment creation and poverty reduction.

A.K. Agarwal in the chapter 'Human Development in Mizoram: An Overview' not only analyses the status of human development in Mizoram, its strengths and weaknesses, but also suggests a strategy for improvement. Through empirical analysis he claims that Mizoram has shown excellent performance not only in the field of education and health but also on Gross State Domestic Product (GSDP) in which the tertiary sector has been playing a dominant role. He also states that one might not notice the relative inadequacy of the state in terms of HDI, Human Poverty Index (HPI), and gender disparity as compared to other states in the region and the country as a whole, but in-depth analysis points towards the need for better services and for evolving an appropriate delivery mechanism with close interaction of various components of human development in the state.

The chapter 'Facets and Factors of Human Development in Tripura', contributed jointly by Sudhanshu K. Mishra and Purusottam Nayak, synoptically presents an account of different facets and factors relating to human development in Tripura which suffered a brutal blow during partition of the country in the form of maimed infrastructure, severed connectivity, and a debilitating burden of immigrants, with all the needs and no resources. They have also systematically presented the geographical and historical forces that have shaped the resource base, infrastructure, connectivity, socio-economic milieu, and, consequently, the economy of the state, determining the level of human development. Their study reveals that in spite of a great population burden on her fragile economy, the state has secured an appreciable score in matters of education and health. The authors opine that human development of the state needs to be harnessed to promote economic growth in terms of increased productivity and higher per capita income.

The next chapter, 'Human Development in Assam: An Analysis', is jointly contributed by Hiranmoy Roy and Kingshuk Adhikari. The authors report that the state is lagging far behind other major Indian states in terms of various socio-economic indicators, including the measures of HDI, HPI, and poverty. Their findings also reveal an inverse relationship between human development and poverty on the one hand, and widespread variation of human development across districts, on the other.

Debasis Neogi, in 'Development and Deprivations in Arunachal Pradesh', highlights the extent of development and deprivations in the state of Arunachal Pradesh. While presenting his findings, he states that while some parts of the state are well ahead in terms of socio-economic development, the other parts are lagging behind. He opines that uneven development, across districts and among tribal groups, has given rise to inter-tribe disputes. The large chunk of Net State Domestic Product (NSDP) in the state is observed to be contributed by the tertiary sector, of which public administration constitutes the major component. This type of development trend, as observed by the author, seems to be untenable in the long run. The author also analyses the role of basic education in bringing empowerment to the society and explains how such capacity building can lead to redressal of deprivation of human beings. Besides, he investigates the aspect of gender discrimination and prescribes mass education in order to remove such discrimination from the society.

The last chapter of the book, 'Human Development and its Correlates in Nagaland', has been contributed by Sudhanshu K. Mishra and Purusottam Nayak. The authors have presented a large amount of data relating to human development in Nagaland, and made an attempt to observe regularities in the same that may be meaningful for devising development policies. Their findings indicate that PCI, HDI, and gender-related development index are poorly correlated with health indicators, but appreciably correlate with educational attainment. The authors conclude that the reliability of data reported by a socio-economic system is dependent on the level of development of the system. Underdeveloped socio-economic systems report highly unreliable data. This is not only regarding the figures of income but also the measures of attainment in matters of health and education. Official data on these variables is thrown up by a system that is administratively motivated and unsupervised with regard to their economic and developmental meaning. Use of such data, whether it pertains to income or any other measure of development, is not dependable for policy decisions meaningful to fostering development.

An overall analysis of various issues discussed in the present volume reveal the following:

1. There is a need to rethink, not only the choice of variables but also the method of construction of HDI. The proposed alternative method, by maximizing the sum of absolute correlation between the composite index and the indicator variables, might be of some use while overcoming the problems associated with construction of composite indices by PCA.

2. In the recent past, the entire region has been experiencing good human development but poor economic growth. There exist widespread variations in the levels of human development across states, regions (rural–urban), among ethnic and other social groups, and between genders. This mismatch probably has given rise to increased disputes among various social groups and tribal populations leading to social tensions reflected in the form of extortions and other secessionist activities. To overcome this, a determined effort is required to harness human development towards achievement of higher economic growth through increased productivity. There is also a need for specific intervention strategies on the basis of sector/group/class/gender/region/ state.

3. Human development is positively associated with the quality of governance. Governance, from the human development perspective, demands greater transparency, accountability, participation, and stringent rules and laws. Judged on these parameters, the quality of governance in the region is not satisfactory and, hence, requires improvement. Besides, local democratic institutions like Autonomous District Councils need to be strengthened and their functioning be made more effective.

4. Revolution of SHGs has not made much headway in the region. SHG as a movement and institution ensures, at the micro level, both economic growth and human development. Further, both these objectives are realized through the method of participation, especially of the poor and the marginalized. There is a need to make this movement more widespread in the region.

5. Besides increased inequality, the quality of public services on the basis of access, use, reliability, and satisfaction are worst in the poverty stricken states in the region. To overcome this, the extremely poor households need up-front intervention through measures such as TPDS.

6. Reproductive health care happens to be an important component of human development. The goal to attain satisfactory human development will remain unfulfilled if the reproductive health needs of married women and children are not properly attended. The situation of reproductive health care in some states of the region is worse than many other in the country. Therefore, immediate efforts are to be made to improve this situation.

7. Higher level of human development is a product of the accumulated benefits that accrue to the society from public investments on social service. Per capita spending on education and health has a relatively stronger impact on human development than growth in per capita income. Hence, public expenditure on social services needs to be continued till the time economic growth itself takes care of it substantially.

8. The country, in general, and the north-eastern region in particular, suffer from the politics of human development. The approach of development theory and practice to poverty has been mechanical. It never goes into the question of the mechanism of generation of poverty. Hence, it is suggested that institutions engaged in development practice should analyse the mechanism of generation of poverty, and based on such analysis should come up with programmes to overcome it.

PURUSOTTAM NAYAK

I

Concept and Measurement Issues

1

Human Development
Concept and Measurement

PURUSOTTAM NAYAK

INTRODUCTION

The development experience of many fast-growing developing countries reveals that their high Gross National Product (GNP) growth rates failed to reduce the socio-economic deprivation of substantial sections of their population. Even developed industrial nations realized that high income is no protection against the rapid spread of problems such as drugs, alcoholism, AIDS, homelessness, violence, and the breakdown of family relations. At the same time, some low-income countries demonstrated that it is possible to achieve high levels of human development if they skilfully use available means to expand basic human capabilities. This establishes the fact that expansion of output and wealth is only a means to development. The end of development is the welfare of human beings. Therefore, the central focus of development analysis and planning must be directed towards people's needs, and oriented towards achievement of this ultimate end. As a first step towards achievement of this end, there is a need to create a database on improved social statistics and new development measures. To cater to this need the concept of human development and its measurement through a measure called Human Development Index (HDI) was introduced by United Nations Development Programme (UNDP) in 1990, in its first *Human Development Report* (*HDR*).

The human development approach to development, as is commonly understood, differs from the conventional approaches to economic growth, human capital formation, human resource development, human welfare, and basic human needs. The following arguments help us in understanding the same:

1. Gross National Product growth is treated as being necessary, but not sufficient for human development. Human progress may be lacking in some societies despite rapid GNP growth or high per capita income levels unless some additional steps are undertaken to improve the same.

2. Theories of human capital formation and human resource development view human beings primarily as means, rather than as ends. They are concerned only with the supply side, with human beings as instruments for furthering commodity production. It is true that human beings are the active agents of all production and wealth creation, but they are also the ultimate end and beneficiaries of this process. Thus, the concept of human capital formation (or, human resource development) captures only one side of human development, but not in its entirety.

3. Human welfare approaches look at human beings more as the beneficiaries of the development process, rather than as participants in it. They emphasize only the distributive policies, rather than production structures.

4. The basic needs approach usually concentrates on the bundle of goods and services such as food, shelter, clothing, healthcare, and water that the deprived population group needs. It focuses on the provision of these goods and services, rather than on the issue of human choices.

CONCEPT OF HUMAN DEVELOPMENT

Human development is a process of enlarging people's choices. In principle, these choices can be infinite and can change over time. But at all levels of development, the three essential choices are for the people to lead a healthy and long life, to acquire knowledge, and to have access to needed resources for a decent standard of living. If these essential choices are not available, many other opportunities remain inaccessible. But human development does not end there. Additional choices, highly valued by many people, range from political, economic, and social freedom to opportunities for being creative and productive, and enjoying self respect and guaranteed human rights.

Human development has two sides:

1. the formation of human capabilities such as improved health, knowledge, and skills; and
2. the use of their acquired capabilities for productive purposes and leisure, or for being active in cultural, social, and political affairs.

Considerable human frustration results if the scale of human development does not finely balance the two sides. In this sense, income is clearly one of the options that people would like to have, albeit an important one. But it is not the sum total of lives. Development must, therefore, be more than just the expansion of income and wealth. Its focus must be on people (UNDP 1990). The *HDR 1991* elaborates the concept of human development along the following lines:

(i) People must be at the centre of human development.
(ii) Development has to be woven around people, not people around development. It has to be development of the people, by the people, and for the people.

Previous concepts of development have often given exclusive attention to economic growth, on the assumption that the benefits of growth would trickle down to various sections of the society. But the past experience does not support this hypothesis much. Higher growth does not necessarily bring higher degree of welfare for every section of the society. Growth needs to be translated into improvements in people's lives.

Human development also encompasses elements that constitute the critical issues of gender and development. There are four major elements in the concept of human development—productivity, equity, sustainability, and empowerment. As far as productivity is concerned, people must be enabled to increase their productivity, and to participate fully in the process of income generation and remunerative employment, to achieve higher economic growth, which is a subset of human development models. Productivity is not the only means to achieve welfare in a society. People must have access to equal opportunities. All barriers to economic and political opportunities must be eliminated so that people can participate in, and benefit from these opportunities. These benefits also need to be distributed over generations. Access to opportunities must be ensured not only for the present generation, but for future generations as well. All forms of capital, such as physical, human, and environmental, should be replenished.

Besides, empowerment is a necessity as regards human development is concerned. People must participate fully in the decision-making process that can shape their lives. Human development is impossible without gender equality. As long as women are excluded from the development process, development will remain weak and lopsided (UNDP 1995).

Development should increase people's choices with two caveats. First, while enhancing the choices of one individual or a section of society, it should not restrict the choices of another. This calls for equity in human relationships. Second, while improving the lives of the present generation, it should not mortgage the choices of future generations (UNDP 1991). In other words, the development process must be sustainable. The concept of human development has gone beyond its basic premises to emphasize the sustainability of the development process. It not only puts people at the centre of the development process but also advocates protection of the opportunities of future generations while respecting the natural systems on which all life systems depend. Sustainable human development addresses equity, both within the generation and among generations, enabling all generations, present and future, to make the best use of their capabilities.

The issue of sustainability has three dimensions: capacity, environment, and institutions. If the development process does not create institutions fully supportive of people's rights, it cannot be sustainable in the long run. Human development, thus, emphasizes on strengthening institutions of both the government and civil society so that the entire development process becomes internally sustainable (UNDP 1995). Human development is not a concept separated from sustainable development, but it can help to rescue sustainable development from the misconception that it involves only the environmental dimension of development. All these approaches have emphasized the need for people centred development with concerns for human empowerment, participation, gender equality, equitable growth, poverty reduction, and long-term sustainability (UNDP 1998). According to Haq (1976), 'the defining difference between the economic growth and the human development schools is that the first focuses exclusively on the expansion of only one choice, that is, income, while the second embraces the enlargement of all human choices, whether economic, social, cultural or political'.

There are at least six reasons for which we talk about and aspire for human development and poverty eradication. First, it is an end in itself; indeed it is the whole purpose of development. Second, it contributes to higher productivity. Third, it lowers reproductivity and, therefore, controls population growth. Fourth, poverty reduction minimizes degradation of environment from soil erosion, deforestation, and desertification. Fifth, the growth of a civil society and democracy leads to greater social stability. Lastly, its political appeal is that it not only reduces civil disturbances but also acts as a means to political stability (Streeten 1995).

MEASUREMENT OF HUMAN DEVELOPMENT: UNDP METHODOLOGY

What does the HDI include? How is it measured? These are some of the few questions which need to be addressed first. HDI is a composite index of three basic components of human development, that is, longevity, knowledge, and standard of living. Longevity is measured by life expectancy. Knowledge is measured by a combination of adult literacy having two-thirds weight and mean years of schooling with one-third weight. Standard of living is measured by purchasing power parity, based on real GDP per capita adjusted for the local cost of living.

The question then arises: Why do we take only these three components to measure human development? In any system of measuring and monitoring human development, the ideal should have been to reflect all aspects of human development, to obtain as comprehensive a picture as possible. In support of the choice of three components of HDI, the following arguments are made in *HDR 1990*: One of the probable reasons is lack of data that imposes some limits on its measurements. Second, comprehensiveness is not always and entirely desirable. Too many indicators may produce a perplexing picture, perhaps distracting policy makers from its thrust. Moreover, some indicators may overlap with existing indicators. Infant mortality, for example, is already reflected in life expectancy. Thus, arbitrary inclusion of more indicator variables may not solve the purpose for which the index is constructed. The crucial issue has, therefore, been emphasis on policy variables.

The next question then arises: How to combine these three indicators measured in three different units? The breakthrough for the HDI, however, is to find a common measuring rod for the socio-economic distance travelled. For each of these three dimensions, the report identified minimum achievements, namely, the lowest national life expectancy, the lowest national level of adult literacy, and the lowest national level of per capita income. It also established a maximum, or a desirable level of attainment for each of these dimensions, and then showed where each country stood in relation to these scales. It was expressed in terms of a numerical value between 0 and 1. Income above the average world income was adjusted using a progressively higher discount rate. The scores for the three dimensions were then averaged in an overall index.

The HDI was constructed in three steps. In the first step, the measure of deprivation of a country was made for each of the three basic indicators using the following formula:

$$I_{ij} = \frac{\text{Max}(X_{ij}) - X_{ij}}{\text{Max}(X_{ij}) - \text{Min}(X_{ij})} \qquad (1.1)$$

The indicator variable (I_{ij}) used in (1.1) refers to the deprivation indicator for the jth country with respect to the ith variable. In the second step, an average deprivation indicator (I_j) was defined by taking a simple average of the three indicators as given below:

$$I_j = \frac{1}{3}\sum_{i=1}^{3} I_{ij} \qquad (1.2)$$

In the third step, HDI was measured as one minus the average deprivation index as follows:

$$\text{HDI}_j = 1 - I_j \qquad (1.3)$$

The human development index attracted a lot of attention among policy makers, development professionals, academics, the press, and the people. Many criticisms were raised against the construction and robustness of the index. As a result of these criticisms, two improvements were brought about in its construction in the subsequent (UNDP 1991). First, knowledge variables, such as adult literacy and years of schooling, were combined to produce a synthetic measure of educational achievement by assigning weights to the two components as follows:

$$E = a_1 \text{ (Literacy)} + a_2 \text{ (Years of Schooling)} \qquad (1.4)$$

The symbols used, that is, E, a_1, and a_2 in equation (1.4), respectively, refer to educational achievement, respective weights of literacy, and mean years of schooling. These weights were assumed as $a_1 = {}^2/_3$ and $a_2 = {}^1/_3$ in the 1991 report, whereas the same were taken as $a_1 = 1$ and $a_2 = 0$ in the 1990 report. Second, modification was made in the treatment of income. As we know, HDI in the 1990 report was based on the premise of diminishing returns from income which was reflected through the use of logarithm of income and assignment of zero weight to income above the poverty line. However, in 1991 the method was revised by using the well-known and frequently used Atkinson formula for measuring utility of income as follows:

$$W(Y) = \frac{1}{1-\varepsilon}(Y^{1-\varepsilon})$$ (1.5)

where $W(Y)$ is the utility or well-being derived from income, and the parameter ε measures the extent of diminishing returns. It is the elasticity of the marginal utility of income with respect to income. If $\varepsilon = 0$, there are no diminishing returns. If ε approaches 1, the equation becomes:

$$W(Y) = \log(Y)$$ (1.6)

The modification adopted in the HDI (1991) was to let the value of ε to rise slowly with rise in income. For this purpose, the full range of income was divided into multiples of the poverty line income (Y^*). Thus, most countries were falling in the income range between 0 to Y^*, some between Y^* to $2Y^*$, even fewer between $2Y^*$ to $3Y^*$ and so on. For all countries for which $Y < Y^*$ (the poor countries), ε was set equal to 0, meaning thereby that there were no diminishing returns. For income between Y^* and $2Y^*$, ε was set equal to ½. For income between $2Y^*$ and $3Y^*$, it was set at ${}^2/_3$ and so on. In general, when $\alpha Y^* \leq (\alpha + 1)Y^*$, it implied that $\varepsilon = \dfrac{\alpha}{\alpha + 1}$ (where α representing constants such as 1, 2, 3, 4, etc., to be multiplied with poverty line income to determine various ranges of income in which a country falls according to its level of income. Thus, we have:

$$\begin{aligned}
W(Y) &= \log(Y) \text{ for } 0 < Y \leq Y^* \\
&= Y^* + 2(Y - Y^*)^{\frac{1}{2}} \text{ for } Y^* \leq Y \leq 2Y^* \\
&= Y^* + 2(Y^*)^{\frac{1}{2}} + 3(Y - 2Y^*)^{\frac{1}{3}} \text{ for } 2Y^* \leq Y \leq 3Y^* \\
&= Y^* + 2(Y^*)^{\frac{1}{2}} + 3(Y^*)^{\frac{1}{3}} + 4(Y - 3Y^*)^{\frac{1}{4}} \text{ for } 3Y^* \leq Y \leq 4Y^* \text{ etc.}
\end{aligned}$$ (1.7)

So, the higher the income relative to the poverty level, the more sharply the diminishing returns affect the contribution of income to human development. Income above the poverty line, thus, has a marginal effect, but not a full dollar-for-dollar effect. This marginal effect is enough, however, to differentiate significantly among industrial countries. The original HDI formulation (UNDP 1990), by comparison, was:

$$W(Y) = \log(Y) \text{ for } 0 < Y \leq Y^*$$
$$= \log(Y^*) \text{ for } Y > Y^*$$

The revision, thus, does not take $\varepsilon = 1$, but allows it to vary between 0 and 1 (UNDP 1991).

The calculation of *HDR* for 1994 was again made different from that of the previous years. Maximum and minimum values were fixed for the four basic variables, that is, life expectancy (85.0 and 25.0 years), adult literacy (100 and 0 per cent), mean years of schooling (15.0 and 0 years), and income (PPP $ 40,000 and 200). For income, the threshold value was taken to be the global average real GDP per capita of Purchasing Power Parity (PPP) $ 5,120. Multiples of income beyond the threshold was discounted using a progressively higher rate (UNDP 1994).

Since the publication of the *HDR 1994*, two changes have been brought out in the construction of HDI relating to variables and minimum and maximum values. First, the variable of mean years of schooling has been replaced by the combined primary, secondary, and tertiary enrolment ratios, mainly because the formula for calculating mean years of schooling is complex and has enormous data requirement. Second, the minimum value of income has been revised from PPP $ 200 to $ 100. This revision has been made because in the construction of the Gender-related Development Index (GDI) for different countries, the minimum observed value of female income of PPP $ 100 has been used as a lower goal post. It is necessary to use this fixed minimum for construction of the overall HDI to maintain consistency between the construction of HDI and that of GDI, and to ensure comparability between the two indices. For HDI, the revision is only marginal, and it has little effect on HDI values. For any component of the HDI, individual indices are computed according to the general formula:

$$\text{Index} = \frac{X_i - \text{Min}(X_i)}{\text{Max}(X_i) - \text{Min}(X_i)} \tag{1.8}$$

For the construction of the dimension indices, maximum and minimum values have been fixed as shown in Table 1.1:

Table 1.1: Dimension Indices of HDI in UNDP Report

Indicators	Scaling Norms for HDI	
	Maximum	Minimum
Life expectancy at birth (years)	85	25
Adult literacy rate (per cent)	100	0
Combined gross enrolment ratio (per cent)	100	0
GDP per capita (PPP US $)	40,000	100

Source: UNDP (2005).

Upto 1999, the Atkinson formula was used to construct the income GDP index in the *HDR*. The basic approach in the treatment of income was driven by the fact that achieving a respectable level of human development does not require unlimited income. To reflect this, income was always discounted in calculating the HDI. To calculate the discounted value of the maximum income of PPP \$ 40,000 which falls between the income range of $6Y^*$ and $7Y^*$, the following formula (constructed before 1999) was used:

$$W(Y) = Y^* + 2(Y^*)^{\frac{1}{2}} + 3(Y^*)^{\frac{1}{3}} + 4(Y^*)^{\frac{1}{4}} + 5(Y^*)^{\frac{1}{5}}$$
$$+ 6(Y^*)^{\frac{1}{6}} + 7(40000 - 6Y^*)^{\frac{1}{7}} \tag{1.9}$$
$$= 6311 \text{ (PPP US\$)}$$

The main problem with this formula is that it discounts the income above the threshold level very heavily, penalizing the countries in which income exceeds the threshold level. It reduces the PPP \$ 34,000 between the threshold and maximum level of income to a mere PPP \$ 321. In many cases, income loses its relevance as a proxy for all dimensions of human development other than a long and healthy life and knowledge. To overcome this problem, the UNDP (1999) brought out a thorough review of the treatment of income and suggested its improvement. Putting the methodology on a more solid analytical foundation by introducing the formula as shown below made the refinement:

$$W(Y) = \frac{\log(Y) - \log\{Min(Y)\}}{\log\{Max(Y)\} - \log\{Min(Y)\}} \tag{1.10}$$

There are several advantages to this formula. First, it does not discount income as severely as the formula used earlier. Second, it discounts all income, not just the income above a certain level. Third, the asymptote starts quite late, so middle-income countries are not penalized unduly;

moreover, as income rises further in these countries, they continue to receive recognition for their increasing income as a potential means for further human development (UNDP 1999).

Subsequently, Anand and Sen (1993, 1995, and 2000) and Chaubey (2002) suggested further modifications to the UNDP formula, but these are yet to be popularized (Nayak and Thomas 2007). Anand and Sen suggested the following two forms for rectification of the transformation adopted by UNDP:

$$= -e^{-\gamma y} \text{ where } \gamma = 0 \tag{1.11}$$
$$= -y^{-\beta} e^{\gamma y} \text{ where } \beta \geq 0 \text{ and } \gamma \geq 0$$

In the first part of function (1.11), γy is the elasticity of the function which is a positive function of income and, therefore, increases linearly with the increase in income. The second part is a more general class which combines the constant absolute inequality aversion and constant relative inequality aversion forms.

Chaubey provided an alternative to these formulations which made the use of the idea of the poverty line and followed the principle of diminishing marginal returns to income:

$$W = Y \text{ for } Y \leq Y^* \tag{1.12}$$
$$= Y^* + Y^* \left\{ \log\left(\frac{Y}{Y^*} \right) \right\} \text{ for } Y \geq Y^*$$

Figure 1.1 below offers a clear overview of how the HDI is constructed:

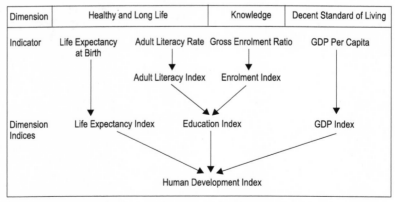

Figure 1.1 : Variables of HDI

Construction of Indices in *UNDP Report 2007–08*

Life Expectancy Index (LEI): The life expectancy index measures the relative achievement of a country in life expectancy at birth. The life expectancy index of India, having life expectancy of 63.7 years at birth for the year 2005, is calculated to be 0.645 as shown below:

$$\text{LEI} = \frac{63.7 - 25}{85 - 25} = 0.645 \tag{i}$$

Education Index (EI): The education index measures a country's relative achievement in both adult literacy and combined primary, secondary, and tertiary gross enrolment. First, an Adult Literacy Index (ALI) and Gross Enrolment Index (GEI) are calculated. Then these two indices are combined to create the EI, with two-thirds weight given to adult literacy and one-third weight to combined gross enrolment. For India, with an adult literacy rate of 61.0 per cent and a combined enrolment ratio of 63.8 per cent in 2005, the education index is calculated to be 0.620 as shown below:

$$\text{ALI} = \frac{61.0 - 0}{100 - 0} = 0.610 \tag{iia}$$

$$\text{GEI} = \frac{63.8 - 0}{100 - 0} = 0.638 \tag{iib}$$

$$\text{EI} = \frac{2}{3}(\text{ALI}) + \frac{1}{3}(\text{GEI}) = \frac{2}{3}(0.610) + \frac{1}{3}(0.638) = 0.620 \tag{iic}$$

GDP Index (GDPI): It is calculated using adjusted GDP per capita (PPP US \$). In the HDI, income serves as a surrogate for all the dimensions of human development not reflected in a long and healthy life, and in knowledge. Income is adjusted because achieving a respectable level of human development does not require unlimited income. Accordingly, the logarithm of income is used. For India with a GDP per capita of PPP \$ 3452 in 2005, the *GDPI* works out to be 0.591 as shown below:

$$\text{GDPI} = \frac{\log(3452) - \log(100)}{\log(40000) - \log(100)} = 0.591 \tag{iii}$$

Human Development Index (HDI): Once the individual indices are calculated determining the HDI is straightforward, it is a simple average of LEI, EI, and GDPI:

$$\mathrm{HDI} = \frac{1}{3}(\mathrm{LEI} + \mathrm{EI} + \mathrm{GDPI}) \tag{iv}$$

$$= \frac{1}{3}(0.645 + 0.620 + 0.591) = 0.619$$

MEASUREMENT OF HUMAN DEVELOPMENT: PLANNING COMMISSION METHODOLOGY

The *National Human Development Report* (*NHDR*) prepared by the Planning Commission of India is an attempt to map the state of HDI in India (Planning Commission 2002). A major objective of the *NHDR* is to bring about a certain conceptual and methodological consensus on the use of human development approach in the country in general, and the framework for identifying indicators and building composite human development indices at the state level, in particular. The work is expected to guide similar initiatives at the sub-state level in future. It seeks to put together indicators and composite indices to evaluate development process in terms of 'ex-post incomes' rather than only in terms of available means of inputs. The report, recognizing the broad-based consensus that exists on the three critical dimensions of well-being, focuses on identifying the various contextually relevant indicators on each of them. These dimensions of well-being are related to the following:

1. *Longevity*: the ability to live a long and healthy life;
2. *Education*: the ability to read, write, and acquire knowledge; and
3. *Command over resources*: the ability to enjoy a decent standard of living and have a socially meaningful life.

The various indicators of these attainments and composite indices capture the process of development and well-being of the people from two perspectives. The first is the conglomerate perspective, which captures advances, made by the society as a whole, and the second is the deprivation perspective that assesses the status of the deprived in a society. Both these perspectives are needed to adequately understand the process of development in any society (Planning Commission 2002: 10).

A composite index of diverse indicators, though it is conceptually and methodologically difficult to put together, has been considered as a useful tool in policy planning in India. It is believed to help in facilitating comparisons with other composite measures. It is expected to help in a meaningful comparison of the human development status across the states. It is, therefore, felt necessary to have core indices that are functionally decomposable at the state and sub-state levels. Keeping these points in view, the *NHDR* included a core set of indices from among the identified indicators that reflect, in some sense, the common concerns, social values, and development priorities of all the states in India, which permitted a meaningful comparison of the human development status across the states. The other concerns that were considered to be reflected in the indices related to their amenability to inter-temporal and inter-spatial analyses, as well as their sensitivity to tracking developmental changes at more frequent intervals of time. The latter implies making use of such indicators that are sensitive to capturing changes, for instance, on an annual basis, as against using only those indicators that primarily capture the accumulated attainments on each of the identified dimensions of well-being that is included in the summary measure. Such a consideration is important when the objective is to have composite human development indices where frequent, or yearly changes, are not on account of changes only in the income variable. This is not the case with the HDI of UNDP, which is presented annually in the human development reports. In their case, the yearly changes in the value of the index is mostly on account of changes in the indicators, that are sensitive to tracking gradual but continuous changes in such aspects of well-being that have conventionally been captured largely through the slow moving indicators, like life expectancy at birth, or even literacy rates.

While taking note of the social valuation and development priorities of India, the scaling and weighting of diverse indicators into a composite index has been done keeping in view the objectives for which the composite indices are being built. In scaling the diverse indicators, the main consideration has been to make attainments on each of them comparable, and at the same time ensuring that the selection of end points, that is, the maximum and the minimum values on the scale for each indicator, are such that they support inter-temporal comparison for a reasonable period of time starting from 1980. The scaling norms that have been selected are expected to remain valid at least till 2020, at a reasonably improved pace of human development. While selecting the norms, the attainments of the best performing state on the concerned indicators and the comparable international norms are also kept in mind.

The issue of weights to combine the identified indicators on each of the three dimensions of well-being is, of course, debatable. The report has adopted a predominantly normative approach as against a purely empirical basis of deriving weights to club different indicators. Conceptually, there are good reasons to suggest that different aspects of well-being have to be co-realizable for an individual to have a meaningful sense of well-being in today's context. It follows that attainments on each aspect of well-being are equally important and, hence, should be equally weighted. Thus, both in HDI as well as in HPI, composite measures reflecting health, educational, and economic attainments/deprivations have been equally weighted as shown in Table 1.2. However, within the composite measure on educational and health attainment, based on a sensitivity analysis, indicators with somewhat distinct attributes have been clubbed using unequal weights so as to reflect appropriately the country's context, development priorities, and the desired policy focus. Accordingly, in case of the composite index on health attainment, life expectancy has been given a 65 per cent weight as against only 35 per cent for infant mortality rate. Similarly, in case of the composite index on educational attainment, while literacy rate has been given a weight of 35 per cent, the indicator capturing intensity of formal education (based on current enrolment rates in successive classes at school level) has been assigned 65 per cent. In case of indicator on economic attainment, namely, inequality adjusted per capita consumption expenditure, an adjustment for inflation over the period had been made to make it amenable to inter-temporal and inter-spatial comparisons. As a result, the composite indices are capable of tracking development across the states and over a period of time for which they have been estimated.

Table 1.2: Indicators of HDI in UNDP and
National Human Development Reports

Attainments	UNDP Indicators	NHDR Indicators
Health	Life expectancy at birth	(1) Life Expectancy at Age 1
		(2) Infant Mortality Rate
Educational	Adult literacy rate combined with enrolment ratio	(1) Literacy Rate 7 +
		(2) Intensity of Formal Education
Economic	Real GDP per capita in PPP $	Per capita real consumption expenditure adjusted for inequality

The formula used for constructing HDI in the *NHDR* is as follows:

$$\text{HDI}_j = \frac{1}{3}\sum_{i=1}^{3} X_i \text{ where } X_i = \frac{X_{ij} - X_i^*}{X_i^{**} - X_i^*} \tag{1.13}$$

In the above equation (1.13), HDI is measured for the jth state, where X_{ij} refers to attainment of the jth state on the ith indicator, X_i^{**} and X_i^* are the scaling maximum and minimum norms, $X1$ refers to expenditure index based on inflation and inequality adjusted per capita consumption expenditure, X2 is the composite index on educational attainment $(X2 = 0.35E1 + 0.65E2)$, where $E1$ is literacy index based on literacy rate for the age group of seven years and above, $E2$ is formal education index based on adjusted intensity of formal education, and $X3$ refers to composite index on health attainment $(X3 = 0.65H1 + 0.35H2)$ where $H1$ is life expectancy index based on life expectancy at age one and $H2$ is infant mortality index based on infant mortality rate. In case of IMR, the reciprocal of the indicator is used.

The different indicators included in the development radars have been scaled and normalized to take a value on a scale ranging from 0 to 5 as shown in Table 1.3. 'As a result, on each indicator including the IMR and poverty ratio, where the reciprocal of the indicator has been used, and the scaled least achievement corresponds to 0 whereas the best achievement is closer to 5. In undertaking the said scaling procedure, desirable norms had to be adopted for the chosen indicators' (Planning Commission 2002: 133). In some cases, the norms are self-selecting, as for instance is the case with access to safe drinking water, or literacy rate, and in some others like per capita consumption expenditure or even infant mortality rate, there is an element of value judgement. In case of the inflation adjusted per capita consumption expenditure (at 1983 prices), the maximum has been pegged at Rs 500 per capita per month. For poverty the minimum has been kept at 5 per cent such that it corresponds to a value of 5 on a scale of 0.5 on the radar. In all other cases, the scaling norms are as follows:

Table 1.3: Dimension Indices of HDI in
National Human Development Report

Indicators	Scaling Norms for HDI	
	Maximum	Minimum
Life expectancy at age 1 (years)	80	50
Infant mortality rate	–	20 per 1000
Literacy rate for 7+ years	100	0
Adjusted intensity of formal education (estimated)	7	0
Inflation adjusted per capita monthly consumption expenditure at 1983 prices (Rs)	325	65

Source: Planning Commission (2002).

REFERENCES

Anand, S. and A. Sen 2000. 'The Income Component of Human Development Index', *Journal of Human Development*, Vol. 1, No. 1.

—— 1995. 'Gender Inequality in Human Development: Theories and Measurement', Occasional Paper No. 19, Human Development Report Office, UNDP, New York.

—— 1993. 'Human Development Index: Methodology and Measurement', Occasional Paper No. 12, Human Development Report Office, UNDP, New York.

Anand, S. and M. Ravallion 1993. 'Human Development in Poor Countries: On the Role of Private Incomes and Public Services', *Journal of Economic Perspectives*, Vol. 7, pp. 133–50.

Chaubey, P.K. 2002. 'The Human Development Index: A Contribution to its Construction', *Indian Journal of Economics*, Vol. 83, No. 328, pp. 95–100.

Haq, Mahboob-ul- 1976. *The Poverty Curtain-Choices for the Third World*, Columbia University Press, New York, p. 35.

Nayak, P. and E.D. Thomas 2007. *Human Development and Deprivation in Meghalaya*, Akansha Publishers, New Delhi.

Planning Commission 2002. *National Human Development Report*, Government of India, New Delhi.

Streetan, P.P. 1995. *Thinking about Development*, Cambridge University Press, pp. 19–20.

United Nations Development Programme (UNDP) 1990, 1991, 1992, 1994, 1995, 1996, 1998, 1999, 2001, 2002, 2004 and 2007–08. *Human Development Report*, United Nations Development Programme, New York.

—— 2005. *Human Development Report*, Oxford University Press, p. 341. http://hdr.undp.orglen/reports/global/hdr2005

2

Concept of Human Development
A Critique

P.K. CHAUBEY

When Mahbub-ul-Haq joined the United Nations Development Programme (UNDP) as a special advisor, he decided, in consultation with some of the prominent economists, to bring out a report, on an annual basis, on the state of affairs in different countries with regard to what may be called human outcomes of development as practised in respective countries. This was to be more or less in contrast to the *World Development Report (WDR)* brought out by the World Bank, since 1978, which was then focusing more on inputs and processes than on outputs and outcomes.

The label of the report was decided by consensus to be *Human Development Report (HDR)* brought out by UNDP, as opposed to say a report on human conditions, for the former does not treat humans as passive beings. The choice of the term stemmed from three considerations:

1. whether, and to what extent do people have a say in matters that concern their lives;
2. whether they have fair opportunities to contribute to development; and
3. whether, and to what extent do they have a chance to a fair share of the fruits of development.

This meant, according to Kaul (2003: 61), Director of Development Studies at the UNDP, searching for a term that described a process of human-centred development. Out of many combinations using humane or human, condition or development, a simple term Human Development (HD) was selected.

It was after the nomenclature of the report that the term 'human development' came to be defined by the collaborators in endeavours to put an annual series of the report. The term HD came to be accepted (Fukuda-Parr and Shiva Kumar 2003: xxi) as:

(i)   expansion of capabilities
(ii)   widening of choices
(iii) enhancement of freedoms; and
(iv)   fulfillment of human rights.

These are the themes pursued in various reports, since 1991, as specific themes. It has been asserted that the central message in the reports is that the end of development is the people's well-being and economic growth (or, for that matter, rising incomes and expanding outputs) is only the means.

As a matter of record, it may be pointed that the UNDP was not the first to use HD as a term. Forgetting for a moment the use of this term by anthropologists, psychologists, and historians in their respective literature, it was a part of the name given to the second part of the third WDR published in 1980: *Poverty and Human Development*. Many of the background papers did use the term HD, and the then President of the World Bank, in his foreword emphasized on the importance of HD saying that health and education, among others, were not only of instrumental significance but the primary ends of development (World Bank, 1980: iii). Though, the WDR of 1980, referred to the above, it did not attempt to make a distinction between HD and Human Resource Development (HRD); it said that it is better to use the former because elements of HRD are themselves ends of development.

Following the third WDR 1980 and preceding by a decade the first HDR 1990, it was Das Gupta (1981: 6) who succinctly defined human development in much the same way as did the contributors to HDRs in the following words: Human development indicates a better ability of people to choose; what they end up choosing is another matter.

The time was ripe and with luck in favour of the UNDP, the idea caught the imagination of one and all. Everybody started paying obeisance to it. A special contribution in the tenth HDR 1999 by Streetan says, 'In 1990, the time had come for a broad approach to improving human well-being that would cover all aspects of human life, for all people, in both high-income and developing countries, both now and in future'. He further says that the approach went far beyond narrowly defined economic development, to cover the full flourishing of all human choices, and that it emphasized the need to put people—their needs, their aspirations, and their capabilities—at the centre of the development effort. He further says that there arose the need to assert the unacceptability of any biases or discriminations, whether by class, gender, race, nationality, religion, community, or generation. As repeated elsewhere, Streetan (1994 and 2003) says, 'Human Development had arrived. It is surprising that such scholars failed to see all such elements in the principles of the state policies and development plans of the countries like India! It is their myopia or opacity of these writings, is difficult to assert'.

Almost two decades ago, an effort was made by Murice D. Maurice, though in terms of capturing essential dimensions of human development, with Physical Quality of Life Index (PQLI). Additional dimensions accepting the criteria of international comparability could be added. The thing it lacked was the imaginative theoretical scaffolding provided by Amartya Sen in terms of capability space in contrast with commodity space, which it verily was. It directly came to index believing that the idea of outcome instead of inputs and processes, that were current in those days, was too obvious.

Unfortunately, HD has been described as an approach, a perspective, a framework, a process, a paradigm, and level of development. For brevity, let us take the process view combining two of the four notions enumerated by Fukuda-Parr and Shiva Kumar and define HD as process of 'enlarging people's choice through expansion of human capabilities' (Chaubey 2001), which is how most of the literature puts it. As Streetan (1994) puts it:

Human development is the process of enlarging people's choices—not just choices among different detergents, television channels or car models but the choices that created by expanding human capabilities and functionings— what people do and can do in their lives. At all levels of development, a few capabilities are essential for human development, without which many choices in life would not be available. These capabilities are to lead long and healthy lives, to be knowledgeable and to have access to the resources needed for a decent standard of living—these are reflected in the human development index. These include political, social, economic, and cultural freedom, a sense of community, opportunities for being creative and productive, self-respect, and human rights. Yet, human development is more than achieving these capabilities; it is also the process of pursuing them in a way that is equitable, participatory, productive, and sustainable.

It goes without saying that the passage is an assertion which is very difficult to process in any concrete shape. But these are the goals a society, with a certain set of values, can think of pursuing with no real end in sight. The distinction between two levels of capabilities just exposes the weakness the very idea of human development inheres. Who chooses to make the distinction between various categories of capabilities! While the concept refers to a set of 'can-be's and can-do's, the index refers to actual achievement in terms of 'beings and doings'. There is a problem with putting beings and doings together, for beings connote the idea of persona while doings that of capability. *Persona* is a stock idea while *doings* are flows. *Functionings* generate from interaction of capability space and commodity space.

It can be conjectured with ease that but for Amartya Sen's conceptual articulation, the idea of human development (index) would have been just an alternative to PQLI, or an improvement of PQLI. Impressing that being well is not the same as being well-off, Sen defines a person's well-being in terms of a vector of functionings, where functioning is an achievement through a choice over commodity vector and exercise of choosing personal utilization function. So, there has to be an interface between capability space and commodity space for achievement of well-being. Take the example of swimming and reading, or driving. Capability of swimming and functioning of swimming are interrelated, but two different things. As has been pointed out by Streetan (2003: 77), 'the use of [these] capabilities can be frustrated if the opportunities for their exercise do not exist or if people are deprived of [these] opportunities as a result of discrimination, obstacles or inhibitions'.

The above articulation clearly gives an impression that the idea is individualistic, though an attempt is made for aggregation because an index is calculated for a set of people rather than for an individual. Yet, an approach which hovers around one's beings and doings is too individualistic and much beyond methodological individualism. As has been rightly pointed out by Streetan again:

Choices change over time and can be infinite, would be mindless and pointless. There are limits and constraints on choices and in fact they need to be combined with allegiances—rights with duties, options with bonds, liberties with ligatures. The exact combination of individual and public action, of personal agencies and social institutions, will vary from time to time and from problem to problem. Institutional arrangement will be more important for achieving sustainability while personal agency may be more important when it comes to the choice of household articles or marriage partners.

The *HDR 1992* pointed out that the UNDP had decided to re-examine the basic concept and its measurement each year. They did it, but they are moving in loops rather than advancing further in the directions indicated above. But, while concluding his piece, Streetan (2003) writes: So 'human development' and human development index are not ultimate insights and other ideas will take their place. We are all free to guess what these will be.

Over six hundred reports have been written titled HDRs, for nations, regions—supranational and sub national—smaller territories, and sections. But growth, from which they wanted to move away by looking at successes in terms of expansion of capabilities despite slow growth of commodity index in a number of countries, is clearly entrapping them, even though a lot more focus has been brought on education and health concerns.

REFERENCES

Chaubey, P.K. 2001. *Human Development Index: Exercises in Methodology and Reconstruction*, Indian Institute of Public Administration, New Delhi.

Das Gupta, Jyotirindra 1981. *Authority, Priority, and Human Development*, Oxford University Press, Delhi.

Fukuda-Parr, S. and A.K. Shiva Kumar 2003. 'Introduction', in Fukuda-Parr, S. and A.K. Shiva Kumar (eds), *Readings in Human Development*, Oxford University Press, New Delhi.

International Bank for Reconstruction and Development (IBRD) 1980. *World Development Report 1980*, Oxford University Press, New York.

Kaul, I. 2003. 'Choices that Shaped the Human Development Report', in Fukuda-Parr, S. and A.K. Shiva Kumar (eds), *Readings in Human Development*, Oxford University Press, New Delhi.

Streeten, P. 2003. 'Shifting Fashions in Development Dialogue', in Fukuda-Parr, S. and A.K. Shiva Kumar (eds), *Readings in Human Development*, Oxford University Press, New Delhi.

——— 1994. 'Human Development: Means and Ends', *American Economic Review*, Vol. 84, No. 2.

United Nations Development Programme (UNDP) 1990–2006. *Human Development Reports*, Oxford University Press, New York.

World Bank 1980. World Development Report, Foreword by Robert McNamara, Washington D.C., p. iii.

3

Construction of an Index
A New Method

SUDHANSHU K. MISHRA

INTRODUCTION

On many occasions we need to construct an index that represents a number of variables (indicators). Cost of living index, general price index, Human Development Index (HDI), index of level of development, etc., are some of the examples that are constructed by a weighted (linear) aggregation of a host of variables. The general formula of construction of such an index (OECD 2003) may be given as:

$$I_i = \sum_{j=1}^{m} w_j x_{ij} \equiv w_1 x_{i1} + w_2 x_{i2} + \dots + w_m x_{im}; \quad i = 1, 2, \dots, n$$

where, w_j being the weight assigned to the jth variable, x_j and remains constant over all observations of $x_j = (x_{1j}, x_{2j}, \dots, x_{nj})$.

The weights $w = (w_1, w_2, \dots, w_m)$ are determined by the importance assigned to the variables $x_j; j = 1, 2, \dots, m$. The criterion on which importance of a variable (vis-à-vis other variables) is determined may be varied and usually has its own logic (Munda and Nardo 2005). For example, in constructing a cost of living index, importance of a commodity is determined by the proportion of consumption expenditure allocated to that particular commodity, and in constructing the HDI, variables such as literacy, life expectancy, or income are weighted according to the importance assigned to them in accordance with their perceived roles in determining human development status.

In many cases, however, the analyst does not have any preferred means or logic to determine the relative importance of different variables. In such cases, weights are assigned mathematically. One of the methods to determine such mathematical weights is the Principal Components Analysis (PCA) [McCracken 2000].

In the PCA (Kendall and Stuart 1968: 285–99), weights are determined such that the sum of the squared correlation coefficients of the index with the constituent variables (used to construct the index) is maximized. In other words, weights in $I = \sum_{j}^{m} w_j x_j$ are determined such that $\sum_{j=1}^{m} r^2(I, x_j)$ is maximized. Here, $r(I, x_j)$ is the coefficient of correlation between the index I and the variable (x_j).

The PCA is a very well-established statistical method that has excellent mathematical properties. From $x = (x_1, x_2, ..., x_m)$, one may obtain m (or fewer) indices that are orthogonal with each other. These indices together explain cent per cent variation in the original variables $x = (x_1, x_2, ..., x_m)$. Moreover, the first Principal Component (often used to make a single index) explains the largest proportion of variation in the variables $x = (x_1, x_2, ..., x_m)$.

SOME PRACTICAL PROBLEMS WITH THE PRINCIPAL COMPONENTS ANALYSIS

Although the PCA has excellent mathematical properties, one may face some difficulties in using it if one desires to construct a single index of the variables that are not very highly correlated among themselves. The method has a tendency to pick up the subset of highly correlated variables to make the first component, assign marginal weights to relatively poorly correlated subset of variables, and/or relegate the latter subset to construction of the subsequent principal components. Now, if one has to construct a single index, such an index undermines the poorly correlated set of variables. As a result, practically speaking, the index so constructed is the weighted aggregation of only the preferred (highly correlated) set of variables. In this sense, the index, so constructed, is elitist in nature that has a preference to the highly correlated subset over the poorly correlated subset of variables. Further, since there is no dependable method available to obtain a composite index by merging two or more principal components, the deferred set of variables never finds its representation in further analysis.

A WIDER VIEW OF CONSTRUCTING AN INDEX

Let us now investigate the possibilities of maximizing $\left(\sum_{j=1}^{m} |r(I, x_j)|^L \right)^{1/L}$ to obtain weights to construct $I = \sum_{j}^{m} w_j x_j$. This is only a Minkowsky generalization of maximization of $\sum_{j}^{m} r^2(I, x_j)$, or (equivalently) $\left(\sum_{j=1}^{m} |r(I, x_j)|^2 \right)^{1/2}$. It can be shown that as $L \to -(\infty)$, the index becomes more and more egalitarian, with an ever stronger tendency to assign weights, such that all or most of the variables, are equally correlated with the index. In so doing, it maximizes the minimal correlation of the index with its constituent variables, or in other words, it gives us the maximin index. However, for $L = 1$, the index is inclusive in nature that assigns reasonable (although smaller) weights to the members of less correlated subset of variables, but has no tendency to undermine the less correlated variables and their representation. This property of the index obtained by maximizing $\sum_{j=1}^{m} |r(I, x_j)|$, or maximizing the minimal correlation, is attractive and useful. The objective of this chapter is to illustrate this fact.

THE METHOD OF OPTIMIZATION

The method of constructing indices by the Principal Components is available in many software packages such as STATISTICA or SPSS. However, the method to construct indices by maximin correlation, or maximization of the sum of absolute correlations, is not available. We have obtained all indices (I-2, I-M and I-1) by solving max $\left(\sum_{j=1}^{m} |r(I, x_j)|^L \right)^{1/L}$ such that $I = \sum_{j}^{m} w_j x_j$, where w_j are the decision variables. It is an intricate non-linear optimization problem. Any powerful non-linear programming software may possibly be used for optimization (see Kuester and Mize 1973 for classical methods and FORTRAN programs). However, we have used the Differential Evolution (DE) method of Global Optimization (which is in the broader family of the genetic algorithms). The optimization may also be done by the Particle Swarm method often used in Artificial Intelligence (see Mishra 2006). We have found that the Repulsive Particle Swarm (RPS) method performs as effectively as the Differential Evolution method. We have not presented the results of the RPS optimization to avoid duplication of results. The FORTRAN codes of the programs (Mishra 2007) may also be obtained from the author on request.

WORKING ON REAL LIFE DATA

Sarker *et al.* (2006), in their paper argued that HDI should include income equality measures (EQ) also in addition to the three measures of life expectancy (LE), education (ED), and per capita gross domestic product at the purchasing power parity with the US $ per capita income (PCI), conventionally incorporated into it. They computed the per capita income distribution-adjusted composite index (DAPCHDI) of human development and showed that the ranking of countries on the basis of this type of HDI (that includes income distribution as one of the component indices) differed substantially from the ranking calculated in the *Human Development Reports* (*HDR*) of United Nations Development Programme (UNDP, published annually). They suggested, therefore, that within-country income distribution should be given its due importance in international comparison of countries.

Sarker *et al.* 2006 used data on life expectancy, educational index, and per capita income from the *Human Development Report* of UNDP for 2004. From the information on Gini coefficients of income distribution available in the *HDR* for various years, they also constructed an index to measure equality in distribution of per capita income. They used the Gini coefficients data over a span of 13 years (1990–2002). Under the constraints of data availability on income distribution, they chose 125 countries for construction of distribution-augmented HDI. The indices were subjected to the PCA and two composite indices of human development, one (PCHDI), without incorporating equality index, and the other (DAPCHDI), with its inclusion were obtained.

Haq (2003) noted that there is no a priori rationale for assigning different weights to different constituent indices. Each dimension of development is important, but the importance of each dimension may be different for developed and developing countries. Hence, he pleaded for equal weights on the principle of insufficient reason to discriminate among the constituent indices. On the other hand, as we have already mentioned, the PCA, a blindly empiricist method, has a tendency to undermine poorly correlated variables and instead favours highly correlated variables to make a composite index. The inclusive index (obtained by minimizing the sum of absolute correlation) gives due weights to poorly correlated variables too (by the proposed method), while the principal component index is largely elitist, favouring highly correlated variables and undermining the poorly correlated ones.

With this background, we re-computed the *DAPCHDI* with the data given by Sarker *et al.* (2006) in their paper to compare our composite index with theirs. As per the UNDP method *HDR 2005* or the *HDR 2006* adds little to the *HDR 2004* (as shown in Figure 3.1) database. We computed DAPCHDI by our new method, which maximizes the sum of absolute coefficients of correlation between the composite index and the constituent variables. We call them $NHDI_2$ (which is an I-2 type index) and $NHDI_1$ (I-1 type of index), respectively.

We have re-computed the DAPCHDI from the four indices, namely LE, ED, PCI, and equality index (EQ). The data for 125 countries, given by Sarker *et al.* (2006) in their paper, is reproduced in Table 3.1 below. We also reproduce the *HDR 2004* ranks (R_1), PCHDI ranks (R_2), and values, as well as the DAPCHDI ranks (R_3) and values obtained by Sarker *et al.* 2006. It may further be noted that computation of *I* (PCA) by the traditional method gives the same correlation coefficients (loadings) to variables (LE, ED, PCI, and EQ) as does the direct optimization method.

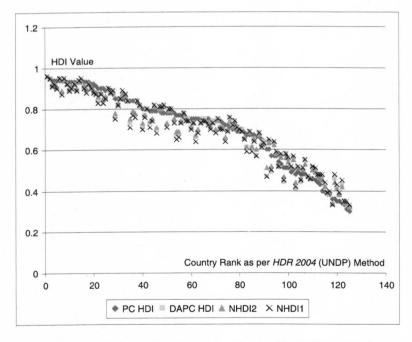

Figure 3.1: HDI Values of 125 Countries Obtained by Different Methods

Table 3.1: Composite Indices of Human Development in Select Countries
Obtained by Different Methods

Select Countries	Ranks by Different Methods					Human Development Indices: Different Aspects				Composite Indices of HDI			
	R_1	R_2	R_3	R_4	R_5	LE	ED	PCI	EQ	PC HDI	DAPC HDI	New Indices $NHDI_2$	$NHDI_1$
Norway	1	1	1	1	1	0.90	0.99	0.99	0.96	0.96	0.96	0.96	0.96
Sweden	2	2	2	2	2	0.92	0.99	0.93	0.98	0.95	0.95	0.95	0.95
Canada	3	3	11	11	11	0.90	0.98	0.95	0.81	0.94	0.91	0.92	0.91
Netherlands	4	6	10	8	10	0.89	0.99	0.95	0.82	0.94	0.92	0.92	0.92
Australia	5	4	14	13	14	0.90	0.99	0.94	0.76	0.94	0.90	0.91	0.90
Belgium	6	5	3	3	3	0.90	0.99	0.94	0.98	0.94	0.95	0.95	0.95
USA	7	7	23	20	26	0.87	0.97	0.98	0.64	0.94	0.88	0.89	0.87
Japan	8	8	4	4	5	0.94	0.94	0.93	0.98	0.94	0.95	0.94	0.95
Luxembourg	9	10	9	10	9	0.89	0.91	1.00	0.86	0.93	0.92	0.92	0.92
Ireland	10	14	18	16	17	0.86	0.96	0.98	0.75	0.93	0.89	0.90	0.89
Switzerland	11	9	12	12	12	0.90	0.95	0.95	0.81	0.93	0.91	0.91	0.90
Austria	12	11	8	9	8	0.89	0.96	0.95	0.87	0.93	0.92	0.92	0.92
UK	13	12	17	17	19	0.88	0.99	0.93	0.74	0.93	0.89	0.90	0.89
Finland	14	13	6	6	6	0.88	0.99	0.93	0.94	0.93	0.93	0.93	0.94
Denmark	15	15	5	5	4	0.86	0.98	0.96	0.99	0.93	0.94	0.94	0.95
France	16	16	13	14	13	0.90	0.96	0.93	0.81	0.93	0.91	0.91	0.90
New Zealand	17	17	19	19	21	0.89	0.99	0.90	0.74	0.93	0.89	0.90	0.88
Germany	18	18	7	7	7	0.89	0.95	0.94	0.91	0.93	0.92	0.92	0.92
Spain	19	19	15	15	15	0.90	0.97	0.90	0.82	0.92	0.90	0.91	0.90
Italy	20	20	21	21	23	0.89	0.93	0.93	0.74	0.92	0.88	0.89	0.88
Israel	21	21	24	23	24	0.90	0.94	0.88	0.76	0.91	0.88	0.88	0.87
Singapore	22	23	30	29	32	0.88	0.91	0.92	0.61	0.90	0.84	0.86	0.83
Greece	23	22	26	25	27	0.89	0.95	0.87	0.76	0.90	0.87	0.88	0.87
Hong Kong China (SAR)	24	24	32	30	33	0.91	0.86	0.93	0.59	0.90	0.84	0.85	0.83
Portugal	25	25	28	27	28	0.85	0.97	0.87	0.69	0.89	0.85	0.86	0.85
Slovenia	26	26	16	18	16	0.85	0.96	0.87	0.91	0.89	0.89	0.90	0.90
Korea Rep.	27	27	22	24	22	0.84	0.97	0.86	0.84	0.89	0.88	0.88	0.88
Czech. Rep.	28	28	20	22	18	0.84	0.92	0.84	0.97	0.87	0.89	0.88	0.89
Argentina	29	29	47	45	49	0.82	0.96	0.78	0.40	0.85	0.76	0.78	0.75
Estonia	30	30	34	34	34	0.78	0.98	0.80	0.72	0.85	0.82	0.83	0.82
Poland	31	31	29	31	29	0.81	0.96	0.78	0.84	0.85	0.85	0.85	0.85
Hungary	32	32	25	26	20	0.78	0.95	0.82	1.00	0.85	0.87	0.87	0.89
Slovakia	33	33	27	28	25	0.81	0.91	0.81	0.96	0.84	0.87	0.86	0.87
Lithuania	34	35	33	33	31	0.79	0.96	0.77	0.83	0.84	0.84	0.84	0.84
Chile	35	34	60	49	64	0.85	0.90	0.77	0.30	0.84	0.73	0.75	0.71

Contd...

Table 3.1 (Contd)

Select Countries	Ranks by Different Methods					Human Development Indices: Different Aspects				Composite Indices of HDI			
	R_1	R_2	R_3	R_4	R_5	LE	ED	PCI	EQ	PC HDI	DAPC HDI	New Indices $NHDI_2$	$NHDI_1$
Uruguay	36	36	43	43	44	0.84	0.94	0.73	0.56	0.84	0.78	0.79	0.77
Costa Rica	37	37	45	44	47	0.88	0.87	0.75	0.52	0.84	0.77	0.78	0.76
Croatia	38	38	31	32	30	0.82	0.90	0.77	0.89	0.83	0.84	0.84	0.84
Latvia	39	39	36	35	35	0.76	0.95	0.75	0.82	0.82	0.82	0.82	0.82
Mexico	40	40	66	63	72	0.81	0.85	0.75	0.35	0.80	0.71	0.73	0.70
Trinidad &Tobago	41	41	46	47	45	0.77	0.87	0.76	0.65	0.80	0.77	0.77	0.76
Bulgaria	42	42	40	39	40	0.77	0.91	0.71	0.83	0.80	0.80	0.80	0.80
Malaysia	43	45	63	58	63	0.80	0.83	0.75	0.46	0.79	0.73	0.74	0.71
Russian Fed.	44	46	57	48	55	0.69	0.95	0.74	0.54	0.79	0.74	0.75	0.74
Macedonia	45	44	35	36	36	0.81	0.87	0.70	0.91	0.79	0.82	0.81	0.82
Panama	46	43	73	67	79	0.83	0.86	0.69	0.31	0.79	0.70	0.71	0.68
Belarus	47	47	39	40	39	0.75	0.95	0.67	0.86	0.79	0.80	0.80	0.81
Albania	48	48	38	38	38	0.81	0.89	0.65	0.91	0.78	0.81	0.80	0.81
Bosnia & Herzegovina	49	49	37	37	37	0.82	0.84	0.68	0.95	0.78	0.82	0.81	0.82
Venezuela	50	50	64	65	66	0.81	0.86	0.67	0.47	0.78	0.72	0.73	0.71
Romania	51	51	42	41	42	0.76	0.88	0.70	0.87	0.78	0.80	0.79	0.80
Ukraine	52	53	41	42	41	0.74	0.94	0.65	0.89	0.78	0.80	0.79	0.80
Saint Lucia	53	52	54	51	57	0.79	0.88	0.66	0.60	0.78	0.74	0.75	0.73
Brazil	54	54	81	78	81	0.72	0.88	0.73	0.25	0.77	0.67	0.69	0.65
Colombia	55	55	80	77	80	0.78	0.84	0.69	0.29	0.77	0.67	0.69	0.66
Thailand	56	56	58	57	59	0.74	0.86	0.71	0.59	0.77	0.73	0.74	0.73
Kazakhstan	57	57	44	46	43	0.69	0.93	0.68	0.84	0.76	0.78	0.78	0.78
Jamaica	58	58	49	50	51	0.84	0.83	0.61	0.70	0.76	0.75	0.75	0.74
Armenia	59	59	52	54	54	0.79	0.90	0.57	0.70	0.75	0.75	0.74	0.74
Philippines	60	60	67	66	68	0.75	0.89	0.62	0.53	0.75	0.71	0.71	0.70
Turkmenistan	61	61	62	61	60	0.70	0.93	0.63	0.64	0.75	0.73	0.73	0.73
Paraguay	62	62	82	81	85	0.76	0.85	0.64	0.30	0.75	0.66	0.67	0.64
Peru	63	64	78	74	78	0.74	0.86	0.65	0.45	0.75	0.69	0.70	0.68
Turkey	64	63	59	60	58	0.76	0.80	0.69	0.66	0.75	0.73	0.73	0.73
Azerbaijan	65	65	51	56	53	0.78	0.88	0.58	0.73	0.75	0.75	0.74	0.74
Jordan	66	66	53	53	50	0.76	0.86	0.62	0.74	0.75	0.75	0.74	0.74
Tunisia	67	67	61	62	61	0.79	0.74	0.70	0.66	0.75	0.73	0.73	0.72
China	68	68	69	69	69	0.76	0.83	0.64	0.56	0.74	0.71	0.71	0.70
Georgia	69	69	55	59	56	0.81	0.89	0.52	0.73	0.74	0.74	0.73	0.73
Dominican Rep.	70	71	76	73	76	0.70	0.82	0.70	0.50	0.74	0.69	0.70	0.68

Sri Lanka	71	70	50	52	48	0.79	0.83	0.60	0.78	0.74	0.75	0.74	0.75
Ecuador	72	72	70	70	71	0.76	0.85	0.60	0.58	0.74	0.71	0.71	0.70
Iran	73	73	71	71	70	0.75	0.74	0.70	0.60	0.73	0.70	0.71	0.70
El Salvador	74	74	83	83	87	0.76	0.75	0.65	0.38	0.72	0.65	0.66	0.64
Guyana	75	75	77	75	75	0.64	0.89	0.63	0.59	0.72	0.69	0.70	0.69
Uzbekistan	76	76	48	55	46	0.74	0.91	0.47	0.94	0.71	0.76	0.74	0.76
Algeria	77	77	65	68	62	0.74	0.69	0.68	0.76	0.70	0.72	0.71	0.72
Kyrgyzstan	78	78	56	64	52	0.72	0.92	0.46	0.89	0.70	0.74	0.73	0.74
Indonesia	79	80	68	72	65	0.69	0.80	0.58	0.78	0.69	0.71	0.70	0.71
Vietnam	80	79	72	76	67	0.73	0.82	0.52	0.74	0.69	0.70	0.70	0.70
Moldova	81	81	74	79	73	0.73	0.87	0.45	0.74	0.69	0.70	0.69	0.69
Bolivia	82	82	84	84	82	0.64	0.86	0.53	0.56	0.68	0.65	0.66	0.65
Honduras	83	84	91	90	90	0.73	0.74	0.54	0.34	0.67	0.61	0.61	0.59
Tajikistan	84	85	75	80	74	0.73	0.90	0.38	0.77	0.67	0.69	0.68	0.69
Nicaragua	85	83	90	91	91	0.74	0.73	0.54	0.34	0.67	0.61	0.61	0.59
Mongolia	86	86	85	85	84	0.64	0.89	0.47	0.57	0.67	0.65	0.65	0.64
South Africa	87	88	94	92	95	0.40	0.83	0.77	0.25	0.66	0.57	0.60	0.57
Egypt	88	87	79	82	77	0.73	0.62	0.61	0.78	0.66	0.68	0.67	0.68
Guatemala	89	89	89	88	89	0.68	0.65	0.62	0.48	0.65	0.62	0.62	0.61
Morocco	90	90	87	87	88	0.72	0.53	0.61	0.67	0.62	0.64	0.63	0.63
Namibia	91	91	108	103	111	0.34	0.79	0.69	0.00	0.60	0.47	0.51	0.47
India	92	92	86	86	83	0.64	0.59	0.55	0.82	0.60	0.64	0.63	0.65
Botswana	93	93	105	100	105	0.27	0.76	0.73	0.17	0.57	0.49	0.52	0.50
Ghana	94	94	88	89	86	0.55	0.65	0.51	0.87	0.57	0.63	0.62	0.64
Cambodia	95	95	92	93	92	0.54	0.66	0.50	0.65	0.57	0.58	0.58	0.59
Papua New Guinea	96	96	99	99	101	0.54	0.57	0.52	0.43	0.54	0.52	0.52	0.52
Laos	97	97	95	94	94	0.49	0.64	0.47	0.72	0.53	0.57	0.56	0.58
Swaziland	98	100	113	107	113	0.18	0.74	0.64	0.21	0.51	0.44	0.47	0.45
Bangladesh	99	98	93	95	93	0.60	0.45	0.47	0.83	0.51	0.58	0.56	0.58
Nepal	100	99	97	97	97	0.58	0.50	0.44	0.73	0.51	0.55	0.54	0.56
Cameroon	101	102	102	102	100	0.36	0.64	0.50	0.56	0.49	0.51	0.51	0.52
Pakistan	102	101	96	96	96	0.60	0.40	0.49	0.81	0.50	0.56	0.55	0.57
Lesotho	103	106	117	114	118	0.19	0.76	0.53	0.17	0.48	0.41	0.44	0.42
Uganda	104	103	101	101	99	0.34	0.70	0.44	0.60	0.49	0.51	0.51	0.52
Zimbabwe	105	107	114	111	114	0.15	0.79	0.53	0.30	0.48	0.44	0.46	0.45
Kenya	106	104	104	104	103	0.34	0.74	0.39	0.56	0.48	0.50	0.50	0.51
Yemen	107	105	98	98	98	0.58	0.50	0.36	0.80	0.48	0.55	0.53	0.55
Madagascar	108	108	107	108	110	0.47	0.60	0.33	0.50	0.47	0.47	0.47	0.47
Nigeria	109	110	112	112	112	0.44	0.59	0.36	0.43	0.46	0.46	0.46	0.46
Mauritania	110	109	100	105	102	0.45	0.42	0.52	0.68	0.46	0.51	0.50	0.52
Gambia	111	111	103	106	104	0.48	0.40	0.47	0.70	0.45	0.50	0.49	0.51

Contd...

Table 3.1 (Contd)

Select Countries	Ranks by Different Methods					Human Development Indices: Different Aspects				Composite Indices of HDI			
	R_1	R_2	R_3	R_4	R_5	LE	ED	PCI	EQ	PC HDI	DAPC HDI	New Indices NHDI$_2$	NHDI$_1$
Senegal	112	112	106	109	106	0.46	0.39	0.46	0.63	0.44	0.48	0.47	0.48
Guinea	113	113	109	110	107	0.40	0.37	0.51	0.65	0.43	0.47	0.46	0.48
Tanzania	114	114	110	113	109	0.31	0.62	0.29	0.70	0.40	0.46	0.45	0.48
Cote d Ivoire	115	115	116	116	116	0.27	0.47	0.45	0.55	0.39	0.42	0.42	0.44
Zambia	116	116	121	120	120	0.13	0.68	0.36	0.39	0.38	0.38	0.39	0.39
Malawi	117	117	119	119	119	0.21	0.66	0.29	0.44	0.38	0.39	0.39	0.40
Central African Rep.	118	118	124	123	124	0.25	0.43	0.41	0.21	0.36	0.33	0.34	0.33
Ethiopia	119	119	111	115	108	0.34	0.39	0.34	0.87	0.36	0.46	0.44	0.48
Mozambique	120	121	118	118	117	0.22	0.45	0.39	0.67	0.35	0.41	0.41	0.43
Guinea Bissau	121	120	120	121	121	0.34	0.39	0.33	0.51	0.35	0.38	0.38	0.39
Burundi	122	122	115	117	115	0.26	0.45	0.31	0.80	0.34	0.43	0.42	0.45
Mali	123	123	122	122	122	0.39	0.21	0.37	0.44	0.33	0.35	0.34	0.35
Burkina Faso	124	124	123	124	123	0.35	0.16	0.40	0.49	0.31	0.34	0.34	0.35
Niger	125	125	125	125	125	0.35	0.18	0.35	0.44	0.30	0.32	0.32	0.33

Source: Sarker et al. 2006 (adapted from HDRs of UNDP); PCI is named as GDP in HDR/Sarker et al. 2006.

The HDI indices computed by us are NHDI$_2$ (principal component) and NHDI$_1$ (that minimizes the sum of absolute correlation coefficients), and the ranks obtained by different countries are R_4 and R_5, respectively. These HDI indices too are presented in Table 3.1. Note that ranks, as computed by us, are based on more accurate NHDI$_2$ and NHDI$_1$ figures.

In our analysis, the constituent indices of HDI obtain different weights and are differently correlated with their composite HDI indices. These weights and correlation coefficients are given in Table 3.2 and Table 3.3, respectively.

Table 3.2: Weights Assigned to the Constituent Indices by Different Methods

Indices	LE	ED	PCI	EQ
DAPCHDI	0.30	0.25	0.25	0.20
NHDI2	0.270909751	0.275588551	0.289481714	0.164019853
NHDI1	0.239643184	0.258695275	0.265657700	0.236003815

Table 3.3: Correlation of Composite HD Indices with Different Constituent Indices

Index	LE	ED	PCI	EQ	SAR	SSR
NHDI2	0.923635411	0.870389039	0.890306269	0.567829911	3.25216063	2.72575551
NHDI1	0.914036295	0.845974366	0.865869176	0.639601336	3.26548117	2.70995428

SAR=Sum of Absolute correlation coefficients; SSR=Sum of Squared correlation coefficients

Table 3.4: Correlation Matrix of Different Ranks and HD Indices Obtained by Different Methods

Ranks/ HD Indices	Ranks obtained by Different Methods					HD Indices obtained by Different Methods			
	R1	R2	R3	R4	R5	PCHDI	DA PCHDI	$NHDI_2$	$NHDI_1$
R1	1.00000	0.99969	0.96199	0.97512	0.95372	-0.97103	-0.95206	-0.96446	-0.94855
R2	0.99969	1.00000	0.96289	0.97568	0.95443	-0.97105	-0.95320	-0.96515	-0.94960
R3	0.96199	0.96289	1.00000	0.99736	0.99878	-0.94587	-0.98259	-0.98089	-0.98573
R4	0.97512	0.97568	0.99736	1.00000	0.99478	-0.95589	-0.98075	-0.98235	-0.98284
R5	0.95372	0.95443	0.99878	0.99478	1.00000	-0.93923	-0.98202	-0.97900	-0.98633
PCHDI	-0.97103	-0.97105	-0.94587	-0.95589	-0.93923	1.00000	0.97141	0.98302	0.96251
DAPCHDI	-0.95206	-0.95320	-0.98259	-0.98075	-0.98202	0.97141	1.00000	0.99783	0.99865
$NHDI_2$	-0.96446	-0.96515	-0.98089	-0.98235	-0.97900	0.98302	0.99783	1.00000	0.99569
$NHDI_1$	-0.94855	-0.94960	-0.98573	-0.98284	-0.98633	0.96251	0.99865	0.99569	1.00000

It may be noted that $NHDI_1$ trades off SSR only slightly to assign higher weights to EQ index. In exchange, the weights of LE, ED, and PCI are reduced. Overall, $NHDI_1$ weights are more egalitarian than the $NHDI_2$ weights. Finally, in the Table 3.4 we present the matrix of correlation coefficients (based on figures in Table 3.1) among and across different ranks, and composite *HDI* measures.

The *HDRs* assign subjective (or arbitrary) weights to indices of life expectancy, education, and income. Inclusion of equality index to HDI naturally raises the question as to the weight to be assigned to it. It is also required to reduce the weights assigned to other indices. An attempt may be made to obtain weights by the Principal Component Analysis. However, the Principal Component Analysis has a tendency to undermine the variables with weaker correlation coefficients. It may be elitist in favouring the highly correlated indices. Variance, or explanatory power of a composite index, cannot be the sole guide to assign weights. Representation of individual indices in the composite HDI also matters. The *HDR* has taken an extreme stand of assigning equal weights to all indices and suffers from an excessive bias to pragmatism. However, the new method of obtaining weights and constructing an HDI suggested by us is inclusive in nature, and takes care of weakly correlated indices and, also, gives them proper representation in the composite HDI.

CONCLUDING REMARKS

In this exercise, we have shown that the principal component indices are elitist and they have a tendency to undermine the importance of poorly correlated variables. On the other hand, I-1 is more inclusive and has a tendency to represent even the poorly correlated variables. The I-M indices are egalitarian in nature. Conventionally, the HD index is constructed by assigning equal weights to all the constituent measures (such as literacy, income, life expectancy, etc.). The I-M index does almost the same, but with an added mathematically-oriented methodological justification. The I-1 (inclusive) type of index is a compromise between I-2 (elitist) and I-M (egalitarian) types of indices.

It would depend on the analyst, whether he is interested in egalitarian, inclusive, or elitist method of constructing indices when the constituent variables are not very highly correlated among themselves. This chapter has opened up the option to choose the method of constructing a desired type of index.

REFERENCES

Haq, Mahbub-ul- 2003. 'The Birth of the Human Development Index', in Fukuda-Parr, S. and A.K. Shiva Kumar (eds) *Readings in Human Development*, Oxford University Press, London.

Kendall, M. G. and A. Stuart 1968. *The Advanced Theory of Statistics*, Vol. 3, Charles Griffin and Company, London.

Kuester, J.L. and J.H. Mize 1973. *Optimization Techniques with Fortran*, McGraw-Hill Book Company, New York.

McCracken, K. 2000. 'Some Comments on the Seifa96 Indexes', Paper presented in the 10th Biennial Conference of the Australian Population Association, Melbourne, Australia, www.apa.org.au/upload/2000-7B_McCracken.pdf

Mishra, S. K. 2007. 'A FORTRAN Computer Program for Construction of Composite Indices: Alternative to the Indices obtained by the Principal Components Analysis'. http://www1.webng.com/economics/make-indices.html

—— 2006. 'Global Optimization by Differential Evolution and Particle Swarm Methods: Evaluation on Some Benchmark Functions', SSRN. http://ssrn.com/abstract=933827

Munda, G. and M. Nardo 2005. 'Constructing Consistent Composite Indicators: The Issue of Weights', EUR 21834 EN, Institute for the Protection and Security of the Citizen, European Commission, Luxembourg.

Organisation for Economic Co-operation and Development (OECD), 2003. *Composite Indicators of Country Performance: A Critical Assessment*, DST/IND(2003)5, Paris.

Sarker, S., B. Biswas, and P.J. Soundrs 2006. 'Distribution-Augmented Human Development Index: A Principal Component Analysis', GSP, College of Business, Utah State Univ., USA, www.usu.edu/cob/econ/graduatestudents/documents/papers/developmentpaper.pdf

United Nations Development Programme (UNDP), 2004, 2005, and 2006. *Human Development Report*, Oxford University Press, New York.

II

Issues at the All India Level

4

Economic Growth and Human Development
Chain Relationship

SAUNDARJYA BORBORA

INTRODUCTION

Human development has now been accepted as the ultimate objective of human activity and has replaced economic growth, which was emphasized till the 1980s. This changed perception dates back to the earlier basic needs approach as well as Sen's concept of capabilities. The first *Human Development Report 1990* of United Nations Development Programme (UNDP) stated that 'the basic objective of development is to create an enabling environment for people to enjoy long, healthy, and creative lives', and defined human development as 'a process of enlarging peoples choices'. It should be noted that there is a strong connection between economic growth and human development. Economic growth provides the resources for investments for sustained improvements in human development and in the other way, improvements in the quality of labour force is an important factor for economic growth. That is, to the extent that greater freedom and capabilities to improve economic performance and human development will have a positive impact on growth. In the same way, to the extent that increased income will increase the range of choices and capabilities enjoyed by households and governments, economic growth will have a positive impact on human development. The chapter tries to analyse this chain relationship, on the basis of review of theoretical studies and empirical analysis, which may be important for policy prescription.

THE CHAIN RELATIONSHIP

The prime objective of economic growth and any human activity is human development, when such activities visualize human welfare and a better standard of living, and economic growth is a very important way for advancing it. Similarly, advancement in human development can be an important contributor to economic growth. Thus, there are these two distinct chains: one is from economic growth to human development, as resources from the growth process are allocated for different areas contributing to human development; and the other is from human development to economic growth, contributing to the increase of national income.

Economic Growth to Human Development

Economic growth influences human development mainly through two links: the influence of household activity and spending on human development, and influence of government policies and expenditure. Income growth helps in increasing the capabilities of individuals and consequently the human development of a nation since it encapsulate the economy's command over resources (Sen 2000). As an example, it can be noted that while the people in the state of Kerala have high life expectancies and literacy rates, comparable to those of many developed countries, the very fact that they cannot enjoy many benefits enjoyed by such countries demonstrates the importance of GDP as a tool for achieving a wide range of capabilities. Besides, GDP has a strong influence on literacy and health of the people, both through household expenditure and government programmes. Thus, it can be seen that higher income facilitates the achievement of human development.

The impact of economic growth on human development also depends on the environment of the society. The income distribution at the micro level (that is, within a household) as well as at the macro level (that is, across the households) also has influence on human development. At the micro level, individual and household consumption can be an important element in advancing human development and may respond more efficiently to the needs of the population than do the government programmes. But, individual consumption always does not necessarily contribute towards human development. In societies, where women contribute a large share to household income and have more influence in household decision making, expenditures on human development-oriented goods are likely to be high. Several studies support this view. Some of the studies are: among the Gambian household, the larger the proportion of food under women's control, the larger is the household calorie consumption (Von Braun 1988). In the Cote d'Ivoire, it has been shown that an increase in women's share of income was associated with higher spending on food, and reduced spending on alcohol and cigarettes (Hoddinott and Haddad 1991).

At the macro level, the distribution of the increased income will have a higher influence on human development. Since poor households spend a higher proportion of their income on goods that directly promote better health and education, economic growth, whose benefits are directed towards poor, will have a greater influence on human development through increased food expenditure and education. Birdsall et al. (1995) showed that if the distribution of income in Brazil were equal to that in Malaysia, school enrolment among the poor children would have been 40 per cent higher.

Government policies and expenditures also have an important effect on human development. The allocation of resources to improve human development is a function of total public sector expenditure and its share to the human development sectors. This can be expressed in the form of three ratios (UNDP 1991). These are:

1. public expenditure ratio, defined as the proportion of Gross National Product (GNP) spent by various levels of government;
2. HD-allocation ratio, defined as the proportion of total government expenditure allocated to the human development sectors; and
3. HD-priority ratio, defined as the proportion of the total HD-sector expenditure going to 'priority areas'. Within the HD-sectors, some expenditure is more productive in terms of impact on human development than others; for example, basic education at the early stage of development is generally recognized to have a better impact on human development than tertiary education.

The government expenditure complements private expenditure in this process and most of the effects of economic growth on human development are likely to flow through government budgetary expenditures (Anand and Ravallion 1993). The achievement of human development through government expenditure depends on effectiveness of expenditure targeting and delivery. The priority sectors, such as primary education and health, which have highest potential for human development improvement, should be identified. These expenditures should be distributed to benefit the low-income groups and government should have an efficient institutional capacity to deliver the goods. The effectiveness of public expenditure is conditional on the quality of governance and accountability (Rajkumar and Swaroop 2002).

Human Development to Economic Growth

Human development, in turn, has also important effects on economic growth. It is well accepted and, also, evidence suggests that healthy and educated people contribute more to economic growth. Higher levels of human development affect the economy through enhancing capabilities and, consequently, impact on creativity and productivity. More specifically, each of the components of human development is likely to have an impact on economic growth. In agriculture, using data from Malaysia, Ghana, and Peru, it was found that each extra year of schooling by farmers is associated with an annual increase in output by 2–5 per cent (Birdsall 1993). In addition to direct effect on productivity, education also affects the rate of innovations and technological adaptation as seen in the case of the Green Revolution in India (Foster and Rosenzweig 1995). Education alone cannot transform an economy. The quantity and quality of investment, choice of technology, and overall policy environment are the other important determinants of economic performance.

Health and nutrition is another component which has a positive impact on economic growth, although it has its own importance. Strauss and Thomas (1998) reviewed a large number of literature showing improvement in productivity and income, with improvements in health and nutrition. Labour productivity gains have been observed to be associated with calorie intake increase in poor countries (Cornia and Stewart 1995). Education and health may also a have strong indirect effect on economic growth through their effect on distribution of income. As education and health improve, and become more broadly based, low-income people are in a position to seek out economic opportunities. Equal distribution of income is known to favour growth for both economic and political economy reasons. Education may also affect per capita income growth via impact on population growth.

THE VIRTUOUS AND VICIOUS CYCLES

The above discussion brings out the fact that there exist a two-way relationship between economic growth and human development. This is supported by theory and evidence. It also points out that nations may enter either a virtuous cycle of high growth and commensurate gains in human development, or a vicious cycle of low growth and low human development. In these states, levels of economic growth and human development are mutually reinforcing, either leading to an upward development or a poverty trap. The persistence of these cycles depends on linkages between economic growth and human development. Some countries may also have lopsided development in the short period, with relatively good growth and relatively poor human development, and vice versa.

There may be a number of reasons for lopsided growth, such as poor public expenditure policy, low social expenditure, and inequitable distribution of income. A study by Ranis et al. (2000) finds that eight economic growth-lopsided nations, during 1960–70, moved into a vicious cycle of low economic growth and low human development. This suggests that economic growth not accompanied by improvement in human development may be unsustainable. Studies also show that a high level of human development in early stages of growth process with right policy decisions translate into a virtuous cycle of good economic growth and human development complementing each other (Ramirez, Ranis, and Stewart 1998). Policies like encouraging higher investment, technological innovation, and improved distribution of income can link up human development into sustainable economic growth. This suggests that human development seems to be necessary prerequisite for sustainable growth. Human development may also exhibit a threshold effect, that is, a country must attain a certain HD level before economic growth becomes sustainable.

CONCLUSION

The foregoing analysis reveals that there is a correlation between economic growth and human development, and the one affecting the other, both directly and indirectly. Government policies also have strong implications. If human development improvements are a prerequisite for economic growth, government policy, and public expenditure may be targeted in social sectors such as education and health along with good governance. This will help the state to move above the threshold level in human development. It is necessary to identify the weak links, appropriate policies might be implemented to strengthen the links, and such policies may be dynamic in nature with changes in the development process. In the early stages, priorities may be given to education and health, and at a later stage, higher education, technology, and better health facilities may assume a greater role.

The important lesson that emerges is that the view 'grow first and worry about human development later' (Ranis *et al.* 2004) is not supported by evidence. But the present perception is that a focus on human development must be made from the beginning of the growth process. Economic growth will not be sustained if it is not accompanied by improvement in human development.

REFERENCES

Anand, S. and M. Ravallion 1993. 'Human Development in Poor Countries: On the Role of Private Incomes and Public Services', *Journal of Economic Perspectives*, Vol. 7, No.1, pp.133–50.

Birdsall, N. 1993. 'Social Development in Economic Development', World Bank Policy Research, Working Paper Series, 1123, Washington D.C.

Birdsall, N., D. Ross, and R. Sabot 1995. 'Inequality and Growth Reconsidered: Lessons from East Asia', *World Bank Economic Review*, Vol. 9, No. 3, pp. 477–508.

Cornia, G.A. and F. Stewart 1995. 'Two Errors of Targeting', in F. Stewart (ed.) *Adjustment and Poverty: Options and Choices*, Routledge, London.

Foster, A.D. and M.R. Rosenzweig 1995. 'Learning by Doing and Learning from Others: Human Capital and Technical Change in Agriculture', *Journal of Political Economics*, Vol. 103.

Hoddinott, J. and L. Haddad 1991. 'Household Expenditures, Child Anthropometric Status and Intra-household Division of Income: Evidence from the Cote d'Ivoire', Research Program in Development Studies, Woodrow Wilson School, Discussion Paper 15.

Rajkumar, A.S. and V. Swaroop 2002. 'Public Spending and Outcomes: Does Governance Matter?', World Bank Working Paper No. 2840.

Ranis, G. 2004. 'Human Development and Economic Growth', Economic Growth Centre, Yale University, Discussion Paper No. 887.

Ranis, G., F. Stewart, and A. Ramirez 2004. 'Economic Growth and Human Development', in Sakiko Fukuda-Parr and A.K. Shiva Kumar (eds), *Readings in Human Development*, Oxford University Press, New Delhi.

——— 2000. 'Economic Growth and Human Development', *World Development*, Vol. 28, No. 2.

Ramirez, A., G. Ranis, and F. Stewart 1998. 'Economic Growth and Human Development', QEH Working Paper Series–QEHWPS18. http://www3.qeh.ox.ac.uk/pdf/qehwp/qehwps18.pdf/

Sen, A. 2000. 'A Decade of Human Development', *Journal of Development*, Vol. 1, No. 1.

Strauss, J. and D. Thomas 1998. 'Nutrition and Economic Development', *Journal of Economic Literature*, Vol. 36, No. 2, pp. 766–817.

United Nations Development Programme (UNDP), 1996, 1991, and 1990. *Human Development Report*, Oxford University Press, New York.

Von Braun, J. 1998. 'Effects of Technological Change in Agriculture, on Food Consumption, and Nutrition: Rice in a West African Setting', *Economic Development and Cultural Change*, Vol. 37.

5

Transformation of Economic Growth to Human Development
A Long-Run Study of Indian States

SANTANU RAY

INTRODUCTION

Economists in the war-stricken world of the 1940s emphasized on economic growth with the belief that expansion of income/output is an end in itself, and that growth does trickle down. Economic Growth (EG) improves the quality of life of the people, at least in the long run. However, the global experience suggests that the transformation of economic prosperity to the well-being of the people is not automatic. Growth, in the new development paradigm of the 1990s, has been identified as a necessary but not sufficient condition for achieving Human Development (HD). Moreover, the economic growth that fails to enhance human development is unlikely to sustain. A virtuous cycle requires that growth must be accompanied or preceded by parallel improvements in human development. An economy may be on a mutually reinforcing upward spiral with high levels of human development leading to high income growth, and growth in turn promoting human development. Conversely, weak HD may result in low growth and consequently poor progress towards HD. Hence, human development is not just an end product of the development process but an important input as well, and also a key ingredient in the process of economic prosperity. Because of the strong two-way relationship, it is extremely important for any economy to promote both growth and human development to sustain progress in either.

India's growth performance over the last two decades became a topical issue. After a sluggish growth rate in the first three decades of independence, India's turnaround in the 1980s attracted attention all over the world. The acceleration, on the other hand, raised several questions. It is often said that the recent growth trend in India is not an inclusive one, and failed miserably to expand the well-being of the people in the human development sense. This chapter seeks to answer the question whether the state-level growth achievements in India are transformed into human development. Using Indian disaggregated data for a period of three decades (1970–71 to 2000–01), a growth-human development relationship is scrutinized. Thus, the present chapter examines whether the economic growth achieved by Indian states in the last three decades has any statistically significant influence in determining the present level of human development.

THEORETICAL FRAMEWORK

Human Development Report 1996 provides a standard framework for discussing the relationship between economic growth and human development, and emphasizes on the quality of growth, that matters, to achieve progress in human development. The framework was further advanced and updated in a series of articles by Ramirez *et al.* (1998), Ranis *et al.* (2000), Ranis and Stewart (2000), Boozer *et al.* (2003), and Ranis and Stewart (2005). They argue that there exists a strong relationship between economic growth and human development. In Chain-A, growth provides resources to permit sustained improvements in human development, while in Chain-B, improvements in the level of education and health, key ingredients of human development, contribute to future growth. They hypothesize that transformation of growth into human development would be stronger when there is a higher income equality, greater allocation of resources toward human development, larger share of government allocation to human development related social expenditure, greater contribution of social capital, and a more effective human development improvement function. The empirical analysis suggests that in most cases, EG and HD run parallel. Most of the developing economies are within the vicious cycle mode—with below average HD and EG, and few economies are facing lopsided realities where HD and EG are not coherent.

LITERATURE SURVEY

India's position in the above framework is far away from satisfactory. *Human Development Report 1996*: 81 notes: '...India—remains in the weak links quadrant with low human development and low growth during the 1960s and 1970s. It moves to lopsided development in 1980–92 as growth accelerates while progress in human development remains slow...'. Ramirez *et al.* (1998) examine the significance of the relationship, for the chains as a whole and for particular links in them, with the help of cross-country statistics. They find Indian performance in the 1960s and 1970s, in a vicious cycle category. However, in the 1990s India moved to the *EG*-lopsided group. Almost the same views have been expressed about India by Ranis and Stewart (2000) and Boozer *et al.* (2003). Using data from 69 developing countries, Ranis and Stewart (2005) extend the analysis for the period 1960–2001. They point out categorically that India remained in a vicious cycle for first two decades; however, her movement toward *EG*-lopsided quadrant during the 1980s received a reversal in the 1990s.

In parallel efforts, Mazumder (1995 and 2000) scrutinized the causal relationship between human well-being and economic prosperity. Human well-being in this framework is captured by the core indicators such as life expectancy at birth, adult literacy rate, and infant mortality rate, while economic achievements by per capita real gross product. Key findings in Mazumder (2000) reveal that the relation varies significantly with different income groups.

At the national level, empirical studies on the causality between economic growth and human development have been attempted in both ways. Few scholars find that economic growth determines the level of human development, however, others argue for reverse causality. Dholakia (1985: 112–18) tested both the hypotheses of neoclassical school. A higher human capital formation would lead to higher growth of the TFP in a region and of human capital approach where human capital base of a region plays an important role in determining the growth of output and TFP, using data from 15 major states for the period 1961–71. However, Indian data could not support any of these hypotheses even at 10 per cent level of significance. Geeta Rani (1995) finds that economic progress in India is one of the important factors that determine the level of human development. Dholakia (2003) finds that human development indicators positively influence income with a lag of about eight years, whereas income per capita affects the other within two years. Using Indian mortality statistics, World Bank (2004) documents that both household living standards and national income levels have a positive effect on the reduction of infant mortality (under age one). This result is for Indian infant mortality in five years preceding 1998–99. Foster and Rosenzweig (1996) focus attention on the relation between education levels and economic growth in rural India during the Green Revolution. They concentrate mainly on the agricultural transformation in that period, and show how initial education levels translated into subsequent economic growth through new opportunities, created by technical change. Gupta and Mitra (2004) investigate the possible links between economic growth, poverty, and health, using panel data for 15 major states covering a period from the early 1970s to late 1990s. Their results indicate that though growth tends to reduce poverty, significant improvements in health status are also necessary for poverty to decrease. The study explores a two-way relationship between growth and health status: better health condition of the people enhances economic growth by improving productivity and higher growth allows better human capital formation.

In another attempt, Duraisamy and Mahal (2005) examine the same relationship between the rate of economic growth, health indicators, and poverty levels of 14 major Indian states for the period 1970–71 to 2000–01. They document a strong association between income growth and health indicators: with the increase in income life expectancy increases significantly and infant mortality falls sharply. However, poverty level and income growth on an average are inversely related. Bhalotra (2006) arrives at the result that unconditional growth elasticity of under-five mortality in India is about –0.7, which means that a 10 per cent increase in per capita income is associated with a 7 per cent reduction in mortality. This result corresponds to the under-five mortality statistics of 14 major Indian states for the period 1970 to 1994. Trivedi (2006) studies the relation between income levels and levels of educational capital in Indian states. The key findings are that the stock of educational capital, proxied by the secondary school enrolment rate, has a significant positive impact on steady-state level of per capita income and also on attendant growth rates. Other interesting set of findings is that both male and female educational capitals are positively related to the steady-state incomes, or that gender-gaps in education reduce long-run incomes. Drawing data mainly from the Planning Commission (2002) for 15 major states of India and covering a period from 1980–81 to 2000–01, Ghosh (2006) found strong evidence of regional convergence in human development despite significant divergence in real per capita income.

PRESENT STUDY

It is evident from the previous section that several attempts have been made to correlate economic progress with human well-being in the Indian sub-national context. However, there is a dearth of empirical studies aimed to find out the cause-and-effect relationship between the two. The present study intends to seek the role of economic growth in determining the level of human development using a limited version of Granger-Causality Test.

We narrow our focus to the 16 most populous states for which consistent time series data are available. The older boundaries of the states of Bihar (including Jharkhand), Madhya Pradesh (including Chhattisgarh), and Uttar Pradesh (including Uttaranchal) are considered for the entire period of three decades. The focused states in this study include Punjab (PJ), Haryana (HR), Himachal Pradesh (HP), Uttar Pradesh (UP), Madhya Pradesh (MP), Maharashtra (MH), Gujarat (GJ), Rajasthan (RJ), Bihar (BH), Orissa (OR), West Bengal (WB), Assam (AS), Andhra Pradesh (AP), Karnataka (KK), Kerala (KR), and Tamil Nadu (TN). These included states have a combined population of 987.92 million, accounting for over 96 per cent of India's total population (Census 2001); and 2.87 million square kilometers, accounting for 87 per cent of India's total geographical area. The variation in economic performances and disparity in level of living within the focused area are large.

First, we computed the growth rates of each of the included states for the last three consecutive decades and then construct a HDI for the states, following the United Nations Development Programme (UNDP) formulated *HDR 1999* methodology, so that the position of the Indian states could be viewed in a global perspective. The states are classified on the basis of their achievements in per capita income and HDI. And finally, using a limited version of Granger-Causality Test we examine the significance of the transformation of economic prosperity into human development.

INDICATORS AND DATA SOURCES

The period chosen for this study covers three decades: 1970–71 to 2000–01. A brief discussion is presented here on the data sources of different variables/indicators that are involved in this study.

Estimates of Economic Growth

Per Capita Net State Domestic Products (PCNSDPs) are taken as an indicator of measuring economic performances of the states. First, we obtain the data directly from EPWRF (2003: Annexure 1 and Appendix 11.6) for the period 1980–81 to 2000–01 at constant 1993–94 prices. For the states of Bihar, Madhya Pradesh, and Uttar Pradesh, we merged the data of Jharkhand, Chhattisgarh, and Uttaranchal, respectively, in case they were provided separately. Now a deflator is constructed for each of the included states, using the price index of the respective state to convert the figures of 1970–71 prices into 1993–94 prices.

Human Development Index

United Nations Development Programme (1999) methodology involves a number of indicators. We present the sources of the dataset of the indicators that are directly involved in the computation of HDI.

Life Expectancy at Birth

The Registrar General of India estimates life-tables for major Indian states on the basis of 6 or 5-year averages of age-specific death rates. Using these values of state-specific life expectancy at birth, regression lines for each of the major states of the country are fitted applying Ordinary Least Square method. From the regression line, the estimate of life expectancy at birth, for a particular state in a particular year, is commonly obtained by the researchers for different purposes. These estimates are widely referred and used in socio-economic researches. We obtained the same from Planning Commission (2002) and MSPI (2006).

Adult Literacy Rate

Planning Commission (2002) provides data on adult literacy rate for the years of 1981 and 1991, while from the Census of India (1971) and (2007), we collected the adult literacy rates for the years 1971 and 2001, respectively. Srivastava (2002) also provides useful feedback on adult literacy rates of Indian states for different census years.

Combined Enrolment Ratio

This is comparatively a complicated indicator. Indrayan et al. (1999) had computed Combined Enrolment Ratio (CER) for major Indian states using official information from different sources. We adopt their figures for the years of 1971, 1981, and 1991. Using information from Geeta Rani (2007) and applying the same formulation of Indrayan et al. (1999), we have estimated the CER for the states of India of the year 2001.

GSDP Per Capita in PPP US $

The income component of HDI is captured by the indicator of real per capita GDP in Purchasing Power Parity (PPP) term. For Indian states the corresponding indicator is Gross State Domestic Product (GSDP) at factor cost. These are estimated for all included states since 1980–81 by the Central Statistical Organisation (CSO). Prior to 1980–81, Net State Domestic Product (NSDP) used to be estimated. To overcome this problem, the NSDP per capita figures of 1970–71 are multiplied by the state-specific ratio of gross to net in the year 1980–81 to obtain GSDP per capita for 1970–71. Throughout this study we use the conversion factor (from official exchange rate to PPP exchange rate) of UNDP (2003), which corresponds to the data for the year 2001. World Development Indicator (2003) notes that these calculations were made on the basis of data on GDP at market prices (at constant 1995 US $) and GDP per capita at PPP US $.

TRENDS OF GROWTH AND HUMAN DEVELOPMENT (1970–71 to 2000–01)

Trend of Income and Growth

For the analysis of inter-state income differentials over the study period, real PCNSDP at constant 1993-94 prices of each state, for every fiscal year, are plotted in Figure 5.1 in logarithmic scale.

Figure 5.1 shows clearly that the top four positions, in terms of per capita income, are uninterruptedly occupied by the states of Punjab, Haryana, Gujarat, and Maharashtra, although there had been some minor changes of positions among themselves. On the other end, in early 1970s, four poorest states, namely Bihar, Orissa, Uttar Pradesh, and Andhra Pradesh, continued to maintain their positions till the end of 1990s, except Andhra Pradesh. In the mid-1980s, Assam entered in the group of four poorest states. Apparently, there is a trend of divergence in inter-state income disparity as the gap between two bold lines has widened over time. This trend is not only true for Punjab and Bihar. The income divergence is obvious for all the 16 major states of India, on which we avoid discussion in the present chapter.

From our dataset we now review the growth performances across the states in three successive decades. The annualized growth rate of an individual state is obtained by fitting log-linear growth curves. The state-wise annual rate of growth of per capita state income for three successive decades are shown in Figure 5.2.

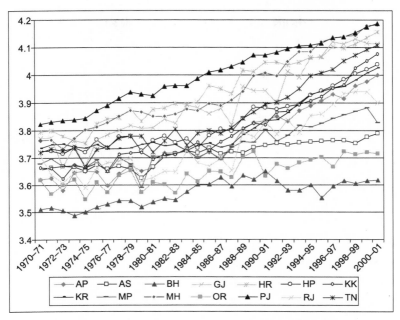

Figure 5.1: Real Per Capita Net State Domestic Product (in Log Scale)

Source: Author's calculation, based on EPWRF (2003).

During the 1970s the growth performance of the country was recorded as low as 0.89 per cent per annum. Maharashtra and Punjab are the only two states which could achieve growth rates over 3 per cent. The coefficient of variation of growth rates across the included states was about 76 per cent indicating that decadal growth performance was quite uneven. During the 1980s, the national growth rate accelerated steeply to 3.43 per cent. All states recorded positive growth with a minimum at 1.14 per cent for Assam. Impressive performances were shown by Haryana (4 per cent), Rajasthan (3.89 per cent), Maharashtra (3.6 per cent), and Punjab (3.4 per cent). The coefficient of variation was much less (about 30 per cent) compared to the previous decade. During the 1990s, when national income growth accelerated further to 3.97 per cent the inter-state variation of growth rates (50 per cent) had considerably widened. The traditionally poorer states such as Bihar, Orissa, and Uttar Pradesh along with Assam and Rajasthan, showed poor performance.

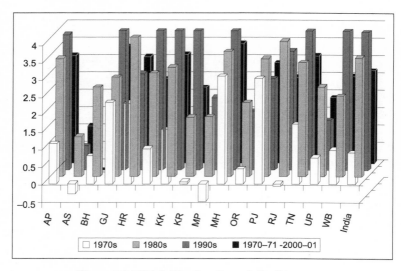

Figure 5.2: Widely Varying Growth Performances

Source: Author's Calculations, Based on EPWRF (2003).

Trend of Human Development

Following the UNDP (1999) methodology, we computed HDIs for India and included states in the UNDP format. Additional information, we have computed is Non-income Human Development Index (NIHDI), which is simply obtained as the mean of health as well as educational indices of the concerned region. Hence, for the jth state

$$NIHDI_j = \frac{1}{2}[(\text{Life Expectancy Index})_j + (\text{Educational Index})_j] \quad (5.1)$$

Figures 5.3 and 5.4 depict, respectively, the levels of HDI and Non-Income Human Index scored by India and Indian states in four years: 1971, 1981, 1991, and 2001. The values are in ascending order in respect of the initial year of the study. In 1971 and 1981, India scored the values of HDI which are classified in UNDP literature as low human development (that is, below 0.500). Kerala was the only state in 1971 and Kerala, Maharashtra, and Punjab were the three states in 1981 that could cross the boundary of low human development. In 1991 India emerged as a member of a medium human development nation taking ten states in the list. In 2001 all included states excepting Bihar entered into the group of medium human development.

The construction of HDI of Indian states for 2001 is comparable to the values obtained by 175 nations in (UNDP 2003: Table-1; 237–40). Interestingly, Kerala, the best performer among Indian states scores a value in HDI equivalent to China which ranks 104 in the list of 175 countries. At the other end, Bihar, the poorest performer scores

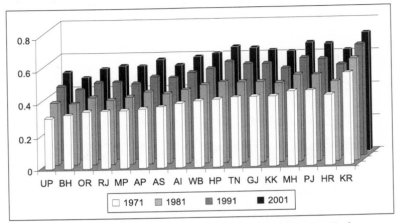

Figure 5.3: Four-Decade Trend in Human Development Index

Source: Author's Elaboration from Secondary Sources.

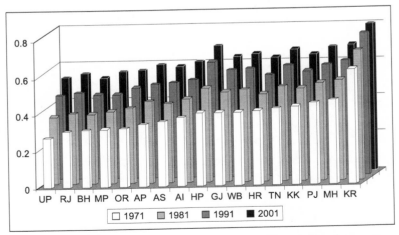

Figure 5.4: Four-Decade Trend in Non-Income Human Development Index

Source: Author's Elaboration from Secondary Sources.

equivalent to Yemen with a rank of 148. Hence, it follows that when India as a nation is placed at a rank of 127, the cross-state variation is marked over a range of 45 nations of the world.

Classification of Indian States

The states are plotted in the scatter diagram (as shown in Figure 5.5) according to their achievements in per capita GSDP, in PPP terms (horizontal axis) and HDI scores (vertical axis) for the year 2001. In Table 5.1 they are classified on two scales:

1. National average; and
2. Average of 94 Developing Nations (the list is provided in UNDP 2003: 247).

Table 5.1: Classification of Indian States 2001

Sl. No.	State	State Code	Basis of Classification	
			National	Global
1	Andhra Pradesh	AP	Vicious	Vicious
2	Assam	AS	Vicious	Vicious
3	Bihar	BH	Vicious	Vicious
4	Gujarat	GJ	Virtuous	Income-Lopsided
5	Haryana	HR	Virtuous	Income-Lopsided
6	Himachal Pradesh	HP	Virtuous	Vicious
7	Karnataka	KK	Virtuous	Vicious
8	Kerala	KR	HD-Lopsided	HD-Lopsided
9	Madhya Pradesh	MP	Vicious	Vicious
10	Maharashtra	MH	Virtuous	Virtuous
11	Orissa	OR	Vicious	Vicious
12	Punjab	PJ	Virtuous	Virtuous
13	Rajasthan	RJ	Vicious	Vicious
14	Tamil Nadu	TN	Virtuous	Vicious
15	Uttar Pradesh	UP	Vicious	Vicious
16	West Bengal	WB	HD-Lopsided	Vicious

In the former scale seven states—namely Gujarat, Haryana, Himachal Pradesh, Karnataka, Maharashtra, Punjab, and Tamil Nadu—are classified in the virtuous quadrant indicating above average performances in both aspects while exactly seven states—namely Andhra Pradesh, Assam, Bihar, Madhya Pradesh, Orissa, Rajasthan, and Uttar Pradesh—are in the vicious cycle showing below average performances in both. Kerala and West Bengal are two states falling into the quadrant described as HD-lopsided reality indicating above average performance in human development not accomplished with parallel expansion of income. However, when the average of developing nations is used as the scale of classification, only two states, Maharashtra and Punjab could maintain their positions in the virtuous cycle quadrant. Gujarat and Haryana move from virtuous to income-lopsided quadrant; Himachal Pradesh, Karnataka, and Tamil Nadu from virtuous to vicious cycle, while West Bengal from HD-lopsided to vicious cycle. Kerala still remains in the HD-lopsided quadrant. This phenomenon is depicted in Table 5.1. It is worth mentioning that India as a nation falls into the vicious cycle in the latter scale.

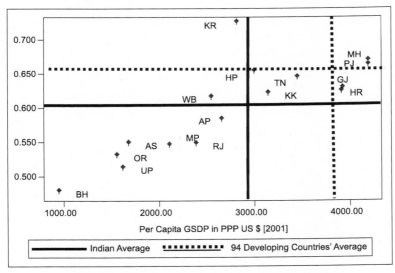

Figure 5.5: Scatter Diagram of Indian States, 2001

EMPIRICAL ANALYSIS

In this section we apply some econometric tools to examine the role of income on non-income HDI. First in Table 5.2 Spearman's rank correlation coefficients between per capita income and non-income human development index are depicted for all four selected years of our study: 1971, 1981, 1991, and 2001. The coefficients are found to be statistically significant at 1 per cent level of confidence, which suggests that the influence of income in determining non-income component of human development cannot be ruled out.

Table 5.2: Rank Correlation Matrix

Variable	Year	Non-Income Human Development Index			
		1971	1981	1991	2001
Per Capita	1971	0.693	0.682	0.678	0.662
Net State	1981		0.753	0.739	0.750
Domestic	1991			0.639	0.641
Product	2001				0.738

Note: All coefficients are statistically significant at 1 per cent level (two-tailed)
Source: Author's calculation

To examine the relationship empirically we assume that the current (2001) level of non-income component of human development is determined by previous levels of non-income components as well as by the previous levels of incomes. This chapter introduces lagged variable model of transformation of economic growth to human development. The time lags used here are 10 years, 20 years, and 30 years and denoted by the suffixes 2001, 1991, 1981, and 1971. The specific model is given by:

$$h_t = \sum_{i=1}^{n} \alpha_i y_{t-1} + \sum_{j=1}^{m} \beta_j h_{t-j} + u_t \text{ and more specifically,} \qquad (5.2)$$

$$h_{2001} = \alpha_1 y_{1991} + \alpha_2 y_{1981} + \alpha_3 y_{1971} + \beta_1 h_{1991} + \beta_2 h_{1981} + \beta_3 h_{1971} + u_t \ (5.3)$$

where h represents the non-income component of human development and y is the per capita income in a specific year. The disturbance term u_t is assumed to be serially independent with zero mean and finite covariance.

Equation (5.3) postulates that the current level of non-income component of human development is determined by past levels of non-income components as well as by past values of per capita income. To establish the influence of per capita income on non-income human development we should get that the coefficients of income in the equation are statistically different from zero as a group, that is, $\sum \alpha_i \neq 0$ irrespective of $\sum \beta_j \neq or = 0$. The basic hypothesis set here is,

$H_0 : \sum \alpha_i = 0$ that is, lagged terms of per capita income do not belong to the equation implying that the rate of transference from income to non-income human development in case of Indian states is insignificant.

The basic hypothesis (H_0) can be tested against the following alternative hypothesis (H_1):

$H_1 : \sum \alpha_i \neq 0$ that is, lagged terms of per capita income belong to the equation, implying that the rate of transference from income to non-income human development in case of Indian states is significant.

A number of steps are involved to decide about H_0. First we obtain the regression of the equation in a restricted form: the current non-income human development index (h_{2001}) is regressed on all lagged terms of non-income human development indices (h_{1991}, h_{1981}, h_{1971})— not including the lagged per capita income terms. This restricted form of equation is denoted by the suffix R . Next unrestricted regression of the equation (suffixed as UR) is obtained involving the lagged terms of both income and non-income variables, that is, (h_{1991}, h_{1981}, and h_{1971}) as well as (y_{1991}, y_{1981}, and y_{1971}). Regression results are depicted in Table 5.3. And finally, from these two regressions we compute the

value of F as $F = \dfrac{(R^2_{UR} - R^2_R)/m}{(1 - R^2_{UR})/N - k} = 3.2146$; where m is the number of

lagged terms in y, k is the number of parameters to be estimated in the unrestricted regression, and N is the total number of observations.

Table 5.3: Results of Empirical Analysis

Regression	Sum of Standardized Coefficients		Coefficient of Determination		F-value
	α	β	R2	Adjusted R2	
Restricted (R)	-	0.72	0.983	0.979	3.2146
Unrestricted (UR)	0.08	0.94	0.993	0.988	

This has the F-distribution with m and (N-k) degrees of freedom. However, it is observed that $F_{0.05,(4,9)}$ = 3.63 and $F_{0.10,(4,9)}$ = 2.69. Hence, if we go for 10 per cent level of confidence the computed value of F exceeds the critical value which suggests that the H_0 can be rejected and H_1 can be accepted. Considering the huge variability in the dependent variable the rejection of H_0 at nearly 7 per cent level of confidence is not unjustified. Therefore, per capita income levels of Indian states play a positive role in determining the non-income component of human development in the long run, that is, economic growth has been crucial for the expansion of human capability.

CONCLUSION

In this chapter we have focused attention on the role of economic variables in enhancing human development in India's sub-national context. We examine whether economic achievements in sub-national levels influence the average of other two components of human development: health and educational attainments. Even though we take the results of our empirical analysis on a positive note the disturbing level of regional disparities in both income and non-income components of human development, is a matter of great concern. The real task for the policy makers is to bridge the gap within a reasonable time frame. An unprecedented effort will be needed to halve the regional variation in both economic prosperity and levels of human development.

REFERENCES

Bhalotra, S. 2006. Childhood Mortality and Economic Growth. UNU-WIDER Research No. 2006/79. http://www.wider.unu.edu/publications/rps/rps2006/rps 2006-79.pdf

Boozer, M., G. Ranis, F. Stewart, and T. Suri 2003. 'Paths to Success: The Relationship between Human Development and Economic Growth', Discussion Paper No. 874, Economic Growth Center, Yale University. http://www.econ.yale.edu/~egcenter/

Census of India, 2001. Educational Level, Census Data Finder—B Series Tables, Economic Tables: Educational Levels. (published in 2007) http://www.censusindia.gov.in

—— 1971. Social and Cultural Tables: Series I Part IIC (ii) compiled in 1976 by Registrar and Census Commissioner of India.

Dholakia, R.H. 2003. 'Regional Disparity in Economic and Human Development in India', *Economic and Political Weekly*, Vol. 38, No. 40, pp. 4116–72.

—— 1985. *Regional Disparity in Economic Growth in India*, Himalaya Publishing House, Bombay.

Duraisamy, P. and A. Mahal 2005. 'Health, Poverty, and Economic Growth in India' in *Financing and Delivery of Health Care Services in India. Back ground Papers of the National Commission on Macroeconomics and Health*, Ministry of Health and Family Welfare, Government of India. http://www.who.int/macrohealth/action/Background%20papers%20report.pdf

Economic Survey, 1999–2000, 2000–01, and 2001–2002. Government of India, Ministry of Finance, New Delhi.

Economic and Political Weekly Research Foundation (EPWRF), 2003. 'Domestic Product of States of India 1960–61 to 2000–01', *Economic and Political Weekly Research Foundation*, Mumbai.

—— (various issues). http://www.epw.org.in/showepwRF.php

Foster, A.D. and M.R. Rosenzweig 1996. 'Technical Change and Human-Capital Returns and Investment: Evidence from Green Revolution', *American Economic Review*, Vol. 86, No. 4, pp. 931–53.

Fosu, A.K. 2002. 'Transforming Economic Growth to Human Development in Sub-Saharan Africa: The Role of Elite Political Instability', *Oxford Development Studies*, Vol. 30, No. 1, pp. 9–19.

Geeta Rani, P. 2007. 'Secondary Education in India: Development and Performance', Paper Presented in 43rd Annual Conference of the Econometrics Society of India, Indian Institute of Technology, Mumbai. http://www.hss.iitb.ac.in/ties07/paper/ts5/psA/1.doc

——— 1995. 'Human Development in India: A District Profile', *Arthavijnana*, Vo. 41, No. 1, pp. 9–30.

Ghosh, M. 2006. 'Economic Growth and Human Development in Indian States', *Economic and Political Weekly*, Vol. 41, No. 30, pp. 3321–29.

Gupta, I. and A, Mitra 2004. 'Economic Growth, Health and Poverty: An Exploratory Study for India', *Development Policy Review*, Vol. 22, No. 2, pp. 193–206.

Indrayan, A., M.J. Wysocki, A. Chawla, R. Mukar, and N. Singh 1999. '3-Decade Trend in Human Development Index in India and its major states', *Social Indicators Research*, Vol. 46, No. 1, pp. 91–120.

Mazumder, K. 2000. 'Causal Flow between Human Well-Being and Per Capita Real Gross Domestic Product', *Social Indicators Research*, Vol. 50, No. 3, pp. 297–313.

——— 1995. 'Classification of Countries: A Socio-Economic Approach', *Social Indicators Research*, Vol. 34, No. 2, pp. 261–73.

Ministry of Statistics and Programme Implementations (MSPI) 2006. *Selected Socio-Economic Statistics, India*, Central Statistical Organisation, Ministry of Statistics and Programme Implementations.

Planning Commission 2002. *National Human Development Report 2001*. http://planningcommission.nic.in/reports/genrap/reportsf.htm

Ramirez, A., G. Ranis, and F. Stewart 1998. 'Economic Growth and Human Development', QEH Working Paper Series, No. 18. http://www.qeh.ox.ac.uk/pdf/qehwps18.pdf

Ranis, G. and F. Stewart 2005. 'Dynamic Links between the Economy and Human Development', http://www.un.org/esa/desa/papers/2005/wp8_2005pdf

——— 2000. 'Strategies for Successful Human Development', *Journal of Human Development*, Vol. 1, No. 1, pp. 49–69.

Ranis G., F. Stewart, and A. Ramirez 2000. 'Economic Growth and Human Development' *World Development*, Vol. 28, No. 2, pp. 197–219.

Srivastava, A.B.L. (ed.) 2002. 'Some Significant Features of Literacy Data and Projection of Literacy Rate for the Population of Age group 15+', CIL's TSG-DPEP, New Delhi. http://www.educationforallinindia.com/page171.html

Trivedi, K. 2006. 'Educational Human Capital and Levels of Income: Evidence from States on India, 1965–92', *Journal of Development Studies*, Vol. 42, No. 8, pp. 1350–78.

United Nations Development Programme (UNDP) 1990 to 2007–08 *Human Development Report.* http://www.undp.org.in

—— 2007. 'Measuring Human Development: A Premier', http://hdr.undp.org/en/media/primer_complete.pdf

World Bank, 2004. *Attaining the MDGs in India,* The World Bank (Human Development Unit, South-Asia Region), Washington D.C.

World Development Indicator, 2001–03, The World Bank, Washington D.C.

6

Effect of Structural and Conditional Rigidities
A Case Study of a Poverty Reduction Programme

ARINDAM BANIK AND PRADIP K. BHAUMIK

INTRODUCTION

The reduction of income poverty is largely associated with long term economic growth. There seems to be a broad consensus among analysts and policy makers that per capita income growth is a major element of sustainable poverty reduction. However, similar rates of growth can have different impact on income poverty, under different conditions and rigidities.

A whole range of mixes of the two major approaches, of higher economic growth and better income distribution, has been used by different governments to achieve the objective of poverty reduction—again with mixed results (Cox and Jimenez 1995). While the East Asian countries have generally been very successful in eradicating poverty, the South Asian ones have been able to achieve rather modest successes. Latin American countries achieved little progress in poverty reduction, largely due to low economic growth, while Africa actually witnessed an increase in its poverty (Fan 2003).

Over the years, a welter of studies has explored the impact of poverty alleviation programmes—largely in developing countries (Cox and Jimenez 1995; Fan and Rao 2003; ADB 1993). In fact, impact assessment studies are routinely conducted for almost all poverty alleviation programmes at different stages of programme implementation, either by the implementing agencies themselves or by independent research organizations. Most of these studies evaluate the programmes in terms of their ability to achieve the stated objectives of the programme, deviations from programme guidelines for implementation, efficiency of targeting, and gaps between targets and achievements. Few of such studies delve deeper to analyse the possible causes for the observed performances, or isolate the effect of one poverty alleviation programme so as to make it more effective.

Yet, such analytical studies could be very useful in designing programmes for public spending. In a study to identify the relative role of different government spending on agricultural growth and rural poverty reduction, using state-level data for 1970 to 1993 and a system of multiple simultaneous econometric equations (Fan, Hazell, and Thorat 1999), it was shown that additional government expenditure on roads had the largest impact on poverty reduction as well as a significant impact on productivity growth. Additional government spending, on agricultural research, and extension, followed by additional government spending on education had the second and the third highest impact on rural poverty reduction.

In another study (Fan and Hazell 1999), the districts in India were classified into three categories: irrigated, high-potential rain-fed, and low-potential rain-fed. The study concluded that for each type of investment—that is, on roads, irrigation, electrification, etc.—the highest marginal impact on agricultural production and poverty alleviation occurs in one of the two rain-fed lands, while irrigated areas rank second, or last. Such differential marginal impacts could be exploited while redesigning these public investment programmes.

In this chapter we specify an econometric model that addresses the determinants of beneficiary households failure to use government support due to structural and conditional rigidities and, yet, is still tractable enough to permit the estimation with the help of standard techniques. Under the Supply of Improved Toolkits to Rural Artisans (SITRA) programme, improved toolkits were provided to poor rural artisans all over India to ensure increased income of the beneficiary artisans besides achieving improved quality, enhanced production, and reduction in migration to urban areas.

Unlike the alleviation programmes, success of poverty reduction programmes requires the active participation of poor beneficiaries. Consequently, poverty reduction programmes also need to motivate the recipients of benefits to actively participate in economic activities at higher levels. Most of the studies on poverty alleviation and reduction programmes emphasize structural bottlenecks, asymmetric information, and rent-seeking behaviour. This chapter provides an analytical characterization of the beneficiaries in a situation of much structural and conditional rigidity, where all the beneficiaries do not move from a passive state to an active state, and take advantage of the government intervention despite their having access to the benefit. Our interest lies in understanding which attributes, if any, affect the beneficiary artisans' decision to use the improved toolkit or not, and what could be the rationale for such differences. We use ordered logit analysis to achieve this end.

The plan of the remaining chapter is as follows: Section II discusses the SITRA programme and its design, and provides the background for its evaluation. It then details the methodology, sample selection, and data collection used in the study. A closer look at the conditional and structural rigidities faced by the poor rural artisans, the beneficiaries of SITRA programme, is provided in Section III, which then leads to the development of the econometric model described in Section IV. Section V presents the results of the ordered logit model and analyses its implications. The chapter ends with the concluding remarks in Section VI.

THE SITRA PROGRAMME

Initially, during the first three five-year plans (1951–66), India adopted a development strategy to achieve higher growth rates, assuming that poverty would be alleviated through the trickle down effect of growth. When that did not happen, the need for direct intervention in favour of the poor was recognized. Consequently, a variety of anti-poverty programmes were designed and implemented over the years, encompassing the entire spectrum from wage employment programmes on one end through programmes for rural housing and for social assistance, to programmes for self-employment and asset creation on the other. Together with economic growth, these anti-poverty programmes succeeded in reducing the head count index of poverty from 37.27 per cent in 1993–94 to 27.09 per cent in 1999–2000 in the rural areas (Planning Commission 2002).

THE INTEGRATED RURAL DEVELOPMENT PROGRAMME

The Integrated Rural Development Programme (IRDP) was launched in 1978 with the aim of improving the asset base of the poor and involving them in the production and income-generating process of the economy. It has been a major self-employment programme, and has been financed partly by bank credit and partly by government subsidies. Although, there were similar programmes for farmers earlier, this was the first time that economic activities under the animal husbandry, small business, and services sectors were included.

IRDP and Its Sub-Programmes

The IRDP has been extensively debated and evaluated both by government agencies (GoI 1987a, 1987b, 1988a, 1988b, and 1989) and independent researchers (Sen 1996; Gupta 1995; Drèze 1990; and Kuriam 1987). While most of these studies have brought many limitations of IRDP to the fore and criticized some aspects of the programme, like its insistence on lifting poor households above the poverty line, almost all of them felt there were many positive aspects and some significant achievements to the credit of the programme.

After its launch in 1978, the IRDP has been modified, enlarged, and diversified to target narrower constituencies such as women, youth, and artisans as shown in Table 6.1. All of these were introduced as sub-programmes of IRDP but implemented as stand-alone programmes. Based on the recommendations of a committee constituted by the Planning Commission to review self-employment and wage-employment programmes, the government merged the IRDP and allied programmes into a single programme, called Swarnajayanti Gram Swarozgar Yojana (SGSY), with a shift in emphasis from the individual beneficiary to a group-based approach. The SGSY was launched on 1 April 1999.

Supply of Improved Toolkits to Rural Artisans

Artisans from a variety of crafts, except weaving, tailoring, needle-workers, and beedi-workers, were to be supplied suitable improved hand tools, or a set of tools. The average cost of a toolkit was Rs 2,000; in the case of power-driven tools, the average cost was Rs 4,500. Ninety per cent of the cost of the toolkit was subsidized and 10 per cent was to be contributed by the beneficiary.

Prototypes of improved tools were developed by the government design and technical development centres. The state governments were authorized to choose models/tools to suit the specific needs of their artisans. Improved toolkits were developed for cane-bamboo workers, carpenters, cobblers, leather goods makers, and jewellery makers, to name a few (GoI 2000c).

Table 6.1: Poverty Reduction Programmes for Self-employment

Programme	Launched in	Programme Objectives
Integrated Rural Development Programme	1978	To improve the asset base of the poor and involve them in the production/income generation processes of the economy
Training of Rural Youth for Self-Employment †	August 1979	To provide basic technical and entrepreneurial skills to poor rural youth to enable them to take up self-employment in secondary and tertiary sectors of the economy
Development of Women and Children in Rural Areas†‡	1982-83	To enable economic empowerment of women and to involve poor rural women in economic activities and matters concerning the rural community
Supply of Improved Toolkits to Rural Artisans†	July 1992	To enable poor rural artisans to enhance the quality of their products, increase their production and income, and ensure a better quality of life with the use of improved toolkits
Ganga Kalyan Yojana†	February 1997	To provide irrigation through borewells and tubewells to individuals and groups of poor, small, and marginal farmers
Swarnajayanti Gram Swarozgar Yojana‡	April 1999	Conceived as a holistic programme of micro-enterprise development in rural areas with emphasis on organising the rural poor into self-help groups, capacity building, planning of activity clusters, infrastructure support, technology, credit, and marketing linkages

Notes: †Introduced as sub-programmes of IRDP but implemented as stand-alone programmes. ‡ On 1 April, 1999, the IRDP and allied programmes were merged into a single programme known as Swarnajayanti Gram Swarozgar Yojana (SGSY).

Under SITRA, there was 50 per cent reservation for Scheduled Caste (SC) and Scheduled Tribe (ST) communities. In the absence of SC/ST beneficiaries, the implementing agency could allocate the SC/ST share to other categories of artisans. There was no provision of reservation for women and physically handicapped persons. However, if eligible, preference was to be given to such persons over others.

EVALUATION OF SITRA

Evaluation studies of SITRA were conducted to probe the apparent difference in performance in Gujarat and Maharashtra in western India (GoI 2000a), and Bihar and Haryana in northern India (GoI 2000b). But a comprehensive evaluation of SITRA at the all India level was conducted during 2000 and it brought out many interesting facets of SITRA (GoI 2000c). The empirical part of the present chapter is based on the data collected during this evaluation study.

Methodology for Sample Selection and Data Collection

The data used in this chapter was collected from primary sources based on fieldwork conducted during January to July 2000. The study covered 30 states and union territories (UTs) of India. In the first stage of the multistage sampling used, 20 per cent of the total numbers of districts in each state, subject to a minimum of two districts, were chosen. The districts were selected through purposive sampling to ensure that these districts were adequately representative of the state with respect to geographical distribution and special conditions of the state, if any. A total of 129 districts were chosen at the end of the first stage.

Thirty per cent of the blocks (rounded upward) were selected in each district in the second stage through circular systematic sampling using the Directory of Blocks as the frame of reference, with some modifications to accommodate blocks having watershed development programmes. From each of the selected blocks, five gram panchayats were chosen using convenience sampling. A gram panchayat is the lowest administrative unit in India. In some cases, a gram panchayat may consist of only one village, while in others it may have a number of villages, hamlets, or *padas*. The selection of villages/gram panchayats was done carefully so that these would properly represent the implementation of the SITRA programme in the blocks. Individual artisans were the final sampling units.

The Government of India (GoI) enumerated Below Poverty Line (BPL) households in two censuses, in 1992 and 1997. The list of BPL households in each village was obtained with due care being taken to identify the reference year. Wherever available, the BPL household list from the 1997 BPL census was used. In all other cases, the 1992 BPL census list was used. From this list of BPL households, a frame of artisans (individuals, not households) was prepared and beneficiaries and non-beneficiaries under SITRA were identified. From the frame of BPL artisans, five beneficiaries (selected randomly), or all of the beneficiaries, in case there were less than five, were selected as beneficiary respondents and the schedule for beneficiaries filled up for each of them. A total of 6,788 beneficiary artisans were covered in the entire study.

Conditional and Structural Rigidities among Poor Rural Artisans—A Close Look

Sustainable poverty reduction, or eradication, cannot be achieved simply by a redistribution or transfer of funds or productive assets.

It requires the beneficiary to make use of the funds or the assets, and engage in some economic activity. Or else, if the beneficiary continues to remain in an economic inactive or passive state, a simple asset or funds transfer may result in only transient consumption after liquidation of the asset or funds. In this section, we take a close look at the profile of beneficiary rural artisans to understand their socio-economic background, in general, and to appreciate their conditional and structural rigidities, in particular. Later, we shall test if such rigidities affect the beneficiary artisan's movement from passive to active state in so far as the use of improved toolkits is concerned.

Table 6.2 reveals the beneficiary artisan's experience in craftsmanship among the different states of India. At an all India level, young artisans having up to 10 years of experience formed about 62 per cent of the total respondent artisans. However, there were wide differences from the all India averages. While states such as Andhra Pradesh, Jammu and Kashmir, Maharashtra, Kerala, Orissa, and Pondicherry had artisans with longer experience in craftsmanship, it was shorter in states such as Arunachal Pradesh, Himachal Pradesh, Madhya Pradesh, and West Bengal.

The level of education and technical training of the beneficiary artisans are shown in Table 6.3. The rate of illiteracy (cannot read or write) at the all India level was reported to be 29 per cent among the artisan beneficiaries. Interestingly, while the rate of illiteracy among artisan beneficiaries was one of the lowest in Kerala (about 3 per cent), the state also had a large percentage of rural artisans with formal education up to SSC/HSC level but with no technical training, either formal or informal. The role of formal or informal technical training appears to be an insignificant factor, implying that the artisans are in the present profession by inheritance.

Table 6.4 presents the landownership of artisan beneficiaries along with their primary occupation and earnings from craftsmanship. Average landholdings tend to be higher in hilly and difficult terrain, for example, in Jammu and Kashmir, Lakshadweep, Manipur, Sikkim, etc. and low in fertile plains such as Haryana, Punjab, Tamil Nadu, etc. The average landholding in UP appears very high (5.044 hectares) again because of dominance of hilly districts in the sample. The primary occupation of the beneficiary artisans is also summarized in Table 6.4 and it can be observed that while only 3 per cent of the beneficiary artisans reported their primary occupation as craftsmanship in Arunachal Pradesh, the figure was 100 per cent or close to 100 per

Table 6.2: Artisan Beneficiaries' Experience in Craftsmanship

Sl. No.	State/UTs	Total no. of sample artisan beneficiaries	Percentage of sample artisan beneficiaries with experience in craftsmanship of			
			0–5 years	6–10 years	11–15 years	More than 15 years
1	A&N Islands	105	55.24	18.10	9.52	17.14
2	Andhra Pradesh	308	23.70	18.51	21.75	36.04
3	Arunachal Pradesh	139	82.01	17.99	0.00	0.00
4	Assam	66	37.88	31.82	10.61	19.70
5	Bihar	772	32.38	37.44	10.10	20.08
6	D&N Haveli	25	32.00	60.00	8.00	0.00
7	Daman & Diu	44	84.09	11.36	2.27	2.27
8	Goa	12	25.00	41.67	16.67	16.67
9	Gujarat	186	32.80	26.34	12.37	28.49
10	Haryana	131	22.14	22.14	16.03	39.69
11	Himachal Pradesh	16	43.75	31.25	12.50	12.50
12	Jammu & Kashmir	120	24.17	20.00	10.83	45.00
13	Karnataka	241	18.67	34.85	19.92	26.56
14	Kerala	301	16.94	24.58	21.59	36.88
15	Lakshadweep	10	100.00	0.00	0.00	0.00
16	Madhya Pradesh	531	44.63	40.49	9.23	5.65
17	Maharashtra	351	7.41	20.80	30.20	41.60
18	Manipur	67	50.75	38.81	7.46	2.99
19	Meghalaya	–	(-)	(-)	(-)	(-)
20	Mizoram	154	29.22	37.66	20.13	12.99
21	Nagaland	96	50.00	46.88	3.13	0.00
22	Orissa	495	20.40	21.82	18.38	39.39
23	Pondicherry	34	11.76	29.41	11.76	47.06
24	Punjab	173	15.61	42.20	21.39	20.81
25	Rajasthan	144	42.36	27.08	8.33	22.22
26	Sikkim	89	32.58	65.17	2.25	0.00
27	Tamil Nadu	249	8.43	42.97	28.51	20.08
28	Tripura	134	22.39	36.57	22.39	18.66
29	Uttar Pradesh	1095	37.08	26.58	14.34	22.01
30	West Bengal	339	45.02	33.92	11.50	8.85
	All India	6427	31.49	30.62	15.19	22.70

Notes: Figures in Column 3 for each State and UT are numbers of beneficiary artisans in sample. Figures in Columns 4 to 7 for each State and UT are percentages of total beneficiary artisans in sample.
Source: Quick evaluation survey conducted during January–July 2000.

Table 6.3: Education and Technical Training of Artisan Beneficiaries

Sl. No.	State/UTs	Total no. of sample artisan benefi- ciaries	Percentage of sample artisan beneficiaries who can/have had					
			cannot read or write	can read or write	some schooling (up to 4 years)	5–9 years of school	SSC/ HSC	Technical Training (formal/ informal)
1	A&N Islands	105	14.29	29.52	1.90	38.10	15.24	0.95
2	Andhra Pradesh	310	45.81	6.77	4.52	25.48	15.48	1.94
3	Arunachal Pradesh	142	76.06	14.08	4.23	4.93	0.70	0.00
4	Assam	66	18.18	15.15	7.58	15.15	43.94	0.00
5	Bihar	858	37.06	35.20	7.34	8.39	11.54	0.47
6	D&N Haveli	25	80.00	4.00	8.00	4.00	4.00	0.00
7	Daman & Diu	50	28.00	8.00	6.00	34.00	24.00	0.00
8	Goa	12	0.00	33.33	25.00	41.67	0.00	0.00
9	Gujarat	189	28.57	10.58	16.40	34.39	10.05	0.00
10	Haryana	131	22.14	37.40	4.58	22.90	10.69	2.29
11	Himachal Pradesh	16	25.00	12.50	6.25	25.00	31.25	0.00
12	Jammu & Kashmir	125	61.60	8.80	4.00	17.60	7.20	0.80
13	Karnataka	242	23.97	7.85	27.69	28.51	11.16	0.83
14	Kerala	301	2.66	9.63	15.61	29.57	39.87	2.66
15	Lakshadweep	11	0.00	0.00	9.09	54.55	36.36	0.00
16	Madhya Pradesh	701	38.94	16.26	9.70	25.39	9.70	0.00
17	Maharashtra	352	20.17	15.63	17.05	27.84	18.75	0.57
18	Manipur	71	15.49	52.11	11.27	12.68	7.04	1.41
19	Meghalaya	–	(–)	(–)	(–)	(–)	(–)	(–)
20	Mizoram	157	5.10	31.85	23.57	35.67	3.82	0.00
21	Nagaland	99	18.18	59.60	12.12	7.07	3.03	0.00
22	Orissa	521	39.16	16.89	15.93	22.26	5.57	0.19
23	Pondicherry	34	0.00	0.00	20.59	64.71	11.76	2.94
24	Punjab	173	27.17	24.28	5.20	26.01	16.18	1.16
25	Rajasthan	153	32.68	22.88	11.76	28.10	4.58	0.00
26	Sikkim	89	4.49	33.71	46.07	15.73	0.00	0.00
27	Tamil Nadu	249	13.65	43.78	13.65	23.29	5.22	0.40
28	Tripura	135	6.67	18.52	33.33	36.30	5.19	0.00
29	Uttar Pradesh	1127	29.64	15.00	9.94	27.33	17.66	0.44
30	West Bengal	344	12.21	43.90	19.77	20.35	3.20	0.58
	All India	6788	28.93	21.91	12.64	23.41	12.52	0.59

Notes: Figures in Column 3 for each State and UT are numbers of beneficiary artisans in sample. Figures in Columns 4 to 7 for each State and UT are percentages of total beneficiary artisans in sample.

Source: Quick evaluation survey conducted during January–July 2000.

Table 6.4: Artisan Beneficiaries Landownership, Primary Occupation,
and Average Earnings/Wages from Craftsmanship

Sl. No.	State/UTs	Total no. of sample artisan beneficiaries	Average land owned (ha)	Percentage of sample artisan beneficiaries with experience in craftsmanship of			Avg. Earnings/ Wages from Craftmanship (Rs. per annum)
				Crafts-manship	Agri-culture	Manual Dom. Labour	
1	A&N Islands	105	0.33	33.33	39.05	27.62	4,535.23
2	Andhra Pradesh	310	0.282	78.39	0.00	21.61	4,046.77
3	Arunachal Pradesh	142	0.927	2.82	94.37	2.82	5,233.09
4	Assam	66	0.429	80.30	16.67	3.03	4,892.42
5	Bihar	858	0.308	84.85	7.23	7.93	2,663.63
6	D&N Haveli	25	0.287	72.00	16.00	12.00	4,500.00
7	Daman & Diu	50	0.265	22.00	32.00	46.00	5,070.00
8	Goa	12	0.708	100.00	0.00	0.00	6,958.33
9	Gujarat	189	0.189	93.12	2.12	4.76	7,099.47
10	Haryana	131	0.095	94.66	1.53	3.82	5,751.90
11	Himachal Pradesh	16	0.457	50.00	25.00	25.00	5,250.00
12	Jammu & Kashmir	125	1.136	80.00	18.40	0.80	4,326.40
13	Karnataka	242	0.532	74.79	3.31	21.90	5,213.63
14	Kerala	301	0.138	93.69	3.65	2.66	14,191.70
15	Lakshadweep	11	1.455	18.18	54.55	27.27	2,909.09
16	Madhya Pradesh	701	0.650	74.18	16.26	9.56	5,474.10
17	Maharashtra	352	0.232	92.33	1.99	5.68	5,901.98
18	Manipur	71	1.682	50.70	42.25	7.04	2,987.32
19	Meghalaya	–	–	(–)	(–)	(–)	–
20	Mizoram	157	1.522	84.08	12.74	3.18	4,754.77
21	Nagaland	99	1.347	17.17	69.70	13.13	2,627.77
22	Orissa	521	0.387	86.76	7.10	6.14	4,140.01
23	Pondicherry	34	0.000	58.82	2.94	38.24	11,691.20
24	Punjab	173	0.017	89.02	1.16	9.83	5,034.68
25	Rajasthan	153	0.707	63.40	11.11	25.49	4,403.92
26	Sikkim	89	1.039	17.98	71.91	10.11	7,210.11
27	Tamil Nadu	249	0.037	99.20	0.40	0.40	6,094.37
28	Tripura	135	0.030	85.93	2.96	11.11	6,022.22
29	Uttar Pradesh	1096	5.044	76.28	12.68	13.87	4,260.33
30	West Bengal	344	0.239	86.34	4.07	9.59	4,019.18
	All India	6757	1.19	77.59	12.51	10.36	5,039.20

Notes: Figures in Column 3 for each State and UT are numbers of beneficiary artisans in sample. Figures in Columns 4 to 7 for each State and UT are percentages of total beneficiary artisans in sample.
Source: Quick evaluation survey conducted during January–July 2000.

cent in Goa and Tamil Nadu. Average earnings from craftsmanship varied between a low of Rs 2,627 in Nagaland and a high of Rs 14,192 in Kerala. It can also be observed that states and UTs with relatively high percentage of artisans, with craftsmanship as their primary occupation, tended to have correspondingly high earnings from craftsmanship. Kerala, having high literacy and being periodically ruled by communist governments, tended to have strong labour awareness and unions that ensured relatively high wage rates. The large scale emigration from rural Kerala to the Middle East may also have contributed to such high earnings from craftsmanship.

Table 6.5 presents the typical products produced and sold by the beneficiary artisans. The percentage of artisans, reportedly selling their services/work as per the customer's needs, seems to dominate at both the all India and state levels. Indeed, the figure is as high as 94 per cent in Assam and 88 per cent in Tamil Nadu, Himachal Pradesh, and Kerala. In contrast, a majority of the artisans in Rajasthan and Andhra Pradesh produce only custom products, produced on order. Finally, the artisans who sell standard products, to be sold in the market, appear to constitute 31 per cent of all beneficiary artisans in Bihar and 36 per cent in Orissa.

The extent of use of the improved toolkits provided to the beneficiary artisans is captured in Table 6.6. About 36 per cent of all beneficiary artisans reported using all the tools in the toolkit, while another 32.5 per cent used some of the tools. As many as 19.5 per cent beneficiary artisans in Karnataka and 13.9 per cent in Orissa did not use any of the tools. On the other hand, in Gujarat, Haryana, Jammu and Kashmir, and Tamil Nadu more than 50 per cent of all beneficiary artisans used all the tools received.

Econometric Model

The econometric analysis adopted in this study is limited to the ordered logit model, a technique used most frequently in cross-sectional studies of dependent variables that take on only a finite number of values possessing a natural ordering. The ordered logit model, also known as the cumulative logit model, estimates the effects of independent variables on the log odds of having lower, rather than higher scores on the dependent variable.

$$Ln\left(\frac{p(Y \le j)}{p(Y > j)}\right) = \alpha_j - \sum_{k=1}^{K}\beta_k X_k \text{, for } j = 1 \text{ to } J - 1 \qquad (6.1)$$

Table 6.5: Typical Products Produced and Sold by Artisan Beneficiaries

Sl. No.	State/UTs	Total no. of sample artisan beneficiaries	Percentage of sample artisan beneficiaries who sell		
			Standard Products Produced and kept for sale	Service/Work as per the customer's needs	Custom Products produced on order
1	A&N Islands	104	10.58	64.42	25.00
2	Andhra Pradesh	218	6.42	38.99	54.59
3	Arunachal Pradesh	141	31.91	21.99	46.10
4	Assam	66	0.00	93.94	6.06
5	Bihar	773	31.44	62.87	5.69
6	D&N Haveli	2	0.00	100.00	0.00
7	Daman & Diu	19	15.79	57.89	26.32
8	Goa	12	8.33	91.67	0.00
9	Gujarat	183	6.01	68.85	25.14
10	Haryana	125	10.40	80.80	8.80
11	Himachal Pradesh	16	0.00	87.50	12.50
12	Jammu & Kashmir	121	9.09	43.80	47.11
13	Karnataka	241	5.39	63.07	31.54
14	Kerala	293	5.80	87.37	6.83
15	Lakshadweep	7	14.29	71.43	14.29
16	Madhya Pradesh	529	2.08	69.57	28.36
17	Maharashtra	344	7.27	64.53	28.20
18	Manipur	62	14.52	66.13	19.35
19	Meghalaya	–	(–)	(–)	(–)
20	Mizoram	156	8.97	33.33	57.69
21	Nagaland	98	15.31	61.22	23.47
22	Orissa	492	36.38	36.59	27.03
23	Pondicherry	34	2.94	82.35	14.71
24	Punjab	171	6.43	73.10	20.47
25	Rajasthan	134	14.93	20.15	64.93
26	Sikkim	88	0.00	71.59	28.41
27	Tamil Nadu	248	4.84	88.31	6.85
28	Tripura	133	21.80	9.77	68.42
29	Uttar Pradesh	1030	11.75	57.48	30.78
30	West Bengal	342	11.99	64.62	23.39
	All India	6182	13.99	59.06	26.33

Notes: Figures in Column 3 for each State and UT are numbers of beneficiary artisans in sample. Figures in Columns 4 to 7 for each State and UT are percentages of total beneficiary artisans in sample.

Source: Quick evaluation survey conducted during January–July 2000.

Table 6.6: Artisan Beneficiaries Using Toolkits

Sl. No.	State/UTs	Total no. of sample artisan beneficiaries	Percentage of sample artisan beneficiaries who are			
			No/Using Some	Using Some	Using Most	Using All
1	A&N Islands	104	3.85	23.08	27.88	45.19
2	Andhra Pradesh	310	7.74	39.68	48.06	4.52
3	Arunachal Pradesh	141	0.00	27.66	47.52	24.82
4	Assam	66	4.55	40.91	9.09	45.45
5	Bihar	770	0.26	47.79	22.47	29.48
6	D&N Haveli	25	20.00	0.00	52.00	28.00
7	Daman & Diu	50	6.00	18.00	38.00	38.00
8	Goa	12	0.00	50.00	8.33	41.67
9	Gujarat	186	0.00	8.06	20.97	70.97
10	Haryana	131	1.53	25.95	12.21	60.31
11	Himachal Pradesh	16	6.25	37.50	25.00	31.25
12	Jammu & Kashmir	124	0.00	0.81	33.06	66.13
13	Karnataka	241	19.50	41.08	21.16	18.26
14	Kerala	295	9.15	14.58	16.61	59.66
15	Lakshadweep	11	45.45	18.18	9.09	27.27
16	Madhya Pradesh	533	5.07	46.72	21.95	26.27
17	Maharashtra	345	8.41	42.90	15.65	33.04
18	Manipur	67	1.49	17.91	50.75	29.85
19	Meghalaya	–	(–)	(–)	(–)	(–)
20	Mizoram	157	0.64	38.22	16.56	44.59
21	Nagaland	97	25.77	1.03	29.90	43.30
22	Orissa	512	13.87	47.46	19.53	19.14
23	Pondicherry	34	5.88	52.94	17.65	23.53
24	Punjab	171	9.36	68.42	8.19	14.04
25	Rajasthan	139	4.32	23.02	55.40	17.27
26	Sikkim	89	0.00	0.00	19.10	80.90
27	Tamil Nadu	248	4.03	16.53	21.37	58.06
28	Tripura	131	0.00	16.79	21.37	61.83
29	Uttar Pradesh	1102	5.26	25.68	27.13	41.92
30	West Bengal	342	0.58	21.35	42.11	35.96
	All India	6449	5.75	32.49	25.68	36.08

Notes: Figures in Column 3 for each State and UT are numbers of beneficiary artisans in sample. Figures in Columns 4 to 7 for each State and UT are percentages of total beneficiary artisans in sample.
Source: Quick evaluation survey conducted during January–July 2000.

In the equation (6.1), α_j are intercepts indicating log odds of lower rather than higher scores when all independent variables equal zero. Note that the effects of the independent variables $\beta_k X_k$ are subtracted from, rather than added, to the intercepts. This is done so that positive coefficients indicate increased likelihood of higher scores on the dependent variables. The intercepts for $J - 1$ category express the categorical nature of the dependent variable, while a parallel odds restriction to let independent variables have the same effects on all cumulative logit results in a parsimonious model for ordinal data. As ordered, logit models are not linear in their parameters, they are estimated by using maximum likelihood techniques.

Table 6.7 defines all the variables used in the model. The dependent variable BDUT represents the beneficiary artisan's decision regarding use/non-use of toolkits. This has four categories: 0 = using none, 1 = using some, 2 = using most, and 3 = using all.

The issue of the artisan's decision to use or not to use the support provided may form a major contribution to poverty literature. In most cases, the policy makers are confused between poverty reduction and alleviation strategies. The former is the long-run type and the latter is the short-run type. The SITRA programme is a poverty reduction type of programme but some of the criteria for choosing beneficiaries are not self-fulfilling.

The independent variable AGE is demographic and may contribute to conditional rigidity of the beneficiary artisan. This factor is defined by the beneficiary artisan's age (1 = up to 19 years, 2 = 20–39 years, 3 = 40–59 years, and 4 = 60 years and above). While categories 1, 2, and 3 are preferred while selecting beneficiaries, the programme will be successful if they can successfully use the improved toolkits. If this variable significantly affects the artisan's decision to use the toolkit, then it should be used for targeting policies.

The variable LED defines the level of education and skill of the beneficiary artisan. This has been measured in five categories (such as, 1 = cannot read and write, 2 = can read and write, 3 = some schooling, 4 = SSC/HSC, and 5 = technical training). If LED is found positive, then this could perhaps be interpreted as the skill and training of the artisan affecting the likelihood of use of the toolkits. The variable could also affect the way an artisan adopts and adapts the new technology represented by the improved toolkits. These variables could lead to a higher or lower wage inequality depending on the sign of the coefficient.

Table 6.7: Definition of Variables

Dependent Variable	
BDUT	Beneficiary artisan's decision regarding use of toolkits
	0 using none
	1 using some
	2 using most
	3 using all

Independent Variables	
AGE	Age of beneficiary artisan
	1 upto 19 years
	2 20 – 39 years
	3 40 – 59 years
	4 60 years and above
LED	Level of education/skill
	1 cannot read/write
	2 can read/write
	3 some schooling (upto 4 years)
	4 SSC/HSC
	5 Technical training (formal/informal)
EAM	Number of earning members in the household
TYPPR	Typical products produced or services sold
	0 standard product produced and kept for sale
	1 sell the service/work as per customer's needs
	2 custom produce on order
BHIC	Beneficiary household's income from artisanal work/crafts (in Rs p.a.)
BHTI	Beneficiary household's total income in an agriculture year (in Rs p.a.)
BHPQT	Beneficiary artisan's perception regarding the quality of the toolkits
	0 poor/none are good
	1 some are good
	2 most are good
	3 all are good
TNUD	Toolkit is not used due to
	1 not in usable condition
	2 does not know how to use toolkits
	3 not in beneficiary household's possession or sold it
	4 tool(s) does/do not relate to the craft of the beneficary artisan
	5 no demand for products made using tool kit

With the help of EAM of the beneficiary household, we seek to capture the economic pressure within the household. This is measured simply by the number of regular earning members in the household. There are many sample beneficiary households with zero earning members and some with as high as four or five earning members. We would like to account for the effect of this variable on the probability of a beneficiary artisan using the improved toolkit.

The variable TYPPR measures an interesting characteristic of an artisan—how exactly is the labour offered in the market. If this variable is found significant, then skilled artisanal labour may not be homogenous and supply of improved toolkits might actually raise wage inequality. The sign and significance of the coefficient for this variable would reflect, for example, if artisanal labour used for standard or commoditized products is valued differently from the same used in customized products or services. While all the previously listed ones represented conditional rigidities faced by the beneficiary artisan, this variable would be part of the structural rigidity faced by the beneficiary artisan.

The beneficiary household's income from artisanal work/crafts is represented as BHIC, while the total income of the household is captured in the variable BHTI. Both these variables are measured in Rupees per annum. It is realized that these variables are difficult to measure, particularly in the rural setting, and that too among poor rural artisans.

Finally, the variables such as BHPQT and TNUD are captured as proxies of structural rigidity variables. BHPQT measures the beneficiary artisan's perception regarding the quality of the toolkit. This is measured in four categories (such as, 0 = poor/none are good, 1 = some are good, 2 = most are good, and 3 = all are good). Intuition suggests that poor condition of the toolkit may deter the beneficiary artisan from using it. Likewise, TNUD may affect the outcome of the beneficiary artisan's decision to use or not to use the given toolkit. TNUD is captured in five categories (such as, 1 = not in usable condition, 2 = does not know how to use the toolkit, 3 = not in beneficiary artisan's possession, 4 = tool(s) does/do not relate to the craft of the beneficiary artisan, and 5 = no demand for the products made using the toolkit).

ANALYSIS

In Tables 6.8(A) to 6.10(B), we report the maximum likelihood estimates of the ordered logit model on a selection of eight explanatory variables as detailed above. The estimation, using the SPSS software package, was performed on the dataset consisting of 6,788 observations (beneficiary artisans). We could not use 4,187 observations because of some missing data. Thus, only 2,601 observations were considered for the purpose of the ordered logit analysis [Table 6.8(A)].

Table 6.8(B) shows the value of Chi-square as 1,524.101 with 24 df and is the most relevant value here. This is the likelihood ratio test that all coefficients for all independent variables are equal to zero. This null hypothesis can be rejected since the test is highly significant. The pseudo R-square measures indicate that the model performs fairly well [Table 6.8(C)]. The Nagelkerke R^2 value will usually be the most relevant value to report. It corrects the Cox and Snell value so that it can theoretically achieve a value of 1. It is to be mentioned here that pseudo R^2 measures confound goodness of fit and explanatory power of the model.

Tables 6.9(A) and 6.9(B) provide the estimation results of the ordered logit model. All the explanatory variables are significant, except AGE, TYPPR, and BHTI. The variable level of education (LED), by the artisan reveals an interesting negative, and strongly significant coefficient. *Ceteris paribus*, artisans with lower general education are more likely to use the toolkits. It is to be noted that a small and negligible percentage (only 0.5 per cent) of sample beneficiaries had any technical training, either formal or informal.

The negative coefficient of EAM, that is, number of earning members in the beneficiary household, indicates that beneficiary

Table 6.8 (A): Case Processing Summary

		N
BDUT	0	240
	1	1675
	2	591
	3	95
Valid		2601
Missing		4187
Total		6788

Table 6.8 (B): Model Fitting Information

Model	-2 Log Likelihood	Chi-Square	df	Sig
Intercept Only	4973.085	1524.101	24	.000
Final	3448.984			

Table 6.8 (C): Pseudo R-Square

Cox and Snell	.443
Nagelkerke	.519
McFadden	.305

Table 6.9 (A): Parameter Estimates

		Estimate	Std. Error	Wald	df	Sig
Threshold	[BDUT = 0]	−.234	.399	.346	1	.557
	[BDUT = 1]	4.746	.407	136.146	1	.000
	[BDUT = 2]	8.327	.447	347.236	1	.000
Location	AGE	−3.972E−02	.079	.250	1	.617
	LED	−.171	.034	25.109	1	.000
	EAM	−.137	.045	9.346	1	.002
	TYPPR_	−2.097E−02	.073	.082	1	.774
	BHIC	−2.658E−05	.000	7.348	1	.007
	BHTI	1.496E−05	.000	2.481	1	.115
	BHPQT	2.723	.082	1097.563	1	.000
	TNUD	.174	.035	24.196	1	.000

Table 6.9 (B): Parameter Estimates

		95 per cent Confidence Interval	
		Lower Bound	Upper Bound
Threshold	[BDUT = 0]	−1.016	.547
	[BDUT = 1]	3.949	5.543
	[BDUT = 2]	7.451	9.203
Location	AGE	−.195	.116
	LED	−.238	−.104
	EAM	−.225	−4.922E−02
	TYPPR	−.164	.122
	BHIC	−4.579E−05	−7.361E−06
	BHTI	−3.656E−06	3.357E−05
	BHPQT	2.562	2.884
	TNUD	.105	.244

households with fewer earning members are more likely to use the toolkits than ones with more earning members. This is likely due to the fact that having fewer earning members in the household puts greater pressure on the artisan to try out different options to change the economic status of the household.

Interestingly, the beneficiary household's income from artisanal work/crafts (BHIC) increases the probability of not using the toolkits. The rationale for this may be similar to what was discussed above in case of EAM. Surprisingly, the total income of the beneficiary household (BHTI) does not affect the decision to use the toolkit.

The beneficiary household's positive perception regarding the quality of the toolkits (BHPQT) indicates the higher probability to use the toolkits. In particular, this model sheds light on how the quality

Table 6.10 (A): Parameter Estimates - I

BDUT		B	Std. Error	Wald	df	Sig
0	Intercept	8.626	.900	91.834	1	.000
	AGE	−.252	.250	1.015	1	.314
	LED	.212	.108	3.818	1	.051
	EAM	.546	.165	10.983	1	.001
	TYPPR	−.282	.221	1.626	1	.202
	BHIC	7.044E−05	.000	3.361	1	.067
	BHTI	−2.566E−05	.000	.489	1	.484
	BHPQT	−5.916	.264	502.143	1	.000
	TNUD	−1.097E−02	.100	.012	1	.913
1	Intercept	8.571	.795	116.352	1	.000
	AGE	−.179	.219	.670	1	.413
	LED	.194	.096	4.114	1	.043
	EAM	.495	.153	10.424	1	.001
	TYPPR	4.356E−02	.187	.054	1	.816
	BHIC	4.024E−05	.000	1.257	1	.262
	BHTI	−8.277E−06	.000	.058	1	.809
	BHPQT	−3.490	.213	267.775	1	.000
	TNUD	−.396	.078	26.041	1	.000
2	Intercept	5.276	.758	48.495	1	.000
	AGE	−.262	.208	1.578	1	.209
	LED	−7.560E−02	.092	.681	1	.409
	EAM	.336	.146	5.299	1	.021
	TYPPR	−.238	.175	1.845	1	.174
	BHIC	1.639E−05	.000	.223	1	.637
	BHTI	1.100E−05	.000	.110	1	.740
	BHPQT	−1.370	.192	51.137	1	.000
	TNUD	1.847E−02	.067	.077	1	.782

of toolkits affects the beneficiary artisans decision to use these. This gives us more insights about the structural condition of the toolkit market, their appropriateness to a particular skill category, and then the quality of the toolkits. This variable appears to be one of the most powerful and significant.

The TNUD (toolkits are not used) variable appears to have increased the probability of the beneficiary artisan of not using the toolkits. Our result, therefore, implies that the impact of such inference may have serious consequences. This may be due to the fact that the toolkits are not in usable condition because there is strong nexus between local level decision maker and the toolkit manufacturer. Hence, the toolkits are not used by the beneficiary artisans.

Table 6.10 (B): Parameter Estimates - II

BDUT		Exp (B)	95 Per cent Confidence Interval for Exp (B)	
			Lower Bound	Upper Bound
0	Intercept			
	AGE	.777	.476	1.269
	LED	1.236	.999	1.528
	EAM	1.727	1.250	2.385
	TYPPR	.754	.489	1.163
	BHIC	1.000	1.000	1.000
	BHTI	1.000	1.000	1.000
	BHPQT	2.695E-03	1.606E-03	4.522E-03
	TNUD	.989	.812	1.204
1	Intercept			
	AGE	.836	.545	1.283
	LED	1.214	1.007	1.465
	EAM	1.641	1.215	2.216
	TYPPR	1.045	.724	1.506
	BHIC	1.000	1.000	1.000
	BHTI	1.000	1.000	1.000
	BHPQT	3.049E-02	2.007E-02	4.631E-02
	TNUD	.673	.578	.784
2	Intercept			
	AGE	.770	.512	1.158
	LED	.927	.775	1.110
	EAM	1.399	1.051	1.863
	TYPPR	.788	.559	1.111
	BHIC	1.000	1.000	1.000
	BHTI	1.000	1.000	1.000
	BHPQT	.254	.174	.370
	TNUD	1.019	.894	1.161

CONCLUSION

A large volume of literature has been generated, in India and abroad, in understanding the consequence of public expenditure in rural areas. While much of this literature has focused on farm and non-farm aspects on various economic issues, the present study uses field data to analyse the effect of structural and conditional rigidities on moving a beneficiary from the passive to active state with the help of data collected under the SITRA programme.

As mentioned earlier, most such studies have concentrated on evaluating the effectiveness of government interventions in meeting the stated programme objectives and targets, gaps between desired and actual targeting of beneficiaries, and adherence to programme guidelines. The few studies which have been conducted to find the differential marginal impact of different government interventions have all used secondary macro data. The study reported in this chapter uses micro-level data obtained from primary sources, comprising a fairly large sample of poor beneficiary artisans.

The ordered logit framework allows us to identify factors that explain the beneficiary artisan's decision, to use or not to use, the support provided by the government. We are, thus, able to show that discreteness does matter, in the sense that simpler linear regression analysis cannot capture the important features of conditional and structural rigidities. With this application, we hope to have demonstrated the flexibility and power of ordered logit model as a tool for investigating the dynamic aspect of poverty reduction programmes.

When looking at the explanatory variables, we find that, indeed, there is strong evidence that governments are confused about the concept of poverty reduction and alleviation strategies. This finding is important for two reasons. First, it means that there are two different types of stakeholders in poverty reduction programmes, that is, those who would remain passive even after the receipt of the benefit, and others who are likely to move from passive to active state. Identifying aging artisans as beneficiaries of the programme may not bear much fruit as they are unlikely to become economically active due to their conditional rigidities.

What do our results suggest for policy? Our findings could provide a rationale for a policy in this context. A thorough understanding of the conditional and structural rigidities faced by a beneficiary artisan and how these affect his economic behaviour would be very useful in both designing and implementation of poverty reduction programmes. It should be noted that while appreciation of significant conditional rigidities are useful while designing such programmes, particularly while targeting the beneficiaries, structural rigidities are important while implementing and monitoring these programmes

Narrower targeting on less-favoured artisans who are more likely to use the toolkits and, hence, increase their income from craftsmanship and so promote both economic growth and poverty reduction, again leading to a win-win situation, is one such possibility. Although, such conclusions appear counter-intuitive initially, they may appear entirely plausible if the cost of working with improved toolkits is factored in an artisan's decision on the supply of skilled artisanal labour with improved toolkits. The role of opportunity costs have been studied in workfare programmes where self-selection has been explained using opportunity cost of a beneficiary (Ravallion and Datt 1995), but surely its role extends far beyond workfare to all poverty reduction programmes in explaining the economic behaviour of different beneficiaries. A deeper understanding of the costs and consequences of selection of beneficiary households in specific programmes could be quite valuable for scholars and policy makers.

REFERENCES

Asian Development Bank (ADB) 1993. *Poverty in Developing Asia: Salient Issues and Lessons*, Economics and Development Resource Centre, Asian Development Bank, Manila.

Cox, Donald and Emmanuel Jimenez 1995. 'Private Transfers and the Effectiveness of Public Income Redistribution in the Phillippiners' in Dominique van de Walle and Kimberly Nead (eds.) *Public Spending and the Poor: Theory and Evidence*, John Hopkins University Press, Baltimore, pp. 450–88.

Drèze, J. 1990. Poverty in India and the IRDP Delusion, *Economic and Political Weekly*, Vol. 25, No.39, pp. A 95-A 104.

Fan, S. 2003. 'Public Investment and Poverty Reduction: What have We Learnt from India and China?', Presented at: ADBI Conference on Infrastructure Investment for Poverty Reduction: What do we know?, Tokyo.

Fan, S. and P. Hazell 1999. Are Returns to Public Investment Lower in Less-Favoured Areas? An Empirical Analysis of India, EPTD Discussion Paper No. 43, International Food Policy Research Institute, Washington, D.C.

Fan, S., P. Hazell, and S. Thorat 1999. *Linkages between Government Spending and Poverty in Rural India*, Research Report 110, International Food Policy Research Institute, Washington, D.C.

Fan, S. and N. Rao 2003. 'Public Spending in Developing Countries: Trends, Determinants and Impact', EPTD Discussion Paper No. 99, International Food Policy Research Institute, Washington, D.C.

Government of India (GoI) 2000a. Impact Assessment of SITRA in Western Region, Ministry of Rural Development, New Delhi (mimeo).

―――― 2000b. Evaluation of Supply of Improved Toolkits to Rural Artisans Programme in Haryana and Bihar, Ministry of Rural Development, New Delhi (mimeo).

―――― 2000c. Quick Evaluation of Supply of Improved Toolkits to Rural Artisans Programme, Ministry of Rural Development, New Delhi (mimeo).

―――― 1989. Concurrent Evaluation of IRDP: The Main Findings of the Survey for January 1989–March 1989, Ministry of Agriculture, New Delhi (mimeo).

Government of India (GoI) 1988a. Concurrent Evaluation of IRDP: The Main Findings of the Survey for January 1987–September 1987, Ministry of Agriculture, New Delhi (mimeo).

—— 1988b. Concurrent Evaluation of IRDP: The Main Findings of the Survey for January–December 1987, Ministry of Agriculture, New Delhi (mimeo).

—— 1987a. Concurrent Evaluation of IRDP: The Main Findings of the Survey for October 1985–September 1986, Ministry of Agriculture, New Delhi (mimeo).

—— 1987b. Concurrent Evaluation of IRDP: The Main Findings of the Survey for January 1987–June 1987, Ministry of Agriculture, New Delhi (mimeo).

Gupta, S.P. 1995. 'Economic Reform and Its Impact on Poor', *Economic and Political Weekly*, Vol. 30, No.22, pp. 1295–1313.

Kuriam, N.J. 1987. 'IRDP: How Relevant Is It?', *Economic and Political Weekly*, pp. A161–A178.

Planning Commission, 2002. *Tenth Five Year Plan (2002-07)*, Planning Commission, GoI, New Delhi.

Ravallion, M. and G. Datt 1995. 'Is Targeting through a Work Requirement Efficient? Some Evidence for Rural India', in D. van de Walle and K. Nead (eds.), *Public Spending and the Poor: Theory and Evidence*, Johns Hopkins Press, Baltimore.

Sen, A. 1996. 'Economic Reforms, Employment and Poverty: Trends and Options', *Economic and Political Weekly*, Vol. 31, No.35, pp. 2459–79.

7

Public Distribution System
An Instrument for Improving Human Development

R. GOPINATH

INTRODUCTION

In the existing world of inequalities, the role of the state becomes inevitable in providing basic requirements to poor people; else, the goal of achieving universal human development is not possible. Public delivery systems have their importance in the context of a developing economy, where many of the households depend on public services to meet their basic needs. It, consequently, brings food security to the poor people and, thus, acts as a first step towards improvement of human development. Proponents have argued that the rationing system plays an important role in ensuring household food security (Swaminathan 2000; Chopra 1981).

Public food delivery systems have been playing a crucial role in many developing economies which are characterized by high levels of poverty and low income. In India, the central and state governments have their monopolies over these services. As is apparent from the analysis and discussions in the following paragraphs, access to food is a major issue for a huge section of the Indian population. Six decades after independence, the country still houses the largest population of malnourished people in the world. Direct programmes for poverty alleviation, income generation, and food distribution, through various schemes have been in operation right from the beginning. The PDS, MDMS, ICDS, and AAY are the key food delivery schemes in operation to address the issues of access to food and nutrition security. These programmes, even though started in different periods and by different governments, have a common goal of improving human development with a focus on health and nutrition of the people, in general, and the poor, in particular. Among these, the Public Distribution System (PDS) could be called the flagship scheme of public food delivery system. It is the oldest and widest scheme in India in terms of coverage. Today, the PDS with a network of more than 4.62 lakh Fair Price Shops (FPSs) distributes commodities to about 2,277.55 lakh cardholders (1,294.39 lakh APL cardholders; 760 lakh BPL cardholders; 223 lakh AAY card holders in May 2006), is perhaps the largest distribution network of its type in the world.

UP TO 1960: WAR-TIME RATIONING MEASURE
The beginning of the PDS, however, can be traced to the period of World War II when rationing system was introduced as a war-time rationing measure. In the 1950s, PDS was extended into some rural areas. But these areas were largely food-deficit regions and the remit of PDS was mainly concentrated in urban areas. After independence, the Food Grains Policy Committee Report of 1950–51 strongly emphasized the importance of controlled system of procurement and distribution of foodgrains. As a corollary to the above, Food Grains Enquiry Committee (1957) recommended opening more FPSs in India (Chopra 1981). In 1958, when the government decided to import wheat from USA under PL 480, PDS was used to control the distribution of imported grains. During 1958–66, quantity of grain distributed through PDS by the government was higher than its procurement, and, thus, growing dependence on import of grains (Swaminathan 2000).

DURING 1960s–70s: PRICE SUPPORTING MEASURE AND REDISTRIBUTION OF IMPORTED GRAINS
The Green Revolution changed the dynamics of foodgrains management in the country. As a great response from farmers to policy support in the 1960s, it provided a powerful thrust to the development of PDS. Surplus grains were mainly produced in the north-western region, particularly in Haryana and Punjab; others remained as deficit regions. Thus, distribution of foodgrains across all regions of the country became another objective of PDS. After 1966, the focus changed towards offering of fair prices to farmers to protect them from market anomalies. Therefore, the government had to adopt a two-pronged strategy: one was to control market prices, and the other to distribute essential commodities to public. The severe drought in

1965–66, further called for the expansion of PDS. The Food Grains Policy Committee of 1966 also emphasized equitable distribution of grains from surplus producing states to deficit ones at reasonable prices (Chopra 1981 and Swaminathan 2000).

In 1966, a study team on FPSs, headed by V.M. Dandekar, suggested market-oriented prices for the FPSs to increase its share in the market. As a result of these suggestions, the number of FPSs was increased to 114,200 in 1967, catering to a 280 million population. It distributed nearly 13.2 million tonnes of foodgrains in 1967. Further, both the number of FPSs and the number of commodities distributed through PDS were increased in 1970s (Chopra 1981).

DURING THE 1980s: INSTRUMENTS OF POVERTY ALLEVIATION

Under the Sixth Five Year Plan (1980–85), PDS was used as a stable and key instrument to control prices, reduce fluctuations, and achieve equitable distribution of essential consumer goods, particularly food grains. Essential Supplies Program (ESP) was introduced in 1982, as the 17th point of the 20-point programme of the then government with the same objectives. The ESP emphasized on expanding PDS outreach through more FPS outlets including mobile FPSs. The number of FPSs was increased from 2.30 lakhs in January 1980 to 3.02 lakhs in January 1984. The Government of India supplied essential commodities (wheat, rice, levy sugar, imported edible oil, kerosene, and soft coke) and the individual states had the liberty to add other items also. The government also introduced a new ministry, namely, Ministry of Food and Civil Supplies and one department, namely, Department of Food and Civil Supplies. Consumer Advisory Committees were also constituted at district, block, and *tehsil* levels in order to inspect the functioning of PDS (Program Evaluation Organization 2005).

The Seventh Five Year Plan period witnessed further reinforcement of these measures. PDS was added to the Minimum Needs Program in 1987–88 to ensure availability of essential items at reasonable prices to the vulnerable sections of the population. In most parts of the country, up to 1997, the PDS was universal and all households, rural and urban with a registered residential address, were entitled to rations made available through a network of FPSs. Eligible households were given a ration card that entitled them to buy fixed rations of selected commodities. The exact entitlement (quality, range of commodities, and prices), however, varied across states (Swaminathan 2003).

Maintaining price stability and ensuring availability of foodgrains, at reasonable prices to the poor and vulnerable sections of the society, across the country became the major objectives of PDS. This entailed movement of foodgrains from the surplus producing states to the deficit ones under the procurement and allotment mechanisms. As a matter of fact, regional variation in food production existed across the country (Table 7.1). The impact of the Green Revolution was primarily seen in Punjab, Haryana, and Eastern Uttar Pradesh. This region still accounted for a high proportion of production compared to other regions, particularly west, central and south. The gap between north, north-west, and other regions had been increasing over time.

Table 7.1: Region-wise Food Grains Production

(Triennial average in per cent)

Zone	1960–62	1972–74	1984–86	1990–93	2000–03
North-North West	26.1	30.4	39.8	38.84	44.41
West-Central	29.1	25.0	23.0	18.34	12.69
East	23.2	22.7	20.2	17.78	22.09
South	21.5	21.9	17.0	16.39	15.37

Note: The summary of all regions in a particular period is not hundred, because the Union Territories are excluded from the given data.
Source: Figures are taken from a) Utsa Patnaik, 1991. 'Food Availability and Famine: A Longer View', *Journal of Peasant Studies*, Vol. 19, No. 1, pp. 1–25; b) www.indiastat.com

Punjab and Haryana are the major states contributing a substantial amount of foodgrains to the central pool for redistribution as shown in Table 7.2.

Madhya Pradesh and Himachal Pradesh also contribute significant amount of foodgrains to the central pool. Deficit states like Kerala, Gujarat, the north-eastern states, Jammu & Kashmir, and A&N Islands are clearly getting benefited from PDS, as is revealed from a comparison of the per capita cereal production and consumption figures.

In a predominantly agricultural country like India, food security is largely dependent upon central and state government policies and mechanisms in relation to farm products, procurement and storage of foodgrains, and delivery through the PDS. This is substantiated by the work of Vyas (2005), who asserted that food subsidies help the poor

Table 7.2: Deficit of Cereal Production to Consumption (1999–2000)

(Grams per day)

State	Per Capita Net Production P	Per Capita Availability (including PDS grains) (Prod-Proc+ Allot) P1	Per Capita Consumption C
Andhra Pradesh	411.546	299.431	406.231
Arunachal Pradesh	454.710	752.570	508.802
Assam	360.889	453.059	419.431
Bihar	397.750	442.937	454.669
Goa	379.043	605.730	355.244
Gujarat	174.154	230.788	318.502
Haryana	1,488.653	1,320.423	330.570
Himachal Pradesh	568.452	700.639	420.410
Jammu & Kashmir	315.441	535.517	474.074
Karnataka	412.933	476.617	369.382
Kerala	58.765	250.398	324.126
Madhya Pradesh	700.030	703.661	414.887
Maharashtra	262.138	317.261	349.491
Manipur	380.109	552.476	531.876
Meghalaya	213.889	481.342	379.915
Mizoram	266.603	700.406	433.048
Nagaland	239.402	446.956	483.356
Orissa	352.734	406.111	500.106
Punjab	2,502.899	1,900.464	337.163
Rajasthan	419.083	418.094	452.504
Sikkim	433.709	895.273	405.660
Tamil Nadu	334.539	431.801	340.567
Tripura	385.541	572.393	436.957
Uttar Pradesh	626.544	643.406	434.398
West Bengal	442.962	497.661	430.389
A & N Islands	192.647	496.728	358.064
D & N Haveli	283.926	404.890	374.679
Delhi	7.504	183.293	284.445

Sources: Government of India, 1999–2000. Ministry of Food and Consumer Affairs; Government of India, 2001. National Sample Survey Organization, 55th Round.

to withstand inflationary pressures and reduce inter-state variations. Thus, a subsidized PDS, with well-defined target groups, is seen as an essential item of social investment.

The state-wise proportion of quantity distributed to bottom 20 per cent of households in rural areas. Orissa, with 21 per cent of population under bottom 20 per cent, received about 7 per cent of cereals only under the PDS and the targeting effectiveness was just 0.34, implying worst performance of the distribution channels in PDS. As a universal programme, ideally the ratio of share of foodgrain purchases to population share should be around one. A share greater than one in Rajasthan and Haryana, for instance, indicates that the population obtained a more than proportionate share of grain from the PDS. Uttar Pradesh with 0.45, Bihar (0.70), and West Bengal (0.86) targeting effectiveness ratio also have scope to increase their effectiveness under the PDS mechanism. In terms of share of grains reaching the bottom 20 per cent of the group, Rajasthan topped the list, followed by Haryana and Jammu & Kashmir. Orissa and Punjab, however, did not have a high fraction reaching the consumer. In the case of Punjab, this has to be understood in the light of the fact that it is a foodgrain surplus region and most households should be having sufficient foodgrains for their consumption, but the same argument is not applicable to Orissa (Parikh 1994: 1-34).

REVAMPED PUBLIC DISTRIBUTION SYSTEM (RPDS)

One of the major criticisms against PDS in 1990 was cost ineffectiveness. Parikh (1994) said, 'The cost effectiveness of reaching the poorest 20 per cent households through PDS cereals is very small. For every rupee spent, less than 22 paisa reaches the poor in all states, excepting in Goa and Daman and Diu, where 28 paisa reach the poor. This is not to suggest that PDS does not benefit the poor at all, but only to emphasize that this support is provided at a high cost'. The High Powered Committee on Agricultural Policies and Programs commented on the FCI that they were unable to reduce costs, despite recommendations of various committees constituted for the purpose. Subsidy to the FCI rose from Rs 276 crore in 1980–81 to Rs 650 crore in 1989–90, an increase of 3.81 times, whereas the quantity distributed was only marginally higher during the same period. There was also the problem of diversion of foodgrains from PDS to the open market, observed to be close to one-third of total distribution (Srinivasan and Jha 2001). One of the problems of the PDS experience was that its benefits did not flow to certain vulnerable sections of the population due to their disadvantageous geographical location, poor communication, and low purchasing power.

In order to address these defects and ensure that PDS reached out to the remotest corners of the country, the structure was revamped and the RPDS was introduced by the Prime Minister on January 1,

1992. This involved geographical targeting with special schemes for relatively backward areas, tribal belts, certain designated hilly places, and urban slums. The main objective of reform in the PDS was to target the poor by using various exclusion criteria. The RPDS focused on 1,752 blocks, falling under Desert Department Program, Drought Prone Area Program, Integrated Tribal Development Projects, and Designated Hill Areas, identified as areas with disadvantage. Foodgrains (wheat and rice) at the rate of 20 kg/month along with levy sugar, and edible oils were distributed to the RPDS blocks at subsidized prices.

Reviewing the RPDS, the Performance Evaluation Organization (1995) of the Planning Commission, however, observed that during the period 1992 to 1994, allotment of commodities did not show any uniformity of proportion to the actual requirement of the states or the food habits of the population. The commodities under RPDS also did not cater to the local needs and preferences. There was irregular supply of commodities to FPSs, irregular opening of FPSs, inadequate storage facility, transport, and financial matters. RPDS was not able to address the socio-economic and cultural dimensions of consumers with regard to their preferences for commodities.

TARGETED PUBLIC DISTRIBUTION SYSTEM (TDPS)

Further, there was a change from a universal PDS to a Targeted Public Distribution System (TPDS) introduced on 1 June 1997. Under this scheme, beneficiaries were classified into Below Poverty Line (BPL) and Above Poverty Line (APL) categories, based on the poverty line defined by the Planning Commission with quantity and price differential in allotment and sale. It identified beneficiaries based on the methodology prescribed by the expert group of the Planning Commission headed by the late Professor Lakdawala. Initially 10 kg of foodgrains were allotted per month, which was revised to 20 kg per month in April 2000, and further to 35 kg in March 2002, at subsidized rates. There were different prices for APL and BPL consumers and in 2001, a third price was introduced for *Antyodaya* cardholders. In March 2000 a differentiation was made in the issue price at which the FCI sold grains to state governments for PDS purpose, at half the economic cost incurred by FCI for BPL households and full economic cost for APL households. The TPDS was also supposed to extend specially subsidized foodgrains to the beneficiaries of Employment Assurance Schemes and Jawahar Rozgar Yojana.

Problems with TPDS

Inadequate Food Subsidy

Food subsidies given by the government remained less than one per cent of GDP. Especially after 1990s, at constant prices, the expenditure on food subsidy rose in mid-1980s, remained stagnant in 1989–90, dipped in 1992–93, hovered between 0.45–0.60 per cent of GDP between 1993–94 to 2000–01, and rose to almost 1 per cent in 2002-03 according to the Economic Survey, Ministry of Finance. The last was, however, due to accumulation of stocks due to increasing issue price.

In sum, the poor people have had to bear the brunt of increasing prices due to inflation. As per the wholesale price index with 1993–94 as the base year, one rupee purchasing power in the month of May 2006 was equal to 37 paisa in 1990–91 (Upadhyay 2006) implying increase in the general prices of food products in the market. The poor had to buy those food products at higher prices even under PDS due to stagnation in the amount allocated for food subsidies.

In fact, under TPDS, state governments were asked to identify the different categories of poor whose numbers were already decided by the Central Government. This led to genuine problems in implementation. It was believed that eligibility on the basis of APL and BPL would help reduce food subsidies; instead they increased during the period. It was Rs 2,340 crore (or 0.43 per cent of GDP) in 1990–91 and increased to Rs 23,200 crore (or 0.66 per cent of GDP) in 2003–04 (*Economic Survey 2006–07*). This was largely due to increasing costs of holding higher stocks. The main reason for increasing stocks was due to increasing issue prices (Chandrasekhar and Ghosh 2005).

Errors of Exclusion

One of the major criticisms of targeting is the extent to which targeting errors leave out those who genuinely deserve to be in a particular program (Swaminathan 2003). Errors of targeting due to imperfect measurement are of two types: Type I error and Type II error. The Type I error refers to exclusion of genuinely poor or deserving households from a program. This shows the failure to reach the target population. On the other hand, inclusion of non-eligible persons or households into a program is Type II error. This error is because of mistakes of excessive coverage. These targeting errors arise in welfare programs due to imperfect information, measurement of household characteristics, corruption, and inefficiency. Error of wrong inclusion results in higher cost due to inclusion of ineligible beneficiaries. Errors of wrong exclusion lead to welfare costs by leaving out the genuinely eligible people.

After introducing structural adjustment programs, many developing countries including India followed conservative targeting schemes that minimized inclusion errors (due to inclusion of some member of the non-target group) but increased the chances of excluding the target group. The Indian case of TPDS is a strong case where many poor people got excluded from PDS due to exclusion errors. TPDS yielded more type I error in all states except Tamil Nadu, where the state followed universal PDS (PEO Report 2005).

The states where poverty ratios were relatively higher also had higher level of errors of exclusion, for example, Orissa with 47 per cent poverty ratio and 26.56 per cent error of exclusion and Uttar Pradesh with 31 per cent and 26.75 per cent, respectively. But a state, for example, Gujarat with only 14.7 per cent poverty level also recorded a high error of exclusion at 45.84 per cent due to inefficient management. Excepting a few states, TPDS excluded a large number of poor from access and defeated the very purpose for which the system was changed (ORG Report 2005). An evaluation by the Planning Commission in 2005 indicated that 57 per cent of BPL households were not included in TPDS.

Problems with the Identification of People below and above Poverty Line

Under TPDS, income-poverty criterion is used to divide the beneficiaries into BPL and APL. The concept of income-poverty is based on a poverty line developed by the Planning Commission in 1993–94, based on the projected population in 2000. There have been several doubts raised as to whether the poverty line representing a very low level of absolute expenditure is the best criterion for identifying households with variable levels of income on the margin.

Indian poverty lines have been based on the estimates of normative nutritional requirement of an average person in the rural and urban areas. The nutritional requirements have been derived from the age-sex-occupation specific nutritional norms, based on demographic data of 1971 census. The rupee value has been updated for reflecting price changes, but the basket of goods and services has not been changed over the period. A country of our size with diverse characteristics is bound to have different prices for products and services at different points. Hence, a common poverty line could either overestimate, or underestimate, across regions. The two main criticisms of income poverty line estimation are that the rupee value of the poverty line at current prices is insufficient to meet the normative calorie requirement taking into account other essential expenditure, and secondly, mere use of calorie intake as a measure of nutritional adequacy would lead to harm in terms of measurement of poverty and design of poverty alleviation programmes. The definitions of BPL and APL have been shown to be arbitrary as are the numbers, calculated on Planning Commission estimates made several years ago (Swaminathan 2000).

Increasing Issue Prices and Declining Quantity Distributed under TPDS

The Central Issue Price of rice experienced a single-fold increase for BPL families and double-fold increase for APL families during the period 1990 to 2002, from Rs 289 in 1990 to Rs 565 per quintal for BPL and Rs 830 per quintal for APL in 2002. Wheat prices also increased by 100 per cent for BPL and around 200 per cent for APL families during the same period from Rs 234 to Rs 415 per quintal for BPL families and Rs 610 for APL families (www.indiastat.com). Increasing issue prices led to reduced offtake, which in turn was also the cause of increasing buffer stocks during the 1990s (Patnaik 2006). Total buffer stocks in FCI increased from 15.81 million tonnes in 1990–91 to 21.82 million tonnes in 1997–98 (www.indiastat.com). It further increased to 44.98 million tonnes in 2000–01. The buffer stock crossed 50 million tonnes in 2001–02 and foodgrain export was resorted to, at BPL prices, to bring down the stocks, even as many eligible people remained unreachable by the PDS.

There was a clear fall in offtake in the year of introduction of TPDS and, subsequently, following a further price change and differentiation in 2000 as shown in the graph presented below (www.indiastat.com).

This trend was due to decline in offtake under the PDS system, especially among APL families. The level of foodgrains purchased by APL families through PDS was 100.82 lakh tonnes in 1999–2000 which reduced to 42.2 million tonnes in 2005–06 (*Economic Survey 2006–07*). This was due to the increase in issue prices and decline in the volume

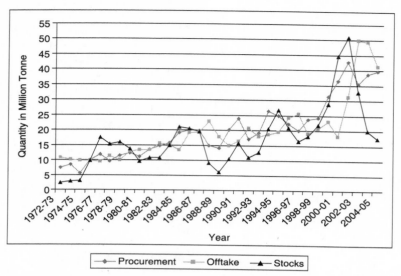

Figure 7.1: Procurement, Offtake, and Stocks of Rice and Wheat under PDS in India (1971–72 to 2004–05)

of foodgrains to APL households. The offtake level increased due to the declining issue prices of rice for BPL families (Rs 795/quintal in 2001 and Rs 565/quintal in 2002) and introduction of Antyodaya Anna Yojana and Food for Work Programs.

The erroneous policies followed by the government, including ever increasing issue prices and exclusion of large deserving population under the TPDS, led to a decline in offtake and fall in average sales realization. The net effect of increasing costs and declining revenues resulted in increasing unit subsidy. The subsidy on rice rose from 17.74 per cent in 1993–94 to 23.8 per cent in 1998–99, and that for wheat from 9.83 per cent to 19.7 per cent during the same period. Quantity distributed through FPSs also declined under TPDS. One of the main reasons for declining PDS offtake from the late 1990s onwards was the narrowing down of price differential between PDS and market prices. The TPDS issued foodgrains at 50 per cent of economic cost to BPL cardholders and 100 per cent of economic cost to APL cardholders. The basic philosophy behind TPDS was to phase out the APL families gradually rather than in one go. Therefore, they fixed the price of goods for APL families at 90 per cent initially and 100 per cent later (Srinivasan and Jha 1999). The central issue prices (CIP) for

APL was very close to the market price. Hence, consumers preferred to buy grains in the open market, instead of from FPSs.

According to the norms of the Indian Council for Medical Research (ICMR), a person has to take 330 gm of cereals per day to meet his minimum nutritional needs. This requires 11 kg of cereals per month or 55 kg for a family with five persons. Data on per capita allocation of food grains under TPDS for BPL households shows that no state was able to meet the ICMR norms of per day calorific requirements (www. indiastat.com and www.census India.net).

Inefficient Functioning of Fair Price Shops

Fair price shops run by private traders in some parts, cooperative departments and governments in other parts also came under attack by researchers. The users from different sections reported that the information about availability of ration was not reaching them properly. More than half the respondents, both in urban and rural areas, reported that they were aware about the availability by word of mouth from another consumer (ORG Report 2005). Information through notices at ration shops and announcements in villages could reach only to 30 per cent in the rural and 25 per cent in urban target households. People in tribal areas and small hamlets, where ration shops were far away from their settlements, could find it more difficult to get information about rations. It often happened that stocks were not available when they approached the FPS; they either did not get information when stocks arrived, or did not have had the purchasing power at that point of time.[1] The rural people had to spend more time, money and energy to get rations from the FPS because they had to commute, on an average, a distance of 2 km to get rations (ORG Report 2005). About 32 per cent of villages in rural areas did not have ration shops within their respective villages.

The ORG survey of 1,000 FPSs (650 rural and 350 urban) revealed that more than 35 per cent of ration shops in urban areas and more than 50 per cent in rural areas were either opened or opened only less than 20 days a month (ORG Report 2005). On an average, they opened only for 15 days causing inconvenience to them in the remaining days. Table 7.3 provides details on the household perception on quality of grains lifted from the FPS and overall level of satisfaction. It reveals that a large percentage of damaged stock of grains was sold at the price charged for normal stock.

Table 7.3: Perception about Quality of Grains Lifted from Ration Shop (unweighted)

		Locality		Status as per Ration Card		
		Urban	Rural	APL	BPL	AAY
Wheat	Acceptable	55.4	61.8	56.2	60	58.5
	Sometimes acceptable	36.5	33.2	31.0	34.3	36.0
	Bad	5.7	3.3	6.9	4	4
	DK/CS	2.4	1.7	5.9	1.8	1.4
Rice	Acceptable	48.9	52.1	46	51.7	51.4
	Sometimes acceptable	43.4	41.9	42.7	42.4	42.5
	Bad	6.8	5.2	9.2	5.3	5.4
	DK/CS	0.9	0.8	2.2	0.6	0.6

Source: ORG Centre for Social Research (2005): IX.1

CONCLUSION

The PDS as a public delivery system started functioning in India in 1930 and has been supported both by the central and state governments. After reviewing the working of public distribution system and analysing some secondary data, it is found that number of problems are associated in the implementation of the scheme. PDS as a scheme has failed miserably in choosing the criteria on the basis of which people are categorized, either as below or above the poverty line. As a result of this, some of the eligible families are excluded and some non-eligible families are included under the scheme. This has resulted in decline of quantities distributed through TPDS and the very purpose of the scheme has been defeated. Therefore, there is a need to address the obstacles involved in smooth functioning of the scheme.

NOTE

1. MSSRF survey of villages where community food grains banks have been setup in Jeypore Block, Koraput, Orissa.

REFERENCES

Chandrasekhar, C.P. and J. Ghosh 2005. Public Food Stocks: The Mess and the Wasted Opportunity, www.networkideas.org

Chopra, R.N. 1981. *Evolution of Food Policy in India*, MacMillan India Limited, Delhi.

National Commission on Farmers 2006. 'Serving Farmers and Saving Farming', Fifth and Final Report, Ministry of Agriculture, Government of India, New Delhi.

ORG Centre for Social Research 2005. 'Evaluation of Targeted Public Distribution System and Antodaya Anna Yojana', Report submitted to Ministry of Consumer Affairs, New Delhi.

Parikh, K.S. 1994. 'Who Gets How Much From PDS—How Effectively Does It Reach the Poor?' *Sarvekshana*, January–March 1994, pp. 1–34.

Patnaik, U. 2006. 'Poverty and Neo-Liberalization in India', www.networkideas.org

——— 1991. 'Food Availability and Famine: A Longer View', *The Journal of Peasant Studies*, Vol.19, No.1, October, pp. 1–25.

Paul, S., Suresh Balakrishnan, K. Gopakumar, Sita Sekhar, and M. Vivekananda 2004. 'State of India's Public Services', *Economic and Political Weekly*, February 28, pp. 920–33.

Program Evaluation Organization, (PEO) 2005. Performance Evaluation of Targeted Public Distribution System, Planning Commission of India, New Delhi.

Srinivasan, P.V. and S. Jha 1999. 'Food Security through Price Stabilisation', *Economic and Political Weekly*, November 20–26.

Swaminathan, M. 2005. 'Liberalization and Policies of Food Security: The India Experience', www.macroscan.com

——— 2003. 'Liberalization and Policies of Food Security: The Indian Experience', Paper presented at the meeting of the Ethiopian Economic Association, Addis Ababa, January 3–5.

——— 2000. *Weakening Welfare: The Public Distribution of Food in India*, Left Word Books, New Delhi.

Upadhyay, Ashok 2006. 'Inflation is Destroying the Well-earned Rupee', *The Hindu Business Line*, 22 November.

Vyas, Vijay S. 2005. *Food Security in Asian Countries in the Context of Millennium Development Goals*, Academic Foundation, New Delhi.

8

Status of Human Development in Orissa

P.K. Tripathy and Bhabagrahi Mishra

INTRODUCTION

The issue of human development (HD) has been discussed extensively in the last one and half decade throughout the world and has got extensive coverage in the various *Human Development Reports* (*HDRs*) of the United Nations Development Programme (UNDP). Elucidating the concept of HD, the UNDP Report 1997 described, 'The process of widening people's choices and the level of well-being they achieve are at the core of the notion of human development'. It added, 'Income clearly is only one option that people would like to have, though an important one. But it is not the sum total of their lives. Income is also a means, with human development the end'.

The Human Development Index (HDI) is an important tool for monitoring long-term trends in human development. The first *HDR* was published by UNDP in 1990, which calculated HDI for various countries and it got updated in subsequent reports. It measures the average achievements in a country in three basic dimensions of HD:

1. A long and healthy life, as measured by life expectancy at birth,
2. Knowledge as measured by the adult literacy rate and the combined primary, secondary and tertiary gross enrolment ratio, and
3. A decent standard of living as measured by the GDP per capita.

After nearly 11 years, the Planning Commission launched its first *HDR 2001* which presented indices for the country as a whole and across the states, and separately for rural and urban areas. Although, the *National Human Development Report (NHDR)* used the same broad attainment dimensions as UNDP namely, longevity, educational attainment, and economic attainment, it departed in the use of indicators (variables):

1. Longevity—(i) Life expectancy at age 1 and (ii) Infant mortality rate
2. Educational—(i) Literacy rate for age 7 and above (ii) Intensity of formal education, and
3. Economic—Per capita real consumption expenditure adjusted for inequality.

Again, after nearly three years, the *Orissa Human Development Report 2004* (GoO 2004) was launched (the 12th state to do so), supported by UNDP and the Planning Commission, which presented district-wise HDI on the basis of the broad measures of attainment outlined in the UNDP report, but again with different indicators (variables):

a. Health attainment—Infant mortality rate due to non-availability of life expectancy data at the district level,
b. Educational attainment—Combination of overall literacy rate and combined gross enrolment ratio, and
c. Standard of living—District domestic product (DDP).

METHODOLOGICAL ISSUES

The computation of HDI involves construction of an index for each of the three dimensions. Dimension Index (DI) is estimated as a function of actual value (AV), minimum value (MINV), and maximum value (MAXV) as $DI = \dfrac{AV - MINV}{MAXV - MINV}$

1. The *life expectancy index* (LEI) measures the relative achievement of a country in life expectancy at birth as,

$$LEI = \frac{AV - MINV}{MAXV - MINV}$$

2. The *education index* (EI) is estimated with two-thirds weight of *adult literacy index* (ALI) and one third weight to *gross enrolment index* (GEI) as,

$$\frac{2}{3}(ALI) + \frac{1}{3}(GEI)$$

3. The GDP index is estimated using adjusted GDP per capita. In the HDI, income serves as a surrogate for all the dimensions of HD not reflected in a long and healthy life, and in knowledge. Income is adjusted because achieving a respectable level of HD does not require unlimited income. Accordingly, the logarithm of income used is as follows:

$$GDPI = \frac{\log(AV) - \log(MINV)}{\log(MAXV) - \log(MINV)}$$

4. HDI is a simple average of the three dimension indices as,

$$HDI = \frac{1}{3}\{LEI + EI + GDPI\}$$

The *NHDR* (2001) computed HDI as a simple average of the three component indices, viz.,

1. Inflation and inequality adjusted per capita consumption expenditure,
2. Composite indicator of education attainment (CIEA), and
3. Composite indicator on health attainment (CIHA).

The CIEA and CIHA are obtained as follows:

$$CIEA = 0.35(LRAG7) + 0.65(AIFE)$$
$$CIHA = 0.65(LEA1) + 0.35(IMR)$$

LRAG7, AIFE, LEA1 and infant mortality rate (*IMR*), respectively are Literacy Rate for the Age group 7, Adjusted Intensity of Formal Education, Life Expectancy at Age 1, and infant mortality rate. In case of IMR the reciprocal of the indicator is used.

The computation of HDI in the *HDR of Orissa 2004* has the following deviations:

1. The health index is seen through infant mortality rate,
2. The education index is a composite index of overall literacy rate with two-third weight, and combined gross enrolment ratio with one-third weight, and
3. The standard of living index in terms of DDP per capita at 1993-94 prices (real DDP per capita).

While in *NHDR* inverse of IMR was used for computation of the health index, the Dimension Index (DI) has been obtained as

$$\frac{MAXV - AV}{MAXV - MINV}$$

State IMR estimates are obtained from the Sample Registration System. In the context of variations in the demographic profile sphere of material production and infrastructure development in the following, an attempt has been made to classify the districts on the basis of a Composite Index (CI) computed on the basis of the Sudarshan-Iyengar method.

Sudarshan–Iyengar Methodology

This method enables us to calculate the indicator of the overall level of development of different districts by giving arbitrary weights to the individual indicators reflecting their relative importance and adopting the inverse ratio of standard deviation. Let X_{ib} represent the size of the value of the ith development indicator in b^{th} block of the state (where $i = 1, 2, ... m$ & $b = 1, 2, ..., n$).

$$Y_{ib} = \frac{X_{ib} - Min(X_{ib})}{Max(X_{ib}) - Min(X_{ib})} \tag{8.1}$$

where $Min(X_{ib})$ and $Max(X_{ib})$ are respectively the minimum and maximum of $(X_{i1}, X_{i2}, ..., X_{in})$ and Y_{ib} is the standard variable.

If, however, the indicator X_{ib} is negatively associated with development, for example, the infant mortality rate or the unemployment ratio which should decline as the district develops then (8.1) can be written as:

$$Y_{ib} = \frac{Max(X_{ib}) - X_{ib}}{Max(X_{ib}) - Min(X_{ib})} \tag{8.2}$$

Obviously, the scaled values Y_{ib} vary from 0 to 1. From the matrix of scaled values $Y = [Y_{ib}]$, a measure for the level or stage of development for different districts is constructed as follows:

$$Y_b = W_1 Y_{1b} + W_2 Y_{2b} + ... + W_m Y_{mb} \tag{8.3}$$

where Y_b is the overall block index and it is assumed that the weights vary inversely as the variation in the respective indicators of development, or more specifically:

$$W_i = \frac{K}{SD(Y_i)} \text{ where } K = \left\{ \sum_{i=1}^{m} \frac{1}{SD(Y_i)} \right\}^{-1} \tag{8.4}$$

The Overall Index Y_b also varies from 0 to 1.

REVIEW OF LITERATURE

Review of some selected literature on aspects of HD in India reveals various problems encountered in the computation of the indices and results, many times not justifiable. Vyasulu and Vani (1997) reveal for the state of Karnataka a high intra-state disparity in development, suggesting sustained political support to an across-the-board improvement in each district. Bhattacharya (1998) provides evidence of high variation in HDI across districts of West Bengal with a bias in favour of urbanized regions, which corresponds to the all India pattern. Krishnaji (1998) indicated that the focus of UNDP (1998) was on inequalities in consumption across nations, and between poor and rich everywhere. Twenty per cent of the world's people in the highest income countries account for 86 per cent of total private consumption expenditure, and the poorest 20 per cent a miniscule 1.3 per cent. Chaubey (2000) pointed out the lapses in the construction of HDI proposed by UNDP, particularly the income component of the index. Sau (1999) emphasized that we have to ascertain the origin, evaluation, and effect of caste, and suggested that a village-level version of the HDI can be used for an indirect estimate of caste bias and that census should collect data on health, education, and earning of the people. Pradhan, et al. (2000) indicated wide disparities in level of living in terms of economic and social indicators in rural and urban India. Grace et al. (2001) examined the behaviour of HDI with variation in demographic, socio-economic, health, dietary habits and nutritional status, and studied the correlation of these indicators with HD. Lieten (2002) emphasized issues of land reforms and education from the experience of Kerala and extended the argument of a close relationship between political intervention on the equity front, and progress on the human development front. Kerala represented the unique distinction among Indian states having abolished feudal landlordism to a large extent and rural labour households having access to land with increasing entitlement. Two important measures were needed to improve the educational levels: a reorganization of educational system in favour of universal primary education and a judicial regulation of school management. Purkayastha and Chakraborty (2005) highlighted, in the context of Assam, that a measured chunk of society consisted of marginal and small farmers, who needed to be handled with care, with due attention to their food security.

RESULTS AND DISCUSSION

The *HDR 2004* of UNDP ranks countries in the HDI range 0.8 and above in the High Human Development (HHD) group. Countries in the HDI range 0.5 to 0.8 in the range of Medium Human Development (MHD) group and countries in the HDI range of less than 0.5 in the Low Human Development (LHD) group. It covered 177 UN member countries. Table 8.1 presents the average HDI for different groups of countries with high variation in the indices of most developed and most underdeveloped countries. It is found that the high income countries have highest values of HDI and the high income OECD countries have still higher level of HDI, and, on the other hand, the least developed countries have the lowest level of the component indices as well as the HDI indicating a strong association between level of income and HDI.

Table 8.1: HDI and the Component Indices of Different Countries

Countries	LEI	Education	GDP	HDI
HHD Countries	0.87	0.95	0.92	0.915
MHD Countries	0.70	0.75	0.63	0.695
LHD Countries	0.40	0.50	0.41	0.438
High Income	0.89	0.97	0.94	0.933
Middle Income	0.75	0.84	0.68	0.756
Low Income	0.57	0.59	0.51	0.557
Developing	0.66	0.71	0.62	0.663
Least Developed	0.43	0.49	0.42	0.446
High Income OECD	0.89	0.97	0.94	0.933

Source: Human Development Report 2004.

Norway notched first rank with a HDI of 0.956 followed by Sweden (0.946). The US ranks 8th and UK 12th. Other important countries of the group are Japan, Hong Kong, UAE, and Cuba. The MHD countries included Russia, Malaysia, India, China, Iran, and South Africa. LHD countries are Pakistan, Nigeria, Zambia, and Syria. Among the 177 countries, 55 were in HHD range, 86 in MHD range, and 36 in LHD range.

The interrelationships of different indices, viz., Health Index, Education Index, and GDP Index with HDI can be examined from Table 8.2. It is observed that in the case of HHD countries, all the components are highly correlated with HDI. However, while GDP is highly correlated with the health index, it has low correlation with the education index. Education also has low correlation with LEI.

In case of MHD countries, although all the components are highly correlated with HDI, GDP index has low correlation with health as well as education index. In case of LHD countries, only education is highly correlated with HDI and GDP index has low correlation with other two indices. GDP, being a major determinant for health and education status of any household, the absence of high correlation with health and education index may be attributed on the one hand to the accuracy of data for the relevant variables, and on the other to aggregation of micro level units to macro aggregates. The problem is more in case of LHD countries where the degree of monetization is very low and there is lower level of development of market forces. The data compiled, very often through statistical surveys, suffer to a significant extent due to improper reporting as well as enumeration. Besides, the indicators themselves have different significance in countries with higher development of market forces and countries where either markets do not exist or are inefficient.

Table 8.2: Correlation Coefficients of Different Components of HDI

Country	Components	LEI	Education	GDP	HDI
HHD Country	LEI	1.000	0.288	0.596	0.780
	Education	–	1.000	0.310	0.654
	GDP	–	–	1.000	0.873
MHD Country	LEI	1.000	0.364	0.109	0.723
	Education	–	1.000	0.320	0.797
	GDP	–	–	1.000	0.615
LHD Country	LEI	1.000	–0.267	0.098	0.420
	Education	–	1.000	0.028	0.673
	GDP	–	–	1.000	0.483

The Planning Commission 2001 of India, as noted earlier, computed HDI for different states using different variables representing three types of attainments as specified in UNDP Report. Table 8.3 depicts the HDI for India and 14 major states for the years 1981 and 2001.

The major states of the Indian Union are classified into High Income States (HIS) consisting of Maharashtra, Punjab, Haryana, and Gujarat, the Middle Income States (MIS) consisting of Tamil Nadu, West Bengal, Karnataka, Andhra Pradesh, and Kerala, and the Low Income States (LIS) consisting of Rajasthan, Madhya Pradesh, Uttar Pradesh, Orissa, and Bihar. Orissa, belonging to LIS has low per capita income, next only to Bihar. In 1981, there is almost correspondence

Table 8.3: HDI of Different States during 1981 and 2001

States	1996–99		1981		2001	
	Per Capita SDP (1980–81 prices)	Rank	HDI	Rank	HDI	Rank
HIS Category						
Maharasthra	5032	1	0.363	3	0.523	3
Punjab	4389	2	0.411	2	0.537	2
Haryana	4025	3	0.360	5	0.509	4
Gujarat	3918	4	0.360	4	0.479	6
MIS Category						
Tamil Nadu	3141	5	0.343	7	0.531	5
West Bengal	2977	6	0.305	8	0.472	8
Karnataka	2866	7	0.346	6	0.478	7
Andhra Pradesh	2550	8	0.298	9	0.416	10
Kerala	2490	9	0.500	1	0.638	1
LIS Category						
Rajasthan	2226	10	0.256	11	0.424	9
Madhya.Pradesh	1922	11	0.245	13	0.394	12
Uttar Pradesh	1725	12	0.255	12	0.388	13
Orissa	1666	13	0.267	10	0.404	11
Bihar	1126	14	0.237	14	0.367	14
All India	2840	–	0.302	–	0.472	–

between levels of HDI with level of income of the states with the only exception of Kerala, which has the highest HDI, though it is a MIS. In 2001, there are minor changes with Haryana in HIS category, Tamil Nadu in MIS category, and Rajasthan and Uttar Pradesh improving slightly in HDI. One notices a decline in ranking in case of Gujarat of HIS, Karnataka and Andhra Pradesh of MIS, and Uttar Pradesh and Orissa of LIS category. It is further noticed that the HDI for the country as per Planning Commission Report in 2001 is 0.472, which is much lower than the UNDP index of 0.595 in 2004.

The State of Orissa has witnessed improvement in HDI from 0.267 in 1981 to 0.404 in 2001 as per *National Human Development Report*. However, the relative position of the state among major states has declined from 10th position to 11th position during the same period. During both points in time, HDI of Orissa is found lower than the all India average. The HDI values obtained for different districts of the state by Government of Orissa (2004) are presented in Table 8.4. The component indices present variation among the districts. The average income index of the state is 0.545, which varies from a minimum of

Table 8.4: HDI Values for Different Districts of the State

Districts	DDP 1977	Health Index	Income Index	Education Index	HDI	Composite Index
Angul	10877	0.481	0.748	0.76	0.663	0.367
Balasore	3961	0.442	0.466	0.77	0.559	0.407
Bargarh	4765	0.449	0.517	0.727	0.565	0.456
Bhadrak	3916	0.673	0.463	0.803	0.646	0.392
Balangir	4538	0.468	0.504	0.666	0.546	0.285
Boudh	4436	0.423	0.497	0.688	0.536	0.275
Cuttack	6116	0.686	0.587	0.813	0.695	0.652
Deogarh	5022	0.776	0.532	0.698	0.669	0.274
Dhenkanal	5046	0.468	0.534	0.773	0.591	0.379
Gajapati	5498	0.173	0.558	0.561	0.431	0.251
Ganjam	5013	0.404	0.532	0.718	0.551	0.478
J.Singhpur	5340	0.288	0.549	0.833	0.557	0.482
Jajpur	4468	0.333	0.499	0.786	0.54	0.402
Jharsuguda	11210	0.635	0.757	0.773	0.722	0.507
Kalahandi	4043	0.763	0.471	0.585	0.606	0.239
Kandhamal	4743	0.006	0.516	0.645	0.389	0.214
Kendrapara	3964	0.596	0.466	0.815	0.626	0.441
Keonjhar	5286	0.34	0.547	0.704	0.53	0.286
Khurda	7353	0.724	0.639	0.845	0.736	0.734
Korpaut	5148	0.218	0.539	0.535	0.431	0.206
Malkangiri	4436	0.122	0.497	0.491	0.37	0.138
Mayurbhanj	4297	0.782	0.489	0.647	0.639	0.198
Nabarangpur	3787	0.34	0.453	0.516	0.436	0.201
Nayagarh	4236	0.462	0.485	0.766	0.571	0.357
Nuapada	4018	0.692	0.47	0.582	0.581	0.197
Puri	4933	0.622	0.527	0.823	0.657	0.629
Rayagada	5300	0.25	0.547	0.531	0.443	0.151
Sambalpur	6171	0.436	0.59	0.742	0.589	0.57
Sonepur	4353	0.474	0.492	0.731	0.566	0.449
Sundargarh	6823	0.692	0.618	0.74	0.683	0.357
State	5264	0.468	0.545	0.723	0.579	-

0.463 for Bhadrak and maximum of 0.748 for Angul. The health index of the state is 0.468, varying from a minimum of 0.173 for Gajapati and maximum of 0.782 for Mayurbhanj. Similarly, the education index value for the state is 0.723, varying from a minimum of 0.491 for

Box 8.1	
HHD Group (greater than 0.6)	Kalahandi, Kendrapara, Mayurbhanj, Bhadrak, Puri, Angul, Deogarh, Sundargarh, Cuttack, Jharsuguda, Khurda
MHD Group (0.5 to 0.6)	Keonjhar, Boudh, Jajpur, Balangir, Ganjam, Jagatsinghpur, Balasore, Bargarh, Sonepur, Nayagarh, Nuapada, Sambalpur, Dhenkanal
LHD Group (less than 0.5)	Malkangiri, Kandhamal, Gajapati, Koraput, Nabarangpur, Rayagada

Malkangiri to 0.845 for Khurda. The HDI value for the state is 0.579, varying from a minimum of 0.370 in Malkangiri to 0.736 for Khurda.

The different districts in Orissa can be classified into high, medium, and low human development groups on the basis of HDI as follows: The inclusion of Kalahandi, Mayurbhanj, and Deogarh in HHD group and Nuapada in MHD group raises doubts regarding the process of computation of HDI. It is, therefore, necessary to examine the inter-relationships among the component indices. Further, the districts can be classified on the basis of a Composite Index of development using similar procedure of indexing taking eight socio-economic variables, namely,

1. Percentage of Urbanization
2. Percentage of Literacy
3. Intensity of Cropping
4. Fertiliser Consumption per Hectare
5. Net Area Sown Irrigated
6. Percentage of Villages Electrified
7. Percentage of Surfaced Roads
8. No. of Hospital Beds per Lakh of Population

The component indices and the HDI can be correlated with the Composite Index to observe the pattern of relationships. It is revealed in Table 8.5 that health and education are highly correlated with HDI but not DDP. Composite index of development is highly correlated with education and HDI, but not with either health index or income index, thereby indicating that the estimates obtained for income and health do not conform to the level of development and developmental efforts, and as such, the computed HDI fails to reflect the actual variations existing across the districts.

Table 8.5: Correlation Coefficients of Different Components of
HDI in Orissa

High HD Country	Health	Education	DDP	HDI	Composite
Health	1	0.419	0.107	0.885	0.371
Education	-	1	0.289	0.729	0.837
DDP	-	-	1	0.437	0.389
HDI	-	-	-	1	0.662
Composite	-	-	-	-	1

Taking the Composite Index of development, we can classify the districts into High, Medium, and Low development groups as shown in Box 8.2:

Box 8.2	
HDG	Ganjam, Jagatsinghpur, Jharsuguda, Sambalpur, Puri, Cuttack and Khurda
MDG	Sundargarh, Nayagarh, Angul, Dhenkanal, Bhadrak, Jajpur and Balasore, Kendrapara, Sonepur, Bargarh
LDG	Malkangiri, Rayagada, Nuapada, Mayurbhanj, Nabarangpur, Koraput, Kandhamal, Kalahandi, Gajapati, Deogarh, Boudh, Bolangir and Keonjhar

SUMMARY AND POLICY PRESCRIPTIONS

1. As per *HDR 2004* of UNDP, out of 177 countries, there are 55 countries under HHD Group, 86 countries under MHD group, and 36 under LHD group. India with a HDI of 0.595 falls under MHD group (bottom 15th country in the group).

2. As per Planning Commission (2001), the position of Orissa is 11th among the fourteen major states with a HDI value of 0.404 compared to all India level of 0.472. Orissa's relative position in terms of HDI seems to have deteriorated from 10th position in 1981 to 11th position in 2001. However, comparability of National HDI with that of HDI of UNDP is lost due to replacement of income variable by consumption expenditure variable.

3. As per Government of Orissa (2004), the HDI for the state is 0.579 with variation across the districts from 0.370 in case of Malkangiri to 0.736 in case of Khurda. There is non-correspondence between the classification of districts on the basis of HDI and the Composite Index of development obtained on the basis of structural and infrastructural variables. Backward districts such as Kalahandi, Deogarh, and Mayurbhanj are found in HHD group,

Table 8.6: Socioeconomic Parameters used for Categorization of Districts in Orissa

Sl. No.	District/State	% of Urbanization (2001)	% of Literacy (2001)	Cropping Intensity (2002–03)	Fertiliser cons. per hect. (2002–03)	% NAS Irrigated (2002–03)	% of Villages Electrified (2003–04)	% of Surfaced Road (2000–01)	Hospital Beds per Lakh of Population (2003–04)
1	Angul	13.89	68.79	155.49	20.35	16.01	80.3	1651	28.25
2	Balsore	10.89	70.56	135.09	71.07	19.27	93.5	1445	23.36
3	Bargarh	7.69	63.99	128.18	91.34	38.15	98.9	1716	20.36
4	Bhadrak	10.58	73.86	123.78	83.84	17.41	83.8	1504	20.46
5	Bolangir	11.54	55.7	124.16	18.59	10.84	94.1	1422	35
6	Boudh	4.83	57.73	134.57	31.93	36.86	60.8	1402	18.76
7	Cuttack	27.39	76.66	176.44	38.82	45.39	98.6	1722	82.96
8	Deogarh	7.33	60.36	131.34	31.02	22.89	46.6	1536	43.06
9	Dhenkanal	8.71	69.42	144.3	20.7	19.29	93.9	1755	36.08
10	Gajapati	10.19	41.26	151.89	23.75	17.35	50.4	1465	38.34
11	Ganjam	17.6	60.77	144.22	54.65	46.06	86.8	1468	50.33
12	J.Singhpur	9.88	79.08	185	31.51	31.53	96.5	1733	14
13	Jajpur	4.49	71.44	166	41.65	14.1	96	1811	13.73
14	Jharsugud	36.47	70.65	122.08	75.11	14.34	99.7	2107	21.22
15	Kalahandi	7.5	45.94	128.83	36.45	8.04	63.6	1542	36.77
16	Kandham	6.8	52.68	141.18	1.79	10.54	49.1	1103	62.65
17	Kendrapar	5.69	76.81	175.71	24.83	26.81	91.5	1896	20.58
18	Keonjhar	13.64	59.24	140.27	22.87	16.24	85.8	755	32.14

Contd...

Table 8.6 (Contd.)

Sl. No.	District/State	% of Urbanization (2001)	% of Literacy (2001)	Cropping Intensity (2002–03)	Fertiliser cons. per hect. (2002–03)	% NAS Irrigated (2002–03)	% of Villages Electrified (2003–04)	% of Surfaced Road (2000–01)	Hospital Beds per Lakh of Population (2003–04)
19	Khurda	42.92	79.59	161.72	30.58	71.87	94.1	3022	43.05
20	Koraput	16.81	35.72	130	17.53	28.39	53	1099	29.55
21	Malkangiri	6.87	30.53	121.26	23.76	16.85	41.8	786	56.75
22	Mayurbhanj	7	51.91	117.02	27.23	5.27	67.7	1212	35.72
23	Nabarangpur	5.78	33.93	127.75	35.21	6.72	76.8	1490	23
24	Nayagarh	4.29	70.52	150.76	25.43	6.8	73.6	1750	56.53
25	Nuapada	5.66	42	117.79	17.66	3.37	80.9	1665	29.75
26	Puri	13.58	77.96	164.83	35.94	43.4	97.9	3333	46.91
27	Rayagada	13.89	36.15	136.24	20.94	15.19	39.5	894	27.07
28	Sambalpur	27.12	67.25	124	81.94	28.52	72	1434	124.36
29	Sonepur	7.39	62.84	156.36	31.63	56.9	88.6	1783	28.23
30	Sundargarh	34.37	64.86	128.96	17.08	2.88	89.8	1374	34.73
	Orissa	14.99	63.08	138.26	37	21.95	77	1455	38.86

Sources: Statistical Abstract of Orissa—2005; Orissa Agricultural Statistics, 2002–03.

districts such as Keonjhar, Boudh, Balangir, and Nuapada are placed under MHD group. Similarly, Ganjam, Jagatsinghpur, and Sambalpur of HHD group are placed in MHD group and Sundargarh of MHD group is placed under HHD group.

4. Given the absence of correlation of estimated DDP and IMR on the basis of sample registration system, with both the HDI as well as the CI, these variables possibly do not reflect the standard of living criterion as well as health attainments in different districts of the state, and particularly their variability. Only education index is found to be having high correlation with HDI as well as the CI.

5. While one can observe the limitations of the HDI using the variables proposed by the UNDP report mainly in the context of backward countries (low correlation of components of HDI with HDI) as aspects of inequality of income is concealed in Per Capita Income. High literacy in developed economies has different implications than in backward economies. In backward economies, mere literacy with no employment opportunities does not lead to educational attainment nor estimated high LEI or lower IMR is reflective of sound health conditions of the majority of the population including agricultural labourer, marginal, and small farmers and poor artisans.

6. In the context of above observations, it may be argued that alternative variables reflecting the health, educational, and standard of living attainment may be taken, which can capture the variations across the districts in the state as well as across the states in the country. For example, a composite index of property ownership (land and other resources), per capita income obtained on the basis of income on accrual method, and the average man days employed of the working population, shall capture the standard of living index more accurately than either mere per capita income or employment. Similarly, education index must be a composite index of literacy as well as linkage with employment opportunities. Health index must be a composite index of anthropometric measurements and pattern of mortality.

REFERENCES

Bhattacharya, B. 1998. 'Urbanization and Human Development in West Bengal: A District level Study and Comparisons with Inter-State Variations', *Economic and Political Weekly*, Vol. 47, No. 48.

Chaubey, P.K. 2000. 'The Human Development Index: A Contribution to Its Construction', *Indian Journal of Economics,* Vol. LXXVII, No. 328, pp. 95–99.

Grace, M.A., K.V. Rao, and N. Venkatram 2001. 'Suitability of HDI for Ascending Health and Nutritional Status', *Economic and Political Weekly*, Vol. XXXVI. No. 31, pp. 2976–79.

Krishnaji, N. 1998. 'UNDP's Gender Related Development Index', *Economic and Political Weekly*, April 6.

Lieten, G.K. 2002. 'Human Development in Kerala: Structure and Agency in History', *Economic and Political Weekly*, Vol. 16.

Government of Orissa [GoO] 2004. *Human Development Report 2004*, Orissa, Bhubaneswar, Planning and Coordination Department. http://orissagov.nic.in/p%26c/humandevelopment/hdr/HDR_2004.pdf/

Planning Commission 2001. *National Human Development Report 2001*, Government of India, New Delhi.

Pradhan, B.K., P.K. Roy, M.R. Saluja, and S. Venkatram 2000. 'Rural-Urban Disparities: Income Distribution, Expenditure Pattern, and Social sector', *Economic and Political Weekly*, Vol. 35, No. 28 and 29, pp. 2527–29 and 2531–39.

Purkayastha, G. and A. Chakraborty 2005. 'The Human Development in Assam', *Yojana*, Vol. 49, pp. 69.

Sau, R. 1999. 'Human Development Index in Lieu of Caste Census 2001', *Economic and Political Weekly*, Vol. 51.

Unite Nations Development Programme (UNDP), 1990, 1998, 2001, 2004, and 2007–08, *Human Development Report* (Volumes). http://hdr.undp.org/en/reports/global/

Vyasulu, V. and B.P. Vani 1997. 'Development and Deprivation in Karnataka, A District level Study', *Economic and Political Weekly*, Vol. 46.

9

Good Governance
The Force behind Human Development

ASHUTOSH DASH AND PAOHULEN KIPGEN

INTRODUCTION

The quickening pace of change in the national economy, with the introduction of economic reforms, has caught the attention of institutions and agencies concerned with development and sustainable growth. Liberalization of the economy, with increasing privatization and globalization, has certainly brought about structural changes resulting in growth of the economy. However, for progressive and constant growth, there is also a need to develop and change the social structure in terms of proportionate growth in various Human Development (HD) indices such as health, education, and so on. Development is seen as a process of change from an underdeveloped stage to a developed stage. It goes beyond the rise or fall of national income to create an environment in which people can develop their full potential and lead productive and creative lives, in accordance with their needs and interests. HD is viewed both as a process of widening people's choice and the level of their achieved well-being, including a healthy life, political freedom, education, etc. However, without eradication of poverty from society, HD remains the same. Apart from this, people should have the freedom of choice. Inequality in status and power restricts one to adopt choices according to one's own preferences. This has created a gap between different levels of hierarchy, which provides more opportunities to the one higher in the ladder in monopolizing power. Development, apart from economic growth, is expanding the people's choice. Looking at the importance of governance, the chapter in the following pages tries to establish governance as the most dynamic factor in the human development process.

HUMAN DEVELOPMENT AND ECONOMIC GROWTH

The transformation of economy around the globe from a highly controlled, inward looking, and protected economy, to a liberalized, outward looking, and market-oriented economy, has undoubtedly witnessed faster Economic Growth (EG) than before. The performance of many developing economies including India, over the last two decades, has improved appreciably in terms of per capital income, growth in GDP, export and balance of payment, foreign exchange reserves, and standard of living. Though the economies are growing at a faster rate, several of them are simultaneously suffering from the problems of poverty, inequality, unemployment, mass illiteracy, and lack of basic health facilities. It is surprising to note that India has ranked the 128th position in the world with respect to HD indicator (*Human Development Report 2007–08*, UNDP). HD, the vital instrument for growth and development of an economy, is highly neglected in India, and more so in the tribal dominated areas and states.

But is this EG without HD sustainable? The likely answer is 'no'. HD and EG are inseparable. EG requires growth in HD. When HD cannot progress, it effects EG. History has been witness to the fact that nations with lopsided EG in 1960–70 have moved to the vicious cycle of low EG and HD state. On the other hand, out of nations that were HD-lopsided, half have made an entry into the virtuous cycle and the other half to the vicious cycle (Ranis *et al.* 2000). The result is a prima facie evidence of the fact that a high level of HD, early in a nation's history, can with the right policy decisions, translate into a virtuous cycle of good growth and HD supporting each other.

A deep insight into the association of principal components of HD with *EG* uncovers their significant and distinct impact on the growth of a nation through their effect on the distribution. Education, an imperative component, is found to have a strong influence on labour productivity, technology adoption, and innovation (Duflo 2001; Deraniyagala 1995). Though, it will not be appropriate to pronounce that education in isolation can transform a country's economy, at the same time it canot be denied that education creates huge potential in the economy. In the case of Malaysia, Ghana, and Peru, each extra year of a farmer's schooling is associated with an annual increase in output of 2–5 per cent (Birdsall *et al.* 1995). Similarly, improvement in health, another dimension of HD, can contribute significantly to a country's EG. Many studies conclude productivity enhancement to immediately follow the increased consumption of calories, especially in poor countries (Strauss and Thomas 1998). Though, both education and health have the power to hasten EG, education gets a little higher weight as it can also have a significant impact on health.

The crucial point that emerges in the light of the above discussion is that HD seems to be a necessary prerequisite for long-term sustainable growth. The philosophy of 'growing first and then thinking of human development' has been changed. Countries stuck in vicious cycles or lopsided EG may need to achieve at least the threshold HD level that will lead to later sustainable EG. The effects of EG on HD can be channelized through government budgetary expenditures, central or local. The government must identify the priority sectors, and the expenditures for HD should be distributed predominantly to low-income groups where the highest marginal impact would be felt. Increased public expenditure, devoid of efficient allocation and optimum utilization, does not endow with a meaningful result. It is worth highlighting here that the countries that have made their journey from lopsided EG to vicious cycle were suffering from corruption, low social expenditure, and unequal income distribution (Ranis *et al.* 2000). To put it in other words, an excellent governance mechanism coupled with government accountability is a precondition for effectiveness of public expenditure towards the HD objective. The need of good governance was first felt with the collapse of East Asian financial economy, and it was realized that the presence of corruption leads to disaster in the economy. Good governance needs to be embedded with transparency to curb corrupt practices. A country's progress principally depends on its governance quality in society, and productivity in its operations.

GOVERNANCE AND HUMAN DEVELOPMENT

At its broadest, governance, that is, the act of governing, refers to the relationship between the governors and the governed, such as that between the government and the people, and has as its basis the decision-making powers ceded by individuals to those in authority so that the common interests of society can be served. Hence, governance primarily deals with exercise of economic, political, and administrative authority in managing the affairs of a nation, and needs to be transparent and accountable. Social activists, recognizing the importance of governance, advocate for an institutional and political change as HD cannot just automatically happen without economic development, and economic development alone cannot bring progressive HD without good governance. Bad governance is responsible for micro and macroeconomic mismanagement. Studies conducted around the world show that weak governance was to be blamed for the financial crisis in South-East Asia and many parts of this region of the world accompanied by the economic fluctuation, leading to a backward move of human development. The collapse of economies in South-East Asian countries has been attributed to bad governance in both the public and the private sector, mainly due to corruption and lack of disclosure.

Governance, that refers to the exercise of authority in the management of a country's affairs, includes the state, private sector, and civil society. Good governance requires a good balance of power among different actors such as politicians, bureaucrats, and civil society. A proper governance mechanism is supposed to ensure that political, economic, and social priorities are based on social consensus and that of the participation of the poor in decision making over allocation of development resources (as shown in Table 9.1).

Table 9.1: Governance—A Taxonomy

	High EG	Low EG
Better HD	Better Governance (Virtuous)	Vulnerable Governance (Lopsided HD)
Poor HD	Exploitative Governance (Lopsided EG)	Poor Governance (Vicious)

This emphasizes that good governance defines the process and structure that guides political and socio-economic relationships. In the above grid, the existence of a two-way link between HD and EG gives rise to a virtuous cycle of development (better governance), lopsided HD (vulnerable governance), lopsided EG (exploitative governance), and vicious governance (poor governance). EG increases the HD growth. On the other hand, HD growth also contributes towards EG. However, the growth between the two is not equally distributed.

By the late 1990s, the World Bank Institute, from several hundreds of variables measuring perception of governance, had developed six dimensions of good governance—control of corruption, rule of law, government effectiveness, regulatory quality, voice and accountability, and political stability, with absence of violence. Public opinion research discloses that corruption is among the top concerns of the people and leaders around the world. Prior empirical research has uncovered the detrimental impact of corruption on socio-economic development of various nations. Studies conducted by the Inter-American Development Bank (IADB) indicate that in Latin America as a whole, 20 per cent of funds earmarked for government procurement are lost to corruption (Mora 2004). The African union estimates that approximately 25 per cent of the GDP is lost to corruption each year (Thachuk 2005) and in Latin America about 10 per cent of the GDP is lost to corruption (Mora 2004). A classic study in this field by Mauro (1995) underlines that one standard deviation improvement in corruption index leads to an increase in the investment rate by 2.9 per cent of GDP.

The act of corruption can be in many forms and ways, like that of political corruption (government), social corruption (community), and economic corruption (market). The corruption in these three areas is usually committed through manipulation of accounts, bribery, and fictitious statements in balance sheets. Corruption is well thought out as the use of public office for private gains. It exists at all levels and in all fields. In a state where corruption is high, it is the poor who suffer the most, as the effect of corruption is not equally distributed. The ill-effects of corruption result in distortion of economic growth and hamper the functioning of all agencies for development, and also results in low Human Development Index (HDI).

Corruption is anti-poor, anti-national, and anti-economic. It is anti-poor because the effects of corruption are not equally shared by the masses. The government plans and objective of raising HD by reducing poverty through its various programmes such as public distribution system, subsidy goods, and education for all, cannot be attained as planned. The funds sanctioned for a cause may have been diverted/siphoned off for the benefit of a few and to the black market. The experience of north-eastern states of India has been much worse than other states in this context. It is anti-national because the institutional collapses following corrupt practices have severe economic impact on political or financial institutions, which are responsible for the growth of an economy, and for better living standards of a nation.

Not only corruption at the country level (administrators and bureaucrats), but market corruption can also create severe damage from the development point of view. The snowballing corporate collapses such as Enron and WorldCom, due to unprecedented large scale failures arising from unethical activities jointly on the part of corporate executives and the auditors, have severely defiled governance in corporate sector. The collapse of Enron has caused about $ 70 billion loss in market capitalization and the total loss of market capitalization resulting from the deception committed by Enron, WorldCom, Qwest Tyco, and Global Crossing amounts to nearly $ 460 billion (Rezaee 2005). In India, though, such financial collapses did not happen till the recent swindle of Satyam, one cannot say that it's a corruption-free state.

CORRUPTION AND HD—THE INDIAN SCENARIO

In the context of India, it is not that the government is silent on its growth policies and human development; rather, many development plans and projects have been framed and duly sanctioned in an increasing number on an year-to-year basis. However, the country could not progress as expected. With regards to the government expenditure on social sector and rural development, there is an increasing trend on both plan and non-plan expenditure. Social expenditure increased from Rs 11,631 crore in 1995–96 to Rs 55,187 crore in 2005–06. With regards to the rural sector, the expenditure increased from Rs 6,609 crore in 1995–96 to Rs 11,503 crore in 2005–06. However, with increase in expenditure on social development, some states such as Uttar Pradesh, Punjab, and Manipur witnessed a declining HDI. Though, there are achievements in some parts of the country, yet all the states do not show proportionate increase with the expenditure. Social and economic pundits do not believe social resources constraint to be the reason, but advocate mis-governance as the source of all tribulations. Thus, it shows that increase in public expenditure for social and rural development cannot contribute for a fast and progressive growth in HDI, if the governance mechanism of the state is not appropriate.

A look at the corruption and human development scores of India in the new millennium is wearisome—even the scores demonstrate an upward trend (as shown in Table 9.2). The increased scores accompanied with the decreasing ranks indicate that India so far has not been succeeded in putting good governance in place as compared to few of its counterparts who have set their places in high human development category from a medium development category. Of course, corruption in India has dropped marginally over the years, but still poses as the main hindrance in fostering the growth in GDP and FDI in the country. According to the Global Corruption Index, conducted by Transparency International, India stood at 83rd in the ranking of 133 nations (2007). India's Position in 2006 was 71st out of 102 nations. India's score of 2.7 out of 10 is an indication of high corruption rate (higher score denotes low corruption). Still, on an average, 30 per cent of funds sanctioned for HD are being driven away for personal benefit. The politicians, bureaucrats, and not to mention illegal and unlawful militants, all have had a share, with the militants being offered the lion's share. In 1984, the then Prime Minister Rajiv Gandhi, once cited that if Rs 100 is sanctioned by the centre to the state, only Rs 22 reaches its destination, and the rest is lost on the way.

Table 9.2: CPI and HDI Rank of India in the New Millennium

	Corruption		HDI	
Year	Rank	Score	Rank	Score
2001	72	2.7	127	0.590
2002	73	2.7	127	0.595
2003	83	2.8	127	0.602
2004	91	2.8	126	0.611
2005	92	2.9	128	0.619

Source: Transparency International and Human Development Reports.

Apart from being development growth's enemy, corruption also has an impact on the country's security. Politicians having links with militants and other unlawful organizations are a threat to the nation. Moreover, money paid to them, by way of bribes, for installing developmental projects or offer of certain percentage of the funds to enable certain activities to be carried out, is used for procuring arms and is, thus, an anti-national activity. Money collection by the government from the public, to be utilized for the welfare of the society, cannot happen and results in failure in projecting HD growth. Moreover, due to corruption, a huge amount is siphoned off from developmental programmes to some militant groups (as is evident in north-eastern states) by politicians, bureaucrats for their self gain, and this image in the political arena results in creating fear and insecurity among society, and ultimately outcomes in low human development.

PARTICIPATION—MEANS TO CURB CORRUPTION AND PROGRESS GOVERNANCE

The solutions to the problems should be strengthening of the governance system in the areas of politics, society, and economic institutions. Many reforms have also been made for better growth but did not result in any positive outcome. To make the reforms strong, governance, first, has to be strong. Good governance in the form of transparency, anti-corruption, and accountability can be brought through proper participation that generally refers to peoples' involvement in all spheres of economic, social, cultural, and political processes that affect their lives. In economic terms, this means being able to engage freely in any economic activity. In social terms, it means being able to join fully in all forms of community life regardless of colour, caste, and religion. In political terms, it means the freedom to choose and change governance at every level, from the presidential place to the village council. All these participations are intimately linked.

Market Participation

Sustainable human development demands more from the markets, as markets are a means for human development. By and large, the markets make no value judgments as they reward those who have either substantial purchasing power or valuable commodities to sell. This market inefficiency is associated with increasing inequality, poverty, and large scale unemployment. They also place little value on environmental concerns and the needs of future generations. Hence, there is an urgent need to build a bridge between markets and the people, to make markets people friendly. As preconditions, to make markets people-friendly, there must be adequate investment in education and health of people, equitable distribution of land in poor agrarian societies, extension of credit to the poor, public access to information, adequate physical infrastructure, a legal framework to protect property rights, and a liberal trade regime to prepare people for the market. A stable macroeconomic environment, accompanied by a comprehensive incentive system and freedom from arbitrary government control and regulations, can make markets run more efficiently and equitably.

The best form of market participation is through productive and remunerative work, and through self-employment and wage employment. It empowers the people socially by offering a productive role that enhances their dignity and self-esteem, and empowers them politically as they start influencing the decision-making at the work place and beyond. As many parts of the world are witnessing a new phenomenon of jobless growth, the measures that create employment and lead to a people-friendly market, can make a major contribution to employment creation. One of the surest ways of encouraging employment is to promote small business. But to encourage entrepreneurs, the most important factor is the ready access to capital. The capital market is very unfriendly to small enterprises, particularly the poorest ones. Banks often ignore the needs of small entrepreneurs and are generally unwilling to provide credit due to lack of acceptable collateral. This hampers the interest of three groups in the society; small farmers, entrepreneurs in informal sector, and women, in particular. To eradicate this discrimination, the best way is to combine improved availability of credit with measures aimed at enhancing competitiveness. People-friendly markets should encourage and nurture small enterprises for profit, not only of the individual entrepreneurs but for the society as a whole, through a steady increase in output and employment.

The concept of people-friendly markets clearly envisages the State and the market working in tandem. The central fallacy in the old ideological debate was that the State and the market are necessarily separate and even antagonistic, and that one is benevolent and the other not. In practice, both the State and the market are often dominated by the same power structure. This suggests a more pragmatic third option: both the State and the market should be guided by the people, and for that matter people should be sufficiently empowered to extend effective control over both.

Social (Community) Participation

At times, countries have developed the institutions of civil society—a fair judiciary, a responsive executive, a free press to upkeep the traditions of transparency, accountability, and fair play; but for ensuring that such institutions continue to respond to peoples' aspiration, group action is often necessary. Community participation, as a component of development strategy, gained momentum in the 1980s as a consequence of the failure of public agencies and growing deficiency in the level of basic amenities. The energy of the people who form the group and the creative solutions demonstrated by the group helps in persuading the governments of the value of involving participatory community groups. These community organizations may be in form of people's organization, that is, Self Help Groups (SHGs) or Non-governmental Organizations (NGOs), voluntary organizations that work with, and very often on behalf of others. These organizations are basically formed in response to a failure by the government to provide infrastructure or services.

It is argued that the community could help not only in social mobilization but also in raising financial resources that the local authorities need very badly. In many cases, it becomes possible to have substantial reduction in project cost as the prospective beneficiaries provide their labour free, or at a wage rate much below that in the market. Further, the pressure of peer groups under participatory arrangement results in better monitoring, more productive engagement of the beneficiaries in the project, and better recovery of development loans sanctioned to individuals. The community is mobilized not merely for making contributions in terms of ideas and labour but also for sharing a part of the capital and current expenditure. Only, there was demand for making credit available outside the formal institutional structure, which was beyond the access of the slum communities. In several cases, attempts were made to build mechanisms at the community level to ensure timely repayment of loans. The most innovative form of community participation in infrastructural projects, which has been hailed as a major achievement in the 1990s, is the neighbourhood and slum networking schemes, launched with substantial financial support from the central or state governments.

People's participation has become a standard rhetoric in India today. Different actors interpret it differently. One view is that participation means getting people to agree to and go along with a project already designed for them, or to get support of a few leaders. The important question is participation for whose benefit, and on what terms? It must, therefore, be understood as a process by which the people are able to identify their own needs and share in the design, implementation, and evaluation of the participatory action. Thus, the various elements of participation are decision making at various stages, control and management of funds and resources, share in usufruct and final produce, and certainly of benefits.

SUGGESTED GOVERNANCE MODEL
As rightly pointed out by the Chairman of United Nations Development Programme (UNDP 2008) that if corruption is unchecked, it will make more children go to school without books and also suffer

from lack of clean water, medicines, etc. However, though the corruption level is still high, the country should not be penalized, instead corruption has to be contained as it is an urgent need for development. India's economic and human development would have been worse had the government neglected its governance. Many Indian states have now made a holy approach to administration for human development growth by cleansing up corrupt practices. An organization apart from NGOs such as the Joint Administrative Council in Manipur and many such other types of organizations in different parts of the country have moved forward for strengthening good governance.

Many governments have adopted simplification of laws and procedures, like the government of Tamil Nadu, or adopted information technology like the Andhra Pradesh government. Better governance can be ensured by fostering literacy, and increasing and adopting the use of E-Governance where data of all political leaders, government plans and actions, and all activities can be provided. Moreover, civil organizations have been promoted to play greater roles and media is stronger to despose corrupt politicians and guilty bureaucrats like the experience of tehelka.com. Apart from NGOs, other local organizations have played a major role in combating corruption and fostering greater community participation in decision making that affect their lives (Meghalaya—Mait Shaphrang Movement, Manipur—Meira Paibi, Nagaland—Naga Mother Association and also other religious organizations). Financial institutions, especially the micro finance institutions like Gramin Bank, Basics, etc. should be made to focus more on the relationship with civil organizations in terms of their commitment towards poverty eradication. People's participation should be encouraged and decisions on matters affecting their lives should be decentralized, which is profoundly observed in the state of Kerala.

The country achieved slow but progressing growth because of the concern on good governance by the government. Still, it requires providing more economic freedom that would result in better HDI. India's position in world ranking of Economic Freedom is 123 (as per EFI)[1] in 2009, which shows we need to increase economic freedom as this is correlated with HDI. Hence, the need of the hour is good governance and the country is not silent in this regard, though corruption cannot be fully contained. A good governance model (as one shown in Figure 9.1), in democratic countries like India, must be designed to promote judicial and the civil society to come together for restoring public trust. The judiciary along with the civil society can enforce and control the executive. The judicial process should not be soft to any wrongdoer or any executive, and should take timely action without any delay in its justice. This will create a self-check and make the executive ethically driven in its action.

Mass media and civil society should play a major role in developing and thinning out public awareness and controlling corruption. Corruption is easily committed as the corruptor can easily escape without being caught through different routes due to lack of transparency and disclosure. The civil society can control the spread of this disease by making the public aware of their opportunities and rights. Moreover, the media should spread the importance of clean society and should stress more on developmental journalism rather than its general journalism. It can bring out more disclosures of public works that are already undertaken and others that are yet to be undertaken.

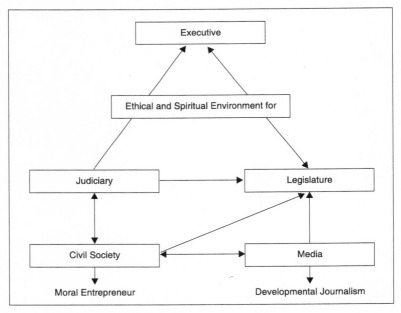

Figure 9.1: Governance Model

For sustainable human development, the governance model requires ethical and spiritual leadership to give highest value to public services with a drive of sacrifice, zeal, and truthfulness. In India, as we have unity in diversity with a culture inspired by spiritualism, society can be brought back to a clean and harmonious form through benevolent and charismatic leadership. Apart from these qualities, the need of the hour is a pious leader to bring change to the degrading society. Hence, to change the present system of our governance, there is a need to change the types of leaders. Leaders who lack basic leadership qualities and who are money chasers and selfish should be replaced by spiritual and effective leaders with strong and strategic vision for a better society. Corruption, which is a biggest challenge to good governance and enemy to democracy, needs to be controlled, even though it cannot be eradicated fully because of human weaknesses. However, if not controlled, it can lead to financial disaster of the economy and slowdown human development. Therefore, there is a need to change the public management system from its present system by adopting the technique of corporate management system. Thus, a corruption-free society will promote a class of entrepreneurs with good morals and will result in higher development.

CONCLUSION

One would agree that good governance is the most important factor in achieving the plan objectives. It is also a factor that could bring a collapse of the economy of a nation like the fallen economies of the South Asian Tigers. The study finds that despite having natural advantages and government initiatives, some states have been witnessing low HD due to poor governance. Even some of the relatively developed states with poor governance are facing the problems of scarcity of food and threat to life and personal security in the face of inadequate state controls on law and order, as in the case of Nagaland, Manipur, and so on. The presence of corruption in the economy has been instrumental in fluctuation of the magnitude of HD as reflected through HDI. Thus, the need of the hour is, apart from achievement of higher economic growth, to bring good governance in all facets of government, public, and markets. One example that can be cited to conclude this study is that as a surgeon requires sharp surgical tools, necessary for the surgery for the betterment of the patient, the same is the case of economic growth, which requires good governance for better human development.

NOTE

1. Economic Freedom Index (EFI) was prepared by The Heritage Foundation and Wall Street Journal. http://www.heritage.org/Index/Ranking.aspx/

REFERENCES

Birdsall N., D. Ross, and R. Sabot 1995. 'Inequality and Growth Reconsidered: Lessons from East Asia', *World Bank Economic Review*, Vol. 9.

Deraniyagala, S. 1995. 'Technical Change and Efficiency in Sri Lanka's Manufacturing Industry', Ph.D Dissertation, University of Oxford, UK.

Duflo, E. 2001. 'The Medium Run Effects of Educational Expansion: Evidence from a Large School Construction Program in Indonesia', Massachusetts Institute of Technology, Department of Economics, Working Paper: 01/46.

Eduardo M.J. 2004. 'Central America: The High Cost of Corruption', accessed from http://ipsnews.net/interna.asp?idnews=26035 on 19 January 2008.

Ghosh, M. 2006. 'Economic Growth and Human Development in Indian States', *Economic and Political Weekly*, July 29, pp. 3321–28.

Mauro, P. 1995. 'Corruption and Growth', *The Quarterly Journal of Economics*, MIT Press, Vol. 110, No. 3, pp. 681–712.

Mora, José, E. 2004. 'Central America: The High Cost of Corruption', Inter Press Service. http://www.worldrevolution.org/article/1624 accessed on 4 February 2009.

Paolo, M. 1995. 'Corruption and Growth', *Quarterly Journal of Economics*, Vol.110.

Ranis, G., F. Stewart, and A. Ramires 2000. 'Economic Growth and Human Development', *World Development*, Vol. 28, No. 2.

Rezaee, Z. 2005. 'Causes, Consequences, and Deterrence of Financial Statement Fraud', *Critical Perspectives on Accounting*, Vol. 16, pp. 277–98.

Strauss, J. and D. Thomas 1998. 'Nutrition, and Economic Development', *Journal of Economic Literature*, Vol. 36, No. 2, pp. 766–817.

Thachuk, K. 2005. 'Corruption and International Security', SAIS Review 25 collected from http://muse.jhu.edu/demo/sais_review/v025/25.1thachuk.html accessed on 19 January 2008.

United Nations Development Programme (UNDP), 2008. *Tackling Corruption, Transforming Lives–Accelerating Human Development in Asia and the Pacific*, Published for UNDP by Macmillian India Ltd. Delhi. http://www2.undprcc.lk/resource_centre/pub_pdfs/p1084.pdf/

10

Politics of Human Development

APURBA K. BARUAH

In the contemporary world, the human development index (HDI) is used to measure the impact of economic policies on the quality of life. This index, as is well known, veers round the measures of life expectancy, literacy, education, and standard of living. The *2006 Human Development Report* (*HDR*), brought out by United Nations Development Programme (UNDP) showed stagnation in the world HDI. This stagnation was noticed despite the continued improvement of developed countries in the areas of concern for such index. The reason was not very difficult to understand. The high rate of growth of life expectancy, literacy, education, and standard of living of the industrially developed countries was offset by a general decline of these indices in the developing countries. The comparatively less developed countries of the regions like the Sub-Saharan Africa and South Asia showed an important decline in life expectancy, literacy, education, and standard of living, even in comparison with the previous year's report. There was no improvement noticed in these indices in the developing countries of other regions too.

As a result, not only has the gap between the rich and poor nations and that between the rich and the poor in the developing countries increased, but also a process of pauperization seems to have set in. We need to notice that the fact of poverty is often recognized in the literature of development in mainstream economics, or rather in the dominant contemporary discourse on development (Chambers 1995; Jodha 1988). Though, in many cases, the term poverty is used more in a comparative manner by referring to conditions of the poorest in a society than to indicate the conditions of the poor, yet there is no attempt at either denying its existence or ignoring it. According to World Bank (2000–01), by the year 2000, 1.3 billion people were living below the poverty line. Where do the majority of these poor live? 633 million live in Asia, 240 million in Sub-Saharan Africa, and six million in Latin America and the Caribbean. Mulien (2002) had pointed out that though the proportion of the poor in relation to the total population below the poverty line had decreased in the world during the last two decades of the twentieth century, yet poverty in areas like Africa had increased substantially. He further showed that the bottom 40 per cent of the population had not benefited from the overall growth. The implication of these findings is clear. Despite globalization of the world economy, that implies free flow of ideas, goods, and capital, the world itself continues to be characterized by polarization, with some people and regions benefiting from it while others faring as poorly as they did before the beginning of the process of globalization, or, worse still, decayed under the impact of this process. The gap between the rich and the poor is widening. The richest 20 per cent of the world's population has been enjoying 85 per cent of the world's income. The poorest 20 per cent of the world shared among them only 1.4 per cent of world's income. We need to constantly remind ourselves that the poor regions of the world remain poor, and poor in the poor regions are becoming poorer, despite all talk about development and growth-oriented policies and principles that the new world order promises.

As mentioned above, it is not that these facts are denied or that existence of poverty itself is disputed. But what should bother us is the fact that most of the discussions of development and poverty in contemporary economic literature are empirical in nature. They state very clearly certain facts about poverty and then sometimes issue prescriptions. While such recognition of poverty is based on presentation of empirically measured facts, the question of mechanism of generation of poverty is left out of the discourse. And without the latter, the process of pauperization cannot be understood. Why, for instance, the per capita annual growth rate varies in striking manners even within the poor regions of the world? According to the UNDP (2006: 334) this rate varies between South Asia at +2.5 to Sub-Saharan Africa at -0.6. Only, when we try to examine why such disparities exist and do not try to explain it away in terms of inefficient state institutions (we will see below that this explanation does not have much merit!) will we understand the issues involved in pauperization, not mere poverty.

But what exactly happens in economics if one focuses on the poorest in the world and tries to take a comparative approach by looking at the richest and the poorest of the countries, and then, within that, tries to scrutinize the lot of the poorest population in the world? The answer to the above question is rather simple. We then arrive at figures that depict the severe deprivation, and I repeat, deprivation in respect of the essential requirements of human existence. And we realize that this deprivation is taking place in the midst of plenty.

When facts about the condition of the poor and the gap between the rich and the poor, both in terms of region and people are presented, we tend to get a picture merely of the poverty that exists among the new found riches. But the picture changes when we also take note of the fact that the condition of the poor is constantly worsening! The fact that the poor's share of the world's riches has actually decreased from 2.3 per cent in 1960 to 1.4 per cent in 1996 explains it strikingly (Castells 1998).

We need to examine the mechanism or process that causes this unfortunate trend. The rich literature on poverty available to us leads us to believe that there is no primary cause of persistence of poverty and more importantly, pauperization. A large section of contemporary literature tends to point to rapid population growth and failure of governments, or states to take remedial steps. The failure of governments is generally attributed to inefficiency of the state-run economies. But it is necessary to ask as to what happens when the state withdraws or when liberalization of a 'Command Economy' takes place? The history of the erstwhile Soviet Union throws some light on this issue. It is common knowledge that in 1917 when the then Russian state ruled by the Tsar underwent radical changes that came to be known as the Russian Revolution and experienced the establishment of the Soviet Union, it carried the legacy of the one of the worst economies of the world. Describing the socio-economic situation of the pre-revolutionary Russia, Boggs and Boggs (1974) said, 'Russia was extremely backward economically. The great majority of the population lived in ignorance, poverty, and squalor on the vast countryside. Not until 1861, the Russian peasants have been emancipated from serfdom. After their emancipation, tens of thousands of the poorest peasants migrated to the cities where they worked in factories for fifteen or sixteen hours a day under the most inhuman conditions'.

This extremely poor economy was transformed by, what now many of us call a 'Command Economy'. Though, most of the liberal economists declare it as the most inefficient economic system, incapable of delivering what is called development, yet, it converted the extremely backward Russian economy of the pre-1917 period into one that by the 1960s could put United States of America, the most advanced of the countries under liberal market and economy, into a difficult situation by sending the first sputnik into space, and also by conquering hunger! The main characteristics of the 'Command Economy', described by its supporters as socialist economy, were connected to the idea of egalitarianism, state-owned industry and agriculture, planned and centralized economic control (Forbes and Thrift 1987; Chapman 1992). This Command Economy established in the Soviet state performed well and delivered goods that were expected of a good economy, and that was why the ideals that established this economy seemed to have inspired country after country. So much so that there came a time when people, particularly the poor in the world, came to believe that their days of woes were over. The practices, processes, and the institutions of Command Economy were of course different from what we call the free market. While the former believed in control, the latter believed in freedom. To put it in other words, the former stressed cooperation, forced or voluntary, the latter emphasized competition.

There is evidence to show that the developmental process, under the socialist economies, with its emphasis on cooperation prospered for the better part of the Cold War, and those state-controlled systems provided employment and a good level of social services. Critics accused it of failing to generate economic competitiveness and of a resultant poor economic performance. This criticism by implication seems to imply that *non-command* economies generate economic competition and, hence, perform better! But from the Russian experience till the 1960s it becomes clear that such a claim is not tenable. What Stiglitz (2002) has said about the transformation in Russia and its consequences is rather revealing. He pointed out that while three quarters of a century of communism may have left its (Soviet Union's) populace devoid of an understanding of market economics, it had left them with a high level of education, especially in technical areas, so important for the new economy. He then goes on to summarize the economic theory explaining the failure of communism. According to that theory, centralized planning was doomed to failure, simply because no government agency could glean and process all relevant information required to make an economy function well. 'Without private property, and the profit motive, incentives—especially managerial and entrepreneurial incentives—were lacking. The restricted trade regime, combined with huge subsidies and arbitrarily set prices, meant the system was rife with distortions' (ibid: 141). Stiglitz further argues that from the above it followed that replacing this system by liberalizing trade would cause a bust of economic output. But to put it in his words '... instead, however, the standard of living in Russia and many of the other East European transition countries, fell' (ibid: 141–2) after the changeover to the non-command mode.

Moreover, as Paulson (1999) pointed out in the context of Africa, even economies governed by the market and, therefore, friendly to economic competition too could not perform better. The end of the Cold War was also the collapse of many socialist economies. That collapse was followed by an unprecedented assertion of ethnic identities in the world under the spell of which many former organized political systems of the East cracked (Amin 1997). This collapse and the attendant consequences have been construed often as the proof of the failure of socialist economy, and also of that philosophy. Experiences of the consequences of liberalization of the former Soviet Union show that the liberalized economy quickly generates unemployment and misery. Some commentators argue that Poland's solidarity movement, the USSR's draining during the Afghan war, Gorbachev's policy of perestroika, contributed to the collapse of Soviet Union and the emergence of hundreds of communities asserting identities (Keith and Salah 1999). These listed causes do not include the failure of the state-controlled economies. There indeed are two clear positions about economic efficiency. Inefficiency of some state-controlled economies cannot be used to hold the entire framework of such economy responsible for the extensive poverty that exists in the world, and, also, the process of pauperization. A logical link between these two phenomena cannot be established.

The liberal analysis of economic development does not explain the process of pauperization. Polarization at the world scale seems to be associated with pauperization. We need to examine if the economic order and the systems of production and marketing, as it takes place, have a tendency of operating on imperialistic lines. It is rather well established in the informed economic literature of the post-cold war world that the capitalist development project, the ideal of liberal economics, was going through a crisis in the 1970s and a series of measures were implemented to overcome that crisis. These measures actually led to a new vision of development that considered the free market to be a panacea for all ills in the economies. It is pointed out that this new vision conceals the realities of exploitative relationships, which in turn helps to defuse the solidarity mechanisms of the oppressed, hides the old structures of dominance, encourages the free floating economic actors, destroys the sense of an alternative social project, and also finds the market for the new products of the system (Biel 2000).

We have to understand that the new concept of development, in fact, is a new variety of imperialism. It is clear from the worsening conditions of the rural poor and the pauperization of a section of the urban population, that the peasants made landless as a result of industrialization and accompanying reforms in the globalized world, is fuelling migrations to metropolises and small towns, leading the political realities of these areas to a volatile situation.

In a working paper, Booth (2005), of the Overseas Development Institute, pointed out that, with a few significant exceptions, the policies supported by concessional lending institutions and development cooperation agencies in the poorest countries had not been implemented in sustained and consistent ways, and a massive body of research suggested the root problem to be lack of local commitment. The questions that we need to ask are: is it possible to elicit greater commitment to equitable and efficient development policies by governments? Are they prepared to debate their policies openly with other actors in their countries? It is common knowledge that when coming face-to-face with such deprivation, liberal economists resort to preaching what we have been calling development. Most advocates of development insist that reduction of poverty is the leitmotif of programmes and policies of development. This idea of development often stresses economic growth and maintains that once a particular growth rate is achieved, the deprivation will disappear. But any informed social scientist today will know that there indeed are two approaches to the issue of development: one that emphasizes growth and the other emphasizes fair distribution of the resources. Shall we look at growth only in terms of per capita income, or in terms of development in living standards of the worlds poorest of the poor? If we look at the latter, then it becomes imperative for us to examine whether our approach to development leads to concentration of wealth or distribution of wealth. The politics of human development actually veers round this issue. In this sense, human development is closely connected with ideology. Ideology is about politics, not merely about apolitical economics. The protagonists of globalization merely speak of the inevitability of globalization and assure everyone that this inevitable economic trend will bring along with it competition in the market. And since market governs everything else, competition will be the order of the day. The argument proceeds further to impress upon all of us that competition is possible only with freedom and, therefore, all restrictions will have to be withdrawn. They also go to great length to spread the message that this is possible in the field of economics only when the state withdraws. But we have shown above that the economic efficiency is in its top gear only when the state takes control. Whether the state will control or it will leave the market to private hands is a matter of politics to which the nature of human development is inalienably connected.

REFERENCES

Amin, S. 1997. *Capitalism in the Age of Globalization- The Management of Contemporary Society*, Madhyam, Delhi, pp. 55–79.

Biel, R. 2000. *The New Imperialism*, Zed Books, London and New York, pp. 174–89.

Booth, D. 2005. 'Missing Links in the Politics of Development: Learning from the PRSP Experiment', Working Paper 256, Overseas Development Institute, London, October.

Castells, M. 1998. *End of Millenium*, Oxford, Blackwell.

Chambers, R. 1995. 'Poverty and Livelihoods: Whose Reality Counts?', Discussion Paper 347, Institute of Development Studies, Brighton.

Chapman, C. 1992. 'The Collapse of Socialist Development in the Third World', *Third World Quarterly*, Vol. 13, No. 1, pp.13–25.

Forbes, D. and N. Thrift 1987. *The Socialist Third World*, Oxford, Basil Blackwell.

Boggs, James and G.L. Boggs 1974. *Revolution and Evolution in the Twentieth Century*, Monthly Review Press, New York and London, pp. 26.

Jodha, N.S. 1988. 'Poverty Debate in India: A Minority View', *Economic and Political Weekly*, Vol. XXII, Nos 45–7, pp. 2421–28.

Keith, S. and Z.E. Salah 1999. 'The Collapse of State Socialism in the Socialist Third World' in Desai, V. and Robert B. Potter (eds) *The Companion to Development Studies*, Oxford University Press, New York.

Mulien, J. 2002. 'Rural Poverty' in V. Desai and R.B. Potter (eds) *The Companion to Development Studies*, Oxford University Press, New York, pp. 147.

Paulson, J. 1999. *African Economies in Transition*, Basingstoke, Macmillan, cited and arguments summarized in Sutton Keith and Z.E. Salah, 'The Collapse of State Socialism in the Socialist Third World' in Desai, V. and R.B. Potter (eds), *The Companion to Development Studies*, p. 21.

Stiglitz., J. 2002. *Globalization And Its Discontents*, Penguin Books, New Delhi.

World Bank 2000–01. *World Development Report: Attacking Poverty*, New York, Oxford University Press, Oxford.

United Nations Development Programme (UNDP) 2006. *Human Development Report.*

III

Issues at the Level of
North-East India

11

Socio-political Transition, Growth Trends, and Development Attainment in the North-East in the Post-Independence Period

M.P. BEZBARUAH

INTRODUCTION

The North-East, comprising of the seven states of Arunachal Pradesh, Assam, Manipur, Meghalaya, Mizoram, Nagaland, and Tripura, constitutes a land surface of 255,083 sq km, where a population of 38.5 million belonging to different ethnic and cultural groups inhabits (NEC 2005). Topographically, the region is a mixture of hills and plains. While Arunachal Pradesh, Meghalaya, Mizoram, and Nagaland are almost entirely hilly, about four-fifths of Assam is plains. Manipur and Tripura have both plain areas and hilly tracts. The hills account for about 70 per cent area and accommodate about 30 per cent of the population of the region, and the plains constituting the remaining 30 per cent of area holds about 70 per cent of its population. Thus, the lower overall density of population of 151 persons per square kilometre for the region is due to the fact that the hills are sparsely populated. The density varies from 13 per sq km in mountainous Arunachal Pradesh to 340 per sq km in Assam, 80 per cent of which is plains. Wide variation in altitude coupled with abundance of rainfall has given rise to wide variations in climatic conditions within the region. This in turn has endowed the region with rich biodiversity. The richness of the biodiversity of the region is almost matched by its ethnic diversity. The region is a meeting place of large number of races, creeds, cultures, and languages (Datta 1995). The impingement of the diversity of physical and cultural environment is to be naturally found in the organization of economic life of the people of the region.

POLITICAL AND ECONOMIC SITUATION AT THE TIME OF INDEPENDENCE

In August 1947, when India attained independence from British rule, the north-eastern region consisted of three broad administrative units. Manipur and Tripura were princely states, and the rest of the region was the undivided Assam province. The administrative arrangement throughout Assam province was, however, not uniform. While the plains were under the effective administration of the provincial government, the hills, inhabited mostly by tribal people, were virtually left out from that system of administration. In fact, the hills were classified as *excluded* or *partially excluded* areas, depending on 'whether the area was inhabited by a compact aboriginal population, or the aboriginal population was mixed with other communities' (Agnihotri 1996). Though, the administration of these areas was vested in the Governor, in effect the tribal groups were left alone to continue with their traditional administrative arrangements. Moreover, most of the excluded areas were subject to the *inner line* restrictions, which restricted the entry of people from other areas to these areas. Thus, the British policy effectively kept the hill tribes isolated from socioeconomic interaction with the population in the plains.

Shifting or '*jhum*' cultivation-based self-contained village was the typical organization of economic life of the hill tribes. Land was owned by the village community and access to it, for individual families for cultivation and other uses, was regulated by the village council or the chief of the village, depending on the form of the administrative organization of the tribe. Families usually also produced clothes and other necessaries for self-consumption. Things such as firewood, house building material, cane and bamboo for making baskets, and other implements were collected from the nearby forests. There were, of course, exceptions to the above described pattern. For instance, tribes like Angamis and Chakesangs of Nagaland adopted settled wet rice cultivation on the terraces developed for the purpose. But such adoptions of improved methods remained isolated phenomena rather than developing into progressive transition from shifting to settled cultivation (Ganguli 1986).

The population in the plains of Assam, Manipur, and Tripura were also by and large dependent on agriculture. But in contrast to the hills, people in the plains practiced settled cultivation with rice as the main crop. There was a small but significant modern non-agricultural component of the Assam economy, developed and dominated almost entirely by colonial capitalists. This sector consisted of the tea industry based on plantation, mining of coal and oil, and oil refining based on minerals, plywood industry and match factory based on forest resources, and railways developed to facilitate the transportation of the output of these industries. Trade and commerce was also a flourishing activity but largely dominated by traders from other parts of the country. Thus, at the time of independence, the indigenous population of the region generally made their living from subsistence agriculture. A small section of people in the Assam plains found employment in the modern non-agricultural sector.

POLITICAL-ADMINISTRATIVE REORGANIZATION IN THE POST- INDEPENDENCE PERIOD

The process of political-administrative reorganization of the region began soon after independence. But it took a long time for the existing set up of seven full-fledged states to emerge. Following their accession to the Indian Union, Manipur and Tripura were given the status of Part C states in the Constitution of India in 1950 and re-designated as union territories in 1956. The hill tract forming the north-eastern part of the region, which constitutionally remained a part of Assam till becoming the union territory of Arunachal Pradesh, was named as North-East Frontier Agency and was administered directly by the central government. For the remaining erstwhile excluded and partially-excluded areas of Assam, autonomous districts with district councils were provided under the 6th Schedule of the Constitution. However, the arrangement did not meet the aspirations of the newly emerging political leadership of many of the hill tribes inhabiting these areas and several tribal groups soon organized movements for greater autonomy. Consequently, the state of Nagaland came into being in 1963, and the state of Meghalaya and the union territory of Mizoram were also carved out of Assam in 1972. In the same year Manipur and Tripura attained full-fledged statehood and the union territory of Arunachal Pradesh came into being. Arunachal Pradesh and Mizoram were upgraded to full statehood in 1986 (Agnihotri 1996).

Unfortunately, the successive reorganizations of the region did not succeed in resolving the question of tribal ethnic identity. Instead, formation of the smaller states seems to have encouraged other ethnic groups to organize themselves into struggles for demands ranging from more autonomy to separate statehood, to complete self-determination. Besides causing frequent disruptions to normal life through agitations, these movements have also contributed, directly or indirectly, towards perpetuation of insurgency and bloodshed in the region. Needless to emphasize, that such things vitiated the environment required for developmental activities to flourish.

Reorganization of the region was, thus, largely an offshoot of the process of integration of the excluded and partially excluded areas of the colonial period to the administrative network of independent India. In that sense, the seeds of these developments were embedded within the region's pre-independence administrative set up itself. But the events of 1947 also had significant exogenous impact on the economy and society of the region. Partition of the country at independence cut off the region's approach routes to the rest of the country and the world through East Bengal. Consequently, the narrow corridor of North Bengal remained the only link of the region with the rest of the country, and the region got burdened with a transport bottleneck and high cost of movement of man and material, to and from it. This, in turn, has hindered economic integration of the region with the rest of the country and reduced the attractiveness of the region as a destination of investment. Moreover, partition also caused an influx of refugees to the region. There had been an inflow of immigrants to the region even in the decades before independence and indeed the inflow of population in those days had some positive contributions to the region's economy. As Ganguli (1986: 20) puts it, 'there was growth of agricultural production through extension of cultivation over larger and larger areas (in Assam plains), which was possible owing to the immigration of farm population from the neighbouring districts of Bengal'. However, the sudden increase in the rate of immigration following partition and the consequent step up in the rate of growth of population in the post-independence period has had several adverse consequences. The worst affected part of the region is Tripura, where there was a growth of population by 78 per cent within just 10 years, from 1951 to 1961. Exceptionally higher rate of growth of population in the decades following independence has put pressure on the region's natural resources of land and forests, and its inadequate social and economic infrastructure besides acting as a drag on the per capita indicators of development. Moreover, the heavy influx of population has also been at times the source of considerable social tension in the region.

THE ECONOMY: TREND AND COMPOSITION

Though, Net Domestic Product (NDP) statistics are available for Assam right from 1950–51, the figures for the other north-eastern states could be found only from 1970–71, or an even later date. Indeed, detailed macro economic data for all the seven states of the region are available from 1980–81, only. However, the NDP figures at constant prices could not be obtained for the two states, namely Mizoram and Nagaland. Therefore, the NDP and the per capita income series at constant prices could not be constructed for the region as a whole. Growth rates can meaningfully summarize the trends in economic performance only when such rates are computed from the series at constant prices. Hence, instead of trying to work out growth rates of NDPs or per capita income levels, an alternative line of analysis has been adopted. The NDP per capita figures of the region and its constituent states at current prices have been expressed as percentage ratios of the per capita income of the country at current prices. The trends in these ratios (Table 11.1) give an idea of the performance of the region and its constituent states in comparison to the performance of the national economy.

Trends till the First Three Decades of Planning

For the early years, data is available for Assam only. In 1950–51, Assam's per capita Net State Domestic Product (NSDP) was higher than India's NNP per capita. But during the first and Second Five Year Plan period, the position of Assam gradually declined, vis-à-vis the all India picture. Since 1961–62, Assam's NSDP per capita has remained below India's per capita NNP. In Tripura, Meghalaya, and Manipur also, NSDP per capita has been less than India's per capita NNP from 1970–71, the year from which we have data for these states, to 1980–81.

Trends Since 1980–81

In the entire period since 1980–81, NDP per capita of the region remained below India's per capita income, and in the post-1991 years (that is, in the post reforms period), the gap has widened further. The regional trend is shared by the more populous state of Assam,

Table 11.1: Per Capita NSDP of North-Eastern States as Percentage of
NNP Per Capita of India

Year (1)	ARP (2)	ASM (3)	MAN (4)	MEG (5)	MIZ (6)	NAG (7)	TRP (8)	N.E. Region (9)
1950-51	N.A.	105.11	N.A.	N.A.	N.A.	N.A.	N.A.	N.A.
1960-61	N.A.	104.20	N.A.	N.A.	N.A.	N.A.	N.A.	N.A.
1970-71	67.59	86.71	72.62	N.A.	N.A.	75.29	74.40	N.A.
1975-76	67.16	92.15	77.96	N.A.	N.A.	89.14	76.37	N.A.
1980-81	96.37	78.77	87.05	83.49	79.07	88.83	80.18	80.38
1985-86	124.64	95.67	85.05	82.41	97.36	94.90	74.17	93.25
1987-88	117.67	93.14	97.74	88.94	124.09	103.03	73.72	93.19
1988-89	114.70	83.39	85.94	80.01	104.79	96.51	78.47	84.38
1989-90	102.63	85.66	82.25	88.25	95.13	99.71	73.28	85.70
1990-91	108.31	85.91	79.79	87.80	89.79	98.33	67.63	85.23
1991-92	116.44	83.58	83.17	87.29	106.03	99.77	65.70	84.22
1992-93	120.06	79.42	80.22	84.19	105.39	100.18	60.41	80.59
1993-94	113.56	74.32	75.96	89.64	108.18	118.71	71.96	78.74
1994-95	103.29	73.31	68.93	82.95	99.28	114.88	63.86	75.94
1995-96	107.95	68.98	67.93	85.14	107.92	108.95	65.31	73.19
1996-97	93.53	63.94	68.42	79.93	105.59	102.08	15.64	53.09
1997-98	91.62	62.69	69.28	80.82	97.53	102.72	76.01	68.49
1998-99	89.99	61.31	67.61	82.76	93.63	86.19	76.49	66.98
1999-2000	87.48	64.51	70.78	83.76	95.42	80.60	84.45	69.88
2000-01	92.53	67.47	69.54	92.11	116.40	110.97	96.02	75.01
2001-02	93.90	66.54	75.81	94.52	117.78	113.04	103.91	76.34
2002-03	87.17	67.52	76.37	93.96	124.18	N.A.	104.43	N.A.
2003-04	91.60	69.20	77.76	95.51	N.A.	N.A.	N.A.	N.A.

Notes: Basic data taken from 'Indian Economic Statistics-Public Finance 1991', Ministry of Finance (Economic Division), Government of India, p. 82 for the early years and from various issues of the *Economic Survey of the Government of India* for 1980–81 onwards. The regional NDP per capita has been estimated as the weighted average of NDP per capita of the seven states with respective population shares as the weights. Both NSDP and NNP are expressed at current prices.

Manipur, and till recently, Tripura. In contrast to the broad regional trends, in Arunachal Pradesh, Nagaland, and Mizoram the per capita NDPs had crossed India's NNP per capita in the mid-1980s and generally remained above the national figure in the following decade. However, this apparent sign of prosperity in these states was misleading. As explained in an earlier work of the present author (Bezbaruah 2001) and this can also be seen from the sectoral compositions of the economies in the region portrayed in the following sub-section, the observed high growth was not propelled by growth of agriculture or manufacturing, or even trade and commerce, but by expansion of such activities as public administration and construction, which was necessitated by the expansion of the administrative apparatus in these newly formed states, and financed by liberal fiscal transfers from the centre to these special category states. Such high growth rates, unless stimulated by genuine economic forces, are unlikely to be sustainable for long. Indeed, the growth impetus of that decade in some of these states has already petered off. For instance, in Arunachal Pradesh the per capita income level has since fallen behind the all India level.

The figures for the last few years suggest that there has been a turnaround of some sort, since 2000–01, in a number of states in the region, resulting in a reduction in the gap between the levels of per capita income of the country and the region. In Tripura, Nagaland, and Mizoram, per capita income levels have surpassed the national level. Institutional reforms in Tripura, and to some extent in Nagaland too, might have contributed to this revival through greater mass participation in development programmes.[1] In Mizoram persistence of peaceful conditions has obviously helped consolidation of economic growth. After stagnating below 3 per cent throughout the 1990s, the growth of real State Domestic Product in Assam has accelerated to 3.93 per cent in 2000-01 and to 5.8 per cent in 2004-05 (Government of Assam 2006: 5–6).

Sectoral Composition

For a better insight in to the nature of economies of the region, it may be useful to have a look at the sectoral composition of the domestic product presented in Tables 11.2 and 11.3. Table 11.2 traces the trend in the sectoral composition of the region as a whole over the period 1980–81 to 1995–96. Table 11.3 gives a more recent and a more detailed picture.

The data on sectoral composition for the period 1980–81 to 1995–96 shows that the share of agricultural and allied, and the others group (comprising of banking and insurance, real estate and ownership of dwellings, public administration and other services) in NDP of the region was much higher than the corresponding share in India's NDP. On the other hand, the share of manufacturing, mining, electricity, and construction group, and that of the services of transportation, trade, hotels, restaurants and storage was lower in the region than at the national level. The share of the manufacturing sector in fact fell to a low level of only 6.05 per cent by 1995–96 and construction

Table 11.2: Percentage Share of Sectors in NDP of the North-Eastern Region at Current Prices

Sector	Year			
	1980-81	1985-86	1990-91	1995-96
1. Agriculture & Allied	51.88	45.35	39.83	40.68 (30.14)*
2. Mining, Manufacturing Etc.	11.56	21.06	23.43	17.67 (24.75)#
2.1 Manufacturing			9.83	6.05
2.2 Construction			6.48	8.68
3. Transport, Trade Etc.	12.18	12.54	11.73	13.19 (22.95)
4. Others	24.38	21.05	25.01	28.46 (22.16)
4.1 Public Administration			7.14	8.33
Total (= 1+2+3+4)	100	100	100	100

Notes: * Includes the share of Mining and quarrying. # Excludes the share of Mining and Quarrying. 1. Agriculture and allied include agriculture, fishing, forestry, and logging; Mining and manufacturing include mining and quarrying, manufacturing, construction, electricity, gas and water supply; transport, trade, etc include transport, storage, trade, hotels and restaurants; and Others include banking and insurance, real estate, ownership of dwellings, business services, public administration, and other services. 2. Figures within parentheses are sectoral shares in India's GDP at current prices in 1995-96.
Sources: 'National Accounts Statistics of India-6, Net State Domestic Product', Economic and Political Weekly Research Foundation, Economic and Political Weekly, Vol XXX, No. 5, December 23, 1995.
2. North-Eastern Development Finance Corporation, Guwahati.

has emerged as the dominant activity in the secondary sector. Table 11.3 confirms that these broad regional features are shared more or less by the economies of all the states in the region. There was no improvement in the share of manufacturing even by 1999–2000, and construction continued to be the dominant activity in the secondary sector. Though, the tertiary sector has assumed similar proportions in the region as in the country—and in some states has grown to even much higher proportions, the composition of this sector does not speak well of the robustness of the economies of the region. While public administration and other services command higher shares in the economies of the region than in the national economy, the services such as trade, transport, communication, and financial services command smaller shares.

HUMAN DEVELOPMENT ATTAINMENT

In the recent past, the area in which the region seems to have done better than the nation as a whole is the social sector, particularly in the spread of literacy. Table 11.4 reveals that the region, on the whole,

Table 11.3: State-wise Percentage Share of Sectors in NDP of the North-Eastern Region at Current Prices in 1999-2000

Sectors	ARP	ASM	MAN	MEG	MIZ	NAG	TRP	N.E. Region	India
1. Agriculture	33.48	35.51	22.52	23.20	21.62	24.00	26.96	31.76	
2. Forestry and Logging	5.01	1.58	4.23	1.06	0.60	3.65	1.50	1.91	
3. Fishing	0.89	1.92	2.16	0.67	1.02	0.90	3.65	1.90	
4. Mining & Quarrying	0.86	7.67	0.00	6.86	0.52	0.00	1.08	5.57	
Primary Sector (1 to 4)	40.23	46.68	28.92	31.79	23.76	28.55	33.19	41.15	27.36
5. Manufacturing	2.50	9.04	8.22	2.10	1.24	1.34	2.18	6.94	
6. Construction	12.86	3.82	10.32	8.29	11.53	10.37	9.62	6.05	
7. Electricity, Gas & Water Supply	2.88	1.41	3.83	3.58	0.71	1.77	1.98	1.84	
Secondary Sector (5 to 7)	18.24	14.28	22.37	13.97	13.47	13.47	13.78	14.83	24.31
8. Transport, Storage & Communication (Total)	6.06	3.56	3.67	5.25	1.40	13.35	4.53	4.36	
9. Trade, Hotel & Restaurant	4.56	11.28	8.25	12.91	10.50	5.66	15.65	11.07	
Sub Total 8 and 9	10.62	14.85	11.92	18.16	11.89	19.01	20.18	15.43	22.28
10. Banking & Finance	1.86	4.00	1.04	2.28	1.48	1.18	1.69	3.14	
11. Real Estate, Ownership of Dwelling & Business Services	2.34	3.16	2.76	9.23	14.27	11.19	2.80	4.27	
Sub Total 10 and 11	4.21	7.16	3.80	11.51	15.74	12.37	4.49	7.41	12.70
12. Public administration	16.37	7.33	18.35	14.94	17.76	17.16	14.11	10.46	
13. Other services	10.34	9.71	14.65	9.63	17.35	9.43	14.24	10.72	
Sub Total 12 and 13	26.71	17.03	33.00	24.57	35.11	26.59	28.35	21.18	13.36
Tertiary Sector (8 to 13)	41.53	39.04	48.71	54.24	62.75	57.97	53.03	44.02	48.33

Note: Basic data taken from National Income Statistics, Centre for Monitoring Indian Economy, January 2004 for the states and *Economic Survey 2002-03* of Ministry of Finance, Government of India.

somewhat lagged behind the country in literacy in 1971. But by 2001 the literacy rate in the region became higher than the national literacy rate. Individual states such as Mizoram, Tripura, Manipur, and Nagaland marched ahead of the country average, Assam more or less kept pace with the national average and, starting from relative backwardness in 1971, by 2001, Meghalaya and Arunachal Pradesh closed the gaps with the country average. Considering that Arunachal Pradesh had a literacy rate of only 11.30 per cent in 1971, the attainment of the literacy rate of 54.34 per cent by 2001 constitutes a huge progress in just three decades. Another positive feature of the literacy situation in the region is that female literacy rate is significantly higher in the region as compared to the country as a whole. (North-Eastern Council 2000: 126). The infant mortality rate has come down well below the country average in all the states of the region, barring Assam.

The relatively poor attainment of Assam, with respect to components of human development, calls for some more detailed probing. As the *Assam Human Development Report 2003* (Government of Assam, 2003: 175–7) suggests, there are districts, predominantly inhabited by some disadvantaged groups such as scheduled tribes, tea (labour) tribes, and immigrant muslims, which pull down the state level index value of human development. There is, hence, a need for target group oriented approach to accelerate the process of human development in the state.

Table 11.4: Some Indicators of Level of Human Development of the States in North-Eastern Region

States/ Country	Literacy Rate (per cent of Population)		Infant Mortality Rate (Per 1000 life births)
	1971	2001	2005
Arunachal Pradesh	11.26	54.34	37
Assam	33.94	63.24	68
Manipur	38.47	70.53	13
Meghalaya	29.49	62.56	49
Mizoram	53.80	88.80	20
Nagaland	33.78	66.59	18
Tripura	30.98	73.19	31
NE Region	33.52	64.99	–
India	34.45	64.84	56

Note: Regional rate has been calculated as the weighted sum of the rates in the states by taking the respective population size as weights.
Sources: Tables 9.4 and 9.5 of *Economic Survey 2006-07*, Ministry of Finance, GoI.

CONCLUSION

Development experience in the region has been mixed and uneven. While there have been periods of high growth for individual states, the region as a whole has increasingly been lagging behind the country in terms of per capita income. The rapid post liberalization growth of the country is a far cry for the region. While the recent service sector led growth of the country was propelled by expansion of frontier areas like information technology, in the Northeast region pubic administration and other services have been the faster growing services. There is not only a need to enhance the rate of economic growth, but to found the growth process on the inherent strength and endowed resource base of the region. The funds for building up the necessary infrastructure to activate the inherent growth potentials of the region are no longer a constraint. But disruptions caused by persistence of insurgency and the bundh culture makes deployment of such investments difficult, and adds to the cost of any business venture reducing competitiveness and viability in the globalized world of the twenty first century. As India enters the threshold of emerging as a new economic super-power, the North East can ill afford to be left behind any further.

NOTE

1. Tripura is in the forefront among the north-eastern states in implementing the Panchayati Raj Institutions as per the letter and spirit of the 73rd Constitution Amendment Act and though Nagaland is out of the purview of this Act, as also of the 6th Schedule of the Constitution, the state has devised its own institutions called Village Development Boards, which are empowered and entrusted to implement development programs. These boards have a good record of effectively utilizing development funds.

REFERENCES

Agnihotri, S.K. 1996. 'Constitutional Development in North-East India since 1947' in B. Dutta Ray and S. P. Agarwal (eds), *Reorganisation of North East India since 1947*, Concept Publishing Company, New Delhi.

Bezbaruah, M.P. 2001. 'Creation of Smaller States and Economic Progress in India's North-Eastern Region', *Dialogue*, Vol. 2, No 3.

Datta, P.S. 1995. 'Introduction' in P. S. Datta (ed.) *North-East and the Indian State: Paradox of Periphery*, Vikas Publishing House, New Delhi.

Ganguli, J.B. 1986. 'Economic Conditions and Change in North-East India' in A.P. Singha (ed.), *Changing North East India*, Gagan Publishers, Ludhiana.

Government of Assam, 2006. *Budget Speech of Finance Minister 2006–07*, Unpublished document, Dispur Guwahati, pp. 5–6.

—— 2003. *Assam Human Development Report 2003*, Planning and Development Department, Dispur, Guwahati. http://planning commission.nic.in/plans/stateplan/sdr_assam/sdr_assch4.pdf/

North-Earthern Council 2005. *Basic Statistics of North-Eastern Region 2005*, Ministry of Home Affairs, Government of India, Shillong.

—— 2000. *Basic Statistics of North Eastern Region 2000*, Government of India, Ministry of Home Affairs, Shillong.

—— 1995. *Basic Statistics of North Eastern Region 1995*, Government of India, Ministry of Home Affairs, Shillong.

12

Human Development in North-East India

PURUSOTTAM NAYAK

INTRODUCTION

The development and growth of a nation greatly depends upon proper utilization of its human resources. To better utilize them, there is a need to improve the human resources, which is both a means for faster development and also an end by itself. Since the basic objective of development for a nation is to improve the welfare of its people, every nation strives hard not only to increase her wealth and productive resources, but also to ensure a better standard of living for her citizens by providing them with adequate food, clothing, housing, medical facilities, education, etc. However, technical considerations, of the means to achieve human development and the use of statistical aggregates to measure national income and its growth, have at times obscured the fact that the primary objective of development is to benefit the people. National income figures, though useful for many purposes, neither reveal its composition nor its real beneficiaries. Of course, people want higher incomes as one of their options, but it is neither the sum total of human life nor the end in itself. Thus, expansion of output and wealth is only a means and the end of development is the welfare of human beings. To measure the welfare of the people, United Nations Development Programme (UNDP) in its first *Human Development Report* (*HDR*) introduced the concept of human development and its measurement (UNDP 1990). It was introduced as a composite measure of economic progress and human welfare, and intended to be a better substitute to Per Capita Income (measure) that could neither capture nor exhibit exact levels of development of human beings nor that of nations. The measure is popularly known as the human development index (HDI).

Recent development experience has underlined the need for paying close attention to the link between economic growth and human development because many fast-growing and developing countries, having high GNP growth rates, have failed to reduce the socioeconomic deprivation of substantial sections of their population. At the same time some low-income countries have achieved high levels of human development by skillfully using the available means to expand basic human capabilities. Countries like Vietnam, Georgia, Indonesia, and Jamaica having relatively very low per capita GDP (PPP US$ 3071, 3365, 3843, and 4291) could achieve medium levels of human development (0.733, 0.754, 0.728, and 0.736), whereas, Botswana and South Africa, in spite of having very high per Capita GDP (PPP US$ 12,387 and 11,110), achieved a relatively lower level of human development of 0.654 and 0.674 (UNDP 2007–08). Therefore, there is a need for shifting the emphasis from per capita GDP to HDI.

In the last two decades, HDI has been used very widely by governments of various nations for planning. Various scholars and organizations have also undertaken a number of research studies, using this index, to focus on the magnitude of human development of various sections of society in different countries. This has helped a lot in formulating plans for improving the life of neglected sections of societies in different countries. Keeping all these points in view, the present study is undertaken on the status and progress of human development in a backward region like North-Eastern India, comprising of eight states, which is predominantly a region of tribal people.

MEASUREMENT OF HUMAN DEVELOPMENT

Though HDI was proposed by UNDP in 1990, many criticisms were raised against its construction and robustness in subsequent periods. As a result, some improvements were brought about in its construction in the subsequent reports of UNDP. It is now, in its present form, a composite index of three basic components of human development, viz., longevity, knowledge, and standard of living. Longevity is measured by life expectancy. Knowledge is measured by a combination of adult literacy having one-third weight, and mean years of schooling with two-third weight. Standard of living is measured by purchasing power, based on real GDP per capita adjusted for the local cost of living (purchasing power parity or PPP). The HDI sets a minimum and a maximum for each dimension and then shows where each country stands in relation to these scales. It is expressed in terms of a numerical value between 0 and 1. The scores for the three dimensions are then averaged in an overall index. The latest formula used for the first two individual indicators {Life Expectancy Index (LEI) and Education Index (EI)} is as follows:

$$\text{LEI or EI} = \frac{X_i - \text{Min}(X_i)}{\text{Max}(X_i) - \text{Min}(X_i)}$$

The income indicator (GDP Index) is calculated using the following formula:

$$\text{GDPI} = \frac{\log(X_i) - \log\{\text{Min}(X_i)\}}{\log\{\text{Max}(X_i)\} - \log\{\text{Min}(X_i)\}}$$

Finally, the HDI is calculated by taking the average of these three indices (LEI, EI, and GDPI). For the construction of the dimension indices, maximum and minimum values have been fixed as shown in Box 12.1.

Box 12.1: Scaling Norms of HDI Used by					
UNDP			**Planning Commission of India**		
Indicators	*Max(Xi)*	*Min(Xi)*	*Indicator*	*Max(Xi)*	*Min(Xi)*
Life Expectancy at Birth (Years)	85	25	Life Expectancy at Age 1 (Years)	80	50
Adult Literacy Rate (%)	100	0	Infant Mortality Rate (per thousand)	–	20
–	–	–	Literacy Rate (7 + Years)	100	0
Combined Gross Enrolment Ratio (%)	100	0	Adjusted Intensity of Formal Education	7	0
Per Capita GDP (PPP US $)	40,000	100	Per Capita monthly Consumption Expenditure in Rupees (at 1983 prices)	325	65
Source: UNDP (2003)			*Source*: GoI (2002)		

In this regard some changes in the formula of HDI were brought out by the Government of India (GoI 2002) in the *National Human Development Report (NHDR)*. A composite health index consisting of life expectancy, with a weight of 65 per cent, and infant mortality rate, with a weight of 35 per cent, was proposed. Similarly, in case of composite index on educational attainment, while literacy rate was given a weight of 35 per cent, the indicator capturing intensity of formal education (based on current enrolment rates in successive classes at school level) was assigned 65 per cent weight. In case of the indicator on economic attainment, namely, inequality adjusted per capita consumption expenditure, an adjustment for inflation over the period was made to make it amenable to inter-temporal and inter-spatial comparisons. The maximum and minimum values for each dimension as used in *NHDR* are shown in Box 12.1.

AN OVERVIEW OF LITERATURE

There are two types of literature available on human development, one on the methodological aspects, and the other on empirical evidence. As far as the methodological aspect is concerned, numerous efforts have been made to remedy the defects of the traditional measure of economic development and to suggest composite indicators that could serve as either complements, or alternatives to this, for example, Sheldon and Land (1972), UNRISD (1970), Adelman and Morris (1973), UN (1975), OECD (1976), UNESCO (1977), Morris (1979), Hicks (1997), Noorbakhsh (1998), Sagar and Najam (1998), Neumayer (2001), Ogwang and Abdella (2003), Arcelus *et al.* (2005), and Leigh and Wolfers (2006). Since the publication of the first *HDR*, the trend has been towards improvement of the method of measurement of human development, and so far there have been three successive attempts in this regard in 1991, 1994, and 1999 by UNDP.

Few important works on human development which could not be reviewed for want of access to individual papers, are Desai (1991), Jain (1991), Tilak (1991), Anand and Sen (1993, 1995, 1997, and 2000), Pal and Kant (1993), Haq (1995), Bardhan and Klasen (1999), Nagar and Basu (2000), Chakravarty (2003), Chaubey (2002), Bose (2004), and many others. Other important empirical works, in the literature on human development, in the context of India that are readily available are reviewed in the following paragraphs:

Dalal (1991), in his edited volume, pointed out that Indian development goals have been set on the criteria laid down in the *Human Development Report*. There has, however, been significant failure in the implementation of well-constructed policies, as a result of lack of political will and administrative inefficiency. The Government of India in 2002 compiled the HDI, GDI, and HPI for the entire country. However, the data for north-eastern states was prepared by taking the data of Assam (one of the big states in the region) as a representative one. Shiva Kumar (1991) ranked 17 Indian major states by constructing the HDI using UNDP methodology. He compared the rankings of these states with the rankings of countries appearing in the UNDP report. The absence of disaggregated data on health and life expectancy, for the union territories and the North-East, prevented him from the computation of the HDI for these regions.

The subsequent study of Shiva Kumar (1996) revealed that states like Haryana and Punjab, despite being relatively high-income states, were facing the problem of serious gender inequality in basic capabilities. There were 13 countries in the world that had a lower value of GDI than that of states like Bihar and Uttar Pradesh, which pointed to the seriousness of the problem of human development at the global level.

Vyasalu and Vani (1997) conducted a study of human development in Karnataka using HDI. While making the concluding remarks, they suggested that sustained political support to an across-the-board improvement in each district was essential if the HDI was to show improvement. Zaidi and Salam (1998), in their study, correlated various indices denoting life expectancy, educational attainment, and real GDP per capita to other parameters of the economies of 15 major states of India for finding out the causes of varying values of these indicators in different states. The study revealed that public expenditure had a closer association with educational attainment than it had with life expectancy as the latter is influenced by multiplicity of factors, like heredity, race, climatic, and environmental factors, apart from public expenditures on health, nutrition, and sanitation, etc. Viswanathan (1999) in her study, for the state of Madhya Pradesh, highlighted the fact that higher incomes do not always yield higher human development, and that higher human development does not always mean equal benefit to men and women. The study of NCAER (1999), conducted and data collected in 1994, revealed that although relative differentials existed, absolute deprivation was high in most parts of rural India. Among the social groups, the poor spent a disproportionately large amount on health and education. The National Institute of Rural Development (NIRD 1999) conducted a study for the major states of India for the years 1961, 1971, 1981, and 1987–88. The study revealed that HDI scores had gone up in all the states over time. Poverty-stricken states like Bihar and UP were at the lower rung, and Gujarat had made considerable progress on HDI. The ranking of states on HDI has changed significantly during the last three decades. Gender discrimination was conspicuous in 14 states, except Kerala and Karnataka. Rao (2000) made an attempt to bring out the insights provided by the *HDR* for the state of Karnataka. His study revealed that the state was lagging behind even in achieving what is regarded as minimum essential norms of human development.

Mahanty (2000) conducted a study with an alternative set of indicators for Andhra Pradesh for the years 1982–83, 1987–88 and 1992–93 using five different methods of index. He found that while the pattern of human development was relatively stagnant, some districts were lagging behind. For the first time, UNDP (2003) devoted an entire chapter on human development to the North East that busted some popular myths, particularly on literacy rates and the status of women. The report identified several factors that had contributed to the depressing and dismal situation in the region. Vijaybhaskar *et al.* (2004), in their study while highlighting the key findings of the *HDR* of the state of Tamil Nadu, mentioned that though the state had registered considerable progress in literacy and reduction of poverty, it had failed miserably in arresting inter-district and intra-regional differences across gender and caste in human development achievements. Nayak and Thomas (2007) conducted an in-depth study on human development by constructing HDI for all the seven districts of the state of Meghalaya. They analysed the status and trend of human development and deprivation in Meghalaya, vis-à-vis, other leading states in the country, using both primary and secondary data. The study revealed a low level of human development in the state, accompanied with considerable degree of unevenness between rural and urban areas, across different districts, and also between genders. Purohit (2008) in his study analysed the factors that led to disparities of development in terms of various indicators, such as per capita income (PCI), access to basic facilities, and human development, using district-level data for three Indian states, namely, Orissa, Karnataka, and Maharashtra, representing, respectively, a poor, middle-income, and high-income state, and attempted to reflect upon the phenomenon of convergence and divergence and two-way causation between human development and income. The findings of the study indicate a tendency to neglect the development of poorer districts in richer states. Skewed development priorities have favoured better off districts in poorer states. The two-way regression analysis carried out by him indicates the need for a more suitable development strategy, incorporating appropriate state intervention, that might lead to enhanced income through improved skills. The results support the contention that the ongoing process of convergence at the district level might minimize inequality over a longer period of time, provided state intervention is made to counter-act the divergence in the social and economic infrastructure.

A number of studies which have been undertaken to examine the link between human development and economic growth, that were reviewed in the works of Nayak and Thomas (2007), are presented briefly. Anand and Ravallion (1993) viewed development indicators or social outcomes as aggregates of individual capabilities and found that GNP and life expectancy are significantly and positively related. Aturupane *et al.* (1994), in their empirical work, observed that economic growth is negatively related to infant mortality rate. Similarly, taking three income-decomposed health aggregates, that is, life expectancy, infant mortality, and perinatal mortality, Bidani and Ravallion (1995) found that overall per capita health spending has a positive effect on life expectancy at birth and infant mortality rate of the poor people. Geeta Rani (1995) found that economic progress in India is one of the important factors that determine the level of human development. Zaidi and Salam (1998) reported a high positive correlation between Net State Domestic Product (NSDP) per capita and enrolment in higher education. The empirical findings of Chakraborty (1997) based on a non-parametric approach revealed that dependency of life expectancy on income is tethered to time and space; income explains life expectancy only below a certain range, and that range is moving up over time. Some studies confirmed the positive relationship between human development and economic growth using time-series data for developing nations (UNDP 1996 and Ranis *et al.* 2000). Ranis and Stewart (2000) in their study outlined two chains—from economic growth to human development, and from human development to economic growth. Boozer *et al.* (2003), while exploring the dual relationship between economic growth and human development, urged that economic growth is just a means of human development, while human development reinforces economic growth. Strong complementarities between investments in human development and attained sustained economic growth emerged in the study of Muysken *et al.* (2003). In the endogenous growth model, Schaper (2003) found that investment in education is able to enhance economic growth and income equality depending upon the way of financing it. Dholakia (2003), in his study, examined the trends in regional disparity in India's economic and human development over the past two decades. Findings suggested a two-way causality between the two. The structure of the relationship varied over time when human development indicators were the cause and the PCI was the effect, but in the reverse causality case, the structure of the equations was found to be stable over time. Estimation revealed that HDI positively influenced PCI with a lag of about eight years, whereas PCI affected the HDI within two years. World Bank (2004), by using mortality statistics of India, documented that both household living standards and national income levels have a positive effect on the reduction of infant mortality rate (under age 1). Drawing attention to a series of advanced studies in human capital theory, basic needs, as well as welfare approach, Ranis and Stewart (2005) viewed that in most cases, economic growth and human development run parallel.

The review of literature on human development reveals that very few studies have been undertaken to focus on the status and trend of human development of the north-eastern region using HDI. Therefore, the present chapter in this regard is a humble attempt with the main objective of testing the following hypotheses:

1. Human development and its growth in the North-East is too low as compared to many countries of the world, and
2. There exists a yawning gap between females and males, the rural-urban gap, and state-wise variation is significant over time in the region.

THE NORTH-EAST

North-East India, having a population of 39.04 million is basically a region consisting of eight states, namely, Arunachal Pradesh, Assam, Manipur, Meghalaya, Mizoram, Nagaland, Sikkim, and Tripura. Among these eight states, four states have tribal population as a majority; specifically, Mizoram (94.5 per cent), Nagaland (89.1 per cent), Meghalaya (85.9 per cent), and Arunachal Pradesh (64.2 per cent) (North-Eastern Council 2002). The region had a literacy rate of 65.8 per cent as against the all India average of 65.2 per cent. However, literacy rate varied from state to state in the region, from the lowest figure of 54.7 per cent (Arunachal Pradesh) to the highest figure of 88.5 per cent (Mizoram). Per capita NSDP in the states varied from lowest figure of Rs 1,675 in Assam to the highest figure of Rs 3,571 in Arunachal Pradesh, and an average of Rs 2,223 for the region in the year 1997–98 at 1980–81 prices. Per Capita Monthly Consumption Expenditure (PCMCE) was as low as Rs 147.52 in the year 2000 at 1983 prices. Assam had the lowest PCMCE of Rs 99.81 as against highest PCMCE of Rs 228.04 for Nagaland. 34.7 per cent of people in the region were below the poverty line in 2000 as against a national average of 26.1 per cent. The highest percentage of people below the poverty line was estimated for Sikkim (36.6 per cent) and the lowest percentage for Mizoram (19.5 per cent).

Human Development in North-East India

According to the 18th *HDR* (UNDP 2007–08), India has a long way to go. When Norway has a HDI value of 0.968 and 27 other countries in the world are having HDI values above 0.9, the corresponding figure in India is 0.619 (UNDP 2007–08). Though, India is a fast growing developing nation, she is placed at the 128th rank at the global level. Even small neighbouring countries in Asia, like Mauritius (0.804), Sri Lanka (0.743), Maldives (0.741), and Indonesia (0.728), have surpassed India. The country has been witnessing very poor growth in human development. The HDI value in the country during 1975, which stood at 0.411, increased to only 0.476 in 1985, and further to 0.619 in 2005. Thus, the country has witnessed an annual growth of merely 1.7 per cent on an average over a period of three decades.

The findings of the Planning Commission on the magnitude and growth of human development has been quite different from that of the UNDP probably because of differences in their methodology of estimation. HDI value, which was estimated to be 0.302 in 1981, improved to 0.381 in 1991, and subsequently to 0.472 in 2001 (GoI 2002). When UNDP estimates showed a relatively high human development (0.619) with low annual growth (1.7 per cent), estimates of Planning Commission showed a low human development (0.472) with a high annual growth (2.3 per cent) over time.

Rural-urban disparity, which was quite low in 1981 (0.179) and 1991 (0.171), instead of improving, deteriorated and stood at 0.204 in 2000 as shown in Table 12.1 (GoI 2002). Gender disparity continued to be high. When male literacy rate was 75.6 per cent, female literacy was 54.0 per cent in 2001. Besides, there has been widespread disparity across the states in the country. The HDI varied between the highest value of 0.638, in the case of Kerala, to the lowest value of 0.365 for Bihar.

As far as the North-East is concerned, the situation has been no different. During 1981, HDI value varied from the lowest figure of 0.242 for Arunachal Pradesh to the highest figure of 0.461 for Manipur. Similarly, in 1991, the lowest and highest figures were 0.328

Table 12.1: Human Development in North-East India in 2000 and 2001

State/Country	In 2000[†]				In 2001[††]
	Rural	Urban	Combined	Disparity	
Arunachal Pradesh	0.379	0.622	0.411	0.243	0.49
Assam	0.330	0.613	0.362	0.283	0.50
Manipur	0.404	0.640	0.455	0.236	0.59
Meghalaya	0.390	0.671	0.436	0.281	0.52
Mizoram	0.473	0.687	0.552	0.214	0.67
Nagaland	0.477	0.738	0.515	0.261	0.57
Sikkim	0.396	0.571	0.411	0.175	0.60
Tripura	0.397	0.656	0.434	0.259	0.59
INDIA	0.380	0.584	0.435	0.204	0.56

Sources: †The figures are estimated by the author.
†† Government of Tripura.

(Arunachal Pradesh) and 0.548 (Mizoram). The region, though, witnessed further improvement but was not free from glaring unevenness in the last decade of the twentieth century. According to our estimate, Assam witnessed the lowest HDI value of 0.362 and Mizoram the highest value of 0.552 in 2000. Similar findings were observed in the *Tripura state HDR*. The report revealed that the lowest performing state was Arunachal Pradesh, with HDI value of 0.49, as against the highest performing state Mizoram, with a corresponding HDI value of 0.67.

There has been a yawning gap between urban and rural areas. Human development in rural areas of the region has been consistently lower than that in the urban areas. The rural-urban disparity index varied from the lowest figure of 0.113 for Manipur to the highest figure of 0.234 for Tripura in 1981. The situation did not improve much in 1991, and also in 2000. In 2000, the highest disparity was observed in Assam (0.283) and lowest in Sikkim (0.175). The position of Meghalaya in this regard is worth mentioning. Her rank in rural-urban disparity deteriorated over time. Though Meghalaya occupied 3rd rank among all the states in the region in 1981, it deteriorated to last (8th) rank in 1991 and, subsequently, to second last in 2000.

Contrary to popular perceptions, the status of women in the region is far from being on an equal footing with that of men. Particularly, gender disparity has been consistently very high in Tripura and Assam—(GoI 2002) and *Tripura HDR 2007*. Assam is the only state in the region which has been consistently lagging behind the rest of India. Gender disparity was lower in four states, namely, Manipur,

Meghalaya, Nagaland, and Sikkim, in the year 1981 as compared to the all India average. In 1991, Arunachal Pradesh and Mizoram were added to the list of better performing states. In 2001, Arunachal Pradesh, Assam, and Meghalaya were lagging behind other states which were doing well. Gender disparity has been varying widely from one state to another in the region. Surprisingly, when gender disparity has been decreasing over time in all the states in the region, it has deteriorated in Nagaland.

CONCLUSION

The Indian economy, in spite of being a fast-growing developing economy and pursuing the policy of liberalization and globalization since the early 1980s, has not been able to achieve much on account of human development and welfare. HDI in 2001 was as low as 0.56 for the country. While some states in the region have performed better than India, some others have lagged behind. Rural-urban disparity, gender disparity, and uneven human development across the states in the region are quite significant. The disturbing trend of increasing gender disparity in Nagaland and escalating rural-urban gap, particularly in the States of Assam and Meghalaya, is a matter of concern. Therefore, there is an urgent need for taking appropriate action in this regard.

REFERENCES

Adelman, I. and C.T. Morris 1973. *Economic Growth and Social Equity in Developing Countries,* Stanford University Press, Stanford.

Arcelus, F.J., B. Sharma, and G. Srinivasan 2005. 'The Human Development Index Adjusted for Efficient Resource Utilization', Research Paper No. 2005/08, World Institute for Development Economics Research (WIDER), United Nations University.

Anand, S. and A. Sen 2006. 'Human Development and Economic Sustainability', *World Development,* Vol. 28, No.12, pp. 2029–49.

—— 2000. 'The Income Component of Human Development Index', *Journal of Human Development,* Vol. 1, No. 1.

——1997. 'Concepts of Human Development and Poverty: A Multidimensional Perspective', in United Nations Development Programme, *Human Development Report 1997 Papers: Poverty and Human Development,* New York.

—— 1995. 'Gender Inequality in Human Development: Theories and Measurement', Human Development Report Office, Occasional Paper 19, United Nations Development Programme, New York.

Anand, S. and A. Sen 1993. 'Human Development Index: Methodology and Measurement', Human Development Report Office, Occasional Paper No.12, United Nations Development Programme, New York.

Anand, S. and M. Ravallion 1993. 'Human Development in Poor Countries: On the Role of Private Incomes and Public Services', Journal of Economic Perspectives, Vol. 7, pp. 133–150.

Aturupane, H., P. Glewwe, and P. Isenman 1994. 'Poverty, Human Development and Growth: An Emerging Consensus', American Economic Review, Vol. 84, No. 2, pp. 244–49.

Bardhan, K. and S. Klasen 1999. 'UNDPs Gender-Related Indices: A Critical Review', World Development, Vol. 27, No. 6, pp. 985–1010.

Bidani, B. and M. Ravallion 1995. 'Decomposing Social Indicators Using Distributional Data'. <http://www_wds.worldbank.org/external/default/WDSContentservices> (visited on 22 June 2006).

Boozer, M., Ranis, G., Stewart, F., and T. Suri 2003. 'Paths to Success: The Relationship between Human Development and Economic Growth', Discussion Paper No. 874, Economic Growth Center, Yale University. <http://www.econ.yale.edu/~egcenter/> (visited on 15 May 2006).

Bose, A. 2004. 'HDRs: Some Reflections', Economic and Political Weekly, 24 January 2004.

Chakraborty, I. 1997. 'Living Standard and Economic Growth: A Fresh Look at the Relationship through the Non-parametric Approach'. <http://cds.edu/download_files/wp283.pdf> (visited on 15 May 2006).

Chakravarty, S.R. 2003. 'A Generalized Human Development Index', Review of Development Economics, Blackwell Publishing, Vol. 7, No.1, pp. 99–114.

Chaubey, P.K. 2002. 'The Human Development Index: A Contribution to its Construction', Indian Journal of Economics, Vol. 83, No. 328, pp. 95–100.

Dalal, K.L. 1991. (ed.), Human Development—An Indian Perspective, Har-Anand Publications, Based on the papers presented in the National Symposium held in New Delhi, March 1991.

Desai, M. 1991. 'Human Development: Concept and Measurement', European Economic Review, Vol. 35, pp. 350–57.

Dholakia, R.H. 2003. 'Regional Disparity in Economic and Human Development in India', Economic and Political Weekly.

Geeta Rani, P. 1995. 'Human Development in India: A District Profile', Arthavijnana, Vol. 41, No. 1, pp. 9–30.

Government of India 2002. National Human Development Report 2001, Planning Commission, New Delhi.

Haq, M. ul 1995. Reflections on Human Development, Oxford University Press, New York.

Hicks, D.A. 1997. 'The Inequality Adjusted Human Development Index: A Constructive Proposal', *World Development*, Vol. 25, No. 8, pp. 1283–98.

Jain, L.C. 1991. 'Human Development in Rural India—A Blue Print', in K.L Dalal (ed.), *Human Development—An Indian Perspective*, Based on the papers presented in the National Symposium held in New Delhi, March.

Leigh, Andrew and Justin Wolfers 2006. 'Happiness and the Human Development Index: Australia is Not a Paradox', *The Australian Economic Review*, Vol. 39, No. 2, pp. 176–84.

Mahanty, G. 2000. 'Human Development in Andhra Pradesh: A District Level Analysis', *The Indian Journal of Labour Economics*, Vol. 43, No. 2.

Morris, D.M. 1979. *Measuring the Condition of the World's Poor: The Physical Quality of Life Index*, Pergamon Press, Elmsford, New York.

Muysken, J. Yetkiner, I.H., and Z. Thomas, 2003. 'Health, Labour Productivity, and Growth', in H. Hagemann and S. Seiter (eds.) *Growth Model and Growth Policy*, Routledge, London, pp. 187–206.

National Council of Applied Economic Research (NCAER), New Delhi, 1999. *India Human Development Report—A Profile of Indian States in the 1990s*, Oxford University Press, Oxford, p. 7.

National Institute of Rural Development (NIRD), 1999. *India Rural Development Report 1999: Regional Disparities in Development and Poverty*, Hyderabad, p. 86.

Nagar, A.L. and S.R. Basu 2000. 'Weighting Socio-Economic Indicators of Human Development', ICSSR Project Report submitted to NIPFP.

Nayak, P. and E.D. Thomas 2007. *Human Development and Deprivation in Meghalaya*, Akansha Publishing House, New Delhi.

Neumayer, Eric. 2001. 'The Human Development Index and Sustainability—A Constructive Proposal', *Ecological Economics*, Vol. 39, pp. 101–14.

Noorbakhsh, Farhad 1998. 'A Modified Human Development Index', *World Development*, Vol. 26, No. 3, pp. 517–28.

Ogwang, Tomson and Abdou Abdella 2003. 'The Choice of Principal Variables for Computing Some Measures of Human Well-Being', *Social Indicators Research*, Vol. 64, pp. 139–52.

Organization for Economic Cooperation and Development (OECD) 1976. *Measuring Social Well-Being—A Progress Report on the Development of Social Indicators*, Paris Cedex, France. www.springerlink.com/index/T48JP3832U644765.pdf

Pal, S.P. and D.K. Kant 1993. 'An Alternative Human Development Index', *Margin*, Vol. 25, No. 2, Part-II (special issue on Human Development).

Purohit, B.C. 2008. 'Health and Human Development at Sub-State Level in India', *The Journal of Socio-Economics*, accepted on 11th December

2007 for publication in 2008 issue. www.elsevier.com/locate/soceco

Ranis, G. and F. Stewart 2005. 'Dynamic Links between the Economy and Human Development', http://www.un.org/esa/desa/papers/2005/wp8_2005pdf (visited on 27 March 2006).

—— 2000. 'Strategies for Successful Human Development', *Journal of Human Development*, Vol. 1, No. 1, pp. 49–69.

Ranis, G., F. Stewart, and A. Ramirez 2000. 'Economic Growth and Human Development', *World Development*, Vol. 28, No. 2, pp. 197–219.

Rao, V.M. 2000. 'Towards Human Development: Glimpses from India and Selected States', *The Indian Journal of Labour Economics*, Vol. 43, No. 2, pp. 327–38.

Sagar, A.D. and A. Najam 1998. 'The Human Development Index: A Critical Review', *Ecological Economics*, Vol. 25, No. 3, pp. 249–64.

Schaper, C. 2003. 'Growth and Distribution Effects of Education Policy in an Endogenous Growth Model with Human Capital Accumulation', in H. Hagemann and S. Seiter (eds.), *Growth Model and Growth Policy*, Routledge, London, pp. 136–155.

Sheldon, E.B. and K.C. Land 1972. 'Social Reporting for the 1970's—A Review and Pragmatic Statement', *Policy Sciences*, Vol. 3, No. 2, pp. 137–51.

Shiva Kumar, A.K. 1991. 'UNDP's Human Development in India—A Computation for Indian States', *Economic and Political Weekly*, October 12, pp. 2343–45.

—— 1996. 'UNDP's Gender-Related Development Index—A Computation for Indian States', *Economic and Political Weekly*, April 6.

Tilak, J.B.G. 1991. 'Human Development Index of India', *IASSI Quarterly*, Vol. 10, No. 2, pp. 132–38.

United Nations 1975. *Towards a System of Social and Demographic Statistics*, Studies in Methods, Series F. No. 18, Sales No. E. 74.XVII.8.

United Nations Development Programme (UNDP) 1990, 1991, 1994, 1999, 2003, 2006 and 2007–2008: *Human Development Report*.

United Nations Educational, Scientific and Cultural Organization (UNESCO) 1976. *The Use of Social Indicators in Development Planning—A Case Study of Sudan*, Study undertaken by Nancy Baster for UNESCO. http://unesdoc.unesco.org/images/0001/000190/019055eb.pdf

United Nations Research Institute for Social Development (UNRISD) 1970. *Contents and Measurement of Social Development*, Report No. 70.10, Geneva. http://www.roiw.org/1971/379.pdf

Vijayabhaskar M., P. Swaminathan, S. Anandhi, and G. Balagopal 2004. 'Human Development in Tamil Nadu', *Economic and Political Weekly*, February 21, 2004.

Viswanathan, R. 1999. 'Human Development Report for Madhya Pradesh —Some Hidden Truths', *Economic and Political Weekly*, May 29.

Vyasalu, V. and B.P. Vani 1997. 'Development and Deprivation in Karnataka: A District Level Study', *Economic and Political Weekly*, November 15.

Zaidi, N.A. and M.A. Salam, 1998. 'Human Development in India: An Inter-state Comparison', *Indian Journal of Economics*, Vol. 78, No. 371, April.

World Bank, 2004. *Attaining the MDGs in India*, Washington D.C.

13

Severity of Poverty and Status of Public Services in North-Eastern States

NIRANKAR SRIVASTAV

INTRODUCTION

Poverty reduction has been noticed as a significant phenomenon during the past two decades in India. The proportion of people Below Poverty Line (BPL) remained stagnant, around 50 per cent, during plan periods till late 1970s. But this witnessed a declining trend, thereafter. This reduction was noticeable during 1980–90, that is, from 51 per cent in 1977 to 39 per cent in 1987–88, and further to 26 per cent in 1999–2000 (GoI 2001–02). Credit for this trend is mainly given to higher economic growth, improvements in real wages, and impact of poverty alleviation programmes. In the literature on poverty, the issues of relative welfare and levels, extent, and severity of poverty has been discussed with some regularity. Most of these studies are, either available at an all India level, or at best for a few selected larger Indian states. The north-eastern states are outside the purview of many such studies.

In this chapter the focus is on analysing the poverty status and process of poverty reduction in the North-East. The three conventional poverty measures, viz., Head Count Ratio (HCR), Poverty Gap Eatio (PGR), and Foster-Greer-Thorbecke (FGT) are used to quantify the level of poverty. A series of such measures were used to analyse poverty reduction during 1993–2000. In order to highlight the dispersal of poverty levels among the poor, the three sub-groups under BPL, namely, extremely poor, very poor, and moderately poor, are categorized and identified. This treatment helps in investigating the trend of poverty reduction.

Next, this chapter focuses on poverty and status of public services. Various studies suggest that a two-way relationship may exist between poverty and quality of public services such as drinking water, health care, public distribution system, public transport, and primary education. This study attempts to deal with the following research questions:

1. What is the prevalence of the extent and severity of poverty in north-eastern states?
2. What are the trends in poverty reduction in urban and rural areas?
3. What is the relationship between poverty reduction and status of quality of public services?

The rest of the chapter is organized as follows. First, we discuss the data and methodological issues. Then we deal with the poverty status in the North-East. This is followed by an analysis of dispersal of poverty between rural and urban areas along with temporal changes. After this, the status of access to public services is discussed leading to a conclusion and policy implications.

DATA AND METHODOLOGICAL ISSUES

In this chapter we use data from the socio-economic survey conducted by the National Sample Survey Organisation (NSSO) for two quinquennial 50th and 55th rounds. The reference years are 1993–94 and 1999–2000. During these two rounds of survey, the NSSO collected data on household level consumption expenditure for the agriculture year, that is, from July to June. The socio-economic survey data of NSSO has its reputation for reliability and suitability for the type of study at hand. This data set has two major advantages; firstly, this is in the form of unit record for household level. Secondly, this is the only detailed data that covers the states of north-eastern India.

The official poverty incidence in India is reported at the state level, divided into rural and urban sectors, in a number of studies, for example, GoI (1993, 1997, and 2001). But, in the situation where there exists substantial inter- and intra-state differences in the level of development and incidence of poverty, the state-level analysis does not provide enough insight into the process leading to change in poverty incidence. As pointed above, we wanted to carry out the analysis at a more disaggregated level. Therefore, we used sub-state (NSSO region) level poverty incidence in the rural and urban sector. This enabled us to do the regional disparity analysis at a fairly disaggregated level.

Level of Living and Poverty Line

For measuring welfare of the population, traditionally, per person income or expenditure has been used. The consumption expenditure is the preferred indicator of standard of living and in turn it indicates the welfare at the household level. To capture this, Average Per Capita Consumption Expenditure (APCTE) is estimated, for the entire population disaggregated by states and NSSO regions, for rural and urban sectors separately.

The poverty norm z, which we use in this chapter, is the Official Poverty Line (OPL) based on the official norm that was derived by a task force in 1979 (GoI 1979). The all India poverty norm for rural and urban sector was derived using the food energy intake method. The task force estimated that, on an average, a representative Indian needs 2435 kilocalories in the rural sector and 2095 kilocalories in the urban sector per day. The cost of these calories worked out to be Rs 49.07 and Rs 56.64 per person at 1973–74 prices for the rural and urban sector, respectively, assuming that education and health care will be provided by the state. The Expert Group (GoI 1993) recommended that the all India poverty norm is to be deflated using state-wise price indices, keeping the average calorie requirement fixed. We have used the state-wise poverty lines that were derived by the Expert Group (1993), and reported in GoI (1997).

It is to be noted that the GoI (1997) recommended that for smaller states and union territories (UTs), the poverty ratios of neighbouring larger states be adopted, as the price data for these states and UTs are not available. For example, the poverty ratios of Assam have been assigned to remaining six north-eastern states and Sikkim. The modification that we introduced in this chapter is that we used the poverty line of the neighbouring larger states in place of poverty ratios as suggested in GoI (1997), and expenditure distribution of the concerned states to calculate the poverty incidence.

Poverty Measures

The simplest index of poverty is HCR, which is defined as:

$$\text{HCR} = \frac{q}{n} \times 100 \tag{13.1}$$

where the population consists of n individuals with per capita total expenditure (PCTE), y_i, ranked in ascending order; q is the number of persons below the poverty line z. HCR gives the proportion of the population that has PCTE below the poverty line. One of the main shortcomings of HCR is that it is insensitive to the depth of poverty of the poor person, thus violating what Sen (1976), defined as the monotonicity axiom. This axiom ensures that any poverty index should increase if there is a drop in the income of any poor individually, *ceteris paribus*.

The weighted Poverty Gap Index (PGI) satisfies the above axiom, which is defined as:

$$\text{PGI} = \frac{1}{q.z} \sum_{i=1}^{q} (z - y_i) \tag{13.2}$$

where n, q, y_i and z are as defined above. But this measure is insensitive to income transfer against the poor, thus violating Sen's Weak Transfer Axiom—the requirement that any transfer of income from a poor person to any one richer should increase poverty, so long as no one crosses the poverty line as a result. There are several such measures described in literature, which satisfy the transfer axioms.

Foster, Greer, and Thorbecke (1984) developed an index (commonly known as FGT index) which has almost become standard in literature for its simplicity and useful properties, besides satisfying various poverty axioms and being population sub-group consistent. Recall that we are computing aggregate poverty measures as a weighted sum of population sub-groups, state, and NSSO region. FGT (α), a generalized index, is a normalized weighted sum of the poverty gaps of the poor, with weights given by those poverty gaps themselves raised to an appropriate power. The FGT index is defined as:

$$\text{FGT}(\alpha) = \frac{1}{n.z^{\alpha}} \sum_{i=1}^{q} (z - y_i)^{\alpha}, \alpha \geq 0 \tag{13.3}$$

where n, q, y_i and z are same as defined above. For $\alpha=0$, the FGT (α) equals HCR, for $\alpha=1$, the index equals PGI. For greater values of α, it satisfies the criteria of diminishing transfer sensitivity. In case of $\alpha=2$, FGT index is defined as:

$$\text{FGT}(2) = \frac{1}{n.z^2} \sum_{i=1}^{q} (z - y_i)^2 \tag{13.4}$$

The advantage of using weights independent of position in the distribution ensures decomposability of the index across different household types.

In this chapter we have estimated poverty using all the three poverty indices discussed above. Recall that for α=0, from equation 13.3 we get HCR; for α=1, it yields PGI and for α=2, it is FGT as shown in equation 13.4. The persons living below poverty line were further divided in three sub-groups, namely, moderately poor, very poor, and extremely poor, as per specifications shown in Box 13.1.

Box 13.1	
Category	Persons whose per-capita expenditure is in the following range of state specific poverty line
Extremely poor	Less than 50 per cent
Very poor	Greater than 50 per cent and less than 75 per cent
Moderately poor	Greater than 75 per cent and below poverty line (BPL)
Total	Total number of persons below BPL

Data on status of public services is based on an all India level survey conducted by a civil society organization, namely Public Affairs Centre, which prepared state-level report cards for rural and urban regions for the year 2001 (Samuel *et al.* 2004). The five basic public services covered are: drinking water, health care, road transport, public distribution system, and primary school. The data on access, use, reliability, and full satisfaction revealed by the households were made available in this survey.

Poverty Status in North-Eastern States

Recall that unit record data is being used from the last two quinquennial rounds of household survey to calculate the incidence of poverty and other poverty indices. Thus, poverty ratios for all the states of the north-eastern region for rural and urban areas along with all India level are reported in Tables 13.1 and 13.2. It is observed from Table 13.1 that poverty in rural areas in the region was only marginally higher in 1993–94, although in 1999–2000, the all India figure (26.5 per cent) is much lower than region (33.31 per cent). While the all India figure shows a steady and continuous fall in poverty incidence, the region has shown an uneven variation over time.

The state-wise breakup of poverty indices in the region highlights the intra-state variations. Table 13.3 clearly shows that there is indeed

Table 13.1: Incidence of Poverty in North-Eastern States in 1993–94

State/ All India	Extremely Poor	Very Poor	Moderately Poor	Poor (BPL)
Rural Poverty (in per cent)				
ARP	2.5	16.1	25.3	48.4
ASS	0.7	12.3	33.0	45.3
MAN	0.1	2.3	16.9	19.2
MEG	0.2	2.9	21.4	24.3
MIZ	0.0	1.3	4.9	6.2
NAG	0.0	0.0	1.9	1.9
SIK	0.0	8.1	23.2	31.3
TRI	0.9	8.7	14.6	23.3
India	2.0	14.7	22.1	36.8
Urban Poverty (in per cent)				
ARP	0.4	1.9	3.9	5.8
ASS	0.2	1.2	6.8	8.0
MAN	0.2	0.4	6.5	6.9
MEG	0.0	0.1	1.7	1.8
MIZ	0.0	0.0	0.0	0.0
NAG	0.0	0.0	0.0	0.0
SIK	0.0	0.0	0.1	0.1
TRI	0.1	1.8	4.2	6.0
India	2.9	15.1	17.7	32.8

Source: Computed from NSSO 50th and 55th round Consumer Expenditure data.

a differential incidence of poverty among the states in the region. This supports the hypothesis that poverty indices, that is, HCR, PGI, and FGT would vary from state to state. The temporal change from 1993–94 to 1999–2000 is not uniform. There is a marked improvement for the majority of states. In both the periods, Assam registers the highest figures as compared to the rest of the sates. A very low level of poverty index (2.85 per cent in the year 1999–2000) could be explained by favourable socio-economic characteristics prevailing in the 1990s, like very high level of literacy rates. The finding that Nagaland has a very low poverty index (0.21 per cent in the year 1999–2000) is not reliable because it was estimated out of limited data due to the known reason that major areas of the state were inaccessible.

As shown in Table 13.3, the poverty status in urban sector among the states is quite low compared to the all India level. Actually, poverty is declining over time, for both the region and the country as a whole. However, the gap between these two has been very glaring. The region has a HCR value less than 5 per cent in 1999–2000 compared to the

Table 13.2: Incidence of Poverty in North-Eastern States in 1999–2000

State/ All India	Extremely Poor	Very Poor	Moderately Poor	Poor (BPL)
Rural Poverty (in per cent)				
ARP	0.0	6.3	17.1	23.4
ASS	1.9	14.8	25.4	40.2
MAN	0.0	2.4	11.7	14.1
MEG	0.0	0.2	5.8	6.0
MIZ	0.0	0.1	2.7	2.8
NAG	0.0	0.0	0.2	0.2
SIK	0.2	3.2	18.5	21.7
TRI	0.2	3.2	13.5	16.7
India	0.8	8.2	18.3	26.5
Urban Poverty (in per cent)				
ARP	2.2	4.1	0.9	5.0
ASS	0.2	2.1	5.1	7.2
MAN	0.0	0.0	0.5	0.5
MEG	0.0	0.0	0.0	0.0
MIZ	0.0	0.0	0.0	0.0
NAG	0.0	0.0	0.0	0.0
SIK	0.0	1.2	3.6	4.8
TRI	0.0	0.4	1.0	1.4
India	1.2	9.2	14.8	24.0

Source: Computed from NSSO 50th and 55th round Consumer Expenditure data.

all India level (23.98 per cent). This clearly suggests that poverty in the region is concentrated in the rural sectors.

Table 13.2 reveals state-wise incidence of rural and urban poverty categorized into moderately poor, very poor, and extremely poor for 1999–2000. It can be seen that magnitude of poverty in all the three categories are higher in Assam as compared to the all India average. Dispersal of poverty is relatively lower in all other states. One trend, which is emerging, is that the proportion of moderately poor is highest among the poor BPL people, both at national and regional level and for urban and rural areas. Assam has the highest concentration of poor people in the rural region followed by Arunachal Pradesh, Sikkim, and Tripura.

In the urban areas, all the north-eastern states including Assam are depicting lower poverty dispersal than all India level. This reveals that the extent of poverty dispersal is concentrated in rural areas. In order to capture the changes in the poverty status, the incidence of poverty dispersal among the three categories of the poor BPL for the

Table 13.3: Poverty Incidence in North-Eastern Region

State*/	HCR		PGI		FGT	
All India	1993–94	1999–2000	1993–94	1999–2000	1993–94	1999–2000
Rural Poverty						
ARP	41.29	22.50	0.0907	0.0390	0.0302	0.0101
ASS	45.26	40.18	0.0830	0.0844	0.0222	0.0269
MAN	18.94	14.11	0.0230	0.0182	0.0047	0.0041
MEG	24.35	5.96	0.0334	0.0054	0.0073	0.0008
MIZ	6.22	2.85	0.0086	0.0023	0.0018	0.0003
NAG	2.30	0.21	0.0021	0.0003	0.0002	0.0001
TRI	23.64	16.67	0.0532	0.0257	0.0171	0.0064
NER	37.67	33.31	0.0856	0.0680	0.0272	0.0213
India	37.28	26.50	0.0845	0.0518	0.0281	0.0152
Urban Poverty						
ARP	6.05	5.06	0.0136	0.0279	0.0046	0.0204
ASS	7.93	7.23	0.0092	0.0148	0.0023	0.0041
MAN	6.89	0.53	0.0059	0.0002	0.0013	0.0000
MEG	1.81	NA	0.0019	0.0000	0.0003	0.0000
MIZ	1.81	NA	NA	0.0000	0.0000	0.0000
NAG	NA	NA	NA	0.0000	0.0000	0.0000
TRI	NA	2.16	0.0117	0.0029	0.0035	0.0006
NER	6.04	4.63	0.0119	0.0095	0.0038	0.0028
India	31.70	23.98	0.0798	0.0522	0.0291	0.0168

Note: * No statistics is available for Sikkim.
Source: Computed from NSSO 50th and 55th round Consumer Expenditure data.

year 1993–94 are shown in Table 13.1. The change in the incidence of extremely poor, very poor, and moderately poor within the BPL is revealed in Table 13.4. The significant reduction in poverty (10.3 per cent) is noticed along with reduction in the proportion of moderately poor and very poor people. But the real cause of concern is the rise in proportion of extremely poor people by 1.2 per cent in the rural region at the all India level.

Assam shows lower poverty decline along with increase in the proportion of extremely poor people and very poor people in the rural region. Tripura also revealed the increase in the proportion of extremely poor people. This highlights the fact that the process of economic development and state-sponsored poverty alleviation programmes are not working efficiently in these states to tackle the economic problems of extremely poor people. This scenario is differ-

Table 13.4: Change in Incidence of Poverty from 1993–94 to 1999–2000 in
North-Eastern States

State/ All India	Extremely Poor	Very Poor	Moderately Poor	Poor (BPL)
Rural Poverty (in %)				
ARP	−2.5	−9.8	−8.2	−25.0
ASS	+1.2	+2.5	−7.6	−5.1
MAN	−0.1	+0.1	−5.2	−5.1
MEG	−0.2	−2.7	−15.6	−18.3
MIZ	0.0	−1.2	−2.2	−3.4
NAG	0.0	0.0	−1.7	−1.7
SIK	0.0	−4.9	−4.7	−9.6
TRI	+0.7	−5.56	−1.1	−6.6
India	+1.2	−6.5	−3.8	−10.3
Urban Poverty (in %)				
ARP	+1.8	+2.2	−3.0	−0.8
ASS	0.0	+0.9	−1.7	−0.8
MAN	−0.2	−0.4	−6.0	−6.4
MEG	0.0	−0.16	−1.7	−1.8
MIZ	0.0	0.0	0.0	0.0
NAG	0.0	0.0	0.0	0.0
SIK	0.0	0.0	+3.5	+4.7
TRI	−0.1	−1.4	−3.2	−4.6
India	−1.7	−5.9	−2.9	−8.8

Note: Positive (+) and negative (−) signs show increase and decrease of poverty respectively.
Source: Computed from NSSO 50th and 55th round Consumer Expenditure data.

ent in the urban regions. The proportions of extremely poor and very poor people have increased in Arunachal Pradesh, while moderately poor people have increased in Sikkim.

It would be of interest to see the profile of these three types of poor people. The comparative picture highlighting this change is shown in Tables 13.5 and 13.6 for rural and urban regions, respectively.

It is clearly shown that the proportion of very poor and moderately poor people has increased both in rural and urban areas. The extent of poverty has increased among rural labour. Almost half of very poor people (47.8 per cent) belong to the class of landless labour in rural regions and other half (47.9 per cent) belong to persons having landholding up to one hectare. The proportion of 'go-hungry' people has declined slightly, both in the rural and urban areas during this period. In the urban areas, the extent of poverty among the very poor has

Table 13.5: Profile of Very Poor and Moderately Poor in Rural Areas (in per cent)

	SC+ST		Labour (Ag+Non-Ag)		Landless		Land-holding up to 1.0 Ha		Not Got Enough to Eat*		Female Headed Households
	1993–94	1999–2K	1993–94	1999–2K	1993–94	1999–2K	1993–94	1999–2K	1993–94	1999–2K	1993–94
Very Poor	47.2	50.7	56.5	61.3	47.0	47.8	36.7	47.9	12.0	11.0	6.6
Mod. Poor	39.1	42.1	44.2	51	38.7	42.4	38.5	51.5	7.3	5.4	5.9

Note: * Inadequate food either throughout the year or in some months.

Table 13.6: Profile of Very Poor and Moderately Poor in Urban Areas (in per cent)

	SC+ST		Casual Labour		Not Got Enough to Eat*		Female Headed Households
	1993–94	1999–2K	1993–94	1999–2K	1993–94	1999–2K	1993–94
Very Poor	29.0	32.0	30.9	40.3	5.4	4.9	9.5
Mod. Poor	22.8	26.6	20.1	26.0	2.5	2.4	8.2

Note: * Inadequate food either throughout the year or in some months.

increased significantly. A larger proportion of female-headed house-holds belong to very poor and moderately poor classes in urban areas than in rural areas.

Access to Public Services in North-Eastern States

Meghalaya, Mizoram, and Sikkim belong to that category of north-eastern states which have better services than all India in terms of access to public drinking water, health care, and distribution system (Table 13.7).

Table 13.7: Access to Public Services in North-Eastern States

(per cent of households)

State*/ All India	Drinking Water Facilities	Health Care	Road Transport	Distribution System	Primary School
Rural Areas					
ARP	81	36	23	40	23
ASS	09	38	22	72	74
MEG	69	23	15	54	73
MIZ	68	82	83	89	62
NAG	19	12	48	12	82
SIK	90	45	51	98	17
TRI	49	53	15	47	41
India	55	40	50	60	76
Urban Areas					
ARP	87	49	12	97	37
ASS	10	72	34	89	38
MEG	77	15	10	57	13
MIZ	72	64	80	98	39
NAG	20	23	78	68	09
SIK	90	45	51	98	17
TRI	63	34	39	97	24
India	62	41	60	85	42

Note: * No statistics are available for Manipur.
Source: Derived from Samuel *et al.* (2004)

Mizoram is the only state which has better road transportation facili-ties than India as a whole. As mentioned earlier, Assam is the only state in the region, which has highest proportion of poor people along with inadequate (public) drinking water facilities (access to 9 per cent population only), health care and road transportation facilities, distri-bution system, and government aided primary schools. It was expected that access to public services may be better in the urban areas, but the scenario is not very much different from that of the rural areas. Access to various types of public services in Assam is lower than the national average. Thus, it can be concluded that the states in which extent of poverty is high, the access to public services is also poor. This establishes the fact that there is a positive and strong relationship between poverty levels and access to public services. This study supports the findings of Rao (2007) that strong and effective implementation of social and economic safety nets are very much essential for poverty alleviation.

CONCLUSION AND POLICY IMPLICATIONS

The major findings of the study are:

(1) The extent of poverty varies from state to state in the north-eastern region according to the socio-economic and demographic characteristics;

(2) Poverty declined for most of the states in the region;

(3) This declination was more in urban than in rural areas and, again, more in hill states than in the plains states;

(4) The quality of public services on the basis of access, use, reliability, and satisfaction were worst in poverty stricken states;

(5) The extremely poor households needed up-front intervention if these were to be taken out of long standing poverty; and

(6) The incidence of poor, very poor, and extremely poor exhibited substantial reduction across all the states with the exception in Assam during 1993–94 and 1999–2000.

The findings of this study have important implications in identifying the poor regions and call for target-oriented and region-specific poverty reduction programmes. More importantly, by way of policy implications, it also calls for good governance of the delivery system and strong political commitment. Furthermore, this also helps in identifying the areas/states where poverty still exists significantly and reduction in poverty is not as much as in other better performing regions.

REFERENCES

Foster J.E., J. Greer, and E. Thorbecke 1984. 'A Class of Decomposable Poverty Measures', *Econometrica*, Vol. 52, pp. 761–66.

Government of India (GoI) 2001–2. *Economic Survey 2001–02*, Ministry of Finance, New Delhi. http://indiabudget.nic.in/es2001-02/welcome.html

—— 1997. 'Estimates of Poverty', *Press Information Bureau*, March 11.

—— 1993. 'Report of the Expert Group on Estimation of Proportion and Number of Poor', Planning Commission, Perspective Planning Division.

—— 1979. 'Report of the Task Force on Projections of Minimum Needs and Effective Consumption Demand', Planning Commission, Perspective Planning Division.

Rao, V.M. 2007. 'Making Safety Nets Effective for Hardcore Poor', *Economic and Political Weekly*, Vol. XLII, No. 33, pp. 3397–403.

Samuel P., S. Balakrishnan, K. Gopakumar, S. Sekhar, and M. Vivekananda 2004. 'State of India's Public Services: Benchmark for the States', *Economic and Political Weekly*, Vol. 39, No. 9, February 28, pp. 925-30.

Sen, A.K. 1976. 'Poverty: An Ordinal Approach to Measurement', *Econometerica*, Vol. 44, pp. 219–31.

14

Economic Growth, Exclusion, and Human Development

BHAGIRATHI PANDA

INTRODUCTION

The thinking on economic development and consequently, to some extent, the practice to realize it have undergone a sea change over the last seven to eight decades. Although, the idea of economic development can be traced back to the times of the mercantilists and physiocrats, it makes enough sense to search for its initial definition in the capitalist system of the not very distant past. In this system, it was identified with economic growth that is to be brought about by means of increase in per-capita income, governed by the philosophy of laissez-faire. It was also thought that economic growth and, hence, development would act as a panacea against all types of ills afflicting and affecting an economy and society. This notion of development was subscribed to by a majority of the countries in the developed world. Came the great depression of 1929, and as a redeeming strategy, the crumbling laissez-faire-based capitalist system was supplemented with limited public intervention in economic matters. Hence, emerged a new economic system called 'reformed capitalism', under which the notion of economic development was again essentially the same as under the earlier capitalism. However, during the 1940s and 1950s, when many of the colonies achieved independence in Asia and Africa, it was increasingly felt that the concept of economic development cannot be identified with economic growth alone. On the other hand, problems of inequality and unemployment surfaced in many of these newly independent countries. Thus, the challenges to development were reformulated and with that the concept of development too. Since capitalism and its subsequent version, 'reformed capitalism', with their institutions and premises, including the outward expansion of capitalism, that is, imperialism were held responsible for this existing situation of poverty, unemployment, and inequality in the developing countries. As a solution, the economic system of socialism was advocated. Subsequently, it took a firm root in erstwhile USSR and many East European countries. For some time, this system was eulogized as the best economic system. However, soon the enchantment with this institution and economic system withered away and the system collapsed because it became too heavy with too much centralization, corruption, nepotism, and false ideology. Then the neo-liberal gospel influenced by Thatcherism and Reaganomics came for a brief period. Eventually, it too turned out to be an unhappy interlude in promoting development. Today, economic development is understood in terms of material and non-material dimensions in achievement and, more particularly and emphatically, expanding the vector of capability of individuals (incremental capability built). In this sense, it emphasizes both effective participation and achievement (income and non-income). In other words, economic development is identified with human development and accordingly the theories and practices in economic development are getting overwritten by the theories and practices in human development.

THEORETICAL FRAMEWORK
Since this chapter deals with economic growth, exclusion, and human development, it would be in the fitness of things to define them explicitly (although, most of us know what they mean) and provide for a theoretical framework for the study of the relationship among them.

Economic Growth, Human Development, and Exclusion
Economic growth, basically, refers to a steady increase in the real national income of a country. It has also become customary these days to express it as net of population growth. Expressed in the second sense, it gives us per capita real income of a country/state/region.

Human development, as mentioned above in the introductory part, is an evolutionary concept. It is an improvement over the concept of economic development, both in its contents and understanding (whether an end, or a means). Human development has been redis-covered as the ultimate objective of all human activities in a society or economy. This is the ultimate objective of the people, for the people, and by the people. As a concept, it refers to enlargement of people's choices, freedoms, and capabilities, by ways and means that are participatory and sustainable in nature. Although this concept is a rediscovery, in many ways this rediscovery is fundamental, path-breaking, struggle-some, and critical. The genesis of its rediscovery lies as much in the disillusionment and inadequacy of economic growth and its associated institution, market mechanism, as in the urgency of strengthening growth as a mechanism of fulfilling certain dimensions of human development.

Exclusion can be social or economic. However, often both reinforce each other. We can understand exclusion both as a situation and as a process. Exclusion, as a situation, refers to a state of affairs at a point in time. As a process, it refers to the operation of the social, economic, political, and cultural forces that cause, maintain, and accentuate exclusion. Understanding the dynamics of exclusion as a process is much more important than just going by its manifestation or situ-ation. Economic growth and its associated institution, the 'market', excludes sections of people on four counts. They do not have:

(1) Sufficient income which can be translated into purchasing power;
(2) Assets, whether physical or financial;
(3) Capabilities acquired through education, training, or experience, which are translatable into labour and capable of yielding income through wages; and
(4) they do not share market values (as the case with people in some tribal societies).

Exclusion reinforces concentration of wealth and income. It is both anti-economic development and anti-human development. In the ideal state of human development, inclusion (that is, no presence of exclusion) and economic growth go together. However, in practice, this may not be the case very often. When this synergy/equilibrium is not there, it has its obvious negatives for the economy and society at large. In such a situation, the greatest challenge for human living is: how to ensure this symmetry/equilibrium/synergy.

Human Development and Economic Growth—The Chain

Ranis *et al.* (2004) have identified four categories of situations with respect to the relationship between economic growth and human development, namely, virtuous, vicious, human development lopsided, and economic growth lopsided. Virtuous cycle refers to strong human development leading to strong economic growth, which in turn leads to strong growth. In the vicious cycle, poor human development leads to poor economic growth, which further depresses human development. In human development lopsided, strong human development is associated with weak economic growth. In economic growth lopsided, weak human development is associated with strong economic growth.

Arrangement and Relevance of the Chapter

This chapter discusses the north-eastern situation in the above outlined framework along with its various implications. All these are done using whatever limited data is available from secondary sources. Finally, based on the analysis and its implications, the chapter comes up with some relevant suggestions for policy and debate. Further, in the context of the North-East, not many systematic studies have been undertaken, even at the macro level, examining the issue of human development in a framework as stated above, along with a poignant examination of its implications for the economy and society of this region. In this respect, our endeavour is modest, but critical.

In this chapter we have used the definition of economic growth outlined earlier. To be exact, it refers to the growth rate of net state domestic product (NSDP). As far as human development is concerned, an ideal measurement of it should include its multiple dimensions and indicators. However, constructing such an index would be difficult at this stage, particularly in the context of the North-East where there is paucity of data. Hence, to make the analysis relevant, we have adopted the human development index (HDI) values computed by the Planning Commission and presented in GoI 2002. It is pertinent to mention here that these figures relate to the year 1991. The third concept, exclusion, has been explained and shown in terms of poverty and inequality along with measures of some basic economic infrastructural facilities (that is, roads, electricity, irrigation, banking, and credit).

ECONOMIC GROWTH AND THE NORTH-EAST

Table 14.1 clearly shows that both in the 1980s and 1990s, the average growth rates in NSDP for the region as a whole, have been lower than that of the country. In the 1990s, the situation had worsened further. Whereas, for the country as a whole, the average growth rate has marginally increased from 5.5 in the 1980s to 5.8 in the 1990s, for the north-eastern region, it has decreased from 4.4 to 3.6 during the same period. Needless to mention here, that the 1990s were the period of liberalization, privatization, and globalization. The situation has grossly deteriorated in Assam. Except for Arunachal Pradesh and Tripura in all other states growth rates in NSDP have not exhibited any difference during the last 20 years.

Table 14.1: Average Growth Rates in the North-East in 1980s and 1990s
(At Constant 1993–94 prices)

States in NER/ Country	Average Growth Rate	
	1980s	1990s
ARP	9.0	5.5
ASM	4.2	2.6
MAN	4.7	4.8
MEG	5.5	5.5
MIZ	*	*
TRP	5.3	8.5
NAG	8.4	8.5
NE REGION	4.4	3.6
INDIA	5.5	5.8

Note: * Data for Mizoram are not available in constant prices.
Sources: Author's calculations based on data in Domestic Product of States of India, EPW Research Foundation, Mumbai, 2003 and CSO, Government of India.

HUMAN DEVELOPMENT AND THE NORTH-EAST

Table 14.2 shows that in 1991, the HDI value for Manipur, Mizoram, Nagaland, and Tripura has been significantly higher than the all India average. In the urban sector, all the seven north-eastern states are having higher level of HDI compared to the all India level. This situation of low economic growth and comparatively higher human development when put in the framework of Ranis et al. 2004 (outlined earlier in this chapter) places the region in the human development lopsided category.

EXCLUSION AND THE NORTH-EAST

One of the fundamental and critical indicators and causes of absolute exclusion is poverty. Poverty cripples human beings in not allowing

Table 14.2: HD Indices for North-Eastern States, 1991

States in NER/Country	Rural		Urban		Combined	
	Value	Rank	Value	Rank	Value	Rank
ARP	0.300	7	0.572	5	0.328	7
ASM	0.326	6	0.555	6	0.348	6
MAN	0.503	1	0.618	4	0.536	2
MEG	0.332	5	0.624	3	0.365	5
MIZ	0.464	2	0.648	1	0.548	1
NAG	0.442	3	0.633	2	0.486	3
TRP	0.368	4	0.551	7	0.389	4
INDIA	0.340	–	0.511	–	0.381	–

Source: GoI (2002).

them to build and improve on their capabilities. It also severely squeezes their opportunities for work and participation. The magnitude and spread of poverty in the region is given in Table 14.3.

Table 14.3: Poverty Incidence in North-Eastern States at Different Periods

States in NER/ Country	Poverty incidence (HCR)			
	1983	1987–88	1993–94	1999–2000
ARP	14.53	26.04	37.10	21.09
ASS	41.51	37.45	41.45	36.82
MAN	22.74	13.11	15.55	10.75
MEG	33.73	31.39	21.26	4.96
MIZ	22.87	2.81	21.26	1.71
NAG	2.97	NA	4.26	0.14
TRI	37.05	22.31	1.69	14.71
NE REGION	38.91	32.96	21.29	29.70
INDIA	45.57	42.14	35.95	25.87

Source: Kharpuri (2004).

It can be observed from this table that the poverty incidence in the north-eastern region, vis-à-vis, the all India level was lower in 1983, 1987–88, and 1993–94. However, in 1999–2000, it is higher than the all India figure. The poverty situation in the rural sector in the region is given in Table 14.4.

From this table, it is obvious that while at the all India level, the rural poverty incidence has been diminishing continuously, in the north-eastern region it has fluctuated. It decreased from 41.46 in 1983 to 35.84 in 1987–88, and then increased suddenly to 39.54 in 1993–94

Table 14.4: Poverty Incidence in the Rural and Urban Sector of
North-East India, 1983–2000

States in NER/ Country	Poverty Incidence (HCR)							
	Rural				Urban			
	1983	1987–8	1993–4	1999–2000	1983	1987–8	1993–4	1999–2000
ARP	NA	26.43	41.20	22.50	14.53	16.22	6.05	5.06
ASS	43.30	39.75	45.20	40.18	22.14	11.45	7.93	7.23
MAN	25.61	15.81	18.86	14.11	14.74	6.52	6.89	0.53
MEG	38.52	36.18	24.37	5.96	7.67	2.04	1.81	NA
MIZ	27.67	3.93	6.24	2.85	2.44	0.62	1.81	NA
NAG	NA	NA	2.29	0.21	2.97	NA	NA	NA
TRI	39.28	23.73	23.63	16.67	21.91	11.22	NA	2.16
NE REGION	41.46	35.84	39.54	33.31	18.45	8.89	6.04	4.63
INDIA	46.51	42.40	36.85	26.50	42.32	41.16	31.70	23.98

Source: Kharpuri (2004).

and again fell to 33.31 in 1999–2000. Further, rural poverty incidence
in the north-east in both the periods, that is, 1993–94 and 1999–2000,
has been higher than the all India situation. This brings out the fact
that the North-East, in general, and rural North-East, in particular,
reveals increased deprivation vis-à-vis the rest of India. The urban poverty situation reveals a different picture. Urban poverty incidence has
consistently and significantly been lower in the north-eastern region
as compared to all India. This incidence also shows a continuous fall
in this region. Therefore, poverty in the north-east is basically a rural
phenomenon.

Inequality in the region, as measured by the Gini coefficient, has
increased during the period from 1993–94 to 1999–2000 (Table 14.5).
What worries one is the fact that this inequality has increased during
this period in all the north-eastern states, except Meghalaya.

Deficiency of basic infrastructure is both a cause and manifestation
of exclusion. Looked at from this angle, availability and, thus, access
to physical infrastructure in the region is limited vis-à-vis all India.
From Table 14.6, it is obvious that the availability of four selected basic
infrastructure namely, surfaced roads, electricity, irrigation, and banking in the region is much less compared to the country as a whole.

READING AND IMPLICATIONS
Theoretically, there is no conflict between economic growth, inclusion, and human development. Economic Growth (EG) implies

Table 14.5: Incidence of Inequality among the North-Eastern States,
1983 to 1999–2000

States in NER/ Country	Inequality Incidence (Gini Coefficient)			
	1983	1987–88	1993–94	1999–2000
ARP	NA	0.3212	0.2788	0.2907
ASS	0.2609	0.3100	0.2899	0.3125
MAN	0.1901	0.1685	0.1569	0.2190
MEG	0.2830	0.3064	0.2451	0.2126
MIZ	0.2058	0.1992	0.1819	0.2321
NAG	NA	0.1609	0.2010	0.2215
TRI	0.3261	0.2856	0.2829	0.2953
NE REGION	0.2702	0.2940	0.2793	0.2962
INDIA	0.3392	0.3508	0.3414	0.3470

Source: Kharpuri (2004).

Table 14.6: Availability of Selected Infrastructure in the North-Eastern
Region vis-à-vis India

Infrastructure	Indicator Value			Indicator Value		
	Year	NER	India	Year	NER	India
Surfaced roads (per cent)	1982	18	47	1997	26	58
Villages electrified (per cent)	1980	19	45	2001	74	86
Net irrigated area as per cent to net cultivated area	1981	23	28	1997	21	38
Average population('000) per bank office	1981	32	19	2002	21	15

Source: Author's calculation based on data from NEC (1982), RBI (1987 and 2003).

improvement in the material well-being of people that are supposed
to promote better health, education, sanitation, and infrastructure to
all sections of the society. However, for the above mentioned social
and economic development to happen, the economy needs to grow
strongly. Sluggish rate of growth, as we have experienced in the
region in the last five decades, is unlikely to have a significant positive
impact on the marginalized sections of population. The alternative
strategy of development is to focus directly on social and economic
infrastructure facilities such as health, education, sanitation, roads,
power, banking, etc. Such a strategy followed in this region over the
last couple of decades, has brought in mixed success. In the front of
social development, the region has done well in education and health
services. This has helped many of the states in the region to have better
HDI ranking vis-à-vis the country. However, on the front of inequality,

poverty, and provision of fundamental economic infrastructure, the region has not been able to deliver as expected.

The interpretation of this situation may be that the conventional measure of HDI, developed by United Nations Development Programme (UNDP) or Planning Commission of India, by default, does not include many of the other variables of human development which could be important determinants of growth in the context of the north-eastern region. For example, security fulfillment is an important challenge in the region. There is absolute security deficit that does not encourage free flow of investment, particularly private investment of significance to the region. Secondly, government failure is widespread and substantial. Government failure and mundane material development sponsored by the state have created a vested interest group in the north-eastern society, which has monopolized the benefits of state-driven investment and developmental works. This is because of this groups' proximity to the political and administrative power centre. This group deliberately has excluded the vast majority of common people from the fruits of growth and development by depriving them socially and economically. This is a case of degeneration in the north-eastern society and is against its trusted age old social capital of community living and sharing. Although, there are cases at the country level which show that social development does not necessarily promote economic growth (for example, Kerala), but what is worrisome for the North-East is the presence of this divergence with the added presence of the institution of exclusion as discussed above.

Further, the region is struggling hard to adjust to its various social tensions and conflicts, including the threat of terrorism and insurgency. In such a situation, human development lopsided category status, along with the increasing social exclusion, does not augur well for the region. When:

(1) employment generation for the educated youth was very slow in the 1990s because of the sluggish per capita economic growth (1 per cent, adjusted against an average growth of population of 2.6 per cent);

(2) the capacity of the public sector to generate more jobs sinking because of the imperatives of liberalization; and

(3) the local youth have the habit of not migrating in large numbers to other parts of the country where jobs are available; all these could bring added tensions into the social fabric of the north-

eastern society, thereby, further aggravating the already stressed situation. This may take away whatever positives have happened in the field of human development. In such an eventuality, the region may fall into the vicious human development-EG cycle.

THE WAY OUT

The above analysis leads us to suggest some measures to be undertaken to ameliorate the state in which the region finds itself embroiled. Promoting economic growth is the immediate need of the hour. This can primarily happen by accelerating industrialization and having greater value addition therein. However, industrialization in the region is held hostage to:

(1) limited access to and availability of physical infrastructure (credit, transport, communications, power, and irrigation to name a few) including organized marketing;
(2) lack of genuine entrepreneurship culture;
(3) security deficit; and
(4) bad governance.

Now to provide for this infrastructure, governments in the region have to play a proactive role along with developmental NGOs. On the entrepreneurship front, since dearth of genuine entrepreneurs is largely because of certain existing socio-cultural value systems and arrangements in the north-eastern society (for example, system of proxy entrepreneurship, easy money culture, risk avoidance, immobility, etc.) these need to be changed with time. The best way to get it done is to promote Self-Help Groups movement and effective participation. To overcome the third limitation, that is, security deficit, reorientation in the value systems is a must. This is a job to be done primarily by the civil society, academia, government, and peer groups. In the same line, better governance can be provided when governance in the states in the region comes under effective scanning of the civil society, academia, NGOs, and people at large. The argument that 'we need to establish peace first to have growth as a follow up', is gradually becoming elusive. This needs to be reformulated as 'invest first to have growth, without waiting for peace to prevail'. However, this does not exclude the possibility of working simultaneously on promotion of peace and growth in the region.

REFERENCES

Government of India (GoI) 2002. *National Human Development Report 2001*, Planning Commission, New Delhi.

Kharpuri, O.J. 2004. 'Poverty, Inequality, and Human Development in the North-Eastern Region of India', Unpublished Ph.D thesis, North-Eastern Hill University (NEHU), Shillong.

Lin, Y.J. 2004. 'Development Strategies for Inclusive Growth in Developing Asia', Working Paper No. E 2004007, Peking University, China.

North-Eastern Council (NEC) 1982. *Basic Statistics of North-Eastern Region 1982*, Ministry of Home Affairs, Government of Shillong.

Panda, B. 1998. 'Status of and Sociological Constraints to Industrial Development in Arunachal Pradesh', in B. Dutta Ray (eds), *Sociological Constraints to Industrial Development in North-East*, Concept Publishers, New Delhi.

Ranis, G., F. Stewart, and A. Ramirez 2004. 'Economic Growth and Human Development', in Sakiko Fukuda-Parr and A.K. Shiva Kumar (eds), *Readings in Human Development*, Oxford University Press, New Delhi.

Reserve Bank of India (RBI) 2003. *Basic Statistical Returns of Scheduled Commercial Banks in India, 2002*, Vol. 31, Mumbai.

—— 1987. *Banking Statistics—Basic Statistical Returns, 1980–81*, Vol. 11, Mumbai.

Sen, A. 2000. *Development as Freedom*, Oxford University Press, New Delhi.

Umdor, S. and B. Panda 2007. 'Economic Infrastructure in North-East India: An Analysis', *Man and Development*, Vol. 29, No. 1, pp. 113–30.

15

Non-Governmental Organizations and Participatory Development

BISWAMBHAR PANDA

INTRODUCTION

The economic growth India witnessed during the last decade has been stupendous. There has been steady rise of the Indian economy due to its liberal economic policy, rapidly expanding consumer market, and changing consumer behaviour. The tertiary as well as secondary sectors of the country have witnessed an upward swing. The growth in Gross Domestic Product (GDP), decline of poverty, creation and availability of job opportunities, and rise in the purchasing capacity of the people suggest that Indian economy is on track and it is booming. However, despite this growth, apprehensions still loom large that the fruits of growth and development have been confined to some sections of society.

The complex Indian society comprising diverse castes, communities, ethnic groups, minority groups, and disadvantaged groups make the development process more challenging. The existing social hierarchy affects the equal distribution of its resources and the deprived sections (lower castes, women, disabled, poor, etc.) struggle to get their due because of the social stigma ascribed to them. Besides, the elite sections within the disadvantaged groups have benefited the most, thereby creating 'inequality within inequality'. There has been regional disparity in development in the form of urban and rural, hills and plains, and west and the east. The prevalence of illiteracy, poverty, and widespread endemic diseases have made scholars and planners to think hard on development issues.

Though the responsibility lies with the nation state for the overall development of its citizens, due to the complex and heterogeneous structure of Indian society, it warrants contributions from various quarters towards integrated development. Efforts are required from all three domains, such as state, corporate, and civil society to achieve the desired objective of integrated and sustained development. India has a democratic polity not averse to social activism. The corporate sector in India is becoming socially responsible and there has been a spurt of civil society organizations, that is, Non-Government Organizations (NGOs), in recent times. These three vibrant sectors need to work in tandem to mitigate the existing socio-economic problems in the country. Therefore, one can expect the convergence of strategies to meet the common objective, for example, social and integrated development in India where all these three actors are required to make concerted efforts to ensure that all the sections of the society have been involved and benefit from the ensuing growth. The state with its machinery, corporate sector with its agencies, and the civil society with its constituents have respective roles to play. One sector's limitation could be another sector's opportunity to encash its strength and, thus, a complimentary approach to yield better results. For example, government may seek support from NGOs in the implementation of their programmes and also getting feedback for programme innovation and renovation at the grassroots level. Similarly, corporate sector, to stand up to their social responsibility role, may wish to collaborate with both the government and NGOs to reach out to the needy. But all these actors, in order to achieve their objective, need to promote people's involvement and participation in their developmental programmes and schemes which are meant for the welfare of the people. Put differently, while working for the people is important, working 'with the people' is more important. Micro-developmental plans and people's active participation therein seem to be crucial in promoting social development, where the marginalized sections also enjoy the benefits of development.

In the above context, this chapter, following the people-centred development approach, highlights the role of NGOs as an active actor of the civil society in evolving peoples' participation in the process of development. Drawing evidence from literature, a modest attempt has been made to demonstrate the strategies and methods adopted by some of the successful NGOs operating in India in empowering the masses, specially the disadvantaged groups to take active participation in the developmental process and, further, to advocate the adoption of the similar strategies for the North East.

PEOPLE-CENTRED DEVELOPMENT

In the words of Korten (1990: 225), 'The conventional vision that has driven development policy and action equates progress with short-term increases in economic activity. It gives little regard to considerations of justice, sustainability or inclusiveness'. Hence, there is a need for an alternative development vision that emphasizes on the local ownership, and use of local resources to meet local needs. It calls for economic and political democratization which are important for economic and political justice (ibid). People-centred development, which 'put the people first' in the developmental process, strive for inclusive and sustained development. Nerfin (1986, cited in Finger 1994) argued that during the crises of the nature namely economic, financial, ecological, social, cultural, ideological, and political, there is a need for the people to join hands together to get rid of these. There exists an immediate and autonomous power, that is, people's power, contrary to state power, asserts Nerfin. The citizens' associations or movements that do not exercise governmental or economic power constitute the third system. Therefore, the third system can be seen as an expression of people's autonomous power. According to Korten (1990, cited in Finger 1994: 56) citizens' movements play four critical roles:

1. Advocacy—which includes redefining policies, transforming institutions, and helping people to define, internalize, and also actualize a people-centred development vision ;
2. System monitoring;
3. protesting—that facilitates reconciliation with justice; and
4. Implementing development programmes.

Commenting on third system politics, Finger (1994) asserts that third system politics leads to people-centred development. He formulated the following characteristics/principles of people-centred development. First, sovereignty resides with the people, who are the real social actors of positive change; second, to exercise their sovereignty and assume responsibility for their development and their communities, the people must control their own resources, have access to relevant information, and have the means to make the government officials accountable; and third, those who assist the people with their development must recognize that it is they who are participating in support of the people's agenda and not the reverse (ibid: 57–8). Hence, third system politics focuses on increasing people's participation in decision making at different levels of society. Finger advocates further on collective learning and teaching, wherein villages, communities, and cities could be more appropriate learning units considered to be appropriate bodies who can promote traditional problem-solving strategies. 'Teaching and preaching ready-made solutions to individuals must be replaced by collective, vertical, horizontal, and cross disciplinary learning' (ibid: p.64). From the above formulations, it is clear that emphasis has been given to development which is people-centred.

CIVIL SOCIETY, NGOs, AND DEVELOPMENT

Baviskar (2005: 141) asserts that a vibrant and lively civil society is the foundation of modern-open-democratic polity and NGOs are the life-force for the civil society. Civil society, in general, may be referred to that segment of society that interacts with the state, influences the state, and yet is distinct from the state. Civil Society, which remains outside the other two domains, that is, government and business sectors, gets strengthened by intermediary institutions and by the voluntary spirit of the people. According to Beteille (2005: 285), 'the interest in voluntary action, voluntary movements, and voluntary associations has been given a new lease of life by the concern for the creation or revival of civil society, particularly in the countries of Asia, Africa, and Latin America'. According to some modern theories of associationalism, voluntary associations:

1. provide local opportunities for representation;
2. offer opportunities for active citizenship by encouraging participation and, thus, contribute to civil culture;
3. contain the spread of bureaucracy in political organizations; and
4. foster pluralism and diversity (Abercrombie, et al. 2000, cited in Jayaram 2005: 22).

The NGOs along with other civil society actors may be seen as the third important force after the state and the business sector. The constituents of civil society, that is, its organizations and associations, can perform various educative and advocacy roles. And NGOs, through their empowerment programmes at the community level, creation of institutions, and organizations at the grassroots level, can contribute significantly to the development process. They can also provide important feedback to policy debates and planning. NGOs are believed to be endowed with the voluntary and altruistic spirit; and their non-profit (not-for-profit) nature makes them distinct from other sectors. These provide added advantage for them to carry out developmental programmes and projects in a more cost-effective way.

There are different kinds of NGOs namely, process-oriented and product-oriented, national and international, and grassroots, who continue to carry out development programmes at different levels and contribute towards development and change. Owing to its complex nature, the scholars have provided different definitions and classifications for NGOs. The acronyms such as Voluntary Organizations (VOs), Voluntary Development Organizations (VDOs), Action Groups (AG), etc. are used for NGOs in literature. Shah and Chaturvedi (1983) categorize them into three, such as, techno-managerial, reformist, and radical (cited in Baviskar 2005: 139). NGOs, as they claim, make efforts to ensure quality, cost-effectiveness, and accountability due to their people-friendly and people-centred approaches. Over the last couple of decades, there has been a phenomenal rise of NGOs in India. The rise and growth of NGOs in India may be attributed to various factors, such as:

(i) shrinking role of the state (aftermath of globalization);
(ii) growing involvement of enlightened and enthusiastic middle class in the NGO sector;
(iii) professionalism displayed by NGOs towards reaching out to masses and delivering goods;
(iv) recognition from the state, due to pressure from international declarations, summits/protocols;
(v) increasing faith of donor agencies in the NGOs (because of ineffective governance by the state); and
(vi) liberal democratic regime, permissive of activism in the civil society (Panda and Pattnaik, 2005: 42).

There are over 14,000 NGOs registered under the Foreign Contributions Regulation Act and there may be over 30,000 NGOs in India (Baviskar 2005: 139). The United Nations Development Programme (UNDP) *Human Development Report 1993* estimates that NGOs manage to reach 250 million of the poorest people. According to the World Bank, NGOs in India spend to the tune of US$ 520 million a year (Dharmarajan 2001). Owing to their rise, growth, and increasing involvement in development activities, and due to their emergence as one of the significant intermediary institutions between state and the people, NGOs have created a niche for themselves. Even though many of them will fade and disappear, but as a social phenomenon, NGOs are here to stay (Beteille 2005: 290).

PARTICIPATORY DEVELOPMENT AND NGOs

The participation of people refers to people's involvement in various spheres, that is, economic, social, cultural, and political processes. It becomes more significant in the context of human development that advocates development 'for the people'. And it can be fulfilled by the people themselves. When people participate in large numbers in developmental activities, it results in greater utilization of human resources and capacities. This, in turn, enhances socio-economic development. Participation of the people can promote self-confidence and they become aware of their rights and responsibilities. Hence, participation of the people may be seen as an instrument of empowerment. Poor and disadvantageous sections should be given opportunities to participate actively in social development. Basic health care, income-generating activities for the poor, and strengthening of social organizations are considered as the basis of social development policy (Dharmarajan 2001). The decentralization of development can ensure the proper distribution of development where local level institutions have greater roles to play. The NGOs, through their advocacy and awareness programmes, tend to motivate people to participate in these spheres.

Participatory development is a process through which people become more aware of their creative potentials and start taking initiatives to realize these. Development occurs when human beings recognize and realize their potential and responsibilities. In participatory mode of development, people are able to identify their own needs. This increases the efficiency of development activities and programmes and, in turn, it helps mobilizing local resources and hidden skills. For instance, if the people who participate in decision making are the poor, the contributions they make would better reflect their problems and eventually induce positive attitude among them. This can have a spiral effect on others, who are disadvantaged groups in the society. The initiative of a farmer in a village to promote kitchen garden or herbal garden to earn his/her livelihood could act as stimulus for other villagers. Béteille (1969) asserted that while economic growth helps reducing social inequality, social values and norms are significant towards understanding of the existence of social inequality. The large scale participation of people in a development programme may create solidarity cutting across caste, ethnic boundaries, and motivate them further to work collectively. This is important, because it will not only bring economic benefits but also may create social responsibility and arouse collectivism among the people. Public participation is, therefore, a key component of human development. It is through participation people can be aware of their rights and responsibilities. This, in the process enhances collective action, which can be transformed into effective mobilization of the people and end up with social movements to yield social transformation and change.

It is worthwhile to cite some of the glaring examples of people's initiatives endowed with voluntarism which have been able to bring transformative changes in the society. This has been possible due to sheer committed participation of the people in developmental process, irrespective of the social strata they belong to. Ralegan Siddhi, a village in Maharashtra was transformed into a model village due to the people's initiatives. The village has successfully achieved 'growth with equality'. The efforts were made to unite the village by dispensing with differences based on caste and class. The people contributed free labour (*Shramdan*) where one adult from every household contributed his/her labour without wages. The village has successfully campaigned against alcoholism, dowry, and superstition (Awasthi 1998: 74–91). The persistence work of National Institute for Rural Integrated Development (NIRID), a voluntary agency, has successfully motivated the *adivasi* community of Thane, Maharashtra. Through participation of people and massive plantation and watershed programmes, it has successfully arrested environmental degradation (Patel 1998).

NGOs AND PARTICIPATORY METHODS

In the 1970s, the trends in NGO activism in India were centred on agrarian issues. In the 1980s, the focus was shifted towards empowerment, while in the 1990s the focus was on gender and environment. Issues such as social forestry, soil conservation and watershed development, consumer protection, etc., also gained prominence during this phase (Pandey 1991). And today, much emphasis is given to participatory and social development. The participatory modes of intervention deployed by NGOs help bringing people together and chalk out strategies based on indigenous knowledge and experience. The participatory methods such as Participatory Rural Appraisal (PRA), Rapid Rural Appraisal (RRA) are in vogue in development programmes and practices (Chambers 1995). 'PRA is an approach and method for learning about rural life and conditions from, with, and by rural people'. (ibid: 1) Participation generates diversity and provides opportunities to villagers to interpret, apply, and also invent methods for themselves (ibid: 15). PRA has been in vogue in diverse areas of development such as community management of common property resources, child labour, hunger and food, security, poverty assessment, health issues, farmers' attitude and cropping pattern, forest issues such as joint forestry management (JFM), social forestry (SF), etc. Some of the NGOs who have pioneered PRA are MYRADA and Action Aid based in Bangalore, SPEECH at Madurai, and Youth for Action in Hyderabad, etc., and among the international NGOs, Intercooperation in Berne, and Action Aid in London were prominent (ibid: 8). Through participatory approaches, NGOs have started implementing various rural development schemes.

WORKING TOWARDS EMPOWERMENT PROCESS

The process of empowerment may be referred to as power that controls one's own life. According to Mohanty (1995: 1434), 'Empowerment as an objective of economic development should be a welcome addition to the democratic discourse'. The process of empowerment transforms the poor in several ways. It can instill self-confidence among the disadvantaged groups. It enables them to raise questions about the reasons of their poverty and sufferings. The awareness created enthuses them to raise their voice and grievances that takes the form of a collective force. The collective awareness and confidence place them in an advantageous position to bargain, and push for their development and uplift. Once people are empowered, they take more initiatives and engage themselves in mobilizing resources. The empowerment process becomes sustainable only through the creation of sustainable community-based organizations. Like other civil society constituents, the NGOs/voluntary organizations can contribute in this process of empowerment, particularly by raising awareness among the people on various social problems and the opportunities and schemes available to them. Youth for Action, based in south India, has worked in some villages with *harijans* to enhance their confidence and capability (ibid:

42). Micro-finance schemes have been propagated by some NGOs to finance the poor. SEWA, through its micro finance scheme, has been able to muster support and interest from poor women towards capital formation. This has proved the myth that 'poor as a burden on the economy, needing endless subsidies' as wrong (Bhatt 1998: 159). Gram Vikas, an NGO based in Berhampur, Orissa, is promoting community participation through rural health and environment programmes. It is also working towards creating alternative sources of employment and income-generating programmes and constantly encouraging people to save money, which they can use at the time of crisis. It also organizes training programmes for the youth so that they can acquire basic skills on masonry, carpentry, maintenance of electrical appliances, etc., and eke out their livelihood (Gram Vikas Annual Report 1998–99).

NGOs IN NORTH-EAST INDIA

NGOs in the north-eastern region, as intermediary organizations, have significant roles to play. As catalysts, they can instill self-confidence among the people; as a facilitator, they can play advocacy roles and as an agent of development, they can promote people's participation in their development projects. In the process they can form different people's institutions and organizations such as youth clubs, women groups, old age homes, etc. They can also initiate various awareness building mechanisms like village meetings, poster campaigns, organizing rallies, etc., against social problems such as domestic violence against women, drug addiction and alcoholism, in particular. Grassroots NGOs can potentially play significant roles in crucial areas of development such as health, micro finance, and agricultural sector, particularly in floriculture and horticulture at the grassroots level. Awareness programmes need to be carried out vigorously, which in turn help people to understand their problems better and also come up with innovative ideas to solve these problems. For instance, despite receiving abundant rainfall, some areas of the North-East linger with shortage of water for domestic use during winter months. This area of concern can very well be controlled with people's innovative methods of rainwater harvesting. Pisciculture and poultry farming could be viable sources of income for poor villagers. Cottage industries can generate income opportunities at local levels, and local skill and expertise could be utilized and people can engage themselves to make various products from available materials such as wood, bamboo, grass, etc. Vocational training needs to be conducted for village youth and women, which may provide opportunities to improve their financial condition. Formation of Self-Help Groups (SHGs) can help to a great extent to address rural poverty, health issues, and the issues relating to environmental protection.

However, due to lack of empirical studies and documentation, the role of the grassroots NGOs in the North-East could not be outlined in the present chapter. Whether these NGOs apply participatory approaches at the local level needs to be empirically investigated and analysed. Nevertheless, greater responsibility lies on these NGOs to address people's issues and employ participatory strategies. These NGOs can be instrumental in creating SHGs to address socio-economic problems that the people encounter in this region.

CONCLUSION

Participatory development can ensure integrated development where all sections of society would be involved and benefit. This not only brings about economic growth but also dissipates the social inequality in the areas of operation. The micro approaches along with people-centred development objectives can bring considerable dividends by resolving conflicts, avoiding programme uncertainties, and evolving synergy among the key actors of the society. Participatory development may not ensure the development for all people but it certainly creates confidence among people and, most importantly, it provides opportunities to people to share their ideas and knowledge. A development plan armed with indigenous practices and native wisdom can accelerate the developmental process at the grassroots level.

Though NGOs are not the only force within civil society to work towards inclusive growth, they are certainly a force to reckon with in the development domain. Through the application of different people-centred approaches and strategies, the NGOs can inch towards this objective despite the apprehensions raised on their accountability and sustainability.

REFERENCES
Abercrombie, N.S. Hill and B.S. Turner 2000. *The Penguin Dictionary of Sociology*, Penguin Books, London.

Awasthi, R. 1998. 'Rural Development through People's Mobilization: A Case Study of Ralegan Siddhi', in M.L. Dantwala, Harsh Sethi, and Pravin Visaria (eds), *Social Change through Voluntary Action*, Sage, New Delhi, pp. 74–91.

Baviskar, B.S. 2005. 'Non-Governmental Organisations and Civil Society in India', in N. Jayaram (ed.), *On Civil Society: Issues and Perspectives,* Sage, New Delhi, pp. 137–49.

Béteille, A. 2005. 'Civil Society and the Good Society', in N. Jayaram (ed.), *On Civil Society: Issues and Perspectives,* Sage, New Delhi, pp. 273–93.

—— 1969. 'The Decline of Social Inequality?', in André Béteille (ed.), *Social Inequality,* Penguin Books, Harmondsworth, England, pp. 362–80.

Bhatt, E.R. 1998. 'Empowering the Poor through Micro-finance: The SEWA Bank', in M.L. Dantwala, Harsh Sethi, and Pravin Visaria (eds), *Social Change through Voluntary Action,* Sage, New Delhi, pp. 1146–61.

Chambers, R. 1995. 'Rural Appraisal: Rapid, Relaxed, and Participatory', in Amitava Mukherjee, (ed.), *Participatory Rural Appraisal: Methods and Applications in Rural Planning,* Vikas Publishing House, New Delhi, pp. 1–63.

Dharmarajan, S. 2001. *NGOs as Prime Movers: Sectoral Action for Social Development,* Kanishka Publishers, New Delhi.

Finger, M. 1994. 'NGOs and Transformations: Beyond Social Movement Theory', in T. Princen and M. Finger (eds), *Environmental NGOs in World Politics: Linking the Local and the Global,* Routledge, London, pp. 48–66.

Gram Vikas Annual Report, 1998–99. Berhampur, Ganjam, Orissa.

Jayaram, N., 2005. 'Civil Society: An Introduction to the Discourse', in N. Jayaram (ed.) *On Civil Society: Issues and Perspectives,* Sage, New Delhi, pp. 15–42.

Korten, D. 1990. *Getting to the 21ˢᵗ century: Voluntary Action and the Global Agenda,* Kumarian Press, West Hartford.

Mohanty, M. 1995. 'On the Concept of Empowerment', *Economic and Political Weekly,* Vol. XXX, No. 24, pp. 1434–36.

Panda, B. and B.K. Pattnaik 2005. 'Effectiveness of Grassroots NGOs: An Empirical Exploration', *Man and Development,* Vol. XXVII, No. 2, pp. 39–66.

Pandey, S.R. 1991. *Community Action for Social Justice: Grassroots Organisations in India,* Sage, New Delhi.

Patel, P. 1998. 'Participatory Development in Adivasi Villages: Experiences of NIRID, 1979–1997', in M.L. Dantwala (ed.) *Social Change through Voluntary Action,* Sage, New Delhi, pp. 113–29.

Shah, G. and H.R. Chaturvedi 1983. *Gandhian Approach to Rural Development: The Valod Experiment,* Ajanta Prakashan, New Delhi.

16

Inter-District Disparities in Meghalaya
A Human Development Approach

PURUSOTTAM NAYAK AND SANTANU RAY

'...something cannot be improved if it is not measured.'
—Edwin J. Feulner Preface: *2007 Index of Economic Freedom*

INTRODUCTION

Meghalaya is one of the seven north-eastern states that have shown an unimpressive performance during the 1980s and 1990s, in terms of both economic and human development. In addition, the regional dimensions of development in the state are also disturbing. A significant level of disparity exists in levels of income and features of human development amongst the districts/regions. However, to attain a decent level of human development in the state as a whole, the backward districts need special attention. For that, one should have a complete picture of inter-district disparities in the levels of different components of human development. This study, based on a UGC Major Research Project (Nayak and Thomas 2007b), attempts to identify the nature and level of disparities amongst the districts/ regions and to trace the causes of the relatively poor performances of some districts. By identifying the deficiencies and disparities, we can provide a useful basis for reorienting priorities and public actions towards the goal of evolving a people-centred development planning for Meghalaya.

The remainder of this chapter proceeds as follows. After this brief introduction, we present the features of the state from secondary sources. Then, we work out the Human Development Index (HDI) for the state as a whole with district/regional level indices, followed by some statistical measures of the level of disparities that exists in Meghalaya. And finally, the chapter is concluded with key findings and policy recommendations.

STATE PROFILE FROM SECONDARY SOURCES

General Features

Meghalaya is one of the smallest states in India. It is predominantly a tribal state of the North-East. The state is surrounded in the east and north by the state of Assam and in the west and south by Bangladesh. It is a hilly strip in the eastern part of the country, and about 300 km long from east to west and 100 km wide. The state lies between 85°49' and 92°53' east longitude and 20°1' and 20°5' north latitude. It has a geographical area of 22,429 sq km. It covers 0.7 per cent of the total area of the country and 8.6 per cent area of the north-eastern region. However, area-wise it is the third biggest state in the region after Arunachal Pradesh and Assam. It has a rising and falling topography. About 37 per cent of the total area of the state is forests. The state is subject to the vagaries of monsoon. The climate of the state, though, varies with altitude, it is moderate and humid. With an average annual rainfall as high as 1,200 cm in some areas, Meghalaya is the wettest state of India. The state gets adequate rainfall throughout the year and the annual rainfall ranges between 2,000 to 5,000 mm. It is a storehouse of economic minerals. The major minerals that are presently exploited are coal, limestone, clay, and sillimanite.

Meghalaya is mainly the homeland of the three major ethnic groups, namely, the *khasi*, the *jaintia*, and the *garo*. About 45 per cent of the total population in the state belongs to khasi, 32.5 per cent garo, and the rest 22.5 per cent are from various communities such as bengali, assamese, nepali/gurkha, hindi speaking, *koch*, *rabha*, *mikir*, etc.

Originally the state had two districts and three sub-divisions. As per 2001 Census (North-Eastern Council 2005), the state now has seven districts, eight sub-divisions, 39 community development blocks, 16 towns, and 5,780 villages. Most of these administrative units starting from villages to districts are very small. The seven districts in the state are quite different from each other in various respects. South Garo Hills is the smallest district having an area of 1,887 sq km, as against the biggest district West Khasi Hills that has an area of 5,247 sq km. The biggest district covers about 24 per cent of the total area of the state, whereas the smallest district covers only 8 per cent.

Demographic Features

Table 16.1 presents the district-wise demographic features of Meghalaya, mostly from Census 2001 (North-Eastern Council 2005).

Table 16.1: Selected Demographic Features for Districts of Meghalaya

Districts	Area (Sq Km)	Population (in lakhs)	Density	Sex Ratio	Urbanization Rate
(1)	(2)	(3)	(4)	(5)	(6)
East Khasi Hills	2748	6.61	241	984	42.1
	(4)	(1)	(1)	(2)	(1)
West Khasi Hills	5247	2.94	56	971	11.4
	(1)	(4)	(6)	(4)	(3)
Ri-Bhoi	2448	1.93	79	942	6.8
	(6)	(6)	(4)	(7)	(7)
Jaintia Hills	3819	2.96	77	979	8.4
	(2)	(3)	(5)	(3)	(6)
East Garo Hills	2603	2.47	95	960	14.5
	(5)	(5)	(3)	(5)	(2)
West Garo Hills	3677	5.16	140	988	11.3
	(3)	(2)	(2)	(1)	(4)
South Garo Hills	1887	.99	53	943	8.7
	(7)	(7)	(7)	(6)	(5)
Meghalaya	22429	23.06	103	975	19.6

Note: Numbers in parenthesis indicate ranks of the districts in the relevant indicators.
Source: North-Eastern Council (2005).

For easy reference, the rankings of the districts, in terms of indices, are also reported in parenthesis. In terms of area, among the seven districts in Meghalaya, West Khasi Hills is the biggest district, followed by Jaintia Hills with about 23 per cent, and 17 per cent of total geographical area, while Ri-Bhoi and South Garo Hills are the smallest in size with 11 and 8.5 per cent, respectively. Population-wise, East Khasi Hills and West Garo Hills are the most populous districts with about 29 per cent and 22 per cent of state population, while Ri-Bhoi and South Garo Hills again occupy the last two ranks, with roughly 8 and 4 per cent. These two columns in Table 16.1, being the sole determinants of the density of population, create a significant range of differences in density. The highest density is recorded in East Khasi Hills (241); followed by West

Garo Hills (140); again, West Khasi Hills (56) and South Garo Hills (53) are sparsely populated districts of Meghalaya. However, in terms of sex ratio, the matrilineal state shows a wide range of variation. With the state average at 975, the highest sex ratio in favour of women is reported in the West Garo Hills (988), followed by East Khasi Hills (984). Not surprisingly, the last two rankers in the state—South Garo Hills (943) and Ri-Bhoi (942) have sex ratios higher than the national average. The state registers poor urbanization rate (19.6) as compared to the national average (27.78). East Khasi Hills, where the state capital Shillong is located, has the highest urbanization rate of a little over 42 per cent, while in the recent district of Ri-Bhoi, less than even 7 per cent of total population live in urban settlements.

Selected Human Development Indicators

Table 16.2 summarizes secondary information regarding indicators that are often taken as determinants of human development. They include per capita net district domestic product, literacy rate, number of primary and middle schools per lakh population, number of beds in government hospitals, and that of doctors and nurses available for every one lakh population.

We first consider the per capita income during 1993–94 and 1999–2000 in columns 2 and 3 of Table 16.2. In the early 1990s, East Khasi Hills had the highest per capita income (Rs 8,943), followed by Jaintia Hills (Rs 7,748). West Khasi Hills (Rs 5,166) and East Garo Hills (Rs 5,148) were the poorest, occupying the last two ranks. In the late 1990s, the relative income scenario of the state changed marginally. The smallest district of the state—South Garo Hills emerged as the richest district pushing East Khasi Hills to second position. Similarly, a little improvement in per capita income by East Garo Hills changed its position in cooperative settings—West Khasi Hills was demoted to the status of the poorest district. However, in both the years, the list of richest and poorest three districts remained unchanged and the ratio of the income levels between the richest and poorest districts did not change significantly. The ratio, that in a sense denotes the level of income disparity, roughly deteriorated from 1.74 in 1993–93 to 1.83 in 1999–2000. The state lagged behind the national average in literacy. The literacy rates in Meghalaya (columns 4–8) varied from about 75 per cent in East Khasi Hills to 51 per cent in West Garo Hills. But the gap between male and female literacy rates in the state was

Table 16.2: Selected Human Development Indicators for Districts of Meghalaya

Districts/State	NDDP Per Capita (Rs) (at 1993–94 Prices)		Literacy Rate (%) (2001)					No. of Schools (Per Lakh Popn.) (1997–98)		Health Infrastructure (Per Lakh Popn.) (1998–99)		
	1993–94	1999–2000	Total	Male	Female	Rural	Urban	Primary	Middle	Beds in Govt. Hospitals	Doctor	Nurse
(1)	(2)	(3)	(4)	(5)	(6)	(7)	(8)	(9)	(10)	(11)	(12)	(13)
East Khasi Hills	8943 (1)	11477 (2)	74.7 (1)	74.9 (1)	74.6 (1)	63.7 (1)	88.6 (2)	119 (7)	30 (7)	181 (1)	27 (1)	33 (1)
West Khasi Hills	5166 (6)	6546 (7)	65.5 (2)	66.7 (3)	64.2 (2)	63.1 (2)	83.8 (5)	245 (3)	58 (2)	68 (4)	12 (4.5)	7 (6.5)
Ri-Bhoi	6003 (4)	7260 (4)	63.7 (3)	65.8 (4)	61.4 (3)	62.7 (3)	77.1 (7)	152 (6)	40 (4.5)	67 (5)	15 (3)	10 (4)
Jaintia Hills	7748 (2)	10938 (3)	52.8 (6)	50.1 (7)	55.5 (5)	48.9 (6)	91.1 (1)	174 (5)	34 (6)	93 (2)	16 (2)	14 (2)
East Garo Hills	5148 (7)	6774 (6)	61.6 (4)	67.2 (2)	55.7 (4)	57.9 (4)	82.2 (6)	246 (2)	40 (4.5)	73 (3)	11 (6)	9 (5)
West Garo Hills	5628 (5)	7232 (5)	50.8 (7)	57.1 (6)	44.4 (7)	46.1 (7)	85.2 (3)	208 (4)	43 (3)	65 (6)	12 (4.5)	11 (3)
South Garo Hills	7728 (3)	12005 (1)	55.2 (5)	61.6 (5)	48.6 (6)	52.3 (5)	83.9 (4)	345 (1)	63 (1)	61 (7)	8 (7)	7 (6.5)
Meghalaya	6894	9003	63.3	66.1	60.4	57.0	87.1	188	41	101	17	15

impressively low at 6 per cent, against the disturbing differences of about 22 per cent at the national level. The educational infrastructure, captured by the number of primary and secondary schools presented in Table 16.2 (columns 9 and 10) reveals that as such there was no clear association between number of schools and literacy rate. In terms of health infrastructure (Columns 11–13), East Khasi Hills determined the state average as all other districts fell below the state average.

STATUS OF HUMAN DEVELOPMENT IN MEGHALAYA

The new development paradigm intends to shift the attention away from the single indicator of per capita income to other attainments of decent human life, such as education, health, participation in decision making, etc., that people have reasons to value for enhancing their overall well-being and, more importantly, for enjoying freedom in their economic, social, and political life. Therefore, it was felt necessary to incorporate these attainments in the measurement of development. United Nations Development Programme (UNDP) had formulated the Human Development Index (HDI) to prepare *HDR 1990* and modified in *HDR 1994*, which takes three most critical aspects of human life, that is, income, education, and health into consideration. Their appearance in HDI with equal weights has in a sense revolutionized the measurement of development. Despite several limitations, HDI gained unprecedented popularity over the years due to its simplicity and plural attention. Planning Commission of India, however, departed slightly from UNDP methodology in preparing the *National Human Development Report* (*NHDR*) 2001 [GoI 2002]. The Planning Commission's formulation of computing HDI seems to be more pragmatic, especially in the context of India. However, the departure is less in terms of conceptualization of human development and more in the selection of indicators.

Data, Methodology, and Indicators

The primary data used in this chapter covers all the seven districts of the state. Data pertaining to seventeen development blocks of the state, has been selected at random, out of 39 blocks, taking five villages from each block. The sample constituted altogether 1,020 interviewed households to capture the level of well-being in different parts of the state. To compute the level of human development in Meghalaya (Nayak and Thomas 2007a) adopted the guideline provided by the Planning Commission. In the present study, if not mentioned otherwise, we followed the same methodology, that is, HDI = 1/3 (Economic Index + Education Index + Health Index). The indices for health and educational attainment were obtained by

$$\frac{X_{ij} - \text{Min}(F_i)}{\text{Max}(F_i) - \text{Min}(F_i)}$$

where, X_{ij} = Actual Value of component 'i' for district 'j',
Minimum F_{i} = Minimum Value Fixed for i^{th} component, and
Maximum F_{i} = Maximum Value Fixed for i^{th} component.

However, for economic attainment which captures the command over resources, the index was computed by

$$\frac{\log(Y_j) - \log\left\{\text{Min}(F_y)\right\}}{\log\left\{\text{Max}(F_y)\right\} - \log\left\{\text{Min}(F_y)\right\}}$$

where, Y_j = Actual value of economic attainment for district j,
Minimum F_y = Minimum Value Fixed for economic component, and
Maximum F_y = Maximum Value Fixed for economic component.

For an easy reference, the indicators and goal posts (Fixed Maximum and Minimum values of indicators) set for this chapter are summarized in the Box 16.1.

Box 16.1: Indicators of Human Development with Fixed Max-Min Values			
Attainment	*Indicators*	*Goal Posts*	
		Max	Min
Access to Decent Living	1. Inequality Adjusted Real Per Capita Consumption Expenditure (Rs/month)	325	65
Access to Knowledge	1. Adult Literacy Rate	100	0
	2. Intensity of Formal Education	7	0
Access to Long and Healthy Life	1. Life Expectancy at age 1**	80	50
	2. Infant Mortality Rate	120	0

*** As no estimation for this indicator could be made, life expectancy of Assam has been taken as representative figure for Meghalaya.*

Level of Human Development in Districts

The state, as a whole, has scored a HDI value, in our study as low as 0.404, which by any standard falls in the category of low human development group (Table 16.3). Hence, the state has a shortfall of about 60 per cent. The value has marginally improved from the score of 0.365;

assigned in *NHDR* (2001) to Meghalaya during 1991 and crosses the national average of 0.381 of 1991.

Table 16.3: Human Development Index for Meghalaya

Districts	Economic Index (Consumption Expenditure)	Educational Index	Health Index	HDI
(1)	(2)	(3)	(4)	(5)
East Khasi Hills	0.453 (2)	0.552 (6)	0.319 (2)	0.441 (2)
West Khasi Hills	0.252 (6)	0.560 (5)	0.196 (6)	0.336 (7)
Ri-Bhoi	0.353 (3)	0.570 (4)	0.263 (4)	0.395 (4)
Jaintia Hills	0.194 (7)	0.427 (7)	0.412 (1)	0.344 (6)
East Garo Hills	0.269 (5)	0.657 (3)	0.228 (5)	0.385 (5)
West Garo Hills	0.299 (4)	0.790 (2)	0.150 (7)	0.413 (3)
South Garo Hills	0.513 (1)	0.834 (1)	0.284 (3)	0.544 (1)
Meghalaya	0.334	0.615	0.262	0.404

Source: Nayak and Thomas (2007a).

The smallest district of the state—South Garo Hills has obtained the highest HDI value 0.544, which happens to be the only district in entire Meghalaya that crosses the benchmark of medium level of human development. West Khasi Hills has scored the lowest value 0.336. The best performer registers a huge shortfall of over 45 per cent while the poorest district, in terms of human development, has a shortfall of over 66 per cent. For the other five districts, the shortfall in HDI ranges between 45 to 66 per cent, which can simply be described as alarming not only in the global context but it seems disturbing even in the national perspective.

The contribution of three human development attainments to determine the value of the composite index is depicted in Figure 16.1. In all the seven districts, educational attainment is the highest contributor to determine the level of HDI. Except in Jaintia Hills, the economic index that contributes next to education and health attainment in all districts show a huge shortfall, which needs to be addressed immediately.

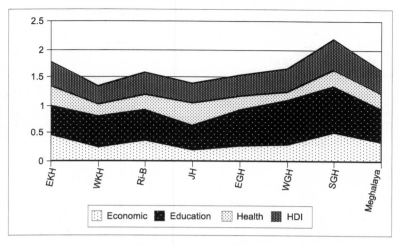

Figure 16.1: Index Values

Level of Human Development in Regions

Meghalaya attained statehood in 1972, covering three matrilineal districts of Assam: Khasi, Garo, and Jaintia Hills districts. In the post-statehood era, both Khasi and Garo districts were divided into three districts each, while Jaintia Hills remained untouched. In order to gain an idea of the regional dimension of human development scenario in Meghalaya, we computed the regional HDI which are population weighted average of the district-level HDI values. It is evident that no region in Meghalaya could touch the benchmark value (0.5) of HDI (Table 16.4).

Table 16.4: Regional Indices of Human Development

Regions	Economic Index (Consumption Expenditure)	Educational Index	Health Index	HDI
Khasi Hills	0.385	0.557	0.278	0.406
Garo Hills	0.315	0.757	0.188	0.420
Jaintia Hills	0.194	0.427	0.412	0.344
Meghalaya	0.334	0.615	0.262	0.404

Source: Computed from data of Nayak and Thomas (2007a).

Garo region topped the list with impressive educational and poorest health attainment. Khasi region topped in economic attainment and ranked second in the other two attainments. Though Jaintia region topped in health attainment, its poor performances in other two attainments placed the region in the last position in overall HDI value.

Linkages Between Income, Consumption, and Non-Income Components

The distinguishing feature of the Planning Commission formulation of computing HDI is that inequality adjusted per capita real Consumption Expenditure (Rs/month) has been taken as economic attainment instead of per capita income, commonly used in UNDP formulation. This particular departure was governed partially by the conceptual requirement of having an indicator which is a direct and better measure of economic well-being for the population (Malhotra 2007). There occurs a significant hike in the magnitude of economic attainment for every district resulting in a moderate increase in overall HDI values. However, nominal change of positions in comparative settings when income, instead of consumption expenditure, is used. To differentiate the same index, obtained from different economic indicators, we refer the composite index as HDI* when the same is constructed on the basis of income. This additional computation helped us to compare the level of human development of Meghalaya with other states in the preceding section.

It is evident from Figure 16.2 that the value of economic attainment for the state as a whole increased by over 51 per cent with a maximum increase in Jaintia Hills district of about 128 per cent, followed by West Khasi Hills of over 110 per cent. On the other hand, least impact of the change in the economic indicator was observed in West Garo Hills (12 per cent), followed by South Garo Hills (37 per cent). The result of these increases in economic indicators has been able to hike the overall composite index of the state by about 17 per cent. Figure 16.3 reveals that the biggest difference between HDI* and HDI was carried out in West Khasi Hills (28 per cent), followed by Jaintia Hills (24 per cent).

Table 16.5 reports the rank correlation coefficient between different indices and examines their level of significance. It shows that per capita income (Income*) is positively and significantly correlated with per capita Consumption Expenditure, Health, HDI, and HDI*. However, per capita Consumption Expenditure is not significantly correlated with health but with Education, HDI, and HDI*. While Education has positive and significant correlations with both HDI and HDI*, Health

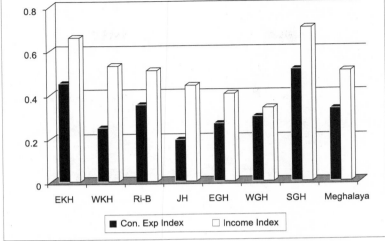

Figure 16.2: Consumption Expenditure versus Income*

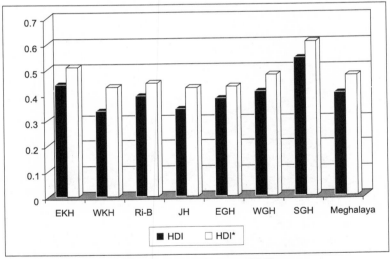

Figure 16.3: HDI versus HDI*

does now have significant association with other indicators except Income*. The negative correlation between Education and Income* and between Health and Education are not statistically significant.

Table 16.5: Correlation Coefficients between Indices

Index	Income*	Con. Exp.	Education	Health	HDI	HDI*
Income*	+1.0	+0.571[s]	−0.036	+0.464[s]	+0.393[s]	+0.464[s]
Cons. Exp.		+1.0	+0.750[s]	+0.123	+0.929[s]	+0.964[s]
Education			+1.0	-0.321	+0.750[s]	+0.607[s]
Health				+1.0	+0.179	+0.001
HDI					+1.0	+0.964[s]
HDI*						+1.0

Note: [s] indicates that correlation is significant at the 0.05 level.
Source: Computed from data of Nayak and Thomas (2007a).

LEVEL OF DISPARITIES IN HUMAN DEVELOPMENT

Dimensions of Inter-District Disparities

The magnitude of disparities in indicators and in corresponding composite index (HDI) is reported in Table 16.6, where population-weighted sample means, standard deviations, coefficient of variations, and Bourguignon Inequality Index (L) are computed. L is given by the natural logarithm of the ratio between the populations-weighted Arithmetic Mean and Geometric Mean of the index. The advantage of L is that it is the only population-weighted, additively decomposable, inequality measure that satisfies Pigou-Dalton condition and, in fact, same as Theil's population-weighted inequality index. This measure is used in several studies such as Ram (1992 and 2006), Pillarisetti (1997), Chelliah and Shanmugam (2000).

Table 16.6: Some Statistics and Inequality Measures for Indices

Inequality Measures Indicator	Mean	Standard Deviation	Coefficient of Variation (%)	Bourguignon Inequality Index (L)
Per Capita Income (Rs./month)	691.07	144.13	20.86	0.0217
Inequality Adjusted Per Capita Consumption Expenditure (Rs./month)	521.92	83.49	15.99	0.0125
Literacy Rate	71.57	8.50	11.88	0.0076
Intensity of Formal Education	3.925	1.28	32.61	0.0496
Infant Mortality Rate	76.00	29.37	38.64	0.0966
HDI	0.404	0.049	12.00	0.0075

Source: Computed from data of Nayak and Thomas (2007a).

The weighted mean, standard deviation, and coefficient of variation have the following well-known expressions:

$$\text{Mean}(X_i) = \sum_{j=1}^{7} p_j X_{ij}$$

where,

p_j = Population share of jth district such that $\sum p_j = 1$

X_{ij} = Actual value of ith component for j^{th} district

Standard Deviation is given by: $SD_i = \sqrt{\sum_{j=1}^{7} p_j (X_{ij} - X_i)}$

Coefficient of Variation is: $CV = \dfrac{SD}{X_i} 100$

And finally, Bourguignon Inequality Index is: $L = \ln\left(\dfrac{\sum p_j X_{ij}}{\prod X_{ij}^{P_j}} \right)$

Table 16.6 reveals that income inequality index (0.0217) is much higher than consumption expenditure index (0.0125). Since, following Planning Commission formulation we used the latter indicator for constructing our composite index, HDI inequality index (0.0075) remains moderate. Two indicators for educational attainment show a very different level of disparities: inequality index for literacy rate (0.0076) is significantly less than that of intensity of formal education (0.0496). Inequality index of infant mortality rate has been the highest among all indicators. The measure of variation suggests altogether a similar picture. The variation in income is as high as about 21 per cent against 16 per cent in consumption expenditure. Again, variations in intensity of formal education (32.61 per cent) and infant mortality rate (38.64) are concernedly higher as compared to other social indicators.

Inter-District Gender Disparities

Human development is a new paradigm that is motivated by a concern for human dignity. Such a perspective of development underscores the role of freedom to shape the life of people—both women and men. India is counted among those countries of the world that are struggling to achieve a certain degree of equality between women and men. To obtain an idea of sex disparities in the unique matrilineal state in the country, we have made an exercise to capture the level of disparities that exists between male and female respondents of our study. As economic attainment (income*/consumption expenditure) could not be separated for men and women, this discussion is limited within the non-income component of HDI, commonly referred in the literature as HDI non-income. Table 16.7 indicates that in the state as a whole, the sex disparity is negative implying a disparity in favour of women. However, the picture varies significantly over districts.

Table 16.7: Gender Disparities in Meghalaya

District/State	HDI non-income		
	Male	Female	Person
East Khasi Hills	0.449	0.440	0.436
West Khasi Hills	0.377	0.380	0.378
Ri-Bhoi	0.413	0.419	0.417
Jaintia Hills	0.401	0.438	0.420
East Garo Hills	0.442	0.432	0.443
West Garo Hills	0.486	0.454	0.470
South Garo Hills	0.567	0.562	0.559
Meghalaya	0.437	0.442	0.439

Source: Computed from data of Nayak and Thomas (2007a).

All three Garo Hills districts and East Khasi Hills districts show an opposite scenario of the state average. Women in these districts are lagging behind their male counterpart.

The magnitude of gender-disparity in Meghalaya, in both directions, is depicted in Figure 16.4, which reveals that in Jaintia Hills, women are enjoying highest opportunities in terms of education and health attainment over men, followed by Ri-Bhoi. On the other hand, in West Garo Hills, women lag most, followed by East Garo, East Khasi, and South Garo Hills.

CONCLUSION

In this chapter we measured the inter-district disparities in Meghalaya in terms of human development indicators. There exists a significant level of disparity both in income consumption and in non-income attainments over the districts. The inequality in economic attainment (income as well as consumption expenditure) happens to be very high. However, both measures of variation and inequality index suggest that few non-income indicators namely, intensity of formal education and infant mortality rate have disparities over economic indicators, which is indeed a cause of considerable concern. In addition, economic inequality is much higher than overall HDI inequality. With

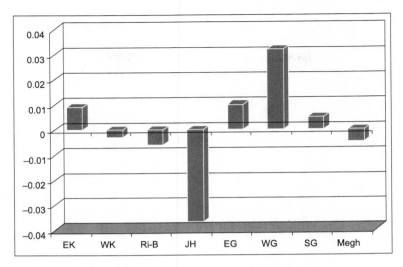

Figure 16.4: Gender Disparity in Meghalaya

a huge shortfall in HDI, the existing level of variation and disabilities imply clearly that there is a need to redesign the public policies that directly affect the welfare of the people.

REFERENCES

Bourgignon, F. 1979. 'Decomposable Income Inequality Measures', *Econometrica*, Vol. 47, No. 4, pp. 901–20.

Chelliah, R.J. and K.R. Shanmugam 2000. 'Some Aspects of Inter-District Disparities in Tamil Nadu', in V. Pandit, *et al.* (eds), *Data Modeling and Policies*, Proceeding of 38th Annual Conference of the Indian Econometric Society, Chennai.

Government of India (GoI) 2002. *National Human Development Report 2001*, Planning Commission, New Delhi.

Malhotra, R. 2007. 'Human Development Measures: From Advocacy to Policy Monitoring at Country Level', *Indian Journal of Human Development*, Vol. 1, No. 1, pp. 103–27.

Nayak, P. 2005. 'Human Development in North-East India', *Journal of NEICSSR*, April.

Nayak, P. and E.D. Thomas 2009. *Human Development and Deprivation in Meghalaya*, Akansha Publishers, New Delhi.

——2007a. *Human Development in Meghalaya*, UGC Major Research Project Report, North-Eastern Hill University, Shillong (mimeo).

—— 2007b. *Human Development and Deprivation in Meghalaya*, Akansha Publisher, New Delhi.

North-Eastern Council 2005. *Basic Statistics of North-Eastern Region 2005*, Ministry of Home Affairs, Government of India, Shillong.

Pillarisetti, J.R. 1997. 'An Empirical Note on Inequality in the World Development Indicators', *Applied Economic Letters*, Vol. 4, No. 3, pp. 145–47.

Ram, R. 2006. 'State of Life Span Revolution between 1980 and 2000', *Journal of Development Economics*, Vol. 80, No. 2, pp. 518–26.

—— 1992. 'International Inequalities in Human Development and Real Income', *Economic Letters*, Vol. 38, No. 3, pp. 351–54.

—— 1982. 'International Inequality in the Basic Needs Indicators', *Journal of Development Economics*, Vol. 10, No. 1, pp. 113–17.

United Nations Development Programme (UNDP) 1990–2006. *Human Development Report*, Oxford University Press, New York.

17

Does Micro Finance Bring Human Development?

A. P. PATI

INTRODUCTION

While attempting to reach at an inference about the effectiveness of Micro Finance (MF) programme in bringing about more human development, this article at the outset tries to establish a linkage between women empowerment and human development. In this brief review of the linkage, economic empowerment of women is the focus. As one of the instruments of the latter, the impact of micro finance is reviewed with the help of existing literature. The efforts at the macro and micro level in the context of India are critically analysed and a conclusion is arrived at.

WOMEN EMPOWERMENT AND HUMAN DEVELOPMENT

Human development, as defined in different literature, does provide a gamut of issues to ponder about. The crux, however, remains with human freedom. It is about building human capabilities—the range of things that people can do, and what they can be. Individual freedoms and rights matter a great deal, but people are restricted in what they can do with that freedom if they are poor, ill, illiterate, discriminated against, threatened by violent conflict, or denied a political voice. That is why the 'larger freedom' proclaimed in the UN Charter is at the heart of human development. So, the most basic capabilities for human development are leading a long and healthy life, being educated, and having adequate resources for a decent standard of living. Other capabilities include social and political participation in society.

Human development, as the end product, gets affected by the prevailing conditions in the larger society. One of them is the basic ability of the masses to survive and sustain their lives. So, poverty is one of the most important indicators. The wind of globalization, although it brought some macro level corrections regarding poverty in the world, for example, extreme poverty fell from 28 per cent in 1990 to 21 per cent today—a reduction in absolute numbers of about 130 million people—it has not been able to converge the poor and rich economies. Some countries, where globalization is cited as a success, are finding it harder to convert rising prosperity into human development. Over the past two decades, India has moved into the premier league of world economic growth, high-technology exports are booming, and its emerging middle class consumers have become a magnet for foreign investors. The incidence of poverty has fallen from about 36 per cent, in the early 1990s, to somewhere around 22 per cent, today. But overall evidence suggests that the pickup in growth has not translated into a commensurate decline in poverty. The record on human development has been less impressive than the record on global integration. In particular, pervasive gender inequalities, interacting with rural poverty and inequalities between states, is undermining the potential for converting growth into human development. Gender inequality is found to be one of the most powerful brakes on human development.

The World Bank reports that societies that discriminate on the basis of gender have greater poverty, slower economic growth, weaker governance, and a lower standard of living. Women are poorer and more disadvantaged than men. United Nations Development Programmes (UNDPs) often quoted *Human Development Report 1995* found that 70 per cent of the 1.3 billion people living on less than $ 1 a day are women (Word Bank 2001). From 1975, the UN International Year on Women, through the Decade on Women (1976–1985) and the global conferences and summits of the 1990s,[1] women participated actively to shape economic, social, and political developments. The UN Millennium Development Goals (MDGs), issued by the UN in 2001, as its third goal, calls for gender equality and womens' empowerment.

The concept of empowerment[2] is related to gender equality, but is distinct from it. Based on a review of literature on the definition and measurement of women's empowerment Malhotra, Schuler, and Boender (2002) conclude that empowerment is a process that marks change over a period of time and requires that the individual being empowered is involved as a significant agent in that change process.

The core of the concept of empowerment lies in the ability of the woman to control her own destiny. It is the process of acquiring the ability to make strategic life choices in a context where this ability has previously been denied. It is defined as agency (the ability to define one's goals and act upon them), awareness of gendered power structures, self-esteem, and self-confidence (Kabeer 2001).

Economic Freedom and Women Empowerment

Women empowerment is a product of numerous factors. Increasing participation in economic affairs, getting equal opportunity in jobs and entrepreneurship, accessibility to political process, education, and health services are some of them. Among these entire variables, the first one is most powerful, that is, economic freedom, which affects the entire spectrum of decision making at the household level. This very fact is also reflected in the calculation of human development index (HDI). Out of three dimensions of human welfare it covers, income is the foremost, others being education and health. Although, across the genders economic empowerment is crucial, the emphasis on women is more because of their prevalent conditions. Amartya Sen (1999) makes a compelling case for the notion that societies need to see women less as passive recipients of help, and more as dynamic promoters of social transformation, a view strongly buttressed by a body of evidence suggesting that the education, employment, and ownership rights of women have a powerful influence on their ability to control their environment and contribute to economic development.

Economic freedom of women has a wholesome impact on the family and the society. Improved financial position of women along with the men, obviously brings more money to look after education, health, and nutrition of the entire family and adds to the disposable income at the hands of the family to handle future contingencies, and to discharge other social responsibilities. This also strengthens the ability to participate in corporate life and ultimately bring social empowerment. So, accelerated and sustained income at the hands of women is one of the important conditions of women empowerment.

MICRO FINANCE AND ECONOMIC EMPOWERMENT OF WOMEN

Historical Perspective

Economic empowerment, as a condition for women empowerment and furthering human development, is conditioned on the availability of income at the hands of women on a sustainable basis. The latter is dependent upon gainful employment of the women, either in the formal or informal sector, or self-employment. Considering the squeezed scope of employment in many developing economies, which is associated with other socio-cultural dimensions, self-employment is a viable option at the hands of women. And, this is greatly influenced by the availability of credit.

Instances of state intervention with credit supply, to bring economic empowerment of individuals across the genders, are plenty in most of the countries, including India. From the early 1970s, women's movements in a number of countries became increasingly interested in the degree to which women were able to access poverty-focused credit programmes and credit cooperatives. Organizations in India like Self-Employed Women's Association (SEWA), among others with origins and affiliations in the Indian labour and women's movements, identified credit as a major constraint in their work with women workers in the informal sector. The problem of women's access to credit was given particular emphasis at the first International Women's Conference in Mexico in 1975 as part of the emerging awareness of the importance of women's productive role both for national economies, and for women's rights. This led to the setting up of the Women's World Banking network and production of manuals for women's credit provision. Other women's organizations worldwide set up credit and savings components, both as a way of increasing women's incomes and bringing women together, to address wider gender issues.

As a mechanism of credit infusion at grassroots level since the early 1980s, micro finance intervention as a strategy of poverty alleviations and micro enterprise creation has been popular among developmental agencies in many countries. Within a few years of its implementation, this became an effective vehicle for empowerment of women. The 1980s and 1990s saw development and rapid expansion of large minimalist poverty-targeted MF institutions and networks like Grameen Bank (Bangladesh) ACCION and Finca among others. In these organizations and others, evidence of significantly higher female repayment rates led to increasing emphasis on targeting women as an efficiency strategy to increase credit recovery. A number of donors also saw female-targeted financially-sustainable MF as a means of marrying internal demands for increased efficiency because of declining budgets with demands of the increasingly vocal gender lobbies (Mayoux 2000).

The Fourth World Conference on Women, in Beijing in 1995, put women's access to credit on the international agenda. The trend was further reinforced by the Micro Credit Summit Campaign starting in 1997, which had 'reaching and empowering women' as its second key goal after poverty reduction (RESULTS 1997). Since then, the number of women receiving MF has increased rapidly. By 1999, the number of poor women receiving micro loans had more than doubled to 10.3 million poor, and by 2005, this had jumped to 69 million, or 84 per cent of the total number of poor people receiving microfinance. Women have now gained an international reputation for their excellent credit performance, making them a priority for poverty-oriented credit programmes.

Recognizing the importance, the year 2005 was also observed as the International Year of Micro Credit. One of the major objectives of this was to promote the role of MF in achieving the MDGs. The UN General Assembly adopted a resolution (A/60/210), recognizing the importance of MF in achieving the MDGs, especially Goal 1 (poverty reduction) and Goal 3 (gender equality and women's empowerment). The resolution calls on member states, the UN system and International Financial Institutions to maximize efforts and adopt policies to facilitate the expansion of MF to help meet the demands of the poor. The 2006 Global Micro Credit Summit adopted a specific target to lift half a billion people out of extreme poverty by providing 175 million of the world's poorest families, especially the women of those families with micro credit, to ensure that at least 100 million families rise above the US$ 1 a day threshold. Micro finance for women have recently been seen as a key strategy in meeting not only MDGs, but also health, HIV/AIDS, and other goals.

Micro Finance is promoted as an entry point in the context of a wider strategy for women's economic and socio-political empowerment, which focuses on gender awareness and feminist organization. The rationale for providing women with loans has been that (Leach and Sitaram 2002) they are disproportionately represented among the poorest in society, discriminated against in the formal labour market, and more vulnerable in times of crisis, as they have fewer resources to draw upon. The assumption is that increasing women's access to MF will enable women to make a greater contribution to household income and this, together with other interventions to increase household well-being, will translate into improved well-being for women, and enable women to bring about wider changes in gender inequality.

Policy makers started realizing that these MF institutions are potentially a very significant contribution to gender equality and women's empowerment, as well as pro-poor development and civil society strengthening. Through their contribution to women's ability to earn an income, these financing activities have the potential to initiate a series of 'virtuous spirals' of economic empowerment, increased well-being of women and their families, and wider social and political empowerment. Micro finance services and groups involving men also have the potential to question and significantly change men's attitudes and behaviour as an essential component of achieving gender equality (Khandelwal 2007).

Evidences

There are four basic views on the link between micro finance and women's empowerment (Mayoux 2000). The obvious reason of incongruity among the views is the time and space considerations, or contextual. All the programmes, although they apparently look similar, are not. The delivery mechanism, the principles of lending, the client groups, the financier, the promoter, state patronage, the basic goal, the business priority, the physical constraints, etc., do vary to a great extent. For example, while many MF institutions seek to empower women as an implicit or explicit goal, others believe they cannot afford to focus on empowerment because it is incompatible with financial sustainability, or because it detracts from the core business of providing financial services. It is worth looking at several institutions that are both focused on empowerment and are financially self-sufficient, such as Working Women's Forum (WWF) in India, which organizes women to achieve better wages and working conditions; ADOPEM in the Dominican Republic, which provides business training and training on democratic processes and civil society; and, OMB in the Philippines, whose commitment to holistic transformation includes leadership training, personal development, and business training. Despite the lack of commonality in most of the cases, the sustainable MF efforts strive for more empowerment. The following observations provide some stray evidence of the MF endeavour and women empowerment.

Strong evidence of MF institutions' contribution to women's empowerment through increased self-confidence and increase self-esteem, and increased participation in decision-making is found in the context of Ghana (Cheston and Kuhn 2002).Women's Empowerment Project in Nepal, for example, showed 68 per cent of women experienced an increase in their decision-making role in the areas of family planning, children's marriage, buying and selling property, and sending their daughters to school (Ashe and Parrott 2001). In Bangladesh, women showed a good deal of empowerment in their capacity to articulate their needs and in their receptivity to new ideas. More impressive was the emergence of women's groups as a dynamic, articulate constituency (Krishnaraj and Kay 2002). For the majority of women borrowers, credit is much more than access to money; it is about women lifting themselves out of poverty, and achieving economic and political empowerment within their homes, their villages, and their countries. For example, 40 per cent of poverty reduction in rural Bangladesh has been attributed to the role of micro credit (Khandker 2005). A number of studies in Bangladesh also show that while for some women it may be empowering, for many others it is marginal, both in economic and socio-political terms (Kabeer 1998 and Schuler et al. 1999). In some cases, it increases domestic violence. Goetz and Gupta (1996) found that an average of 39 per cent of women had little or no control over their loans in the four Bangladesh programmes they studied. Some programmes, with an explicit gender strategy, particularly in India but also in Sudan, had played a significant role as an entry point for mobilizing women around wider gender issues, and challenging domestic violence, alcoholism, and dowry (Mayoux 1998).

In India, women borrowers are given priority in Rosca; 90 per cent of group members are women. The main reason for targeting women over men in rural areas is based on the premise that women make a higher contribution to family welfare. Women generally give priority to investing their earnings in their children, and spending on other household necessities comes second. Therefore, their earnings bring more qualitative benefits to family welfare than the earnings of men. In addition, lending to women is an effective tool for the attainment of socioeconomic empowerment of women (Guha and Gupta 2005). Lakshmanan (2001) in a micro level study in Tamil Nadu, also observed that one of the major contributions of micro finance is towards women's empowerment.

SELF-HELP GROUP-BANK LINKAGE MODEL OF MICRO FINANCE AND EMPOWERMENT

Macro Level Observations

Micro Finance as a whole comprises of several products like micro credit, micro insurance, money transfer, money advice, leasing, etc. The Indian effort, so far, mainly concentrates on the credit and has the patronage of both state and private players. Small credit, although flowing through various MF schemes, the most popular among them is Self-Help Group (SHG).

Identifying the large potential of SHGs, National Bank for Agriculture and Rural Development (NABARD) launched the SHG-Bank linkage model of credit delivery in 1992. The achievement so far is acclaimed as astounding and the programme is considered as the largest MF initiative in the world (Table 17.1). The quantum jump in the last five years is an eye opener for other developmental agencies/programmes, etc. NABARD saw the promotion and bank linking of SHGs not merely as a credit programme, but as part of an overall arrangement for providing financial services to the poor in a sustainable manner, leading to empowerment of the members of these SHGs (Wilson 2002).

Table 17.1: Glimpse of SHG-Bank Linkage Progress in India

Variables	Mar 1993	Mar 1996	Mar 2001	Mar 2006
SHGs linked	255	4,757	263825	2238565
Women's groups (per cent)	70	74	90	90
Families assisted (in million)	0.0051	0.08	4.5	32.98
Banks participating	14	95	314	545
No. of Partners	32	127	1030	4896
Districts covered	26	157	412	583
Aggregate bank loans (Rs in million)	2.9	60.6	4809	113980

Source: NABARD.

The 90 per cent dominance of women clearly designates this as a women-oriented credit intervention programme and reveals the demand of such micro loans at the household level, and its relevance to the family. This rapid expansion of numbers in such a short span of period speaks volume about the insatiable needs of the women and their nature of requirements. Although the growth rate has slowed down in the recent years to less than 40 per cent, still it is too high to sustain. Even if half of this growth rate in next ten years continues, it would perhaps link all the households who need such type of small finance. Though, a much skewed picture emerges from the regional distribution (Table 17.2), its importance at the macro level cannot be sidelined from the angle of its potential of bringing women empowerment and human development.

Table 17.2: The Regional Spread of SHGs

(*Loan amount in Rs Million*)

Year	Var.	North	East	Central	West	South	NE	India
2001-02	Nos.	19321 (4.19)	45892 (9.94)	48181 (10.44)	29318 (6.35)	358689 (77.73)	1490 (0.32)	461478 (100)
	Loan	373 (3.64)	468 (4.56)	569 (5.55)	515 (5.02)	8313 (81.00)	25 (0.25)	10263 (100)
2005-06	Nos.	133097 (5.95)	394351 (17.62)	267915 (11.97)	166254 (7.43)	1214431 (54.25)	62517 (2.79)	2238565 (100)
	Loan	3986 (3.50)	9354 (8.21)	8050 (7.06)	5251 (4.61)	85677 (75.17)	1657 (1.45)	11398 (100)
LGR (2002-06)	Nos.	68.92	78.07	57.13	56.51	43.32	170.95	46.23
	Loan	87.92	119.19	100.76	82.30	85.17	199.35	82.74

Note: LGR refers to linear growth rate.
Source: NABARD.

As women's groups exclusively dominate the SHGs, their empowerment both on the economic and social fronts is one of the greatest opportunities in the mainstream of development activities. Opportunities for earning through deposits and higher off-farm activities improve their disposable income (Namboodiri and Shiyani 2001). Consequently, family incomes substantially increased. There are tremendous social changes too. The women command more respect, get their due affection, and rightful place in the family. Their involvement in family decisions has been substantially enhanced (Dadhich 2001). In addition to meeting financial requirements, the SHG has become a platform for exchange of experiences and ideas beyond social participation by members, especially women (Tilekar *et al.* 2001).

Self-help Groups, intermediated by micro credit, have been shown to have positive effect on women, with some of these impacts being ripple effects. They have played valuable roles in reducing the vulnerability of the poor, through asset creation, income and consumption smoothing, provision of emergency assistance, and empowering and emboldening women by giving them control over assets, and increased self-esteem and knowledge (Zaman 2001). Several recent assessment studies have also reported positive impacts (Simanowitz and Walker 2002). Till now, benefits for the poor, in terms of social empowerment and economic progress through SHGs, have far outpaced benefits from other rural development projects (Ramakrishna 2001). The evidences, as found, are quite encouraging to form a conclusion that the linkage programme has a salubrious impact on the overall economic condition of the women and, consequently, on their empowerment.

The Micro Level Scenario

To test the above findings, a micro level investigation into a state of the most backward region of the country was attempted. North-Eastern India, despite around 3.75 per cent share in population, has only 2.8 per cent of the total SHGs, and their share in loans is further low at 1.5 per cent of the all India total. As per the NABARD data, the regional distribution in the North East is very much skewed in favour of Assam, which commands 90 per cent of the SHGs and 85 per cent of total loans disbursed till 2006. All other states in the region are yet to take off in a big way.

Considering an average state of this region, it is found that the growth of MF activities in Meghalaya is catching up only in recent years. The dominance of women in SHGs is found to be less in comparison to the national level figure (Table 17.3), which is just above 40 per cent. However, the overall banking environment of the state is not conducive for growth of any developmental scheme. The overall recovery rate in the state is below 40 per cent, which indicates very poor response from the borrowers for regeneration activities. Further, since the MF effort in the state is conditioned by the ongoing SGSY scheme, which is subsidy-based, the effectiveness of the former is doubtful. The upgradation of SHGs from Grade I to Grade II (Table 17.4), which is 25 per cent only, and the recovery rate under this scheme (Table 17.5), which is 36 per cent, speak volumes about the precarious nature of MF initiative in the state. This simply indicates that the MF intervention is no better than the overall lending business. So, the overall picture

Table 17.3: District-wise Distribution of SHGs in Meghalaya

Sl. No.	District/State	SHGs	Men SHGs	Women SHGs	Women SHGs (%)
1	Jayantia Hills	402	77	166	8.26
2	East Khasi Hills	684	76	134	6.67
3	Ri Bhoi	426	164	208	10.35
4	West Khasi Hills	729	125	200	9.95
5	West Garo Hills	1520	256	861	42.84
6	East Garo Hills	840	119	283	14.08
7	South Garo Hills	242	27	158	7.86
8	Meghalaya	4843	844	2010	100

Source: Government of Meghalaya, Office of the State Coordinator for SHGs in Meghalaya.

Table 17.4: Upgradation of SHGs under SGSY Scheme
as on 31 March 2006

Sl. No.	District/State	% of SHG Passed Grade I	% of SHG Passed Grade II	% of Grade I SHGs Passed Grade II	% of SHGs taken up Economic Activities
1	Jayantia Hills	53.72	15.59	29.02	9.83
2	East Khasi Hills	36.23	11.52	31.80	6.68
3	Ri Bhoi	90.61	9.39	10.36	9.39
4	West Khasi Hills	67.38	27.16	40.32	11.85
5	West Garo Hills	38.76	2.69	6.94	1.21
6	East Garo Hills	34.99	15.28	43.65	34.99
7	South Garo Hills	34.49	2.85	8.26	0.00
8	Meghalaya	46.26	11.62	25.11	11.26

Source: Department of Community and Rural Development, Government of Meghalaya.

Table 17.5: Recovery Position of SGSY Scheme as on 31 March 2006

(*Figures in Lakh*)

	SBI	OCBs	RRB	MCAB	STATE
SGSY Demand of Loan	339.02	20.22	30.92	38.03	428.19
SGSY Recovery of Loan	120.12	5.17	11.20	16.50	152.99
Overdue with SGSY	218.90	15.43	19.72	21.53	581.18
SGSY Recovery Performance (%)	35.43	25.57	36.22	43.39	35.73

Source: SLBC, Meghalaya, 2006

in the state is not very encouraging for sustainable MF activities and women empowerment. However, looking at the recent growth and state emphasis, this programme could be an effective vehicle for economic empowerment.

Against the sustainability parameter, the evidences in favour of empowerment found elsewhere in India are not vindicated in the case of Meghalaya. An in-depth study at the primary level may bring the real evidences. However, studies conducted in other states by Seibel and Dave (2002), Puhazhendi and Badatya (2002), Harper (2002), and Fernandez (2000) do provide enough support for this programme.

CONCLUSION

Human development requires more than economic growth alone. Economic growth is one of the obvious requirements for accelerated income, poverty reduction, and sustained human development. Credit can never be the single case solution for all problems the poor face. To call it a self-help movement that is successfully eradicating poverty and emancipating women would be misleading. Self-help, as it is largely understood today, is a project that aims to provide relief while masking the causes of the malaise. Women need to be organized to understand and confront the violence of their reality; a violence based on gender, caste, community, political corruption, and a failure of governance (Kannabiran 2005).

Existing evidence of the impact on gender relations of microfinance programmes is limited, and few studies investigate the impact of different programme strategies in any detail. Independent academic research has been done only on a few programmes in Bangladesh and India, and conclusions differ among these, even for the same programmes (Mayoux 1998). There are no magic bullets, no panaceas, no blueprints, no readymade formulae which bring about the radical structural transformation that the empowerment of the poor, and of poor women, implies Kabeer (2005). Apprehension is also found with the new amendment to the NABARD Act to allow new micro finance organizations with meagre capital base (Premchander and Chidambaranatham 2007).

Empowerment cannot be assumed to be an automatic outcome of micro finance programmes, whether designed for financial sustainability or poverty targeting. Unless empowerment is an integral part of the planning process, the rapid expansion of micro finance is unlikely to make more than a limited contribution to empowerment. The growth of micro finance has to necessarily be accompanied by the overall growth in mainstream rural finance. Cost-effective ways of integrating micro finance with other empowerment interventions, including group development and complementary services are still lacking.

In the pursuit to achieve the goal of women empowerment and larger human development, the full potential of micro finance must be realized. To achieve this, MF must be:

1) part of a sectoral strategy for change which identifies opportunities, constraints, and bottlenecks within industries, which if addressed can raise returns and prospects for large numbers of women. Possible strategies include linking women to existing services and infrastructure, developing new technology such as labour-saving food processing, building information networks, shifting to new markets, policy level changes to overcome legislative barriers, and unionization; and

2) based on participatory principles to build up incremental knowledge of industries and enable women to develop their strategies for change (Chen 1996). There is also a need for making the programme more male inclusive (Leach and Sitaram 2002).

So, creating an enabling environment for micro finance and women's empowerment by promoting women's access to public services and employment opportunities, establishing stronger partnerships between the private banking sector and micro finance institutions, gathering information on women's needs and designing products specifically to meet those needs, providing complementary services with microfinance such as literacy classes, business training, and childcare, including women's perspectives and women's empowerment indicators in the design, implementation, and evaluation of microfinance programmes, and tracking empowerment benefits along with institutional financial performance and economic impact indicators will help to achieve human development.

NOTES

1. These conferences included: the Conference on Environment and Development (Rio de Janeiro, 1992) where women's vital role in environmental management and development and the need for their full participation to achieve sustainable development was recognized; the International Conference on Human Rights (Vienna, 1993) where women's human rights were spelled out for the first time; the International Conference on Population and Development (Cairo, 1994) where formal recognition of women's reproductive rights prevailed despite bitter opposition; the World Summit on Social Development (Copenhagen, 1995) where the link between gender equality and poverty was explicitly recognized; and the Fourth World Conference on Women (Beijing, 1995) where advocates won a broad-based agenda for promoting and protecting women's human rights worldwide, while establishing the principle of shared power and responsibility between women and men in all arenas.

2. Bennett (2002) describes empowerment as 'the enhancement of assets and capabilities of diverse individuals and groups to engage, influence, and hold accountable the institutions which affect them'. Kabeer (2001) defines it as 'the expansion in people's ability to make strategic life choices in a context where this ability was previously denied to them.' Both these definitions are considered as operational for women empowerment, also.

REFERENCES

Ashe, J. and L. Parrott 2001. 'Impact Evaluation of PACT's Women's Empowerment Program in Nepal: A Savings and Literacy Led Alternative to Financial Institution Building', Cambridge, MA: Brandeis University.

Bennett, L. 2002. 'Using Empowerment and Social Inclusion for Pro-poor Growth: A Theory of Social Change', Working Draft of Background Paper for the Social Development Strategy Paper, Washington, D.C.: World Bank.

Chen, M. 1996. *Beyond Credit: A Sub sector Approach to Promoting Women's Enterprises*, Canada, Agha Khan Foundation.

Cheston, S. and L. Kuhn 2002. 'Empowering Women through Microfinance', unpublished background paper for the Microcredit Summit + 5, New York, 10–13 November. www.microcreditsummit.org/papers/papers.htm

Dadhich, C.L. 2001. 'Microfinance—A Panacea for Poverty Alleviation: A Case of Oriental Grameen Project in India', *Indian Journal of Agricultural Economics*, Vol. 56, No. 3, pp. 419–26.

Fernandez, A.P. 2000. 'Putting Institutions First Even in Microcredit', Paper presented at the Workshop on Best Practices in Group Dynamics and Micro Credit, Unpublished workshop paper, 15–17 February, Manesar, Gurgaon.

Goetz, A.M. and R. Sen Gupta 1996. 'Who takes the Credit? Gender, Power and Control over Loan Use in Rural Credit Programmes in Bangladesh', *World Development*, Vol. 24, No. 1, pp. 45–63.

Guha, S. and G. Gupta 2005. 'Microcredit for Income Generation: The Role of Rosca', *Economic and Political Weekly*, Vol. 40, No. 14, pp. 1470–3.

Harper, M. 2002. *Promotion of Self Help Groups under the SHG Bank Linkage Programme in India*, NABARD, Mumbai.

Jeffrey A. and L. Parrott 2001. *Impact Evaluation of PACT's Women's Empowerment Program in Nepal: A Savings and Literacy Led Alternative to Financial Institution Building*, Cambridge, MA: Brandeis University.

Kabeer, N. 2005. 'Is Microfinance a "Magic Bullet" for Women's Empowerment? Analysis of Findings from South Asia', *Economic and Political Weekly*, Vol. 40, Nos. 44 and 45, pp. 4709–18.

—— 2001. 'Reflections on the Measurement of Women's Empowerment: In Discussing Women's Empowerment—Theory and Practice', Sida Studies No. 3. Novum Grafiska AB, Stockholm.

—— 1998. 'Money Can't Buy Me Love? Re-evaluating Gender, Credit and Empowerment in Rural Bangladesh', IDS Discussion Paper 363, Brighton, IDS.

Kannabiran, V. 2005. 'Marketing Self-Help, Managing Poverty', *Economic and Political Weekly*, Vol. 40, No. 34, pp. 3716–18.

Khandelwal, A.K. 2007. 'Microfinance Development Strategy for India', *Economic and Political Weekly*, Vol. 42, No. 13, pp. 1127–35.

Khandker, S.R. 2005. 'Microfinance and Poverty: Evidence Using Panel Data from Bangladesh', *World Bank Economic Review*, Vol. 19, No. 2.

Krishnaraj, M. and T. Kay 2002. 'Report of Review of IFAD Gender Mainstreaming Projects in Asia', unpublished paper prepared for IFAD.

Lakshmanan, S. 2001. 'Working of Self-help Groups with Particular Reference to Mallipalayam Self-Help Group, Gobichetizalayam Block, Erode District, Tamil Nadu', *Indian Journal of Agricultural Economics*, Vol. 56, No. 3.

Leach and S. Sitaram 2002. 'Microfinance and Women's Empowerment: A Lesson from India', *Development in Practice*, Vol. 12, No. 5, pp. 575–88.

Malhotra, A., S. Schuler, and C. Boender 2002. 'Measuring Women's Empowerment as a Variable in International Development', www.icrw.org/docs/MeasuringEmpowerment_workingpaper_802.doc

Mayoux, L. 2000. 'Micro-finance and the Empowerment of Women: A Review of the Key Issues', Social Finance Unit Working Paper No. 23, ILO, Geneva.

—— 1998. 'Research Round-Up Women's Empowerment and Micro-finance Programmes: Strategies for Increasing Impact', *Development in Practice*, Vol. 8, No. 2, pp. 235–41.

Namboodiri, N.V. and R.L. Shiyani 2001. 'Potential Role of Self-Help Groups in Rural Financial Deepening', *Indian Journal of Agricultural Economics*, Vol. 56, No. 3, pp. 401–9.

Premchander, S. and M. Chidambaranatham 2007. 'One Step Forward or Two Steps Back? Proposed Amendments to NABARD Act', *Economic and Political Weekly*, Vol. 42, No. 12, pp. 1006–8.

Puhazhendi, V. and K.C. Badatya 2002. *SHG-Bank Linkage Programme for Rural Poor – An Impact Assessment*, NABARD, Mumbai.

Ramakrishna, R. 2001. 'Credit Needs of the Rural Poor and the Role of Self-Help Groups', *Indian Journal of Agricultural Economics*, Vol. 56, No. 3.

RESULTS, 1997. The Micro-credit Summit, 1997. Declaration and Plan of Action.

Schuler, S.R., S.M. Hashemi, and S.H. Badal, 1999. 'Men's Violence against Women in Rural Bangladesh: Undermined or Exacerbated by Microcredit Programmes?', *Development in Practice*, Vol. 8, No. 2, pp.112–26.

Seibel, H.D. and H.K.R. Dave 2002. 'Commercial Aspects of SHG Banking in India', NABARD, Mumbai.

Sen, A. 1999. *Development as Freedom*, Oxford University Press, UK.

Simanowitz, A. and A. Walker 2002. 'Ensuring Impact: Reaching the Poorest while Building Financially Self Sufficient Institutions, and Showing Improvement in the Lives of the Poorest Women and their Families', unpublished background paper for the Microcredit Summit + 5, New York, 10–13 November. www.microcreditsummit. org/papers/papers.htm

Tilekar, S.N., N.J. Naikade, B.J. Deshmukh, and A.A. Patil 2001. 'Women Self-Help Groups Affiliated to "Chaitanya": A Study in Pune District', *Indian Journal of Agricultural Economics*, Vol. 56, No. 3.

United Nations Development Programme (UNDP), 2005. Human Development Report.

Wilson, K. 2002. 'The Role of Self-Help Group Bank Linkage Programme in Preventing Rural Emergencies in India', NABARD, Mumbai.

World Bank, 2001. 'Engendering Development: Through Gender Equality in Rights, Resources, and Voice— Summary, Washington: World Bank'. www.worldbank.org/gender/prr/engendersummary.pdf

Zaman, H. 2001. 'Assessing the Poverty and Vulnerability Impact of Micro-credit in Bangladesh: A Case Study of BRAC', unpublished background paper for World Bank, World Development Report 2000/2001,Washington, World Bank.

18

Public Expenditure and Human Development in North-East India
A Case Study of Meghalaya

P.S. SURESH AND BISWAMBHARA MISHRA

INTRODUCTION

Meghalaya, being an underdeveloped state in the north-eastern part of India, has been witnessing a massive increase in public expenditure during the period from 1972 to 2002. The additional spending undertaken by the state has been partly financed through taxation, a major part through grants-in-aid from the central government, and the remaining through increased public borrowing. For example, the fiscal deficit as a percentage of State Domestic Product (SDP), which stood at about 1 per cent in 1981–82, rose up to 7.48 per cent in 2002–03. Similarly, public debt increased from 1.35 per cent to 6.37 per cent during the same period. Besides, a major chunk of the total public expenditure was earmarked for payment of wages and salaries. This has resulted not only in significant increase in the state government's budget deficit, fiscal deficit, and public debt but also in mounting up the quantum of public expenditure on servicing the public debt. All these facts corroborate the nature of the extra governmental spending that the state government has carried out over the years.

THE PROBLEM

Meghalaya is not only a backward state but also predominantly an agricultural economy, providing means of livelihood to more than 80 per cent of her population. Although, significant developments took place in some spheres in the state since her attainment of statehood, the access to opportunities for a reasonably minimum standard of living remained one of the lowest in the country. The developmental efforts of the state resulted in a paradoxical growth. When the exponential growth of the state income increased to a level of 12.61 per cent, public expenditure increased to a magnitude of 14.68 per cent implying the fact that increased public expenditure could not provide enough stimuli to the state income to grow steadily to the desired level. This, we believe, might have been due to improper implementation of the public expenditure programmes to address the right set of objectives that fiscal policy accords. Thus, the phenomenal growth of public expenditure without a corresponding, proportionate, growth in her SDP brought about an explosive growth of public expenditure. A closer scrutiny of Meghalaya's fiscal figures exhibited a rising trend of public expenditure on the service sector, followed by the primary and manufacturing sectors. The resultant pattern of public expenditure was only a testimony to a lopsided allocation of scarce resources. The neglect of the manufacturing sector over the years resulted in overall backwardness of the state manifested through social tension and unrest. Further, an unabated growth of revenue expenditure in relation to capital expenditure, exhibited the fact that the state could not build up in all these years the capital base required for maximizing long-term growth and development.

According to the *National Human Development Report* (GoI 2002) people must be at the centre of human development. Development has to be woven around people, not people around development. It has to be development of the people, by the people, and for the people. Human development has, thus, two sides:

(1) the formation of human capabilities, such as improved health, knowledge, and skills; and
(2) the use of their acquired capabilities for productive purposes, leisure or for being active in cultural, social, and political affairs.

The scales of human development must finely balance the two sides, otherwise considerable human frustration may be the resultant outcome. Striking a balance between these two requires a smooth and steady growth of per capita income. In this perspective, income is clearly one of the options that people would like to have, albeit an important one. But it is not the sum total of lives. Development must, therefore, be more than just the expansion of income and wealth.

This is substantiated by the findings of several studies, Streeten (1979), Isenman (1980), Grossman (1988), Anand and Kanbur (1991), Griffin (1992), Anand and Ravallion (1993), Drèze and Sen (1995), Haq (1995), Mundle (1998), Noorbakhsh (1998), Sen (1998), and Chakraborty (2001),which claim that per capita income cannot be a sole determinant of achieving human development; public spending on social sectors also has a significant role to play.

In a socialistic and welfare-characterized state, where the state intervenes in almost all the areas of economic activities, shaping and re-shaping of policy environment, not only for civil society but also for the private economic agents, remains a logical offshoot of quality and sustainability of the development programmes, subject to resource constraint. In order to achieve the best of the economic and social progress in terms of a better human development index, the use of public resources/investment must emphasize both efficiency and equity. Such involvement of the government is considered to be of paramount importance. What we are trying to hint at is the fact that the scale of human development remains as a logical offshoot of the allocation policies of the government. The question of allocation of financial resources not only takes into consideration the societal needs and aspirations, but also societal priorities. If one assumes for the moment that these factors remain static, then it can be argued safely that public expenditure programmes that translate societal value judgments into economic realities are instrumental in achieving a higher degree of human development. To what extent economic policies on public expenditure affect the magnitude of human development remains an open question. Keeping consistent with our argument, we thought it imperative to present a brief account of the growth of public expenditure in the state of Meghalaya.

GROWTH OF PUBLIC EXPENDITURE IN MEGHALAYA

It may be mentioned here that it is the size and composition of public expenditure that the community finally looks up to. Underneath the policy controversies regarding the quantum of public expenditure, the ultimate questions about the trends and patterns of these expenditures await dispassionate analysis. Therefore, this section is an attempt in this direction.

In recent years, there has been an enormous growth of public expenditure in the state. In order to understand the intricacies of the problem of public expenditure, it would be proper to analyse first the direction in which public expenditure, both in revenue and capital accounts, has moved during 1989–90 to 2001–02.

Table 18.1: Growth of Public Expenditure in Meghalaya
(*Both Revenue and Capital Account*)

Year	Total Expenditure (Rs in crores)	NSDP (Rs in crores)	Per Capita Expenditure (Rs)	Total Expenditure as a Percentage of NSDP
1989–90	350.69	659.78	2092.42	53.15
1990–91	405.65	767.35	2311.40	52.86
1991–92	492.29	884.22	2773.46	55.68
1992–93	588.60	978.54	3130.85	60.15
1993–94	609.08	1133.38	4666.74	53.74
1994–95	677.97	1258.04	3855.15	53.89
1995–96	796.42	1380.31	3812.45	57.70
1996–97	813.58	1485.28	3761.35	54.78
1997–98	850.72	1690.42	3791.09	50.33
1998–99	1022.93	2079.25	4397.81	49.20
1999–2000	1195.40	2467.13	4974.62	48.45
2000–01	1401.89	2806.20	5303.82	49.95
2001–02	1685.15	2967.36	5764.31	51.57

Sources: (1) Budget in Brief, Government of Meghalaya, 1974–75, 1977–78, 1978–79; (2) Budget at a Glance, Government of Meghalaya: 1984–85, 1986–87, 1987–88, 1989–90, 1992–93, 1993–94, 1994–95, 1996–97, 1998–99, 2001–02; (3) Statistical HandBook, Meghalaya, 1976; (4) Estimates of State Domestic Product of Meghalaya, 1980–81 to 1995–96, Government of Meghalaya, Directorate of Economics and Statistics, Shillong; (5) State Economy, Government of Meghalaya, Directorate of Economics and Statistics.

A close look at Table 18.1 exhibits that the total public expenditure of the state increased several folds over the years. It grew from Rs 351 crore in 1989–90 to Rs1,685 crore in 2001–02, recording an average annual growth of 29.27 per cent. The Net State Domestic Product (NSDP) increased from Rs 660 to Rs 3,267 crore during the same period, showing an average annual increase of 26.90 per cent. Similarly, per capita public expenditure, which grew from Rs 2,092 to 5,764, recorded an average growth of 13.49 per cent. It is observed that growth of total public expenditure is higher compared to individual growth rates of NSDP and per capita expenditure. Thus, increased expenditure of the state over and above her income is in line with Wagner's law of expanding state activity.

Further, it is observed that public expenditure as a percentage of the NSDP declined marginally over the years. This increase in public expenditure may be attributed to the intensive development efforts made by the government through comprehensive economic planning. Through comprehensive planning, the State not only tried to develop various sub-sectors of the economy, but also explored the new bases and sources of additional resources.

The trend in revenue expenditure according to sectors namely, general services, social services, and economic services can be examined in order to ascertain the direction of change that has taken place in the quantum of public expenditure on these sectors. Table 18.2 shows the sector-wise revenue expenditure on different services.

Table 18.2: Sector-wise Revenue Expenditure in Meghalaya

(Rupees in Crore)

| Year | Services | | |
	General	Social	Economic
1989–90	78.58	94.86	85.33
1990–91	87.58	112.65	110.59
1991–92	102.86	137.55	127.64
1992–93	123.89	145.65	140.75
1993–94	149.04	177.91	155.9
1994–95	158.25	162.50	136.20
1995–96	188.42	209.01	182.96
1996–97	205.62	324.40	186.94
1997–98	197.82	253.64	195.22
1998–99	280.34	299.95	235.15
1999–2000	337.44	356.04	234.32
2000–01	435.00	448.64	309.22
2001–02	510.48	498.18	346.17

Sources: (1) *Budget in Brief*, Government of Meghalaya, 1978–79; (2) *Budget at a Glance,* Government of Meghalaya: 1984–85; 1986–87; 1989–90; 1994–95; 1998–99; 2000–01; 2001–02.

It is evident that the revenue expenditure of the state on general services increased from Rs 78.58 crore in 1989–90 to Rs 510.48 crore in 2001–02. The growth rate of the general services on the revenue account is shown by the least squares estimate of the following equation as:

$$Ge = 4.1384e^{0.156t} \ \& \ R^2 = 0.9901 \tag{18.1}$$

where, *Ge* refers to general services expenditures on revenue account expressed in Rs crs. The results suggest that the annual compound rate of growth of the expenditure on general services during the period of study is approximately 15.6 per cent. On the social services front, it is found that the expenditures grew from Rs 94.86 crore in 1989–90 to Rs 498.18 crore in 2001–02. The growth rate of the social services on the revenue account is shown by the least squares estimate of the following equation as:

$$Se = 4.1247e^{0.1681t} \;\&\; R^2 = 0.9910 \qquad\qquad (18.2)$$

where Se refers to social services expenditures on revenue account expressed in Rs crore. It is observed that the annual compound rate of growth of the expenditure on social services on the revenue account during the period is approximately 16.81 per cent. From the above Table 18.2, we can also see that expenditures on economic services on the revenue account increased from Rs 7.02 crore in 1972–73 to Rs 346.17 crore in 2001–02. The growth rate of the general services on the revenue account is shown by the least squares estimate of the following equation as:

$$ECe = 6.8998e^{0.1332t} \;\&\; R^2 = 0.9811 \qquad\qquad (18.3)$$

where ECe refers to economic services expenditures on revenue account expressed in Rs crore. The result shows that the annual compound rate of growth of the expenditure on economic services of the revenue account during this period is approximately 13.32 per cent. It is evident from the above analysis that the revenue expenditures on social services account for the maximum rate of growth, followed by the revenue expenditures on general services, and economic services. This only reveals that over the years, more attention has been accorded to the expansion of the social sector comprising of health, education, social security, etc., by the Government of Meghalaya. In spite of the huge investment carried out by the state government on this particular sector, the human development indicators show a contrasting picture.

In order to substantiate the above statement, it is thought imperative to give insight into the trends and pattern of developmental expenditure and the per-capita expenditure on human and physical capital. Table 18.3 gives the comparative picture on this count.

Table 18.3 indicates that the expenditure on human capital increased consistently, in a significant way, throughout the period of the study. The year 1992–93, showed a remarkable increase in per capita human capital expenditure which keeps on mounting till date. This indicates that the state has consciously followed a policy of heavy investment on

Table 18.3: Developmental and Per Capita Expenditure on Human and
Physical Capital

Year	Developmental Expenditures (Rupees in Crores)			Per Capita Expenditures (Rupees)	
	Human Capital	Physical Capital	Total	Human Capital	Physical Capital
1989–90	94.86	85.33	180.19	589.21	530.00
1990–91	112.65	110.59	223.24	686.87	674.35
1991–92	137.55	127.64	265.19	775.00	719.18
1992–93	149.15	138.80	287.95	833.23	775.42
1993–94	181.46	154.47	335.93	997.00	848.74
1994–95	165.01	135.45	300.46	887.15	728.22
1995–96	212.28	181.74	394.02	1117.25	956.21
1996–97	227.26	186.09	413.35	1171.44	959.24
1997–98	253.64	195.22	448.86	1281.02	985.96
1998–99	299.95	235.15	535.10	1484.90	1164.11
1999–2000	356.04	234.32	590.36	1728.35	1137.45
2000–01	448.65*	309.22*	757.87*	1903.44	1311.94
2001–02	498.18**	346.17**	844.35**	2075.74	1442.37

Note: * Revised Estimate; ** Budget Estimate
Source: (1) *Budget in Brief*, Government of Meghalaya, 1978–79; (2) *Budget at a Glance,* Government of Meghalaya: 1984–85; 1986–87; 1989–90; 1994–95; 1998–99; 2000–01; 2001–02.

human capital than on physical capital. The incompatible fact about the huge investment on human capital has resulted in widespread poverty, which is evident from the number of people living below the poverty line. Further, a lopsided approach that has been followed by the state government in terms of investment decisions, of giving lesser importance to the development of physical capital, has not only slowed down the indicators of human development but also resulted in a slow pace of economic growth of the state. Since the above analysis does not clearly spell out the intricate relationship between public expenditure and human development, an attempt is made in the following section to examine the factors that will account for the slow pace of human development in the state.

DETERMINANTS OF HUMAN DEVELOPMENT IN NORTH-EAST INDIA

The factors responsible for expanding public sector activities in the state economy can be explained through two distinct approaches suggested in economic literature. The first approach relates to the increasing pressure on the demand for public services, due to increasing level of money income and population growth, and its subsequent impact on the density of population and urbanization. The growth of population intensified the need for provision of educational, health, and other basic minimum needs/services. In a welfare-characterized state, provision of these basic services absorbs a major portion of the total public resources. Further, the process of transformation that the state undertakes to lift its economy from a static subsistence agriculture to a stage of self-sustained economy leads to a situation where the state is compelled to make provision for larger investments in infrastructure and other developmental activities, in order to reduce pressure on the subsistence sector and provide employment opportunities in other sectors of the economy. As a result, many non-exclusive public expenditure programmes of the state, which are supposed to be guided by externality conditions, are subsequently brought within the domain of the public sector.

The second approach is the supply side approach. In Meghalaya, where the private sector is not well developed and the process of industrialization is virtually non-existent, the public sector has a dual and greater role to play. On the one hand, it had to be directly involved in the process of production and, on the other, for evolving such programmes that would help to stimulate the private sector participation in developmental activities. The massive investments in the social and economic overheads were made in order to increase the productive capacity of the economy, either by increasing the skills, or organizational capacity, or capital stock in the economy. Thus, factors operating, both from the demand and supply side, made a decisive influence on expanding the size of public sector in the state. A declining trend in public expenditure as a percentage of net state domestic products in the state during and after the mid-nineties may be explained by the gradual withdrawal of the government sector from various economic activities on the ground of either efficiency or competitiveness.

In order to present a cross-section analysis on the relationship between human development and its determinants in the context of the north-eastern region, we consulted data pertaining to human development index (HDI), per capita expenditure on health and education, per capita income from the *National Human Development Report* (*NHDR*), and the budget papers of the respective state governments for the same year. Since we started with the premise that public economic policies, as reflected through public investment on health and education, affect human development, we thought it imperative to take per capita expenditure on health and education as two independent variables along with per capita income as the third variable to regress with HDI, using the model as specified below:

$$HDI_i = a_0 + a_1 PCEH_i + a_2 PCEE_i + a_3 PCI_i + \varepsilon_i \qquad (18.4)$$

where HDI_i, a_i, $PCEH_i$, $PCEE_i$, PCI_i, respectively represent values of HDI, estimates of the parameters of exogenous variables, per capita expenditures on health and education, and per capita income. The estimated parameters of the equation (18.4) are as follows:

Box 18.1						
	a_0	a_1	a_2	a_3	R^2	DW
Estimated Parameters	8784.242	0.39596	0.454641	0.250797	0.8342	2.08437
t-values		2.10537	1.9596	2.8432	0.90168		

The above equation seems to be a viable equation so far as prediction is concerned. The result shows that all the three explanatory variables revealed positive relationship with HDI. The t-estimates of public expenditure, on health and education, were found to be statistically significant, whereas it was not so in the case of per capita income. Further, it exhibited that expenditure on education in the region had a greater impact on human development than that of health expenditure.

As the total variance was distributed over all the three explanatory variables mentioned above, in the second stage of our analysis, we decided to replace two explanatory variables, viz,. per capita expenditure on health and education by a single explanatory variable by combining them. The model that we specified runs as follows:

$$HDI_i = b_0 + b_1 PCEHE_i + b_2 PCI_i + \varepsilon_i \qquad (18.5)$$

where HDI_i, b_i, $PCEHE_i$, PCI_i, respectively represent values of HDI, estimates of the parameters of exogenous variables, per capita combined expenditures on health and education, and per capita income. The estimated parameters of the equation (18.5) are as follows:

Box 18.2					
	b_0	b_1	b_2	R^2	DW
Estimated Parameters	9812.438	0.658596	0.0356	0.89732	2.1990
t-values	8.455461	4.07759	3.6723		

The result of the above estimation exhibited a high coefficient of determination and both the estimates of the parameters were statistically significant. The D-W statistics also showed no sign of auto-correlation. Thus, the results showed that public expenditure on social services had a stronger impact on human development than economic growth, per se.

CONCLUSION

Meghalaya, in the last few decades, has been witnessing a paradoxical and explosive economic growth because of the mismatch between growth rates of state domestic product and public expenditure. Disproportionate growth of the social sector over the years has not only eaten up most of the public investment in the state, but also given rise to a weaker linkage among different sectors. The study reveals that at the regional level, there is a positive functional relationship between public expenditure on social sectors and human development. Further, it reveals that per capita spending on education and health has a relatively stronger impact on human development than per capita income growth. Thus, the findings of the present study support our premise that higher public expenditure on social sector is a prerequisite to better human development.

REFERENCES

Anand, S. and M. Ravallion 1993. 'Human Development in Poor Countries: On the Role of Private Incomes and Public Services', *Journal of Economic Perspectives*, Vol. 7, Issue 1, pp.133–50.

Anand, S. and R. Kanbur 1991. 'Public Policy and Basic Needs Provision: Intervention and Achievement in Sri Lanka', in J. Drèze and A. Sen (eds.), *The Political Economy of Hunger*, Vol. 3, Clarendon Press, Oxford.

Chakraborty, L.S. 2001. 'Public Expenditure and Human Development: An Empirical Investigation', National Institute of Public Finance and Policy, New Delhi, India. www.wider.unu.edu/conference/conference-2003-2/ conference%202003-2-papers/papers-pdf/Chakraborty%20120403.pdf

Drèze, J. and A. Sen 1995. *India: Economic Development and Social Opportunity*, Oxford India Paperbacks.

Government of India (GoI) 2002. *National Human Development Report 2001*, Planning Commission, New Delhi.

Griffin, C. 1992. *Health Care in Asia: A Comparative Study on Cost and Financing*, World Bank, Washington D.C.

Grossman, G.M. and E. Helpman 1994. 'Endogenous Innovation in the Theory of Growth', *Journal of Economic Perspective*, Vol. 8, No. 1, pp. 23–43.

Grossman, P.J. 1988. 'Government and Economic Growth: A Non-Linear Relationship', *Public Choice*, Vol. 56, No. 2, pp. 193-200.

Haq, M.u 1995. *Reflections on Human Development*, Oxford University Press, New York.

Isenman, P. 1980. 'Basic Needs: The Case of Sri Lanka', *World Development*, Vol. 8, No. 3, pp. 237–58.

Mundle, S. 1998. 'Financing Human Development: Some Lessons from Advanced Asian Countries', *World Development*, Vol. 26, No. 4, pp. 659–72.

Noorbakhsh, F. 1998. 'A Modified Human Development Index', *World Development*, Vol. 26, No. 3, pp. 517–28.

Sen, A. 1998. 'Human Development and Financial Conservatism', *World Development*, Vol. 26, No. 4, pp. 733–42.

———. 1981. 'Public Action and the Quality of Life in Developing Countries', *Oxford Bulletin of Economics and Statistics*, Vol. 43, No. 4, pp. 287–319.

Streeten, P. 1979. 'From Growth to Basic Needs', *Finance and Development*, Vol. 16, No. 3, pp. 28–31.

19
Antenatal Care, Institutional Delivery, and Human Development in Meghalaya

KISHOR SINGH RAJPUT

INTRODUCTION

The progress in the field of human development in a country invariably depends on the performance of its health sector, besides improvement in other related areas. The health sector has been given topmost priority in the recent central and state plans, along with efforts to develop the primary and elementary education. This is to bring the people in general at the centrestage of development so as to integrate everyone in the development process and provide benefits to them. Again in the health sector, emphasis has been placed on the reproductive health component, particularly the health needs of married women and children. This change has started taking place only after the International Conference on Population and Development (ICPD 1994), held in Cairo under the auspices of the United Nations Organization (UNO).

The ICPD stressed that the goal to attain satisfactory human development will remain unfulfilled if the reproductive health needs of married women and their children are not properly attended to. Demographers and sociologists consider women as the keepers of nation's health (Basu 2000). If keepers of the health of a nation are not healthy, the immediate family and society, in general, will invariably suffer. Cairo represents a transformation in the ideology of a field—from a regulatory approach to a humanistic agenda, centred on people. Human development factors such as education, especially of women, preparation and opportunities for employment, economic development, and human rights, including the recognition of gender-based inequality and its effect on reproductive processes, all form an integral part of the vision adopted in Cairo.

There is an extraordinary difference in maternal death rates between the developed and developing countries (ICMR 1990). According to the World Bank (1993), about one-third of the total disease burden of women between 15 and 44 years of age in developing countries is linked to health problems related to pregnancy. Every minute, a woman dies as a result of pregnancy or childbirth. Every time a woman in the third world becomes pregnant, her risk of dying is 200 times higher than the risk run by a woman in the developed world (Motashaw 1997). Approximately, seven out of every 100 children born in India die before reaching age of one and five out of every 1,000 mothers, who become pregnant, die of causes related to pregnancy and childbirth. India also accounts for more than one-fifth of all maternal deaths from causes related to pregnancy and childbirth worldwide (Sughathan *et al.* 2001).

Chatterjee (1996) stressed that women in India bear their health problems in a 'culture of silence' and do not seek timely health care; they often do not travel beyond the area of their normal activities to obtain services; they usually hesitate to approach male health workers. Heads of the families, in general, and women, in particular, spend less time, effort, and money seeking health care for women and girls as compared to men. There is substantial evidence to show that Indian women also bear a heavy burden of reproductive morbidity (Bang and Bang 1991; Pachauri 1994).

The situation in Meghalaya is no different. According to the National Family Health Survey (NFHS 1998–99) 63.3 per cent of the surveyed women in the state suffered from anaemia, hardly 30.8 per cent received two or more tetanus toxoid injections, and as low as 17.3 per cent had institutional delivery. Further, the infant mortality rate of the state was higher than the all India figure at 89 per 1,000 live births.

In the recent past, researchers have started placing emphasis not only on the problems of reproductive health but also have been trying to examine the community influences on individual health outcomes, so as to place health-care seeking behaviour in its socioeconomic context. It is hypothesized that use of reproductive health care services is influenced by various socioeconomic and demographic factors. These factors that are studied in this context are urban residence, household living conditions, household income, occupational status, the type of family in which they live and their status, woman's employment in skilled work outside the home, husband's high level of education, young maternal age, etc.

In her studies of Khasi tribal women, Das (2000) observes that the utilization of maternal health care services varies from society to society, and within a society, from group to group, and finally from individual to individual. Her results suggest that better utilization of antenatal services and institutional delivery is found among urban women having higher standard of living, with exposure to mass media, and having greater autonomy.

It is a well-established fact that receiving antenatal care and giving birth in a medical institution under the care and supervision of trained medical personnel promotes child survival and reduces the risk of maternal mortality. The fact that 1,00,000 women in India are estimated to die every year due to problems related to pregnancy and childbirth reinforces the importance of antenatal care during pregnancy under the supervision of trained medical personnel (IIPS 1995).

OBJECTIVES

The basic objectives of the paper are to:

1. provide a brief picture of public sector health infrastructure in Meghalaya;
2. present the antenatal care situation and to analyse the effect of certain selected background variables on it; and
3. present the institutional delivery situation and analyse the effect of certain selected background variables on it.

SOURCES OF DATA AND ANALYSIS

This paper mainly uses the data of the NFHS 1998–99 for Meghalaya state including raw NFHS data collected by the International Institute for Population Sciences, Mumbai. Altogether 945 women, in the age group of 15 to 49 with at least one live birth, were sampled to collect maternal health-related data from 72 villages. To draw meaningful conclusions, besides bivariate tables, logistic regression has been used in the study.

Public Sector Health Infrastructure in Meghalaya

Between 1971–72 and 2004–05, the number of hospitals in Meghalaya increased from seven to eight, but the number of dispensaries declined from 57 to 14. However, the number of Primary Health Centres (PHCs) significantly increased from just nine in 1971–72 to 101 in 2004–05. So is the case with the Community Health Centres (CHCs) and sub-centres (Table 19.1).

Table 19.1: Number of Hospitals, Dispensaries, PHCs, CHCs, and Sub-centers in Meghalaya

Year	Hospital	Dispensaries	PHC	CHC	Sub-Centre
1971–72	7	57	9	NA	NA
2004–05	8	14	101	24	401

Sources: *Meghalaya Socioeconomic Review*, 2003.
Statistical Handbook, Meghalaya 2005.

Though the number of doctors went up, the doctor–population ratio came down. For instance, the number of government doctors increased from 113 in 1971–72 to 498 in 2004–05 (Table 19.2), but at the same time, the doctor–population ratio came down from 1:9,204 to 1: 5,169 (Table 19.3). Likewise, the number of nurses, Auxiliary Nurse Midwives (ANM), and pharmacists also increased. The number of nurses increased from 117 to 956, the ANM from 82 to 754, and the pharmacists from 83 to 168 during the same period.

Table 19.2: Number of Doctors and Para-Medical Staff in Meghalaya

Year	Doctors	Nurses	ANM	Pharmacists
1971–72	113	117	82	83
2004–05	498	956	754	168

Source: *Meghalaya Socioeconomic Review*, 2003.
Statistical Handbook, Meghalaya 2005.

Table 19.3: Doctor–Population Ratio in Meghalaya

Year	Doctors	Population (in '000)	Doctor–Population Ratio
1971–72	113	1040	1 : 9204
2000–01	324	2319	1 : 7157
2004–05	498	2574*	1 : 5169

Source: Meghalaya *Socioeconomic Review*, 2003
Statistical Handbook, Meghalaya 2005. * Estimated population

When we look at the availability of specific hospital beds in Meghalaya, the progress over the years was not very satisfactory (Table

19.4). The number of general beds in government hospitals increased from 983 in 1987 to 2,426 in 2004–05. The progress was far more discouraging in case of maternity beds and paediatric beds. Between 1987 and 2004–05, maternity beds increased from 135 to just 235, whereas paediatric beds increased to 227 from 190. The results suggest that only 4.2 per cent, 5.6 per cent, and 6.9 per cent of the villages had PHCs, CHCs, and Sub-centres respectively. As low as 2.8 per cent villages had the provision for private hospitals and clinics. Likewise, 6.9 per cent of the villages were served by resident private doctors. The percentage of villages having visiting doctors stood at 15.3 per cent.

Table 19.4: Availability of Number and Types of Medical Beds in Meghalaya

Year	General Beds	Maternity Beds	Paediatric Beds
1987	983	135	190
2004–05	2426	235	227

Source: Meghalaya Socio-Economic Review, 2003
Statistical Handbook, Meghalaya, 2005.

Background Characteristics of Women

As high as 26.3 per cent women belonged to the age group of 25–29 years followed by the age group 20–24, constituting 18.4 per cent of women. Only 4.9 per cent of women were in the age group 15–19 as against 8.1 per cent in the 45–49 age group. From the point of view of religion, 72.1 per cent of the women were found to be Christians and 9.9 per cent Hindu. Almost 13.0 per cent of the women reported not to be having any religion, whereas the remaining 5.4 per cent belonged to other religions. Meghalaya, being predominantly a tribal state, 90 per cent of the women belonged to scheduled tribe category. As far as the education of the women and their husbands is concerned, a majority of them belonged to the category of 'literate but less than middle school completed', followed by the illiterate group. For example, 41.3 per cent of the women and 37.6 per cent of their husbands were found to have education of less than middle school. Percentage figures of illiterate women and illiterate husbands stood at 37.4 per cent and 29.9 per cent respectively. On the other hand, 11.9 per cent and 9.5 per cent of the women were found to have education of more than middle school and more than high school, respectively. Likewise, the percentages of husbands having education of more than middle school and more than high school stood at 16.5 per cent and 15.1 per cent respectively.

Work status of the women is another background variable used in the analysis. The analysis shows that 54.0 per cent of the women were found as non-working and the remaining 46.0 per cent worked outside their homes for their livelihood. As far as the rural–urban distribution is concerned, 79.6 per cent of the surveyed women belonged to rural areas.

Antenatal Care and Its Correlates

The likelihood of women receiving antenatal care during pregnancy depends on many factors. Table 19.5 presents the antenatal care of women by her selected background variables. Altogether, 55.1 per cent

Table 19.5: Per cent Distribution of Women having Antenatal Care by Selected Background Characteristics

Selected Background Variables	Antenatal Care	
Place of Residence		
(i) Rural	49.8	(220)
(ii) Urban	87.7	(64)
Religion of the Women		
(i) Christian	57.6	(209)
(ii) Hindu	50.0	(20)
(iii) No Religion	62.3	(48)
(iv) Others	20.0	(7)
Ethnic Background		
(i) Scheduled Tribe	57.4	(264)
(ii) Others	36.4	(20)
Education of the Women		
(i) Illiterate	39.1	(77)
(ii) Literate < Middle School	60.5	(133)
(iii) More than Middle School	66.7	(46)
(iv) High School and Above	96.6	(28)
Work Status of the Women		
(i) Not Working	61.0	(197)
(ii) Working	45.3	(87)
Education of the Husband		
(i) Illiterate	41.5	(71)
(ii) Literate < Middle School	57.4	(116)
(iii) More than Middle School	67.1	(47)
(iv) High School and Above	71.2	(47)
(v) Missing	5.0	(3)
Total	55.1	(284)

Note: Data for women giving birth during the 3-year period preceding the survey.

of the women received antenatal care for the children born during the 3-year period preceding the survey.

The urban women (87.7 per cent) receive far better antenatal care than the rural women (49.8 per cent). Likewise, the scheduled tribe women (57.4 per cent) have shown better antenatal care than the women of other ethnic backgrounds (36.4 per cent). However, women do not show much variation in the antenatal care by their religious background.

Education of women and their husbands is found positively related with antenatal care, that is, higher the educational level, the higher is the likelihood of antenatal care. For example, 39.1 per cent of the illiterate women go for antenatal care as compared to 96.6 per cent of women having more than high school education. Likewise, the percentage figures for antenatal care of women whose husbands are illiterate and more than high school educated stands at 41.5 per cent and 71.2 respectively. As far as the work status of the women is concerned, it is seen that 61.0 per cent of the non-working have gone for antenatal care compared to 45.3 per cent of the women who are working.

Determinants of Antenatal Care

Table 19.6 presents the adjusted effects (odd ratios) of selected background variables on the likelihood of women receiving antenatal care. This analysis is done for rural women and total women, separately. The results carried out on rural women show that women's education, her work status, and her husband's education, come out as the significant determinants of antenatal care after the adjustment of the effects of other background variables used in the model. For instance, women who are less than middle school educated, middle school complete, and above high school are respectively, 2.0 times, 2.1 times, and 9.4 times more likely to have antenatal care as compared to the illiterate women. Likewise, women whose husbands are less than middle school educated, show 1.5 times higher probability of receiving antenatal care as compared to women whose husbands are illiterate. However, working women are less likely to have antenatal care in comparison to their counterparts who are working. As far as the total number of women are concerned, the result shows that urban women are 5.0 times more likely to receive antenatal care than rural women, when controlled for other background variables. However, husband's education loses its

Table 19.6: Odd Ratios of Logistic Regression Analyses of Utilization of Antenatal Care Services

Background Variables	Rural	Total
Religion of the women (rc: Hindu)		
Christian	1.4	1.4
No religion	2.1	2.0
Others	0.7	-
Ethnical background (rc: Scheduled tribe)		
Others	0.6	0.6
Place of current residence (rc: Rural)		
Urban	–	5.0***
Women's education (rc: Illiterate)		
Less than middle school	2.0***	1.8***
Middle school complete	2.1**	1.9**
High school and above	9.4**	16.9***
Work status of women (rc: Not working)		
Working	0.6**	0.6**
Husband's education (rc: Illiterate)		
Less than middle school	1.5*	1.4
Middle school complete	1.2	1.4
High school and above	0.8	0.6
Constant	0.5	0.5

Note: *** Significant at 1 per cent; ** Significant at 5 per cent, and * Significant at 10 per cent.

significance as a predictor variable of antenatal care when the total number of women are considered.

Institutional Delivery and Its Correlates

The background variables of women do exert an influence on the institutional delivery of children (Table 19.7).

When women are considered by their place of residence, it is found that the institutional delivery of the children is significantly higher for urban women. For example, 80.8 per cent of urban women have deliveries in medical institutions, whereas the corresponding figure for rural women stands at only 7.9 per cent. Though the institutional delivery of children by religious affiliation of women does not show much variation, Hindu women (27.5 per cent) comparatively have slightly higher institutional delivery than Christian women (19.3 per cent), women with no religion (15.6 per cent). Likewise, the ethnic back-ground of women hardly makes any difference in the institutional delivery of the children. Like antenatal care, the education of women and their husbands is positively associated with the institutional delivery of the child. Particularly the education of women is very strongly related to institutional delivery. For instance, as compared to 5.1 per cent of illiterate women having institutional delivery, 79.3 per cent of women with high school education and above have institutional delivery. But there is no significant variation in the institutional delivery between the working and non-working women, though the institutional delivery of the child is found to be slightly higher for the non-working women. For instance, as compared to 21.1

Table 19.7: Per cent Distribution of Women having Institutional Delivery by Background Characteristics

Selected Background Characteristics	Institutional Delivery
Place of residence	
(i) Rural	7.9 (35)
(ii) Urban	80.8 (59)
Religion of the women	
(i) Christian	19.3 (70)
(ii) Hindu	27.5 (11)
(iii) No Religion	15.6 (12)
(iv) Others	2.9 (1)
Ethnic background	
(i) Scheduled Tribe	18.3 (84)
(ii) Others	18.2 (10)
Education of the women	
(i) Illiterate	5.1 (10)
(ii) Literate < Middle School	16.4 (36)
(iii) More than Middle School	36.2 (25)
(iv) High School and Above	79.3 (23)
Work Status of the women	
(i) Not Working	21.1 (68)
(ii) Working	13.5 (26)
Education of the husband	
(i) Illiterate	5.8 (10)
(ii) Literate < Middle School	15.3 (31)
(iii) More than Middle School	31.4 (22)
(iv) High School and Above	47.0 (31)
(v) Missing	–
Antenatal care	
(i) No	2.2 (5)
(ii) Yes	31.3 (89)
Total	18.3 (94)

Note: Data for the women giving birth during 3-year period preceding the survey.

per cent of the non-working women, 13.5 per cent of working women have institutional delivery. Lastly, those women having antenatal care have shown higher institutional delivery in comparison to the women without antenatal care during their last pregnancy. For example, the women with and without antenatal care, the respective percentage figures of institutional delivery stand at 31.3 per cent and 2.2 per cent. In all, 18.3 per cent of the women with pregnancy during the three-year period preceding the survey have delivered their children in medical institutions.

Determinants of Institutional Delivery

The adjusted effects of the background variables on institutional delivery are presented in Table 19.8, both for rural and total women.

As far as rural women are concerned, their educational level and work status, their husband's education, and antenatal care are found to be the important determinants of institutional delivery. For instance, women who are more than middle school educated and also women whose husbands are more than middle school educated are respectively 6.0 times and 4.1 times more likely to go for institutional delivery as compared to their respective reference categories, namely illiterate women and women whose husbands are illiterate. Work status of women also makes a difference in the place of delivery of the child. After the adjustment of other background variables, it has been seen that the probability of having institutional delivery increases by 2.6 times for the working women, vis-à-vis, the non-working women. However, the most significant determinant of institutional delivery for rural women has been found to be antenatal care. Women having gone for antenatal care during their last pregnancy have shown 42.0 times higher probability of having institutional delivery as compared to women without having earlier antenatal care. As far as the total number of women are concerned, besides the above mentioned variables for rural women, the place of residence comes out to be another significant determinant for institutional delivery. The chances of urban women going for institutional delivery are significantly higher than the rural women. In fact, the probability of having institutional delivery rises by 43.5 times for urban women in comparison to rural women. Likewise, for total number of women also, it has been seen that women who are literate, working, received antenatal care during their last pregnancy, and whose husbands are literate, are more likely to have deliveries in medical institutions in comparison to women

Table 19.8: Odd Ratios of Logistic Regression Analyses of the Institutional Delivery

Background Variables	Rural	Total
Religion of the women (rc: Hindu)		
(i) Christian	1.1	1.0
(ii) No religion	0.6	0.5
(iii) Others	3.0	3.5
Ethnic background (rc: Scheduled tribe)		
(i) Others	0.8	0.6
Place of current residence (rc: Rural)		
(i) Urban	–	43.5***
Women's education (rc: Illiterate)		
(i) Less than middle school	2.6	3.1**
(ii) Middle school complete	6.0***	8.3***
(iii) High school and above	3.6	11.1***
Work status of women (rc: Not working)		
(i) Working	2.6**	2.1*
Husband's education (rc: Illiterate)		
(i) Less than middle school	1.6	2.4*
(ii) Middle school complete	4.1**	3.8**
(iii) High school and above	2.8	2.9*
Antenatal care (rc: No)		
(i) Yes	41.9***	14.1***
Constant	0.001***	0.001***

Note: *** Significant at 1 per cent; ** Significant at 5 per cent, and * Significant at 10 per cent.

who are illiterate, not working, whose husbands are illiterate, and who had no antenatal care during their last pregnancy.

CONCLUSION

The study indicates that over the years public health infrastructure in Meghalaya has not been satisfactory. Growth of public sector health infrastructure has not been able to keep pace with that of the growth of the population in the state. The antenatal care coverage as well as institutional delivery of children is very low. Given the health infrastructure and the coverage of antenatal care and institutional delivery, the goal of achieving safe motherhood in the near future will remain elusive until and unless drastic improvements take place.

The logistic regression analyses show that place of residence acts as an important determinant of both antenatal care and institutional delivery, that is, urban women have better chances of receiving antenatal care and institutional delivery of children as compared to their rural counterparts. Mother's education as well as husband's education, exerts a positive effect on antenatal care and institutional delivery. Work status of women exerts differential effects on antenatal care and institutional delivery. Antenatal care acts as a very important determinant of institutional delivery. Women having antenatal care during their last pregnancy are more likely to go for institutional delivery of their children as compared to women without earlier antenatal care.

REFERENCES

Bang, R.A. and A. Bang 1991. 'Why Women Hide Them: Rural Women's View Points on Reproductive Tract Infections', *Manushi*, Vol. 69, pp.7–30.

Basu, A.M. 2000. 'Gender in Population Research: Confusing Implications for Health Policy', *Population Studies,* Vol. 54, No. 1.

Cairo Conference, 1994. International Conference on Population and Development (ICPD), September 5–13, United Nations.

Chatterjee, M. 1996. 'Addressing Gender and Poverty Concerns in a Reproductive Health Programme', in Anthony R. Measham and A. Richard Heaver (eds) *Supplement to India's Family Welfare Programme: Moving to a Reproductive and Child Health Approach,* The World Bank, Washington, pp. 30–45.

Das, M. 2000. 'Reproductive Health Issues and Health Seeking Behaviour of Women in a Matrilineal Set-Up: A Study of Khasi Tribal Women', Unpublished PhD Thesis, International Institute for Population Sciences, Mumbai.

Entwisle, B., J.B. Casterline, and A. A. Sayeed 1989. 'Villages as Contexts for Contraceptive Behaviour in Rural Egypt', *American Sociological Review,* Vol. 54, No. 6, pp. 1019–34.

Indian Council of Medical Reserach (ICMR) Bulletin, 2000. 'HIV Infection in India', *Indian Council of Medical Research,* Vol. 20, Nos. 11 and 12, 1990.

International Institute of Population Sciences (IIPS), 1995. *National Family Health Survey (MCH and Family Planning), 1992-93: India,* International Institute for Population Sciences, Mumbai.

Motashaw, N.D. 1997. 'Root Causes of Maternal Mortality: Infancy to Motherhood', *The Journal of Family Welfare,* Vol. 43, No. 2, pp. 4-14.

National Family Health Survey (NFHS-2) INDIA, North-Eastern States (Arunachal Pradesh, Manipur, Meghalaya, Mizoram, Nagaland, and Tripura, 1998–99). ORC Macro, Calverton, Maryland USA and International Institute for Population Sciences, Mumbai, December 2002. http://www.nfhsindia.org/data/ne/neintro.pdf

Pachauri, S. 1994. 'Women's Reproductive Health in India: Research Needs and Priorities', in J. Gittlesohn, M.E. Bentley, P.J. Pelto, M. Nag, S. Pachauri, A.D. Harrison, and L.T. Landman (eds), *Listening to Women Talk about Their Health Issues and Evidence from India*, Har-Anand Publications, New Delhi, pp. 15–39.

Harrison, L.T.L. (eds): *Listening to Women Talk about Their Health Issues and Evidence from India*, The Ford Foundation and Har-Anand Publications, New Delhi.

Sughathan, K.S., V. Mehta, and R.D. Retherford 2001. *Promoting Institutional Deliveries in Rural India: The Role of Antenatal - Care Services*, NFHS Subject Reports, No. 20, IIPS, Mumbai and East-West Center, Population and Health Studies, Honolulu, USA.

World Bank, 1993. 'Investing in Health', *World Development Report*, Oxford University Press, New York.

20
Human Development in Manipur

E. Bijoykumar Singh

INTRODUCTION

Manipur is a small state in this region. It has shared the triumphs and travails like the other states of this region. It has an area of 22,327 sq km. Out of her nine districts, five are in the hills and the remaining four in the valley. The hill districts are known as Senapati, Tamenglong, Churachandpur, Chandel, and0 Ukhrul and the districts in the valley are Imphal East, Imphal West, Bishnupur, and Thoubal. Though, the valley is only one-tenth of the area of the state, most of the people of the state live in the valley. The tribal population, consisting of about 30 per cent of the total population, is mainly from the hill districts. The state has been a remarkable case study of struggle and success. The contribution of this small state in sports and classical dance has been phenomenal. It is also remarkable that this strife-torn erstwhile princely state, since its merger into India in 1949, has managed to transcend adversity. The egalitarian ethos in the Manipuri society has been an asset. This is indicative of a vibrant core in human development of the state.

Human development, in the sense of a long, healthy, and well-informed life, a decent standard of living, and comprehensive well-being of all persons requires a favourable enabling environment, comprising a progressive rise in income and diversifications of the sources of income, and creation of adequate opportunities for gainful employment for all who are willing to work, alleviation of poverty, progressive changes in the pattern of livelihood, expansion and structural changes of private and public consumption, provision of education for all children, adequate health care for all, creation of environment for healthy living, due care for the aging population, greater involvement of women in social empowerment, and participation in decision making in all fields of life. It also needs promotion of the capabilities of youth and expansion of opportunities for productive utilization of their energies, good governance for promoting the general well-being of the people including material and social well-being, self respect, security of life and property, civil peace, safe and secure environment, and freedom of choice and action. Viewed from this perspective, what has been unfolding in the North East, in general, and Manipur, in particular, can be said to be closely interlinked with our experience of development, vis-à-vis, our aspirations. The sense of alienation, neglect, and mistrust are all manifestations of the growing divide.

HUMAN DEVELOPMENT

The most comprehensive measure of human development is the Human Development Index (HDI). It is a composite index mea-suring average achievement in three basic dimensions of human development—a long and healthy life, knowledge, and a decent stan-dard of living. It combines measures of life expectancy at birth, school enrolment, adult literacy, and income to provide a broader view of development. It is, thus, a summary measure to evaluate progress, focusing both on income and human welfare. The United Nations Development Programme (UNDP) has been constructing indices of human development for various countries since it started publishing *Human Development Report (HDR)* in 1990.

In 1981, Manipur had the highest HDI among all the north-eastern states in India and its all India rank was 4th (*NHDR 2001*). Despite having a substantially lower per capita income, the status of the state was raised over most of the Indian states mainly due to high liter-acy, high enrolment, and much better life expectancy. Though, HDI of Manipur had increased by 11.43 per cent during 1981–91, her all India rank dropped to 9th position, and in the region the state was 2nd to Mizoram. The increase in HDI was the lowest in the states among the north-eastern states, much lower than the national aver-age. This indicated nothing but deterioration in the quality of human development-enhancing programmes in the state. In order to assess the performance of economic reforms, let us ask ourselves an interest-ing question: Has HDI increased faster in the era of post-economic reforms covering the 1990s? At the all India level, the percentage increase declined from 26.16 per cent, during 1981–91, to 23.88 per cent, during 1991–2001. Assam is the only north-eastern state whose HDI was estimated for 2001. As regards official data at the national level, HDI for Manipur, like many other smaller states in India, was not constructed for 2001. Like other north-eastern states, the database of Manipur is highly inadequate for routine construction of a measure as comprehensive as the HDI. It is again a reflection of the quality of economic policy of the state. Absence of data requires that one has to infer information on the quality of human development from the correlates of human development. For this purpose, the quality of human resources, the occupational distribution of workers and quality of jobs, and poverty are examined in the following sections.

Quality of Human Resource

As per the 2001 Census (North-Eastern Council 2005), the total population of Manipur was 22, 93,896, of which 49 per cent were females. Crude birth rate, death rate, and infant mortality rates were, respectively, 16.8, 4.6 and 14. During 1991–2001, the population registered a growth of 24.8 per cent. The state has the distinction of having the lowest infant mortality rate among the Indian states. It declined from 32 in 1961 to 11 in 2006. Low infant mortality rate indicates better child care, emanating from sound child care practices, awareness among mothers about hygiene, and nutrition. Expectation of life at birth, which is a summary measure of the mortality experience of a society, reveals the females in the state have a better chance in life in terms of expectation of life as evident from the state and district level data (Government of Manipur and GoI 2007–08). The expectation of life at birth for the state was 68.64 for males and that of 72.42 for females in 1991, as against the corresponding figures of 62.3 and 63.9 at the national level during 2001–05. Besides, the state has a large proportion of people in the working age group and, thus, their productive employment has the potential of being a major demographic dividend. Only 6.7 per cent of the population of the state belongs to the 60 years plus category while 60.5 per cent are in the age group of 15–59 years. The rest of the population belongs to the age group of 0–14 years.

As per 2001 census, the state ranks 15th among the states and union territories in literacy (Table 20.1). Male literacy rate stood at 80.3 per cent, as against female literacy rate of 60.5 per cent.

As regards sex ratio, that is, the number of females per 1,000 males, which is another measure of gender inequality, Table 20.2 shows that

Table 20.1: Literacy: India versus Manipur

	1951	1961	1971	1981	1981	2001
Manipur	12.57	36.04	38.47	49.66	59.89	70.53
India	18.33	28.30	34.45	43.57	52.21	64.84

Note: Literacy rate for Manipur in 1951 is based on sample population and from 1951 up to 1971 censuses relate to population aged five years and above. The rates from 1981 up to 2001 refer to population aged seven and above.
Source: Office of the Registrar General of India, Ministry of Home Affairs, GoI.

Table 20.2: Sex Ratio in India and Manipur

(Females per 1000 males)

Census Year	Sex Ratio	
	India	Manipur
1901	972	1037
1911	964	1029
1921	955	1041
1931	950	1065
1941	945	1055
1951	946	1036
1961	941	1015
1971	930	980
1981	934	971
1991	927	958
2001	933	974

Source: Office of the Registrar General of India, Ministry of Home Affairs, GoI.

it was growing increasingly favourable to women when the reverse was occurring at the all India level.

It peaked in 1931, and started declining thereafter, by which time the declining trend had already been set in at the all India level. The sex ratio in the state became unfavourable to females in 1971. It kept on declining till 1991 and recovered in 2001, though it was still adverse to females. Given the declining trend, it is not known whether this recovery will be sustained in 2011. The phase of adverse sex ratio coincides with high population growth associated with male selective in-migration. Female infanticide and dowry deaths are rare in the state. Overall, women in Manipur take an active part in economic activities and decision making, both at the family and state level. The socially accepted active role played by Manipuri women in anti-alcohol movements and movements against excesses, both by state forces and unlawful organizations, indicate their high social status. Thus, gender inequality looking from different angles would be less in Manipur and the overall quality of human resources must have improved during the post-economic reforms period.

Income and Employment

Structural change and changes in the occupational distribution of the workforce will have an important bearing on human development. The sectoral distribution of workers reveals the level of their relative well-being. Higher the proportion of workers in more remunerative occupations, the higher will be the human welfare. It will be better than a situation with higher per capita income and more people in low-paid occupations. Table 20.3 shows the real per capita income of the state during 1993–94 and 2004–05. The growth of per capita NSDP has been erratic. The annual compound growth rate of state per capita income during this period is 2.91 per cent. Among the northeastern states, only Assam has a lower per capita income.

Table 20.3: Per Capita Income of Manipur

(Income in Rs)

Year	State Per Capita Income at 1993–94 Prices	Growth Rate
1993–94	5846	
1994–95	5558	(–) 4.93
1995–96	5616	1.04
1996–97	6022	7.22
1997–98	6434	6.84
1998–99	6401	(–) 0.51
1999–2000	7097	10.87
2000–01	6851	(–) 3.47
2001–02	7445	8.67
2002–03	7446	0.01
2003–04	7532	1.15
2004–05	8015	6.41

Source: Central Statistical Organization.

In 2004–05, the primary sector contributed 27.95 per cent of real NSDP, while the shares of secondary and tertiary sector were 24.63 per cent and 47.42 per cent, respectively. The share of the primary sector has been falling, while the shares of secondary sector and tertiary sectors have been rising. Much of the decline in the share of primary sector has been accounted by the secondary sector. Among the sub-sectors, agriculture including livestock in the primary sector,

Table 20.4: Distribution of Working Persons by Broad Industry Division (Rural)

(Per 1000 persons)

NSS Round & Year	Agriculture		Mining & Quarrying		Manufacturing		Construction		Trade		Transport		Services	
	M	F	M	F	M	F	M	F	M	F	M	F	M	F
32nd (1973–74)	871	666	–	–	20	239	3	–	14	84	2	–	90	10
38th (1977)	850	767	–	–	24	167	5	–	31	49	3	–	88	17
43rd (1983)	692	799	–	–	31	101	14	–	29	35	16	1	217	64
50th (1987–88)	660	603	1	–	37	262	41	6	38	56	24	–	196	70
55th (1999–2000)	780	696	1	18	22	186	13	–	27	58	20	–	137	42
61st (2004–05)	694	691	5	6	31	172	50	1	53	87	34	–	132	44

Source: NSSO (1986, 1990, 1996, 2001, and 2006).

Table 20.5: Distribution of Working Persons by Broad Industry Division (Urban)

(Per 1000 persons)

NSS Round & Year	Agriculture		Mining & Quarrying		Manufacturing		Construction		Trade		Transport		Services	
	M	F	M	F	M	F	M	F	M	F	M	F	M	F
32nd (1973–74)	256	272	–	4	64	394	21	–	236	224	12	–	411	106
38th (1977)	513	609	9	–	71	228	30	–	51	79	40	–	272	85
43rd (1983)	323	289	1	11	77	196	29	–	151	203	21	–	398	301
50th (1987–88)	309	261	–	–	44	342	38	3	108	195	46	2	437	196
55th (1999–2000)	293	263	13	–	55	215	60	3	164	274	44	19	371	225
61st (2004–05)	313	215	–	–	78	290	65	–	170	261	60	–	310	234

Source: NSSO (1986, 1990, 1996, 2001, and 2006).

construction in the secondary sector, and public administration in the tertiary sector are the most important sub-sectors. Public administration has emerged as the most important sub-sector next to agriculture. Against this backdrop of structural change the occupational pattern has been examined.

Tables 20.4 and 20.5 show how the workers, by principal status and subsidiary status, have been distributed across sub-sectors of the economy. It also shows the pattern of livelihoods of the people over time.

In the beginning, rural male workers were mainly in agriculture and rural females had a more diversified activity matrix. Now, the predominance of agriculture with rural male workers has declined and they have made inroads into female-dominated activities, such as manufacturing and trade. On the other hand, females have made inroads into mining, quarrying, transport, and services. Though, manufacturing remains a predominantly female activity, the proportion of females in this sector declined substantially from 239 in 1973–74 to 172 in 2004–05. Traditionally, Manipuri women have been participating actively in trade. During the period under study, the proportion of women in trade declined and again recovered showing insignificant change. However, the proportion of males in trade has risen substantially.

Urban workers, both male and female, had a much more diversified activity matrix. However, the ranking of the sectors has undergone changes. In 1973–74, for urban males, services was the predominant sector and for females it was manufacturing. In 2004–05, the proportion of urban males in agriculture marginally exceeded the proportion in services sector, which declined from 411 to 310. In the case of urban females, the proportion in the manufacturing sector declined by 26.4 per cent while that in service sector rose by 120.75 per cent. These tables show that the livelihood matrix has undergone significant changes for both sexes and the urban matrix has been more diverse than that of the rural matrix.

A frequently asked question is the employment content of growth. It is also associated with the impact of globalization. If higher growth leading to higher per capita income perpetuates higher unemployment, it is not desirable. This issue is being examined by using elasticity of employment with respect to total real NSDP and income originating in different sectors of the economy. Table 20.6 shows the change of elasticity over a time period covering both pre- and post-economic reforms. The period from 1993–94 to 2004–05 covers post-economic reforms, while the two sub-periods, from 1993–94 to 1999–2000 and from 1999–2000 to 2004–05, represent the early and latter phases of economic reforms, respectively. Data reveals that the experiences in two sub-periods differed significantly.

Table 20.6: Sectoral Employment Elasticities

Sector	1987–88 to 1993–94	1993–94 to 1999–2000	1999–2000 to 2004–05	1987–88 to 2004–05
Agriculture	1.057 (0.7)	1.93 (0.01)	1.589	1.34
Manufacturing	0.296 (0.38)	−0.42 (0.33)	1.437	0.189
Construction	3.66 (0.86)	−0.282 (0.82)	2.078	0.839
Transport	1.15 (0.55)	0.25 (0.63)	0.85	0.734
Trade	1.785 (0.68)	0.643 (0.62)	1.661	1.508
Services	0.758	−0.189	0.209	0.133
All	0.794 (0.52)	0.303 (0.16)	1.322	0.67

Note: The sectoral elasticities for Manipur are derived by dividing the percentage change in employment by percentage change in real NSDP at 1993–94 prices originating in the sector. Figures in parentheses are employment elasticities for all India.
Source: National figures are from Planning Commission (2002): 132.

Elasticity of employment with respect to real NSDP shows the job creating character of economic growth. Over the period from 1987–88 to 2004–05, the elasticity is 0.67. Thus, every one per cent increase in NSDP raised employment by 0.67 per cent. The sectoral variation shows that trade is the most employment elastic sub-sector, followed by agriculture. Services together have the least elasticity. The sub-period analysis of income elasticity for the periods from 1987–88 to 1993–94, 1993–94 to 1999–2000, and 1999–2000 to 2004–05, reveal some interesting features. During the pre-reform period (proxied by the period from 1987–88 to 1993–94) construction as a sub-sector was the most employment elastic. During the period from 1993–94 to 1999–2000, except for agriculture, elasticity not only declined but also became negative in manufacturing, construction, and services. Labour simply got absorbed in the agricultural sector, as usual as the residual sector. Since this period coincided with economic reforms, it supported the hypothesis that economic reforms initially ushered in growth without jobs. An economy with surplus labour, experiencing jobless growth, will have serious problems. Fortunately, during the period from 1999–2000 to 2004–05, employment elasticity of all the sub sectors except agriculture registered impressive growth. Construction re-emerged as the leading sub-sector. The overall employment elasticity was the highest in the sub-periods. The low employment content of growth during 1993–94 to 1999–2000 was reversed during 1999–2000 to 2004–05. It implies that the trend of jobless growth in the initial phase of economic reforms was reversed in the latter phase as decision makers could learn the lessons from the new economic environment.

Unemployment rates rose for every category in the initial phase (Table 20.7). Female unemployment rate doubled during the initial phase of economic reforms, implying a gender bias in jobs. Unemployment rate declined in the latter phase of economic reforms, except for urban females, in sharp contrast to the all India experience of rise in all categories. The gender bias remained with urban jobs. Rural females had the lowest unemployment rate and the urban females the highest. The unemployment scenario in the state had never been as serious as it is made out to be, even though the rates have been rising gradually. Unemployment is an urban phenomenon for both the sexes. It is more acute with urban females. In 1977–78, urban female unemployment rate was only 16.91 per cent of all India urban female unemployment rate. It rose to 69.8 per cent in 2004–05. On the other hand, rural unemployment for both the sexes remained substantially lower than the corresponding all India figures.

Table 20.7: Unemployment Rate in Manipur and India

(by Current Daily Status)

Year	Male				Female			
	Rural		Urban		Rural		Urban	
	Manipur	India	Manipur	India	Manipur	India	Manipur	India
1977–78	2.94	7.1	1.61	9.4	0.18	9.2	2.47	14.6
1983	0.98	7.5	0.51	9.2	–	9.0	–	11.0
1987–88	1.2	4.6	4.4	8.8	1.2	6.7	5.9	12.0
1993–94	2.2	5.6	5.0	6.8	1.1	5.6	3.1	10.4
1999–2000	2.4	7.2	6.6	7.3	2.6	7.0	7.6	9.4
2004–05	1.9	8.0	5.5	7.5	1.1	8.7	8.1	11.6

Source: NSSO (1986, 1990, 1996, 2001, and 2006).

There need not be any complacency in the low level of unemployment rates as revealed in the NSSO data. The low quality of employment is reflected in the preponderance of self-employment and the low productivity of agriculture, the dominant source of livelihood. Construction is the most remunerative occupation while agriculture is the least remunerative one. The productivity of the agricultural sector has been declining from 1987–88 to 2004–05. Productivity of trade also has been declining. It is the service sector that has been showing the highest rise (Table 20.8). If the additional labour cannot be absorbed in more productive work outside the farm sector, there is an urgent need to raise the productivity of agriculture through higher public capital formation in agriculture and improved marketing infrastructure of the produce.

Table 20.8: Productivity per Worker

(Figures in Rs)

Sector	1987–88	1993–94	1999–2000	2004–05
Agriculture	12481 (73.5)	12375 (68.6)	11116 (50)	11054 (52.8)
Manufacturing	6797 (40)	14648 (81)	29473 (133)	25386 (121)
Construction	81261 (479)	41849 (232)	137766 (621)	93869 (448)
Transport	31062 (183)	28939 (160)	36798 (166)	39505 (189)
Trade	34894 (206)	29305 (162)	31764 (143)	27192 (130)
Services	23330 (137.5)	25059 (139)	42719 (193)	57011 (272)
C.O.V.	0.78	0.39	0.83	0.58
All Sectors	16966	18044	22176	20935

Note: Labour productivity in a sector is derived by dividing the real income generated in the sector at 1993–94 prices by the number of workers in it. The figures in parentheses are indices of productivity taking aggregate labour productivity as 100.

Poverty

Due to smallness of the sample size, the poverty ratio of Assam has been used to proxy the poverty ratio for all the states in the northeastern region, including Manipur. As such, the data does not permit interstate comparison of poverty ratio among the north-eastern states. Poverty in Manipur has been gradually declining, and has come down below the national average both for urban and rural areas (Table

20.9). The urban poverty ratio has declined much faster than the rural poverty.

Table 20.9: Poverty in Manipur and India: A Comparative Picture

Year	Rural		Urban		Combined	
	Manipur	India	Manipur	India	Manipur	India
1973–4	52.67	56.44	36.92	49.23	49.96	54.93
1977–78	59.82	53.07	32.71	47.4	53.72	51.81
1983	42.6	45.61	21.73	42.15	37.02	44.76
1987–88	39.35	39.06	9.94	40.12	31.35	39.34
1993–94	45.01	37.27	7.73	32.6	33.78	35.97
1999–2000	40.04	27.09	7.47	23.62	28.54	26.1
2004–05	22.3	28.3	3.3	25.7	17.3	27.5

Source: Planning Commission (2005).

Between the period from 1973–74 to 2004–05, poverty ratio of the state declined by 65.37 per cent against the decline of 49.94 at the national level. While urban poverty ratio declined by 91.06 per cent in the state, rural poverty ratio declined only by 57.66 per cent. Urban poverty declined sharply by 54.25 per cent during 1983 to 1987–88. During the period from 1999–2000 to 2004–05, national poverty ratio increased both in the rural and urban areas. However, there was no such reversal in Manipur. The state's poverty ratio has had ups and downs while national poverty ratio declined for all the years except in 2004–05.

A comparison of the pre- and post-economic reforms performance on this front shows that at the national level, poverty declined faster in the pre-reforms era. During the period from 1973–74 to 1993–94, national poverty ratio declined by 34.52 per cent as against a decline of 23.55 per cent during 1993–94 to 2004–05. In Manipur, poverty declined faster in the post-reforms era. During 1973–74 to 1993–94, poverty ratio declined by 32.38 per cent as against a decline of 48.78 per cent during 1993–94 to 2004–05. At the national level, urban and rural poverty declined by 33.78 per cent and 33.96 per cent, respectively, in the pre-reform era. In the post-reform era, the corresponding figures were 21.16 per cent and 24.07 per cent. As against this, Manipur witnessed a decline of urban poverty by 79.06 per cent in the pre-reform era and by 57.31 per cent in the post-reform era. However, in the case of rural poverty, the percentage decline rose from 14.54 per cent to 50.45 per cent.

What stands out is the coexistence of high poverty and low unemployment rates. Though, urban unemployment rate for both the sexes have been rising, urban poverty ratio has been declining dramatically from 36.92 per cent in 1973–74 to 3.3 per cent in 2004–05. In contrast to this, rural unemployment rates have been lower and poverty ratio higher. This is indicative of the low returns to rural jobs which are dominated by agriculture. Rural workers, because of their poverty, have little choice in their activity matrix and have to remain employed, even at extremely low wages. On the other hand, labour force in the urban area, because they are better off, can afford to remain unemployed while looking for more remunerative jobs.

A comparison of Manipur with some other Indian states shows that per capita income of Manipur is way behind some of the states. She is relatively better in life expectancy at birth and infant mortality rate. Manipur stands out in infant mortality (Table 20.10).

CONCLUSION

The discussion above, on human development in Manipur during the post-economic reforms period, reveals the following:

(i)   Though per capita income in Manipur remained low, trend of other indicators like IMR, literacy rate, and sex ratio are encouraging, reflecting an inner vibrancy in the social core;

(ii) The preponderance of low productivity jobs persisted despite structural change in the economy. The change in occupational distribution of the work force essentially meant transfer from one low paid job to another of similar nature;

(iii) The 1990s saw jobless growth, with female unemployment rate doubling, reflecting a gender bias. Though, there was a reversal in the latter period, female urban employment rate continued to rise;

(iv) Poverty in the state declined substantially, particularly in the urban sector. It declined faster in the post-reforms period in contrast to the slower decline at the national level. The decline in post-reforms period was more substantial in the rural sector than the urban sector; and

(v)   High level of poverty coexisted with low unemployment rate in rural Manipur, implying employment in low paid jobs. In urban Manipur, low poverty coexisted with high unemployment rate,

Table 20.10: Development Indicators of Some Select States in India

State	Per Capita Income (Rs) (2004–05)	NSDP (Rs in lakhs) (2004–05)	Life Expectancy at Birth (2001–05)		Infant Mortality Rate (2006)	Literacy Rate (2001)	Sex Ratio (2001)
			Male	Female			
Punjab	1,6756	4,31,2214	68.1	70.1	44	69.65	874
Tamil Nadu	1,3999	9,01,3787	64.8	67.1	37	73.45	986
Maharastra	1,7864	18,23,8870	65.8	68.1	35	76.88	922
Karnataka	1,3820	7,62,9830	63.4	66.9	48	66.64	964
Assam	7020	2,02,2636	58.3	59	67	63.25	932
Manipur	8015	19,7936	68.64*	72.42*	11	70.53	974
Kerala	1,3321	4,40,5472	71.3	76.3	15	90.86	1058
India			62.3	63.9	57	64.84	933

Note: * Figures refer to the year 1991 and Per capita income and NSDP at constant prices (1993–94).
Source: (i) Central Statistical Organization.
(ii) Economic Survey 2007–08.

implying the capability of job seekers to look for better paid jobs and remain unemployed for a longer period.

REFERENCES

Ahluwalia, M.S. 2000. 'Economic Performance of the States in the Post Reforms Period', in Uma Kapila (ed.), *Indian Economy since Independence*, Academic Foundation.

Government of India (GoI), 2002. *National Human Development Report 2001*, Planning Commission, New Delhi.

North-Eastern Council (NEC) 2005. *Basic Statistics of North Eastern Region 2005*, Ministry of Home Affairs, Government of India, Shillong.

National Sample Statistical Organization (NSSO), 1986. 'Key Results of Last Three Quinquennial NSS Enquiries on Employment and Unemployment', *Sarvekshana*, Vol. II, No. 4, pp. S195.

—— 1990. 'Key Results of Employment and Unemployment Survey All India Part I NSS 43rd Round', Special Report No.1, pp. 108–09.

—— 1996. 'A Note on Employment and Unemployment Situation in India: Fifth Quinquennial Survey, NSS 50th Round (July 1993–June 1994)', *Sarvekshana*, Vol. XX, No. 1, July–Sept.

—— 2001. 'Employment and Unemployment Situation in India 1999–2000', Report No. 458.

——2006. 'Employment and Unemployment Situation in India 2004–05', Report No. 515.

Planning Commission 2005. *India's Five Year Plans Complete Documents*, Academic Foundation.

Sen, Amartya 1997. 'Inequality, Unemployment and Contemporary Europe', The Development Economics Research Programme, No.7, November.

Shetty, S.L. 2006. 'Growth of SDP and Structural Changes in the State Economies: Interstate Comparisons', in Uma Kapila (ed.), *Indian Economy since Independence*, Academic Foundation.

Singh, E. Bijoykumar and N. Bhupendra Singh 2007. 'Nature of Unemployment and Employment in the North East: A Case Study of Manipur', ICSSR Sponsored Project Report, Manipur University.

United Nations Development Programme (UNDP) 1990. *Human Development Report 1990*, Oxford University Press, New York.

21

Human Development in Mizoram
An Overview

A.K. AGARWAL

INTRODUCTION

Human Development Index (HDI) and its family of indices, as introduced by United Nations Development Programme (UNDP), gained
significance and global acceptance since its inception in 1990. According to UNDP, human development is the process of enlarging people's
choices and the raising of level of well-being. From among the valued
choices, the most critical ones are the ability to lead a long and healthy
life, to read, write, and acquire knowledge, to enjoy a decent standard
of living, and have a socially meaningful life. These choices reflected
in three equally weighted dimensions of well-being, namely, longevity,
education, and command over resources, and captured by corresponding indicators, provide the components for composite measures.
Longevity and educational attainments are valued as ends in themselves, and at the same time these are instrumental in the enjoyment of
other aspects of well-being. The inclusion of resources in the notion of
well-being, as also in the composite measures, is explained as a 'catch
all' variable to reflect aspects of well-being not captured by indicators
on education, health, and longevity of people. The approach puts the
people at the centre of development of policy agenda. Transmission
of the benefits of development for human welfare is the crux of the
concept. Hence, rising income and expanding outputs in the human
development framework are seen as the measure and not the end of
development (Malhotra 2007: 104).

LITERATURE ON HUMAN DEVELOPMENT

There has been no dearth of literature on human development right from the introduction of the concept of human development, selection of variables to be included in the construction of HDI, weights to be assigned to different variables under consideration, and finally construction of HDI for different states and sections of the society. Gender disparity, rural-urban unevenness, poverty, and low allocation of resources on social sectors can be noticed for low HDI in many parts of the country. There are some scholars who advocate for high growth and, thereby, high human development, while others argue in favour of a balanced path of development combining the strategies of growth and human development with appropriate weights.

In the literature on HDI, one can identify three categories of studies—those who are critical of the human development approach and have been instrumental in strengthening its conceptual underpinnings, and in identifying relevant dimensions of well-being with corresponding measures (Haq 1995; Anand and Sen 1996, 1997; Streeten 2000; and Noorbaksh 2002) and secondly, those who address the methodological issues of weighing different dimensions of well-being, scaling disparate variables into measures that can be combined into composite indices, and the related refinements in HDI (Haq 1995 and Noorbaksh 1998), and, finally, studies that focus on data related issues and the need for contextualization of various measures to country situations and development priorities (Shariff 2001 and Noorbaksh 2002).

ISSUES OF DEVELOPMENT AT THE NATIONAL AND REGIONAL LEVEL

In India, it has been observed that economically less developed states are also the ones with low HDI. Similarly, the economically better-off states perform relatively better on the HDI. However, there is no clear relationship between HDI and the level of development among the middle income states in the country. It may be noted here that while allocation of adequate public resources is an important factor in furthering human development, it is equally important to put the available resources to efficient and effective use. Human attainments appeared to be better sustained in those parts of the country where there has been social mobilization for human development, and where female literacy and empowerment has encouraged women to have a say in decision making at the household level (Malhotra 2007: 123).

The Planning Commission of India has also been publishing *National Human Development Reports* (*NHDRs*) considering the above three mentioned dimensions, such as:

(1) Longevity— to live long and healthy life;
(2) Education; and
(3) Command over resources to enjoy a decent standard of living and have a socially meaningful life.

But, it has been confining itself to major states as the required data for the purpose is not available for smaller states, including the states in North-East India. In the last few years, human development reports were prepared for Arunachal Pradesh and Assam under the sponsorship of UNDP and Planning Commission, whereas, the report for Manipur is yet to be published. It may be noted here that the proportion of expenditure on education to the total budget of all the north-eastern states was higher than that of the national average during 1998–99. Almost all the states of the North East allocated more than half of their educational budget to primary education (Sharma 2006: 75)

The states of the North-East have experienced high growth rate of domestic product, but this apparent sign of prosperity is not reflective of the true picture of the domestic product, if not examined from the point of view of its composition across sectors. As observed by Bezbaruah (2001), high growth was not propelled by growth of agriculture or manufacturing, or, even trade and commerce, but by expansion of such other activities like public administration and construction, which was necessitated by the expansion of the administrative apparatus in these newly formed special category states (carved out from Assam) and financed by liberal fiscal transfers from the centre. Such high growth rates, unless stimulated by genuine economic processes, are unlikely to be sustainable over time. Another notable feature being observed is the declining contribution of primary sector in the state domestic product besides smaller share of services, such as trade, transport, communication, and the financial services.

HUMAN DEVELOPMENT IN MIZORAM
Analysis of human development in Mizoram involves an assessment of performance of the state, her strength and weaknesses, and identify a strategy for improvement. In this chapter, we have made an attempt to focus on the health and educational aspects of human development,

which tend to influence the present, as well as the potential standard of living of the people in the state.

Mizoram became the 23rd state of India in February 1987. Till 1972, it was one of the districts of Assam after which it became one of the union territories. It is located in the remote north-east corner of India, sandwiched between Myanmar and Bangladesh. Her inter-state border with Assam extends to 123 km, with Tripura 66 km, and with Manipur 95 km. The total geographical area of the state is 21,081 sq km. The *NHDR* (Planning Commission 2002) documents the performance of the states of India in terms of HDI, Gender Disparity Index, and Human Poverty Index. Data reveals that Mizoram performs better than the national average on each one of the indicators of HDI. Thus, the focus of enquiry is not so much on the relative inadequacy of services in the state as compared to the rest of India. The state instead required better services and an appropriate delivery mechanism, whereby various interacting components of human developmen can be visualized together and not as separate indicators and action points.

Mizoram has witnessed remarkable achievement in terms of literacy rate, that is, from 59.90 per cent in 1981 to 88.49 per cent in 2001, being next only to Kerala (90 per cent) (Economic Survey 2003–04, Census 2001). So far as gender-based differential is concerned, it is the lowest in the country at 90.7 per cent for males and 86.7 per cent for females. Rural-urban disparities (80.5 per cent in rural and 96 per cent in urban areas) in terms of literacy rates can be noticed, as is usually noticed in other states of the country. The 61st Round of NSSO also records an almost similar trend. It may be noted here that female median year of schooling is the highest in Mizoram. To achieve the target of cent per cent literacy, the state introduced Sarva Shiksha Abhiyan (SSA) and Eradication of Residual Illiteracy (ERIP) to cover children under the age group of 6–14 years and the population in the age group of 15–35 years, respectively. In spite of all these initiatives, there exist substantial intra-state differences in terms of literacy rate. The district Lawngtlai with 64.74 per cent of literacy rate lagged substantially behind Aizawl, which was having a corresponding figure of 96.51 per cent. When significant disparity between literacy rates of males (70.90 per cent) and females (57.81 per cent) existed in Lawngtlai, virtually no disparity between male (96.75 per cent) and female (96.26 per cent) existed in Aizawl.

According to the NSSO's 61st round on educational profile of the people in the age group of 15 years and above, the percentage of people with education up to primary school was 36.5 per cent and that to middle school completed was 35.8 per cent. Though, gender bias (male 37.2 per cent, female 34.3 per cent) was not noticed to a great extent, but the extent of gain from education to the mass was rather limited. This needs utmost attention of the state government if we want to capitalize on its literate labour force. If we analyse the percentage figures for graduates and above and people in the age group of 18 years and above, it comes to 4.5 per cent and a gap between genders with 6.1 per cent for males and 2.7 per cent for females. This requires immediate government attention, not only to uplift their standard of living but also in adoption of family planning norms to limit the size of the family.

Enrolment rate for primary schools in the age group of 6–11 years was 119, while it was substantially lower around 80 for the age group 11–14 years (*Economic Survey 2003–04*). While compared to other north-eastern states and all India average, the figure seems to be quite satisfactory. Another notable feature is that a sizeable proportion of the children enrolled in primary schools were either too young or older than the prescribed age. The net enrolment ratio was 72.6 per cent for primary schools, as compared to gross enrolment ratio of 113.6 in the same year.

The figures on dropout rates suggest a worrisome trend. Along with high enrolment ratios, the state witnessed high dropout rates (*NHDR 2001*). In 1994–95, a majority of students (63 per cent) belonging to classes I to V left studies even before completing class V. Although, it declined over time, as has been claimed by the state government. In 2006–07, the dropout rates for the primary and middle stage of education were 3.93 and 10.54 respectively while for high schools and higher secondary schools remained at 23 and 70, respectively. It is, of course, hard to believe these figures. Another noticeable feature is the high incidence of dropouts in rural areas as compared to urban areas. This might be due to lack of consciousness about the value of education and also due to engagement of children in work in the villages. It may be noted here that the problem of child labour has almost been absent in the villages in the state, but it cannot be ruled out altogether for the obvious reason that non-enrolment and dropout is mainly due to prevalence of poverty. It may also be noted here that in rural areas the children are required to share the work at the level of households and farms. These factors are critical in understanding the success or otherwise, of any initiative to improve the system of education in the state.

The teacher-pupil ratio in the state is 1:13, which seems to be quite satisfactory. There are very few educational institutions for education beyond the secondary level. As far as higher education is concerned, the (Central) Mizoram University offers professional courses both at the undergraduate and postgraduate level, such as B. Tech, MBA, and MCA, whereas, nursing courses are offered by DOEACC and RIPAN. The weakening force in education has been, of course, in terms of its delivery, that is, in terms of qualified and efficient faculty and manpower. Although, the state government sponsors students for higher studies, it has been unable to offer them gainful employment.

Health is another major indicator of human development. A healthy life is crucial to personal well-being. The health indicators along with demographic-related indicators, which concern society, are important constituents in the framework for evaluating the development process. Success and achievement depends on adequate provision of good health care facilities, in general, and attention to women and children, in particular. Private health care has gained popularity in the state over the last decade due to poor and non-satisfactory health services rendered by the state government. However, the state has a significant role to play in this sector by creating infrastructure, providing access, improving delivery, educating, and developing mass consciousness about hygiene and basic health care. Relatively low dependency ratio above 60 years of age group and low infant mortality rate, including the under-five mortality rate which is lower than the national average, are positive indicators about the overall performance of health in the state. However, as in the case of education, these figures mark some underlying concerns.

It may be noted here that the average annual growth rate of population is 2.59 per cent, as compared to national average of 1.95 per cent. High rate of growth of population, coupled with low infant mortality rate suggests that the state has crossed the first stage of demographic transition. Though, increase in the use of contraceptives by young married couples has been helpful in the decline in the rate of growth of population, still the state has a long way to travel to overcome this problem.

The National Family Health Survey-3 Report indicates fertility rate to be as high as 2.86 (rural 3.33 and urban 2.50). The report further indicates to a strong negative relationship between education of women and total fertility rate. However, it may be noted here that fertility rate has been reduced over time due to women's education and a better standard of living, but not to the desired extent. It may be noted here that with an increase in the standard of living and in the level of education, the demand for private health care has increased. Similarly, urbanization, by making available more choices to the people, has induced a shift in demand for private health care services in the state.

Public health sector had attained dynamic and enthusiastic leadership in the state with 10 hospitals, 10 Community Health Centres (CHCs), 56 Primary Health Centres (PHCs), and 366 sub centres, served by 260 doctors and 26 dentists (Government of Mizoram 2008: 71–77.) The private hospitals, including hospitals run by voluntary organizations, cater mainly to the urban areas; hence, the coverage to the rural poor is quite inadequate. Since the entire rural health care system is highly dependent on the PHC, sub-centres, and CHCs, the more critical aspect of it has been its efficiency and functionality.

Provision of drinking water supply is being made through pumped water supply, rain water harvesting, hand pump, tube wells, submersible pumps, and through improvement of spring sources in the villages. According to a survey conducted in 2003, there are 777 habitations in Mizoram of which 354 are fully covered and 295 are partially covered under the water supply scheme (Government of Mizoram 2008: 79). Thus, the high rate of illness, on account of various water borne diseases, and high morbidity rate in the state can be ascribed to inadequateness of good drinking water. Sanitation facilities for rural habitations are being provided by the government under the total sanitation campaign programme. Normally, toilet facilities are provided to each household and rural and urban differentials hardly exist in the state, in sharp contrast to other parts of the country.

OTHER DEVELOPMENT ISSUES AND THE WAY OUT

Currently, the Mizos either depend on government jobs, in the absence of private entrepreneurship and industrialization, or on agriculture and other allied activities. Efforts need to be made to train the people for settled cultivation in an organized manner, may be through the cooperative sector. The government should make sincere efforts for warehouse facilities, transportation, and marketing facilities for the marketable surplus of agriculture, horticulture, floriculture, and pisciculture, etc. Once the people realize and fetch remunerative prices for their produce, they will be enthused to produce more and, thereby, to raise their standard of living.

Another perceived lacuna with the education in the state is the paucity of professional education, especially in medicine, engineering, and accounting practices, etc. Given the small scale of demand, it is difficult to conceive of all manners of specializations being offered within the state, unless the state chooses to transform itself into an education hub. The Central University, RIPAN, DOEACC, and other private institutions can play an important role in this direction. Since it is a time-taking process, it is desirable to identify a few core specializations in line with the overall strategy of development. These could be developed in the state over a period of time, and for the time being there is a need to encourage students through offering scholarships to pursue these specialized courses in the institutions outside the state.

Information technology can certainly serve as a growth engine for development but there are certain bottlenecks associated with entrepreneurship building, entry barriers in terms of Inner Line Permit System to non-Mizos, infrastructure, etc. These issues need to be tackled by the government. However, information technology as an administrative tool can be effectively used for better governance.

The state can gain from the burgeoning business of health tourism and be the hub of the entire eastern region. Though, it looks a distant dream in current circumstances, but with the expansion of infrastructure facilities like transport and communication, expansion in medical and paramedical colleges, and other related human resource development, availability of trained and specialized medical personnel, along with better equipped medical centres and creation of e-health networking, the dream can come true provided sincere efforts are made in this direction.

Finally, for any approach or development framework to be meaningful and effective in directing public policies and programmes, it has to be anchored in a social context. More importantly, it should reflect the values and development priorities of the society where it is applied. Emphasis has to be laid on expansion in the production of goods and services, and the consequent growth in the per capita income, to a focus on enhancement of human well-being. The deprived and marginalized society should have equal access, not only to productive resources but to lead a socially meaningful life. This will play an instrumental role in sustaining the development process and in enlarging the available opportunities and choices for the people.

CONCLUSION

Mizoram is known as a land of peace, engaging about half of her population in agriculture and allied activities. The state attained a high level of literacy and has performed better on the health front, too. Absence of manufacturing activities and shortage of skilled manpower limit the scope of employment opportunities. The state has attained a satisfactory level of enrolment of children at the primary level but the worry is the high dropout rate. The reasons may be traced in engagement of children in household work and farms besides poverty, especially in rural areas. Another weakening force in the education system is the non-availability of qualified manpower and other supportive infrastructural facilities. The major concern is high growth rate of population due to high fertility rate. Private health care is gaining popularity, especially in urban areas, but the greater concern is the rural areas where more hospitals equipped with adequate infrastructural support are required. The focus should be more on appropriate delivery mechanism for a balanced development of human resources.

REFERENCES

Anand, Sudhir and Amartya Sen 1996. 'Sustainable Human Development: Concept and Priorities', Discussion Paper No.1, Human Development Report Office, UNDP, New York.

——— 1997. 'Concept of Human Development and Poverty: A Multidimensional Perspective', UNDP Human Development Papers 1997; Poverty and Human Development, UNDP, New York.

Bezbaruah, M.P. 2001. 'Creation of Smaller States and Economic Progress in India's North-Eastern Region', *Dialogue*, Vol. 2, No. 3.

Government of India (GoI) 2007–8. *Economic Survey 2007–08*. http://india budget.nic.in/es2007-2008/chapt2008/chap106/pdf

——— 2002. *National Human Development Report 2001*, Planning Commission, New Delhi.

Government of Manipur. 'Health Status and Health Care Services', in Manipur State Development Report (Draft copy), Department of Planning and Coordination, Imphal. http://manipur.nic.in/planning/Draft-MSDR/Draft_SDR_pdf/Chapter%2015_Health.pdf

Government of Mizoram 2008. *Economic Survey Mizoram, 2007-2008*, Planning and Programme Implementation Department, Aizawl.

Haq, M.u. 1995. *Reflections on Human Development*, Oxford University Press, NY.

Malhotra, Rajeev 2007. 'Human Development Measures: From Advocacy to Policy Monitoring at Country Level', *Indian Human Development*, Vol. 1, No. 1, pp. 104–23.

Noorbaksh. F. 2002. 'Human Development and Regional Disparities in Iran: A Policy Model', *Journal of International Development*, Vol. 14, Issue 7, pp. 927–49.

Noorbaksh. F. 1998. 'A Modified Human Development Index', *World Development*, Vol. 26, No. 3, pp. 517–28.

Shariff, Abusaleh 2001. *India Development Report: A Profile of Indian States in the 1990's*, NCAER, New Delhi.

Sharma M. 2006. 'Globalization and Education Hopes and Challenges; A Study of North-East', *Manpower Journal*, Vol. 41, No. 2, April–June, 2006, pp.75

Streeten P. 2000. 'Looking Ahead: Areas of Future Research in Human Development', *Journal of Human Development*, Vol. 1, No.1, pp. 25–48.

United Nations Development Programme (UNDP) 1990–2006. *Human Development Report*, Oxford University Press, New York. http/hdr.undp.org/reports

22

Facets and Factors of Human Development in Tripura

SUDHANSHU K. MISHRA AND PURUSOTTAM NAYAK

INTRODUCTION

For centuries, economists remained preoccupied with gathering more and more information on the means to human well-being and its optimal allocation so as to produce more wealth and well-being, at a lesser cost. However, the real achievement of human well-being was not in focus since it was believed that more of wealth would automatically lead to a higher level of well-being. In due course, it became clear that between wealth and well-being, there are multiple pathways that join them. While some of the pathways may connect higher wealth to meagre well-being; some other pathways may join the commensurate levels of wealth and well-being. It also became clear that those pathways are the results of the socio-cultural and technological environment in which an economy is placed. It was also realized that those pathways evolve over time, and are shaped by historical forces.

In the last two decades or so, there has been a growing involvement of economists in studying aspects of well-being directly. Such studies are concentrating on directly measuring the level of human development, which is defined as an average level of achievement of an economy in ensuring education, health, and income of the people. The objective of this study is to present a synoptic view of the well-being aspect of the economy of Tripura, a constituent state of the north-eastern region of India. Area and population-wise, Tripura is a small state as compared to many other states in India. It is also a state located along the frontiers of the nation. But unlike many other states in the region, the Scheduled Tribes population of Tripura is hardly one-third of the total population.

THE GEOGRAPHY

Tripura is situated between latitudes 22°56' N and 24°32'N and longitudes 90°09'E and 92°10'E. Its maximum stretch measures about 184 km from north to south and 113 km from east to west with an area of 10,492 sq km. Tripura is the third smallest state of the country. It was inhabited by 3.2 million people as reported in Census 2001 (North-Eastern Council 2005). It has Bangladesh on its north, south, and west, stretched along 856 km of its total border of about 910 km. On the east are Assam and Mizoram, two other states of India. Its altitudes vary from 50 to 3,080 ft above sea level at different places, although the majority of the area has an altitude of 50 to 180 ft above sea level.

Central and northern Tripura are hilly regions crossed by four major valleys, carved by the northward flowing rivers. The low valleys in the west and south tend to be open and marshy, although in the south the terrain is heavily dissected and densely forested. North-south trending ranges separate the valleys. The west of Deotamura range is the Agartala plain, an extension of the Ganges-Brahmaputra lowlands, less than 200 feet and drained by numerous rivers. Tripura has a tropical climate and receives ample (more than 80 inches) rainfall during the monsoons. Overall, the terrain of the state is hilly and forested: over 60 per cent is hilly, and around two-third of the land area is classified as forest land. A majority of the population lives in the plains.

GROWTH OF POPULATION

Vis-à-vis other states in the north-eastern region, Tripura has exhibited, in the last century, the second highest growth rate of population. Its population was about 173 thousand in 1901, which increased to 3.2 million in 2001 (North-Eastern Council 2001, 2002). In particular, the growth of population showed an abrupt increase during the 1941–51 Census years. This abrupt increase was brought about by the partition of the country in 1947, which turned out to have an enduring effect on the process of social, political, and economic development in the state. The status and dynamics of human development in Tripura cannot be properly understood without a reference to this catastrophe in the backdrop.

HISTORICAL BACKGROUND

India won freedom with her limbs severed. The partition of the country had directly decisive and enduring effects on Punjab, Bengal, and the north-eastern states. The partition resulted in the geo-political isolation of Tripura (the entire north-eastern region for that matter) and, in particular, made Tripura a landlocked state. The state was cut off from India's railway network as it lost all its rail-heads to the west, south and north, which fell in East Pakistan (now Bangladesh). The distance by road from Agartala to Kolkata was less than 350 km before partition. After partition, the route to Kolkata, via the Siliguri land corridor, became 1,700 km long (Government of Tripura 2007). Tripura is connected with the rest of India by only one road, which runs through the hills to Cachar district in Assam. Thus, the partition affected connectivity, movement of people and goods, prospects of investment, cost of production, etc., ultimately holding back the pace of economic, social, and human development.

Secondly, the partition led to a very large influx of refugees from the then East Pakistan (now Bangladesh) into Tripura. This large scale emergent immigration not only placed a tremendous burden on the resources of the state, but also led to an upheaval in the social composition of its population. The refugees came into the state almost paupers, with dire needs for survival, settlement, and livelihood, and, more importantly, with the traumatic psyche of the endangered. The economy of Tripura was largely dependent on agriculture, forest-based activities, and a modest manufacturing sector, comprising handicrafts and household industries. The major mode of farming in the state was shifting cultivation (*jhum*), which produced little surplus. Only a small proportion of the state's plains were under settled agriculture, and the main crop was rice. Most of the plains were not under cultivation and were covered with cane-brakes and marshes. The severed infrastructure made markets inaccessible and sealed the future of the manufacturing sector for decades to come. There was also a sizeable influx of immigrants during and immediately after the Bangladesh war of independence in 1971. The feeble economy and infrastructure of the state had to bear the burden of a large influx of refugees in three waves, some before the partition (in 1941), hugely just after partition, and sizeably in 1971, with obvious results of strife.

DEMOGRAPHIC FEATURES

Administratively, Tripura is divided into four districts: West Tripura,

South Tripura, Dhalai, and North Tripura. The West Tripura district is the most heavily populated. In the year 2001, about 48 per cent of the population lived in this district (GoI 2007–08). Over the years, the density of population in this district has also been increasing faster than in other districts (Table 22.1). The second district, namely South Tripura, is area-wise almost as large as West Tripura, but its population is only half that of the latter. The third district, Dhalai, is the most sparsely populated. Density-wise, the fourth district, North Tripura, is between West Tripura and South Tripura.

There is a very clear relationship between the proportion of Scheduled Tribes (ST) in the total population (GoI 2007–08) and urbanization, as well as density of population in the state. Increase in the proportion of ST population is associated with decrease in density and urbanization in the districts. The rate of decline is so sharp that it cannot be ignored for its implications to human development.

Table 22.1: District–wise Population Growth, Sex Ratio, and Density, Tripura 1991–2001

Districts/State	Decadal Growth Rate		Sex Ratio*		Density**	
	1981–1991	1991–2001	1991	2001	1991	2001
West Tripura	32.5	18.5	944	951	432	511
South Tripura	40.3	6.8	951	945	236	251
Dhalai	33.7	10.9	931	935	118	131
North Tripura	30.9	26.5	943	951	223	282
Tripura	34.3	16.0	944	948	263	304

Note: Sex ratio = Females per 1000 males; ** Density = persons per sq. km.
Source: GoI: Annual Work Plan and Budget on MDM 2007-08.

The decadal growth of population in different districts of the state reveals that during 1981–91, all the districts had a very high growth of population, while it slowed down substantially during 1991–2001. A 40 per cent growth rate (1981–91) of population in South Tripura followed by 6.8 per cent in the subsequent decade (Table 22.1), indicates a heavy influx of immigration in the district.

As to the age structure of the population, Dhalai has a slightly higher stock of young population, followed by North and South Tripura districts (GoI 2007–08). The West Tripura district has higher stock of population in the working age group 15–59 years. As regards urbanization, West Tripura is more urbanized. Dhalai, South Tripura and North Tripura districts are mostly rural (GoI 2007–08). It also indicates that West Tripura is the hub of economic, social, and cultural activities in the state. Agartala, the capital of the state, is located in the West Tripura district.

Health Aspects

The infant mortality rate and the expectation of life at birth are the indicators of the general health of the population. These indicators are related in a very complicated manner to economic, social, infrastructural, technological, institutional, and administrative development of the people. Table 22.2 indicates that Dhalai district has the largest infant mortality rate and the smallest expectation of life at birth, followed by South Tripura, and North Tripura, in that order.

Table 22.2: Estimated Infant Mortality Rates and Life Expectancy at Birth in Tripura

| District/State | Infant Deaths per 1000 Live Births (2001) | | Life Expectancy at Birth | | | |
| | | | 1991 | | 2001 | |
	Male	Female	Male	Female	Male	Female
West Tripura	33.9	36.6	68	70	73	75
South Tripura	45.2	50.1	65	66	70	71
Dhalai	49.2	54.3	64	65	69	70
North Tripura	37.6	40.0	67	69	72	74
Tripura	41.3	43.5	66	69	71	74

Source: GoI: Annual Work Plan and Budget on MDM, 2007–08.

The West Tripura district has the smallest infant mortality rate and the highest expectation of life at birth. Clearly, these indicators are in tune with the general level of social, economic, infrastructural, and technological development exhibited by those districts. The distribution of public health institutions and facilities is presented in Table 22.3. The figures indicate that health facilities in West Tripura are far superior to those in other districts.

We also present in Table 22.4 some indicators of the health of population in Tripura and the health of children, in particular.

Table 22.4 indicates that in terms of the weight for age indicator, 14.4 per cent of children were severely underweight and another 28.2 per cent were moderately underweight. In the case of height for age, 22 per cent were moderately undernourished and 18.4 per cent were severely stunted. However, the incidence of malnutrition is lower than the national average in Tripura, particularly with respect to severe malnutrition in terms of weight for age.

Table 22.3: Numbers of Public Health Institutions in Tripura (April 2007)

District/State	SDH	CHC	PHC	SC	RD	PPD	BPLP
W. Tripura	3	6	21	257	443	3460	132
S. Tripura	3	3	22	144	130	5903	68
Dhalai	3	–	11	66	107	2877	78
N. Tripura	2	1	20	112	162	3647	67
Tripura	11	10	74	579	842	3799	99

Source: GoI: Annual Work Plan and Budget on MDM 2007–08.
Note: SDH—Sub-division Hospital, CHC—Community Health Centre, PHC—Primary Health Centre, SC—Sub-Centre, RD—Registered Doctor, PPD—Persons per Doctor, BPLP—Beds per Lakh Persons.

Table 22.4: Percentage Distribution of Nutritional Anthropometry
of Children

(below 3 Years of Age)

Particulars	Tripura				India			
	Weight for Age		Height for Age		Weight for Age		Height for Age	
	Below 3SD	Below 2SD	Below 3SD	Below 2SD	Below 3SD	Below 2SD	Below 3SD	Below 2SD
Total	14.4	42.6	22.0	40.4	18.0	47.0	23.0	45.5
Male	14.5	46.6	25.1	46.5	16.9	45.3	21.8	44.1
Female	14.3	38.7	18.9	34.4	19.1	48.9	24.4	47.0

Source: GoI: Annual Work Plan and Budget on MDM 2007–08.

Anaemia among children (6 to 36 months) is highly prevalent in Tripura (GoI 2007–08). In fact, it has the second highest incidence among the north-eastern states, and sixteenth among all states of India. A significant percentage of children had severe anaemia (less than 7gm/dl), which is a matter of grave concern. A survey conducted to investigate the nutrients intake of the rural people revealed that their food had severe deficiencies regarding iron, vitamin A, riboflavin and thiamine (Ibid 2007–08).

Educational Aspects

Education permits a person to inherit the wealth of knowledge amassed over generations, rather the entire history of civilization of the mankind. It also makes a person more acceptable and productive. Education increases the chances of fitness and employability, too. Additionally, education leads to fulfillment. Today, when we have already entered into the age of knowledge and information, education has become all the more important. Economists have found that a larger share of increase in productivity is attributable to education of the people.

Providing education to the people has primarily been a concern of the governments in India. That is why most of the educational institutions in India are run by or heavily supported by the government. Only recently has the private sector entered into the educational sector. Tripura is no exception. As Table 22.5 reveals, the educational infrastructure in Tripura is managed by the government. There are privately run but government-aided educational institutions too, but they are only a small minority.

As it may be seen in Table 22.6, the percentage of children (age group 6–14 years) attending schools in the rural areas is significantly less than that in the urban areas. This is due to several reasons. First, the level of income in the rural areas is significantly lower than that in the urban areas and parents in the former can less support their children than those in the latter. Secondly, availability of educational infrastructure is much inferior and more sparsely located in the rural areas than in the urban areas. Thirdly, the level of education of parents also determines their children going in for education. In this matter, there are gender-based differences also. In patrifocal societies, boys tend to dominate in availing themselves of educational facilities.

Enrolment figures are presented in Tables 22.7 and 22.8. Generally, enrolment decreases with increasing standard, so that in class (standard) VIII only one-third of the total enrolment in class I remain. The remaining two-third drop out. ST boys as well as girls exhibit steepest fall in enrolment from Class I to VIII, followed by the students of the general category and the SC category. The OBC boys as well as girls do not exhibit such tendencies. Similar tendencies are observed when we look into Table 22.9 and Table 22.10, except in West Tripura, where ST students exhibit lower dropout rates.

Literacy rates in Tripura are quite high. Overall, 81 per cent males and 64 per cent females are literate. Literacy in rural areas is only marginally less than in the urban areas. West and North Tripura districts have higher figures for literacy and Dhalai shows the lowest figures. Female literacy is less than 50 per cent in Dhalai.

Economic Aspects

Tripura's economy is primarily agriculture-oriented. A large number of people are engaged in the tertiary sector as well. Like most of the states in the north-eastern region, Tripura also does not have any developed

Table 22.5: Number of Schools in Tripura, 2006–07

District/State	Primary	Primary with Upper Primary	Primary/Up. Primary/ Sec/H. Sec	Upper Primary Only	Upper Primary/ Sec/H. Sec	No Response	All Schools
W. Tripura	682(13)	336(2)	266(22)	0(0)	13(5)	0(0)	1297(42)
S. Tripura	635 (0)	223(0)	133 (2)	0(0)	34(0)	0(0)	1025 (2)
Dhalai	389 (2)	153(0)	47 (0)	0(0)	5(1)	0(0)	594 (3)
N. Tripura	251(37)	271(0)	97 (3)	0(0)	8(3)	0(0)	627(43)
Tripura	1957(52)	983(2)	543(27)	0(0)	60(9)	0(0)	3543(90)

Note: Figures refer to Govt.-managed schools while those in brackets are for privately managed schools.
Source: GoI: Annual Work Plan and Budget on MDM, 2007–08.

Table 22.6: Percentage of Children (Age: 6–14 years) Attending School in Tripura, 1991

District/ State	Rural			Urban			Total		
	Boys	Girls	All	Boys	Girls	All	Boys	Girls	All
W. Tripura	81.5	78.6	80.1	86.6	84.4	85.5	82.5	79.8	81.2
S. Tripura	78.6	73.7	76.2	91.5	88.4	89.9	79.2	74.4	76.9
Dhalai	68	61.5	64.9	84.8	82.9	83.9	68.8	62.6	65.8
N. Tripura	73	69.6	71.3	87.4	83.9	85.7	74.1	70.7	72.4
Tripura	77.5	73.6	75.6	87.1	84.7	85.9	78.7	75	76.9

Source: GoI: Annual Work Plan and Budget on MDM, 2007–08.

Table 22.7: Enrolment Summary in Government Managed Schools in Tripura, 2006–07

Enrolment		I	II	III	IV	V	VI	VII	VIII	I-V	VI-VIII
					Classes					Total	
Gen.	B	14131	12201	12861	12453	11411	9974	8278	7002	63057	25254
	G	13278	11500	12349	11639	11141	10150	8395	6897	59907	25442
SC	B	9194	9339	10476	10045	9342	8777	7131	5951	48396	21859
	G	8520	8609	9499	9188	9231	8911	7126	5780	45047	21817
ST	B	27550	22503	21683	18874	17065	14372	11208	9356	107675	34936
	G	25396	20602	18761	15757	14319	11740	9568	8191	94835	29499
OBC	B	7072	7266	8150	7894	7693	8717	7602	6297	38075	22616
	G	6725	6954	7225	7635	7638	8606	7615	6712	36177	22933
Total	B	57,947	51,309	53,170	49,266	45,511	41,840	34,219	28,606	257,203	104,665
	G	53,919	47,665	47,834	44,219	42,329	39,407	32,704	27,580	235,966	99,691
Percentage to Total											
General		24.50	23.95	24.96	25.77	25.67	24.77	24.91	24.74	24.93	24.81
SC		15.84	18.13	19.78	20.57	21.14	21.77	21.3	20.88	18.95	21.37
ST		47.33	43.55	40.04	37.04	35.73	32.14	31.04	31.23	41.06	31.53
OBC		12.33	14.37	15.22	16.61	17.45	21.32	22.74	23.15	15.06	22.29

Source: GoI: Annual Work Plan and Budget on MDM, 2007–08.

Table 22.8: Enrolment in Privately Managed Government Aided Schools
in Tripura, 2006

District/State	Pvt. Aided	EGS	AIE	Total
West Tripura	2,046	18,792	624	21,462
South Tripura	1,025	7,749	320	9,094
Dhalai	689	12,680	441	13,810
North Tripura	5,198	14,884	532	20,614
Tripura	8,958	54,105	1,917	64,980

Source: GoI: Annual Work Plan and Budget on MDM, 2007–08.

manufacturing sector. As reported (Government of Tripura 2007), the primary sector accounted for 28.6 per cent of income in West Tripura, and its share fell to 20.8 per cent in 2001–02. By contrast, the primary sector contributed almost one-half of the district income in Dhalai in 1993–94, and its share remained as high as 38 per cent in 2001–02. South District was also predominantly agricultural in 1993–94; over the years, however, the share of agriculture has declined substantially. A comparative view of the sectoral composition of income in Tripura and India is presented in Tables 22.11, 22.12, and 22.13. It appears that Tripura is fast catching up with the national figures in the matter of the contribution of the secondary sector in the total income. The share of income from the primary sector is fast declining.

The growth of per capita income in Tripura has been presented in Tables 22.12 (A and B). The data presented in Table 22.12 (A) has been taken from two publications (NEC, Shillong) for two different years, and appears to be inconsistent. Assuming that the latest report is authentic, we have adjusted the data for the years 1990–91 to 1992–93 to match with the rest. The adjusted Table 22.12 (B) may be used to have an idea of movement of per capita NSDP (at constant 1993–94 prices) in some states of the North East.

The data indicates that growth rate of per capita income is the highest in Tripura followed by Arunachal Pradesh. Of late, growth rate of per capita income in Manipur has picked up. Assam is more or less stagnant. Meghalaya, too, is not showing any encouraging trends. In this milieu, the trends shown by the per capita income in Tripura is worth appreciation. Nevertheless, per capita income of Tripura is substantially lower than that of India as a whole.

Human Development Index

The district-wise Human Development Index (HDI) and Gender-

Table 22.9: Dropout Rate in Primary Schools, Tripura, 2006

District/ State	Total			SC			ST			RM		
	B	G	T	B	G	T	B	G	T	B	G	T
W. Tripura	12.29	9.75	11.04	12.52	10.06	11.32	11.05	9.96	10.5	18.88	11.19	15.06
S. Tripura	10.8	13.17	11.97	5.79	6.9	6.35	12.85	16.75	14.77	13.01	9.52	11.26
Dhalai	9.48	12.58	10.89	7.01	15.17	11.06	10.93	13.62	12.12	0	0	0
N. Tripura	12.72	12.01	12.37	13.11	13.91	13.51	18.76	18.77	18.77	12.1	9.93	10.96
Tripura	11.44	11.76	11.6	10.11	10.57	10.34	12.79	14.91	13.81	15.71	10.47	13.05

Source: GoI: Annual Work Plan and Budget on MDM, 2007–08.

Table 22.10: Dropout Rate in Upper Primary Schools, Tripura, 2006

District/ State	Total			SC			ST			Others		
	B	G	T	B	G	T	B	G	T	B	G	T
W. Tripura	21.97	19.47	20.74	23.72	20.07	21.92	19.78	20.36	20.05	32.07	28.48	30.44
S. Tripura	19.05	17.94	18.52	17.02	15.45	16.26	31.90	28.79	30.43	27.71	25.53	26.63
Dhalai	25.37	30.77	27.98	17.47	21.20	19.41	35.11	48.39	41.43	23.64	7.50	16.84
N. Tripura	23.18	23.51	23.34	22.42	22.62	22.52	29.08	28.25	28.71	28.55	29.20	28.86
Tripura	21.86	20.96	21.42	21.57	19.73	20.66	26.94	28.32	27.59	29.89	27.69	28.86

Source: GoI: Annual Work Plan and Budget on MDM, 2007–08.

Table 22.11: Sectoral Composition of NSDP of Tripura and National
Income of India

Sector	Tripura			India		
	1980–81	1990–91	2002–03	1980–81	1990–91	2002–03
Primary	46.7	36.9	30.0	38.9	31.3	22.7
Secondary	10.5	10.3	18.6	19.7	22.0	20.5
Tertiary	42.8	52.8	51.4	41.5	46.7	56.9
Aggregate	100.0	100.0	100.0	100.0	100.0	100.0

Source: Tripura Human Development Report 2007, Government of Tripura.

Related Development Index (GDI) reported in the Tripura Human Development Report 2007 is presented in Table 22.13. The HDI is an arithmetic average of three indices: the education index, the health index, and the income index. However, as we all know, averages under present some figures, while over present some others. In Tripura, the health index is the largest contributor followed by the education index. The income index simply pulls down the HDI. The force of gravitation exerted by the income index on the HDI was more powerful in 1991. Economic development during 1991–2001 has abated this gravitational force. The GDI relates to gender equality. We observe that this index too has improved during 1991–2001.

It would be pertinent to raise a question here as to the economic meaning of HDI. Yes, higher level of human development (as it is) indicates that literacy is widespread, basic minimum health facilities are available, infant mortality is under control, and expectancy of life is higher. Yet, the income index is roughly one-third of the other two indices. The issue of channelizing literacy and life expectancy into productivity—a source of sustained rate of growth or development— is begging the question.

Economic development depends not only on the supply of the brute muscular power that human beings can apply to transformation of the non-human resources to more useful forms, but also on the skill embodied in the manpower applied to the production processes. Skill formation among the illiterate, though very important for economic development, has quite limited scope. Therefore, literacy and some extent of educational proficiency are of fundamental importance. Literacy among the females is of great importance, not only for participation in productive and civic activities, but also for rearing children for a better future. In this respect, Tripura performs better than India as a whole. However, literacy is not sufficient to ensure

Table 22.12(A): Per Capita NSDP (in Rs) of some North-Eastern States at 1993–94 Prices

State/ Country	1990 –91	1991 –92	1992 –93	1993 –94	1994 –95	1995 –96	1996 –97	1997 –98	1998 –99	1999 2000	2000 –01	2001 –02
Arunachal	2710	3012	3013	3364	8407	9424	8635	8693	8829	8520	9013	–
Assam	1594	1575	1557	1583	5737	5760	5793	5796	5664	5785	5867	5989
Manipur	1739	1841	1884	1896	5566	5612	6331	6770	7076	8147	7955	7976
Meghalaya	1733	1764	1617	1681	6705	7221	7225	7413	7935	8333	8460	8827
Nagaland	1976	2006	2239	2170	9410	9646	9880	10287	9118	8726	–	–
Tripura	1642	1681	1709	1856	5364	5707	6239	6828	7396	7967	8372	–
India	7321	7212	7433	7690	8070	8489	9007	9244	9650	10068	10306	10754

Source: ☐ Basic Statistics of North-Eastern Region 2000, NEC, Shillong, Table 173; p. 171.
☐ Basic Statistics of North-Eastern Region 2002, NEC, Shillong, Table 173; p. 238.

Table 22.12(B): Per Capita NSDP (in Rs) of some North-Eastern States at 1993–94 Prices [Adjusted]

State/ Country	1990 –91	1991 –92	1992 –93	1993 –94	1994 –95	1995 –96	1996 –97	1997 –98	1998 –99	1999 2000	2000 –01	2001 –02
Arunachal	6938	7711	7713	8612	8407	9424	8635	8693	8829	8520	9013	–
Assam	5755	5686	5621	5715	5737	5760	5793	5796	5664	5785	5867	5989
Manipur	5350	5664	5796	5833	5566	5612	6331	6770	7076	8147	7955	7976
Meghalaya	6928	7052	6464	6720	6705	7221	7225	7413	7935	8333	8460	8827
Nagaland	8313	8439	9419	9129	9410	9646	9880	10287	9118	8726	–	–
Tripura	4896	5012	5096	5534	5364	5707	6239	6828	7396	7967	8372	–
India	7321	7212	7433	8070	8070	8489	9007	9244	9650	10068	10306	10754

Source: ☐ Adjusted data from Table-15 (A).
☐ Basic Statistics of North-Eastern Region 2002, NEC, Shillong, Table 173; p. 238.

Table 22.13: HDI and GDI in Tripura: 1991–2001

| District/State/India | Education Index | | Health Index | | Income Index | | Human Development Index (HDI) | | Equally Distributed Indices | | | | | | Gender related Development Index (GDI) | |
| | | | | | | | | | Education Index | | Health Index | | Income Index | | | |
	1991	2001	1991	2001	1991	2001	1991	2001	1991	2001	1991	2001	1991	2001	1991	2001
West Tripura	0.66	0.77	0.73	0.82	0.08	0.26	0.49	0.62	0.64	0.77	0.73	0.82	0.03	0.17	0.47	0.58
South Tripura	0.53	0.70	0.67	0.76	0.08	0.24	0.43	0.57	0.51	0.69	0.67	0.76	0.04	0.19	0.41	0.55
Dhalai	0.50	0.61	0.66	0.74	0.05	0.19	0.40	0.51	0.47	0.59	0.66	0.74	0.03	0.16	0.39	0.50
North Tripura	0.63	0.73	0.72	0.80	0.07	0.25	0.47	0.59	0.62	0.72	0.72	0.80	0.03	0.16	0.45	0.56
Tripura	0.60	0.73	0.71	0.79	0.07	0.25	0.46	0.59	0.59	0.72	0.71	0.79	0.03	0.18	0.44	0.56
India	0.52	0.64	0.59	0.78	0.16	0.28	0.42	0.56	0.49	0.62	0.59	0.78	0.12	0.21	0.39	0.54

Source: Tripura Human Development Report 2007, Government of Tripura.

sustained development. When we consider education in relation to development, we must visualize what it may signify. The objectives of education are two-fold:

(i) to rationalize and modernize the attitudes of those who receive education and, in turn, to inculcate and nurture such attitudes among the rest of the society through the educated ones; and
(ii) to impart to the recipients of education knowledge and skill together with the ability to acquire further knowledge and still better skill by their own efforts.

The touchstone of the worth of education is in meeting these objectives. The modernized attitudes relate to efficiency, diligence, orderliness, punctuality, frugality, scrupulous honesty, and rationality in decisions, on actions, analytical rather than dogmatic view to understanding the world, preparedness for change, alertness to opportunities, energetic enterprise, integrity and self-reliance, cooperativeness, acceptance of responsibility for the welfare of the community and the nation, willingness to take the long view, and so on. The skills relate to knowing and the application of knowledge to changing things that may be more useful after such transformation.

HDI does not take into account some vital aspects of human resources that may have a great economic relevance. Human resources, in any region, have three aspects increasingly more important in the sequel:

(1) Physical fitness—relating to physical effort, easily captured by the number of workers, their general health (corporal), number of man-hours devoted to work; etc.,
(2) Dexterity—agility, skill, expertise, ability, and proficiency inculcated by training; and
(3) Attitude, outlook, and mindset—imbibed modernization ideals (in the sense of Gunnar Myrdal, pp. 38–40) and their practice at a mass level.

This third aspect makes *soft resources* or social capital. The first aspect of human resources is perhaps taken care of by the HDI. Literacy or life expectancy does not say anything about dexterity and attitude. Unless these factors are made a component of the HDI, its economic relevance would continue to be elusive. Beyond this, does high value of HDI say anything regarding the people if they are more 'human' in their conduct, their thoughts, and their world view? This is another big question.

CONCLUSION

In this chapter, we have synoptically presented an account of different facets and factors relating to human development in Tripura, a state that suffered a brutal blow of partition of the nation in 1947, that maimed its infrastructure and severed its connectivity with the rest of the nation, and thrust upon it a debilitating burden of immigrants with all needs and no resources. Its miseries did not end at that; it also had to bear the brunt of the Bangladesh freedom struggle and war in 1971. Until the late 1980s, it continued to be exposed to recurring floods of immigrants that strained the very core of its social and economic structure. Its delicate primary sector and feeble household industries could hardly support the population thrust upon it. However, the people of Tripura have shown great courage and an invincible will to scale all the odds against them and keep themselves up to mark in matters of education and health. These two factors win for them a higher score on the HDI. What is needed is that the human resources of Tripura are to be geared to command higher per capita income too.

REFERENCES

Government of India (GoI) 2007–08. Annual Work Plan and Budget on MDM 2007–2008. www.education.nic.in/mdm/Plan_2007-08/GOA /tables.doc

Government of Tripura 2007. *Tripura Human Development Report 2007*, Govt. of Tripura, Agartala.

Myrdal, Gunnar 1971. *Asian Drama: An Inquiry into the Poverty of Nations.* (abridged by Seth S. King), Vintage Books, New York.

North-Eastern Council (NEC) 2005. *Basic Statistics of North-Eastern Region 2005*, Ministry of Home Affairs, Government of India, Shillong.

—— 2002. *Basic Statistics of North-Eastern Region*, Ministry of Home Affairs, Government of India, Shillong.

—— 2001. *Basic Statistics of North-Eastern Region*, Ministry of Home Affairs, Government of India, Shillong.

23

Human Development in Assam
An Analysis

HIRANMOY ROY AND KINGSHUK ADHIKARI

INTRODUCTION

Nowadays, human development is an important area of study which provides information on the standard of living and quality of life of people. Human development, however, differs significantly from human resource development. The former is a wider term, as it includes all the sections of the society and does not treat human beings simply as a factor of production, whereas the human resource development approach emphasizes the need for the development of human capital through education, in-service training, health care, nutrition, and housing in order to raise productivity. The human development approach, on the other hand, concentrates mainly on the provision for basic means of well-being, which inter-alia includes food, education, and healthcare for the people. Human development as well as human resource development put human beings at the centrestage of the development process. The concept of human development is based on the idea that people are the real wealth of a nation and should, therefore, be the main beneficiaries of economic development. The present chapter, in this regard, is an attempt to analyse the issues related to human development in the state of Assam. A brief profile of Assam is provided along with the concepts of human development and its relevance, and finally, data analysis and interpretation about human development.

PROFILE OF ASSAM

Assam is the biggest and most important state in the North East. This state is bordering Arunachal Pradesh in the east, West Bengal,

Meghalaya and Bangladesh in the west, Arunachal Pradesh and Bhutan in the north and Nagaland, Manipur, Mizoram, Meghalaya, and Tripura in the south. Its longitude lies from 88.5°E to 96.0°E and latitude from 24.5°N to 29.0°N. The temperature of the state varies from 60°C to 380°C. The humidity brought into Assam by the south-west monsoon showers gives an average annual rainfall of 120 inches or more, and also creates spectacular sunsets for most part of the year. The monsoons are Assam's life blood, creating a biodiversity that can compete with equatorial rainforests and painting the region with a thousand shades of green. Except for a narrow corridor running through the foothills of the Himalayas, that connects the state with West Bengal, the state is almost entirely geographically isolated from the major part of India.

According to 2001 census, the population of the state is 2.66 crs and is scattered over 23 districts, 125 towns, and 26, 247 villages. Dispur is the current state capital of Assam. Its major towns are Guwahati, Dhubri, Barpeta, Dibrugarh, Tinsukia, Jorhat, Nagaon, Sivasagar, Silchar, and Tezpur. The state has the highest population density among the north-eastern states, that is, 339 persons per sq km. As against decadal growth rate of 21.54 per cent at the national level, the population of the state has grown by 18.92 per cent over the decade 1991–2001. The sex ratio in the state at 935 females to 1,000 males is higher than the national average of 933. Female literacy during the same decade rose from 43.03 per cent to 56.03 per cent. There are so many major tribes and a number of sub-tribes inhabiting the area.

The economy of Assam is mainly based on agricultural activities and oil exploration. The state produces a significant part of the total tea production of the world and produces more than half of India's petroleum. The growth of the state economy seems to be encouraging and is likely to register an upward trend in the coming years. The advance estimates of the State Domestic Product (SDP) for the year 2003–04 indicate that the growth rates of Net State Domestic Product (NSDP) is estimated at 6.2 per cent at constant (1993–94) prices and 10.5 per cent at current prices as compared to the corresponding growth rates of 3.9 per cent and 7.8 per cent for the year 2002–03.

Due to the adverse impact of natural calamities like floods, the performance of the agricultural sector, consistently, has not been up to expectations in the past. In the manufacturing and processing sector, a mixed performance in production has been observed. The overall power supply has been erratic. The installed capacity of power remained, by and large, constant. The generation of power decreased over the period. In order to meet the shortage of power supply, the state continued to purchase power from various other states in the region.

The total number of scheduled commercial bank offices (including regional rural banks) in the state, at the end of March 2005, was 1,235. The volume of deposits and credit of these banks stood at Rs 18,081 crs and Rs 6,219 crs, respectively, at the end of the aforesaid period. The credit-deposit ratio in the state, as on March 2005, was only 34.4 per cent, which was quite unsatisfactory.

As regards employment, the number of persons employed in organized economic activity (comprising both public and private sectors) has decreased. The data available from the employment exchanges of Assam reveals that the total job seekers in the Live Register are on the rise. But placements have decreased. In order to increase employment avenues through generation of gainful employment opportunities, the government has been implementing various schemes such as Employment Assurance Scheme (EAS), Swarnajayanti Gram Swarozgar Yojana (SGSY), and Special Swarnajayanti Gram Swarozgar Yojana (Special SGSY), etc. The concept of Self-Help Groups (SHGs) has been introduced to bring a drastic change in the field of self-employment. It is observed that more and more people of the state are taking keen interest in availing opportunities offered through implementation of these schemes. A positive development is already under way in various key sectors of the rural areas in the state.

In the last few years, the state has been passing through a crisis, such as stringent financial position, insurgency, and recurrence of natural calamities in the form of floods, soil erosion and at times drought, thereby making the task of desired development difficult. Despite such constraints, the state has been able to achieve considerable progress in diverse fields reflected through higher growth of SDP in the last two to three years.

CONCEPT AND RELEVANCE OF HUMAN DEVELOPMENT

Since the publication of the first human development report in the year 1990, human development has emerged as an important area of research. It has its own influence on the social policies to bring dynamic changes in development. Human development is now globally recognized as a crucial aid in measuring, monitoring, and managing socio-economic development (Fukuda-P. *et al.* 2005). Most social scientists agree that Gross National Product (GNP) per capita is a crude and incomplete measure of quality of life, and yet such a measure continues to be widely used while public policy is formulated. Human development approach embraces all aspects of human lives. The defining difference between economic growth and human development schools is that the first focuses exclusively on the expansion of only one choice, that is, income, while the second embraces the enlargement of all human choices, whether economic, social, cultural, or political. The introduction of ethical consideration has been the hallmark of this approach. Human Development Index (HDI) has been used as a tool for measurement of the non-income dimension of quality of life. It is constructed as a composite index of three basic dimensions of development—longevity, knowledge, and income.

United Nations Development Programme (UNDP), in its successive annual reports on human development, has been emphasizing issues on access to education, health, drinking water, sanitation, gender equality, and even societal and institutional arrangements for ventilating the freedom of the people. We, therefore, are introduced with the concepts like Human Poverty Index (HPI), Gender Empowerment Index (GEI), Capability Poverty Measure (CPM), and HDI, apart from traditional measures of poverty such as Head Count Ratio, Gini Coefficient, etc., in the study of quality of life. For measuring well-being of the people, income was taken as a yardstick prior to 1990. This approach to well-being was replaced by the human development approach with the publication of successive *Human Development Reports (HDRs)* of UNDP. The objective of human development has not been simply to produce more goods and services for material well-being, but to increase the capabilities of people. The real wealth of a nation is its people and the purpose of development is to create an enabling environment for a long and healthy life, to access knowledge and education, and to possess the resources needed for a reasonable standard of living, which are the primary social concerns of a society. For the construction of HDI, we have used the UNDP method as follows:

$$I_{ij} = \frac{X_{ij} - \text{Min}(X_{ij})}{\text{Max}(X_{ij}) - \text{Min}(X_{ij})}$$

where I_{ij} indicates individual indicator for the jth district with respect to the ith variable; X_{ij} indicates the actual value of the ith indicator with respect to j^{th} district; $Min(X_{ij})$ indicates minimum value of the ith indicator with respect to j^{th} district; and $Max(X_{ij})$ indicates maximum value of the ith indicator of the jth district. The overall index is calculated as: $HDI = \frac{1}{n} X_{ij}$. To ascertain the relative position of the districts in the development panorama, district development index (DDI) is estimated based on three indicators namely, (a) Indicators of Economic Growth, (b) Indicators of Infrastructure Development, and (c) Indicators of Social Development (Chatterjee and Ghosh 2001).

HUMAN DEVELOPMENT IN ASSAM
The HDI for the state of Assam and her districts were estimated and presented in *Assam Human Development Report (AHDR) 2003*. The HDI for the state was 0.407 and the corresponding figures in different districts ranged from the lowest figures of 0.214 in Dhubri district to the highest of 0.650 in Jorhat district (*AHDR 2003*). Most of the eastern districts in Assam and the districts of Kamrup and Karbi Anglong have had HDI higher than the state average. All the western districts except Kamrup district had HDI lower than the state average. The districts of Nagoan, Hailakandi, Lakhimpur, Karimganj, Dhemaji, and Darrang also had HDI below the state average.

Table 23.1 shows the districts having lower and higher HDI values as compared to that of the state average. It is revealed that Jorhat, Kamrup, Golaghat, Morigaon, Karbi Anglong, Dibrugarh, and Sibasagar were having higher HDI than the state average. All other districts of Assam were having HDI below the state average. The reason for low HDI in west Assam districts could be attributed to factors like lower attainment in the field of education, health services, and limited economic opportunities to earn sufficient livelihoods. The dearth of employment opportunities for educated people was borne out by the increasing number of people with high educational and professional qualifications as revealed from live registers of different employment exchanges. Unemployment continued to be a serious problem, especially among educated youths. Within the state there were considerable inter-district disparities.

The task has been identified to achieve higher growth for all, to bring basic services within the reach of every citizen of the state, and to reduce regional disparities and inequalities among people. Table 23.2 clearly shows that the mean HDI of districts where it is higher than that of the state average is much higher than the mean HDI of those districts where it is lower than that of the state average.

Table 23.1: Districts with Lower and Higher HDI than the State Average

| HDI Below State Average | | HDI Above State Average | |
District	HDI	District	HDI
Barpeta	0.396	Jorhat	0.650
Tinsukia	0.377	Kamrup	0.574
Hailakandi	0.363	Golaghat	0.540
N.C. Hills	0.363	Morigaon	0.494
Sonitpur	0.357	Karbi Anglong	0.494
Nagaon	0.356	Dibrugarh	0.843
Kokrajhar	0.354	Sibasagar	0.469
Nalbari	0.343		
Lakhimpur	0.337		
Goalpara	0.308		
Karimganj	0.301		
Dhemaji	0.277		
Bongaigaon	0.263		
Darrang	0.259		
Dhubri	0.214		
Cachar	0.402		

Source: Assam Human Development Report, 2003.

Table 23.2: Analysis of Data

District	Mean	Standard Deviation	Maximum	Minimum
Districts (15) having higher HDI than that of the State average	0.5133	0.3245	0.650	0.402
Districts (8) having lower HDI than that of the State average	0.0747	0.0518	0.396	0.214

Source: Based on data obtained from Assam Human Development Report, 2003.

The gap between maximum and minimum value of HDI of districts (15) having higher HDI than that of the state average is also much wider than that of districts (8) having lower HDI. The standard deviation of districts (15) having higher HDI than that of state average is much greater than that of districts (8) having lower HDI. This implies that human development level of the districts having higher HDI than that of the state average is much dispersed, or scattered from the mean value. In case of districts (8) having lower HDI, the very low standard deviation reveals that the level of human development in these districts is, by and large, very close to one another.

In order to calculate the composite index, three indices, namely, education index, income index, and infant mortality index were constructed. District-wise data regarding all the three indicators were procured from AHDR (2003). It may be pointed out that due to non-availability of data on life expectancy, the infant mortality rate (IMR) was used as a proxy variable for longevity while constructing district-wise composite index in the report. The composite index was calculated using the UNDP method.

Table 23.3 depicts the comparative picture of districts having lower or higher composite indices than the state average. The districts, namely, Jorhat, Kamrup, and Golaghat are having higher HDI values in all the three independent indices compared to the corresponding state averages. It may be mentioned here that these three districts have contributed significantly to the higher value of the index at the state level. The districts, namely, Hailakandi, Nagaon, Goalpara, Bongaigaon, Darrang, and Dhubri are having lower values in all the three independent indices compared to the state average.

Table 23.3: Districts having Lower and Higher Composite Indices than the State Average

District	Composite Index Below State Average	District	Composite Index Above State Average
Cachar	0.402	Jorhat	0.650
Barpeta	0.397	Kamrup	0.575
Tinsukia	0.377	Golaghat	0.541
Hailakandi	0.363	Morigaon	0.495
N.C. Hills	0.363	Karbi Anglong	0.494
Sonitpur	0.358	Dibrugarh	0.484
Nagaon	0.356	Sivsagar	0.469
Kokrajhar	0.354	Assam	0.408
Nalbari	0.344		
Lakhimpur	0.337		
Goalpara	0.308		
Karimganj	0.302		
Dhemaji	0.278		
Bongaigaon	0.263		
Darrang	0.259		
Dhubri	0.214		

Source: Assam Human Development Report, 2003.

While the income is considered an exclusive measure of well-being, per capita domestic product is one of the three components of

HDI. This is because income is an important determinant of access. Income provides the means that allows people to attain well-being, but income alone is not an indicator of well-being. Nor do per capita income figures necessarily reflect social well-being, whether incomes get translated into long and healthy lives, higher education, and better standard of living is dependent on the choices that people, societies, and governments make. To enhance the level of human development in the state, steps should be undertaken to increase the level of income and employment in the state, and reduce poverty. The average level of income and rates of growth of income in Assam are much below the corresponding averages at the national level. The state has an extremely high proportion of poverty, more than one-third (36.09 per cent) of its population are below the poverty line. The percentage of poor in the state is the highest among the seven states of the North East. Therefore, the policy of the state must be oriented to forge a strong linkage between HDI and HPI so that both become mutually reinforcing.

Commonly, poverty which is defined in terms of inadequacy of income, is a severe failure of basic capabilities. HPI in this context has been constructed to measure deprivation in widest sense—deprivation in basic services and income. The indicators used to measure HPI are the deprivation in longevity, knowledge, and standard of living. The variables used in measuring HPI are:

1. Percentage of people not expected to survive beyond age 40;
2. Percentage of illiterate persons;
3. Percentage of people without having access to safe drinking water;
4. Percentage of people without having access to health care;
5. Percentage of underweight children at birth;
6. Percentage of people without access to sanitary facilities; and
7. Percentage of people not having pucca dwelling house.

The results obtained reveal that there is a wide variation across districts in terms of HDI and HPI (Table 23.4).

In most of the districts where HDI is higher, HPI is correspondingly lower, implying that higher human development is accompanied with higher poverty. The districts in which HPI is lower are Dibrugarh, Sibsagar, Tinsukia, Sonitpur, Nagaon, Nalbari, Lakhimpur, Goalpara, Karimganj, Dhemaji, Darrang, and Dhubri. In these districts, poverty

Table 23.4: District-wise HDI and HPI in Assam

District	HDI	HDI Rank	HPI	HPI Rank
Jorhat	0.650	1	31.33	6
Kamrup	0.574	2	24.72	3
Golaghat	0.540	3	30.84	5
Morigaon	0.494	4	34.06	10
Karbi Anglong	0.494	5	44.44	23
Dibrugarh	0.843	6	24.30	2
Sibasagar	0.469	7	24.28	1
Cachar	0.402	8	39.71	17
Barpeta	0.396	9	35.22	13
Tinsukia	0.377	10	33.71	9
Hailakandi	0.363	11	41.02	19
N.C. Hills	0.363	12	42.66	21
Sonitpur	0.357	13	34.60	12
Nagaon	0.356	14	30.33	4
Kokrajhar	0.354	15	42.73	22
Nalbari	0.343	16	33.04	8
Lakhimpur	0.337	17	32.81	7
Goalpara	0.308	18	39.55	16
Karimganj	0.301	19	40.22	18
Dhemaji	0.277	20	37.03	15
Bongaigaon	0.263	21	35.37	14
Darrang	0.259	22	34.43	11
Dhubri	0.214	23	41.92	20
ASSAM	0.407	–	–	–

Source: Assam Human Development Report, 2003.

is less acute, though HDI is lower. The correlation between HDI and HPI is estimated to be –0.579. Thus, there exists a moderate degree of relationship between HDI and HPI in the state. A district where HDI is lower than the state average, the correlation between HDI and HPI is –0.414. In case of districts where HDI is higher than the state average, the correlation between HDI and HPI is – 0.115.

We have also regressed HDI on HPI to study the causal relationship between them. The following is the estimated equation:

$$HDI = 44.797 - 23.785HPI$$
where $R^2 = 0.34$

What emerges from the analysis is that poverty is a result not only of lower income but also due to human deprivation in terms of health, education, shelter, water supply, and sanitation. There is a gap between income and employment levels, both in the state and the country as a whole. On the part of the state, there is a need to prioritize and target relatively backward areas of the state and disadvantaged people. A development strategy, which is decentralized and seeks to involve a larger community, needs to be developed by the government in the sectors in which the state has potential advantages. In the context of poverty, the adequacy of funding of public initiative is even more urgent.

CONCLUSION

The progress and status of human development in Assam is far from satisfactory. There has been high degree of disparity across the districts as reflected in the levels of attainment in various dimensions of human development in the state. The districts, namely, Jorhat, Kamrup, and Golaghat are performing much better than the state as a whole. Seven districts that are having higher human development as compared to state average are also correspondingly having higher infant mortality rates. In contrast to this, Cachar, N.C. Hills, Nalbari, Lakhimpur, Karimganj, and Dhemaji are having better performance in education accompanied with lower infant mortality inspite of having lower income as compared to the state average. Further, inter-district disparities are also noticed in the HPI. The position of different districts in terms of HDI and HPI varies. Moderate degree of negative correlation between HDI and HPI exists in the state. What emerges from the analysis is that poverty is not only an outcome of lower income but also due to deprivation in health, education, shelter, water supply, and sanitation for the people. Therefore, there is an urgent need to set priorities and target for relatively backward regions of the state and groups of disadvantaged people. A development strategy which is decentralized and seeks to involve a larger community needs to be adopted by the government.

REFERENCES

Basu, K. and S. Richard (eds) 1986. *Social and Economic Development in India*, Sage Publications, New Delhi.

Chatterjee, B. 2002. 'Human Development in India: An Analysis of Inter-State Variations', *Artha Bijnan* (Journal of Bengal Economic Association), December.

Chatterjee, B. and D. Ghosh 2001. *In Search of a District Development Index*, State Institute of Panchayat and Rural Development, Kalyani.

Fukuda, P., K.R. Sakiko, and A.K. Shivakumar 2005. 'Using the Human Development Index for Policy Purposes', in Sakiko Fukuda-Parr and A.K. Shiva Kumar (eds), *Readings in Human Development: Concepts, Measures and Policies for a Development Paradigm*, Oxford University Press.

Government of Assam, 2003. *Assam Human Development Report.*

Government of India (GoI) 2002. *National Human Development Report 2001,* Planning Commission.

Haq, M.u. 1996. *Reflections on Human Development,* Oxford University Press, New Delhi.

Kamalamma, G. 1996. *Health and Nutritional Status in India,* APH Publishing Corporation, New Delhi.

Kamdar, S. and A. Basak, 2005. 'Beyond the Human Development Index, Preliminary Notes on Deprivation and Inequality', *Economic and Political Weekly,* Vol. 44, No. 34, pp. 3759–65, August 20–26.

Mahbub ul Haq Development Centre, 2000. *Human Development in South Asia: The Gender Question,* Oxford University Press, New Delhi.

Nayak, P. 2005. 'Human Development in North-East India', *Journal of NEICSSR,* April.

National Council of Applied Economic Research (NCAER), 1999. *India Human Development Report,* Oxford University Press, New Delhi.

Prabhu, K.S. 2001. *Economic Reform and Social Sector Development A Study of Two Indian States,* Sage Publications, New Delhi.

United Nations Development Programme (UNDP), 1995. *Human Development Report,* Oxford University Press, New Delhi.

24
Development and Deprivation in Arunachal Pradesh

DEBASIS NEOGI

INTRODUCTION

The very notion of development often confronts with conflict in the academic literature. In fact, the process of economic development itself has undergone a number of paradigm-shifts over the last few decades, especially in the aftermath of the World War II. While, on the one side, such changes were inevitable as they were timely responses to the contemporary necessities, on the other, the differences among the scholars originated mostly in the interpretation of the concept and in the outcome of various strategies implemented. In the era of global-ization, the debate has become more intense. When the market has emerged as the driving force of the economy, the development strategy initiated by the state operates with its usual exclusion principle. The produce of development reaches that section of society, which fits well in the market dynamics, ensuring survival of the fittest. However, the development ethicists have put strong objection to such exclusions. They argue that at least some development ideology should be in place to address the problems of the excluded—mostly the poor and the vul-nerable section of the society. There is, in fact, a large, complex, and unresolved empirical question regarding the relative contributions of local and global factors to the wealth and poverty of the societies (Beitz 2001). In this context, the role of different development agents becomes crucial. These agents, at both governmental and non-govern-mental level, have to shoulder the responsibilities of ensuring social upliftment, and for that the best possible development strategy has to be devised.

In spite of India being the largest democracy in the world, development has not been uniform across the states and at the sub-regional level. While some parts of India have progressed rapidly, some others are way behind. The rising regional disparity has invariably slowed down the trickle-down effect of growth on poverty reduction (Bhanumurthy and Mitra 2004). Since long, the region has been encountering various problems associated with its development. Exclusion of some parts of the society from the process of development though existed in the past and was not caused due to market economy, but because of deficient infrastructure. With the advent of globalization, this asymmetry has got additional dimension.

Policy formulation for any region, without taking proper stock of the existing disparity, may lead to further augmentation of the problem. Formulating a too pro-rural policy, for example, may transfer too much burden to the urban sector through inter-sectoral redistributions, which besides offsetting the relative gains to the rural area, fail to add to the net social benefit. In north-eastern India, apart from an asymmetric development and concentration of economic power, a dependency syndrome has started to operate. The dependence is on central grants, which have been flooding the region under various development schemes. But development in the real sense has always been inadequate and devoid of its qualitative dimensions in the region (Meier 1995). Because of such lopsided development practice, the region is considered as one of the most underdeveloped one in the country.

Arunachal Pradesh is one of the remotely located border states of the region. The difficult geographical location along with its geopolitical identity has rendered the state with a special status where even-distribution of the fruits of development has connotations for its strategic sensitivities. However, development and deprivation in the state are in tandem. With the help of some selected parameters, the present chapter analyses the inequalities in the attainment of socioeconomic development across the districts and sectors in the state. It attempts to examine whether the stage of development so far achieved by the districts is compatible to their attained economic growth. It also examines the relative convergence and divergence of such intrastate disparity during the period from 1993 to 2004.

MATERIALS AND METHODS
According to 2001 census, there are 16 districts in Arunachal Pradesh.

However, for the purpose of the present study, only those 13 districts were selected for which required data is available. For the purpose of comparison over time, a few selected socio-economic indicator variables were chosen. Since the state is predominantly an agricultural economy, having 58.44 per cent of the workers as cultivators, the overall development of the state depends to a large extent on development of agriculture. To evaluate agricultural development, some parameters like net area sown, area brought under irrigation, and fertilizer consumption, were considered for analysis. Infrastructure, both physical and social, is very crucial for the development of the state, given her geographical location and topography. A number of parameters were considered for analysis for physical and social infrastructure

The study is based on secondary data (Statistical Abstract of Arunachal Pradesh 1993 and 2004, and the *State Human Development Report 2005*) and uses a number of statistical tools for the purpose of analysis. The coefficient of variation of the parameters, both in 1993 and 2004, finds the relative variation of the respective parameters across different districts in the state. The Ginni C Coefficient suggests relative concentration of these parameters across districts. To make the analysis richer, the chapter also uses Lorenz consistent General Entropy measure. Its sensitivity to both upper and lower parts of the data series is also considered. Composite indices of agricultural development and socio-economic development are constructed. The study also uses graphical presentation to elaborate the findings.

RESULTS AND DISCUSSION

As a first step, let us commence with the analysis of the performance of each indicator for the year 1993. Table 24.1 provides necessary data related to these indicators of socio-economic development of the state. The largest share of population in the state in 1993 was in Lohit district, while Tawang had the lowest share of population. However, indicator-wise, there were differences among the districts. As far as sex ratio is concerned, East Siang was the most advanced district. It had, on the average, 961 females per 1000 males, which is pretty higher than the state average of 859.

The state had a very poor performance in 1993 as regards literacy rate (32.8 per cent) was concerned. Highest literacy rate of 38.5 per cent was observed in Lohit. The female education was, however, not so grim as compared to the overall literacy rate in the state. On the average, 42.88 per cent of the total students enrolled in the primary

Table 24.1: Select Indicators of Socioeconomic Development of
Arunachal Pradesh in 1993

District/State	Columns									
	2	3	4	5	6	7	8	9	10	11
Tawang	3.27	844	24.14	84	0.08	85	29	35.93	90.74	3535.88
W. Kameng	6.53	822	36.48	79	0.17	38	27	42.62	12.86	2969.53
E. Kameng	5.83	961	20.81	48	0.15	23	31	39.54	19.83	5599.44
Papum pare	8.42	830	43.06	6.82	0.08	45	28	42.08	13.71	2696.70
L. Subansiri	9.62	956	24.24	24.18	0.25	28	39	42.06	13.79	2772.23
U. Subansiri	5.79	867	30.83	29	0.13	12	41	44.41	10.64	3577.57
West Siang	10.40	872	35.5	28	0.24	89	36	46.01	14.56	3330.96
East Siang	11.53	861	35.29	51	0.27	52	30	47.71	14.26	2214.29
D. Valley	4.98	788	36.88	30	0.18	70	30	44.49	5.85	3589.00
Lohit	12.69	797	38.47	55	0.13	60	31	41.65	12.16	2675.76
Changlang	11.05	862	33.53	31	0.14	25	40	44.14	17.25	5027.89
Tirap	9.89	862	25.18	33	0.14	41	32	33.89	89.46	4071.81
A. Pradesh	100.00	859	32.8	499	0.17	48	33	42.88	16.73	3178.52

Note: Population share (in per cent); Col.3: Sex ratio; Col.4: Literacy rate; Col.5: Fertilizer used (M.T.); Col.6: Ratio of net area sown to population; Col.7: Ratio of net irrigated area to net area sown; Col.8: Pupil-teacher ratio in Primary Section; Col.9: Per cent of girl students enrolled in primary section; Col.10: Length of road per 100 sq km area; Col.11: Population-doctor ratio.
Source: Government of Arunachal Pradesh (1993).

section were females. The highest proportion of female students in the primary section was in East Siang (47.71 per cent).

The student-teacher ratio in primary schools was the lowest at 27 in West Kameng as compared to the state figure of 33, thereby making it possible for the teachers to give relatively more attention to the individual students in the district. The population-doctor ratio was lowest in East Siang, where one doctor treated, on an average, nearly 2,214 people. This was lower than the state average of 3,179.

As far as agricultural development is concerned, the relative positions of the districts in respect of all the three parameters were different. Use of fertilizer was the highest in Tawang, where 84 Metric Tonnes of fertilizer was used in 1992–93. The highest per capita net area sown was in East Siang district (0.27 hectare). It was much higher than the overall scenario of the state, which was 0.17. In terms of availability of irrigation facility in the sown area, West Siang was in the best position, where almost 89 per cent of the net sown area had irrigation facility. At the state level, the corresponding figure was as low as 48 per cent.

As per 2001 census also, the largest share of population continued to be in Lohit district. This district had 12.69 per cent of total population of the state. In terms of sex ratio, East Kameng had the highest sex ratio. It had 985 females per 1,000 males, which was higher than the state average of 901.

Regarding literacy rate, the capital district Papum Pare had the largest share of literate people at 71 per cent against the state average of 55 per cent. The scenario in female education in the state had improved in 2004 as compared to 1993. The enrolment of girl students in primary education in Arunachal Pradesh, on an average, has remained at 46 per cent. Among the districts, Upper Siang had the largest proportion (50.19 per cent) of enrolled girl students in primary education. The student-teacher ratio was the lowest at 22:1 in both West Kameng and East Siang districts. At the state level, on an average, 35 students were taught by a teacher.

In a similar pattern, the average number of people attended by a single doctor was lowest in Upper Siang district, where a doctor treated nearly 1,400 people. The situation was much better than the average state figure where the population-doctor ratio was 2364:1.

As far as infrastructure development is concerned, road development is an important component. As a matter of fact, it is a pre-requisite to economic development of any region. Arunachal Pradesh, even after entering into the twenty first century, is yet to witness a balanced and uniform road network across the state. In fact, there are still many places which do not have road connectivity and these places remain cut off for months together by the flowing streams. At the state level, the length of roads per 100 sq km area was meagre at 16.72 km. However, among the districts, Tawang had the maximum of 35.58 km per 100 sq km, while upper Dibang Valley had the lowest of 6.96 km of roads per 100 sq km. As regards tele-connectivity, as low as 5 out of every 100 people had telephone connections in the state, the highest being in the capital district, Papum Pare (15).

Provision of drinking water is another area of concern in some parts of the state. About 54 per cent of the total population of the state had access to drinking water. Among the districts, Upper Subansiri had 97.57 per cent of the total population having drinking water facility as against the lowest of 77.82 per cent in West Kameng.

In the field of agriculture, there has been improvement in terms of use of fertilizer over the years in the state. Among the districts, West Kameng had the highest fertilizer consumption of 264 Metric Tonnes in 2004, which was over 14 per cent of the total fertilizer used in the state. The per capita net area sown was the highest in Upper Dibang Valley district (0.40 hectare) while the corresponding figure was only 0.19 hectare at the state level. Out of net area sown in the state, only 18.84 per cent had irrigation facility. Changlang, having access to irrigation, with over 53 per cent of the net sown area, was the best among all the districts.

As far as the extent of poverty is concerned, during the ninth five-year plan, 54 per cent the families in the state lived below poverty line. Upper Subansiri had the highest incidence of poverty: 84 per cent of the families in the district belonged to below poverty line (BPL) category, followed by Tirap with 74 per cent, while the lowest incidence was in Changlang, where only 25 per cent families were of BPL category. East Kameng (69 per cent), Lower Subansiri (67 per cent), and Tawang (66 per cent) were the other districts that had incidence of poverty higher than the state average.

To measure disparity in respect of all the indicators, we considered the coefficient of variation, which is the ratio of standard deviation to the mean of the distribution and Ginni C Coefficient (Pyatt *et. al.* 1980). Between 1993 and 2004, the coefficient of variation (CV) had worsened, though marginally for sex ratio, but substantially in case of per capita net area sown, proportion of net irrigation in net area sown, and pupil-teacher ratio (Table 24.2).

However, this relative variation had reduced in the use of fertilizer, enrolment of girl students at the level of primary school, and the availability of doctor represented by population per doctor. Reduction in disparity was also noticed in the case of physical connectivity (length of road per 100 sq km area).

All these measures provide a clear picture of extent of disparity in the state in its socio-economic perspective. However, these estimates ignored population share effect of the districts. To overcome this, we employed Lorenz-consistent General Entropy (GE) set of measures (Cowell 1995, Fedorov 2002). These measures are sensitive to various parts of the distribution. In Table 24.3, we have presented results of these measures for all the indicators. The GE measure showed improvement over the decade in terms of sex ratio, per-capita net area sown, pupil-teacher ratio in primary education, and share of girl students in total number of students enrolled in primary education. Increased disparity was observed in case of literacy rate, use of fertilizer, road length, and availability of doctor. For c = 2, improvement was noticed

Table 24.2: Coefficient of Variation and GCC Indicators in
Arunachal Pradesh

Indicator	Coefficient of Variation		Ginni C Coefficient	
	1993	2004	1993	2004
Sex ratio	6.21	7.48	0.03165	0.03821
Literacy rate	21.64	17.63	0.11586	0.65089
Fertilizer used (M.T)	54.66	51.55	0.28346	0.03528
Ratio of net area sown to population	37.05	44.45	0.19731	2.08326
Ratio of net irrigated area to net area sown	51.90	76.33	0.28144	0.23549
Pupil-teacher ratio in Primary Section	14.85	25.91	0.07981	0.18235
Percentage of girl students enrolled in primary section	9.47	6.12	0.04922	0.11616
Road Length per 100 sq km area	114.30	48.27	0.45541	0.52259
Population provided with drinking water facility (%)	--	13.39	--	0.00015
Population doctor ratio	28.40	23.79	0.14690	0.00218
Proportion of families below poverty line	--	37.81	--	5.65068
Telephone per 100 population	--	60.97	--	28.0980

in case of overall literacy rate, proportion of girl students in primary section, road length, and population-doctor ratio. However, the disparity had gone up for sex ratio, use of fertilizer, per capita net area sown, availability of irrigation facility in net sown area, and pupil-teacher ratio.

The Theil Index is considered to be the best suited one in the present study for its responsiveness to the entire part of the distribution. It revealed reduction in disparity in sex ratio, literacy rate, per capita net area sown, and length of road. In literacy rate, there was marginal reduction. However, the decrease in disparity was substantial in per-capita net area sown, proportion of girl child enrolled in primary education, and length of road per 100 sq km. The disparity aggravated in case of use of fertilizer, availability of irrigated area, student-teacher ratio in the primary section, and in the population-doctor ratio. Thus, in some cases, convergence was noticed while in some others divergence was found to exist in the extent of disparity. These convergences and divergences are represented in Figure 24.1.

Table 24.3: Results of General Entropy Measure of Inequality

	C = 0		C = 1		C = 2	
	1993	2004	1993	2004	1993	2004
Sex ratio	−0.0684	−0.2206	0.0722	−0.0229	0.610307	0.95079
Literacy rate	0.1480	0.5090	1.9203	1.7647	3.734461	2.113118
Fertilizer used (M.T.)	−8.9287	−3.9771	2.6050	5.5321	10.19506	26.13274
Ratio of net area sown to popn.	0.5420	−4.5614	6.3252	1.9181	11.7119	15.72089
Ratio of net irrigated area to net area sown	−5.2592	−11.8069	4.6905	12.7042	14.57001	61.56257
Pupil-teacher ratio in Primary Section	0.1124	−1.3333	0.9228	1.7470	3.231598	36.51683
Girl student enrolled to total enrolled students in primary (%)	0.2238	−0.7105	0.5966	−0.5608	−1.27395	−1.40675
Length of road per 100 sq km area	−18.2864	−3.6895	11.7646	5.4898	340.5777	98.45004
Popn. with drinking water (%)	—	−0.5828	—	−0.1173	—	1.197206
Population-doctor ratio	−2.7506	−0.4522	0.5251	1.3956	24.79149	13.81042
Proportion of BPL families	—	−3.9764	—	1.7422	—	12.79737
Telephone per 100 population	—	−3.3342	—	11.6019	—	46.1139

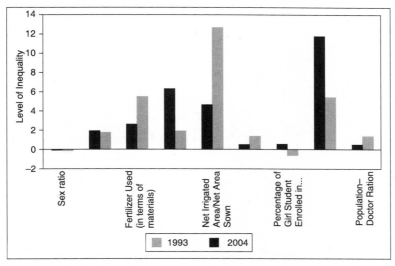

Figure 24.1: Relative Convergence and Divergence of Parameters from 1993 to 2004

On the basis of the above mentioned parameters, we ranked the districts by constructing Composite District Development Index (CDDI) for 1993 and 2004. While constructing HDI, we partly deviated from the norm of United Nations Development Programme (UNDP) by not choosing three dimensions but by taking 10 dimensions for the year 1993 and that of 12 dimensions for 2004. For those parameters, where lower figures indicate better impact on development, such as student-teacher ratio, population-doctor ratio, and below poverty line population, we used rank in ascending order as the component of the index. In each of these cases, the largest value, that is, the worst case was ranked one and the least value was given the highest rank. However, for other parameters, the concerned values were taken into consideration. The development index was computed by simple average of all the indices and presented with ranks in Table 24.4.

$$C_j = \frac{1}{N} \sum_{i=1}^{N} \frac{A_{ij} - L_{ij}}{H_i - L_i}$$

where C_j = Composite District Development Index of district j,
A_{ij} = Actual Value of the ith indicator in district j,

Table 24.4: Composite Development Index and Agricultural
Development Index

District	1993		2004		1993		2004	
	CDI	CDI Rank	CDI	CDI Rank	CADI	CADI Rank	CADI	CADI Rank
Tawang	0.5162	4	0.5576	3	0.67	3	0.39	7
W. Kameng	0.5374	3	0.3832	8	0.58	4	0.35	8
E. Kameng	0.3692	10	0.2970	12	0.36	8	0.20	10
Papum pare	0.4448	7	0.5369	4	0.15	12	0.12	12
L. Subansiri	0.4434	8	0.3553	10	0.45	7	0.33	9
U. Subansiri	0.2898	11	0.4184	7	0.18	11	0.18	11
W. Siang	0.6033	2	0.5620	2	0.71	1	0.50	3
E. Siang	0.6874	1	0.6024	1	0.71	2	0.50	2
D. Valley	0.4577	6	0.3371	11	0.55	5	0.54	1
Lohit	0.4748	5	0.3556	9	0.52	6	0.46	5
Changlang	0.2877	12	0.4570	6	0.28	10	0.46	4
Tirap	0.3770	9	0.2390	13	0.35	9	0.09	13
U. Siang	--	--	0.4982	5	--	--	0.40	6

Note: CDDI—Composite District Development Index; CADI—Composite Agricultural Development Index.

H_i = Highest Value of the ith indicator among all the districts,
L_i = Lowest Value of the ith indicator among all the districts, and
N (Number of parameters) = 10 (in case of 1993) and 12 (in case of 2004).

It was found that East Siang continued to be the most developed district in Arunachal Pradesh followed by West Siang. Both of these districts maintained their respective ranks in 1993 and 2004, though, over the decade, the respective indices witnessed marginal decline. The index for Tawang increased, while that of West Kameng decreased substantially. The socio-economic development of the capital district Papum Pare showed substantial improvement over the decade. In 1993, the development index was 0.4448 with a rank of 7, and it increased significantly to 0.5369 in 2004 with rank elevated to 4th. Lohit, with the largest share of population in the state, had deteriorated over the years. East Kameng was the least developed district and was yet to show any sign of improvement. While Dibang Valley witnessed sharp decline on the development front, Changlang showed remarkable progress in its socio-economic condition. The pace of development of Upper Subansiri was faster than that of Lower Subansiri. The relative development of Tirap also slowed down over the period.

Applying the above method, the Composite Agricultural Development Index (CADI) was also estimated by incorporating the three dimensions of agricultural development namely, fertilizer consumption, per-capita net area sown, and proportion of net irrigated area in the net sown area (Table 24.4). The CADI showed mixed results. While some of the districts improved, development in others remained sluggish. The districts with high CDDI, like East Siang and West Siang, also had higher CADI. The capital district, Papum-pare remained backward. Among the rest of the districts, Dibang Valley improved its relative position from 5th to 1st. However, it witnessed a decline in the value of the index.

In the following paragraphs, we have attempted to analyse the compatibility of such development with economic growth prospect. Table 24.5 provides an estimate of the real per capita Net District Domestic Product (NDDP) of 13 major districts of Arunachal Pradesh along with sectoral growth rate and the HDI ranks of the districts.

The point worth mentioning is that growth rate in the primary sector was negative in a majority of her districts (8 out of 13) though all districts experienced positive growth rates in NDDP. In the case of

Table 24.5: Real Per Capita NDDP and Sectoral Growth Rates of NDDP
(1993–94 to 2000–01)

Districts	NDDP		Growth Rates of NDDP (%)			
	Mean Per Capita (Rs)	Growth Rate	Primary Sector	Secondary Sector	Tertiary Sector	HDI Rank
Tawang	10541	3.46	−4.30	4.34	10.09	6
West Kameng	12391	1.69	6.39	4.82	9.14	3
East Kameng	7237	0.61	−3.71	−0.56	8.79	13
Papum Pare	9334	4.30	−2.33	−0.60	9.38	3
L. Subansiri	6179	2.60	−0.48	−0.37	9.02	11
U. Subansiri	7268	4.90	2.82	−1.43	9.65	10
West Siang	8595	2.73	−1.73	0.28	9.29	5
East Siang	10719	3.00	0.96	0.27	9.04	1
Upper Siang	9878	2.85	6.11	−5.95	9.30	7
Dibang Valley	13328	2.59	0.16	−0.57	9.25	2
Lohit	8450	2.49	−2.63	0.34	9.64	8
Changlang	7167	1.42	−1.70	0.70	8.56	9
Tirap	7602	1.11	−7.54	1.25	9.14	12

Source: Arunachal Pradesh Human Development Report, 2005.

the secondary sector also, negative growth rate was found (6 out of 13 districts). However, growth rate in the tertiary sector recorded significant rise for all the districts. Another point that needs special attention is the incompatibility of the economic growth and development in some cases. Though highest growth rate in NDDP was observed for Upper Subansiri at 4.90 per cent accompanied with the highest mean per capita NDDP, the HDI rank was very low at 10th. In terms of socio-economic development, the district improved its relative rank from 11th to 7th. Similarly, the CADI rank of the district was also very low at 11 and it had the highest incidence of poverty. Similarly, Tawang, which had quite high growth rate in NDDP, experienced a marginal rise in its relative position in socio-economic development with CDDI rank improving from 4th to 3rd. It had a HDI rank of 6. The CADI rank had, however, fallen drastically from 3 to 7. Tawang had as high as 66 per cent of the families residing below poverty line. The capital district Papum Pare had a very high growth rate in NDDP along with a high mean per capita NDDP. The district had negative growth in case of primary and secondary sector. However, significant growth occurred in the tertiary sector. The district was ranked 3rd in terms of HDI and its socio-economic profile had improved significantly (rank improving from 7th to 4th). However, the district had 46 per cent of the families under BPL. The position in agriculture remained stagnant at a very low level. The position of Dibang Valley is noteworthy. The district consistently had the highest mean per capita NDDP during 1993–94 and 2000–01, and its NDDP grew at a moderate rate of 2.59 per cent. The district, though, had negative growth rate for the secondary sector, had positive growth in case of primary sector besides improvement in the tertiary sector occurring almost at par with that of the other districts. Though, in the ladder of HDI, it was placed at a high position (rank 2), in terms of socio-economic development, the district had shown deteriorating performance with its CDDI rank slipping from 6 to 11. However, in terms of agricultural development, the position of the district improved from 5th rank in 1993 to the 1st position in 2004. About 38 per cent of the families in the district lived below poverty line.

Lohit and Changlang, which were among the large districts of the state and which had the highest proportions of population, performed miserably in both socio-economic and human development fronts. In terms of socio-economic profile, the relative position of Lohit dropped from 5th in 1993 to 9th in 2004 with a rank as low as 8th in 2004. The district had 53 per cent of the families in BPL category. For Changlang, though the socio-economic development index improved, its relative position in 2004, in terms of human development, had a rank as low as 9th. However, among the districts, it had the minimum incidence of poverty.

It is observed that growth in the tertiary sector has the maximum bearing on overall economic growth in the state (Table 24.6). There were in fact only two districts (West Kameng and East Siang) where all the three sectors of the economy recorded positive growth. West Kameng had a high mean per capita NDDP and it had a reasonably high HDI rank (at 3). But in terms of the socio-economic performance, the district was found to have deteriorated from 1993 to 2004 and the proportion of BPL families was 49 per cent. The best district in terms of HDI rank was East Siang. Its position remained consistent in the socio-economic and agricultural fronts. However, the percentage of BPL families was 44. The position of West Siang was also noteworthy in this connection. Though, in terms of the chosen parameters of socio-economic development, the district had been consistent and performing well in terms of HDI rank, the position of the district was 5th. However, it was well in tune with its rank in terms of mean NDDP from 1993–94 to 2000–01 (at 5), though the incidence of poverty was quite high in the district with 48 per cent of the families living below poverty line.

Table 24.6: Coefficients of Correlation between Various Parameters

| | Growth Rates in | | | Rank in terms of | |
	Primary Sector	Secondary Sector	Tertiary Sector	Mean NDDP	HDI
Growth Rate of NDDP	0.27	–0.21	0.66	–	–
CDDI Rank	–	–	–	0.32	0.60
CADI Rank	–	–	–	0.22	0.56

CONCLUSION AND POLICY IMPLICATIONS

While undertaking any development initiative, especially in the socio-economic perspective, the government needs to ensure that the fruits of development spread evenly across the region and people. Existence of regional disparity, as a negative offshoot of asymmetric development, has long-ranging repercussions. Arunachal Pradesh, though a tiny state with few districts, is inhabited by a large number of tribes and sub-tribes having differences in behaviour, food habits, clothing, and other socio-economic paraphernalia. Taking into consideration geo-political identity, strategic importance, and tribal sentiments, development on a balanced footing is what is always sought for and is a prerequisite for maintaining political stability and integrity. However, the study reveals disparity and income poverty on a large scale across districts in the state, leading to inefficiency in the utilization of resources. This has led the entire economy into a vicious circle of undernourishment and underdevelopment. This has given rise to inter-tribe disputes, feuds, and social tension. A growing number of untoward incidents in the state are evidence of deterioration in social harmony in the state.

Disparities in social and physical infrastructure have much to do with lack of awareness and ignorance among the tribes. If education is the preliminary step for removal of such ignorance, provisioning of adequate dissemination of information forms the second step in generating awareness in the community. A proper telephone network along with internet facility and village knowledge centre is a pre-requisite for their advancement.

The primary sector of the state is dominated by agriculture while construction occupies the central place within the secondary sector. The tertiary sector is dominated by public administration. There have been fluctuations in the share of public administration in NSDP over the years. The state has a bulk of its income coming from public administration, which is untenable for development in the long run and to employ the unemployed youth. Private-public participation in different sectors of the economy could be an effective strategy of development, of course, without ignoring the agricultural sector. Given the huge demand for processed fruits in the world market, the state has the potential to develop its horticulture.

A number of schemes are available for financing small-scale industries in the state. What is needed is an effective implementation of such schemes. To solve the institutional problems related to marketing, cooperatives have a decisive role to play along with Panchayati Raj Institutions.

REFERENCES

Beitz, C.R. 2001. 'Does Global Inequality Matter?', in Thomas W. Pogge (ed.), *Global Justice*, Oxford, Blackwell.

Bhanumurthy, N.R. and A. Mitra 2004. 'Economic Growth, Poverty, and Inequality in Indian States in the Pre-reform and Reform Periods', *Asian Development Review*, Vol. 21, No. 2, pp.79–99.

Bhattacharjee, R.P. and N. Upadhaya 2002. 'Human Development in North-East India', in B.J. Deb (eds), *Development Priorities in North-East India*, Concept Publishing Company, New Delhi.

Bhattacharya, B.B. and S. Sakthivel 2004. 'Regional Growth and Disparity in India', *Economic and Political Weekly*, March 6, pp.1071–1077.

Cowell, F. 1995. *Measuring Inequality*, second edition, Prentice Hall/ Harvester Wheatsheaf.

Das, K. 2005. 'Can Firm Clusters Foster Non-farm Jobs? Policy Issues for Rural India', in R. Nayyar and A.N. Sharma (eds), *Rural Transformation in India: The Role of Non-farm Sector*, Institute for Human Development, New Delhi.

Drèze J. and A. Sen 1995. *India: Economic Development and Social Opportunity*, Oxford University Press.

Fedorov, L. 2002. 'Regional Inequality and Regional Polarization in Russia, 1990–99', *World Development*, Vol. 30, No. 3, pp. 443–56.

Government of Arunachal Pradesh 1993. *Statistical Abstract of Arunachal Pradesh 1993*, Itanagar. http://databank.nedfi.com/content/arunachal-pradesh

Mehta, A.K. and A. Shah 2003. 'Chronic Poverty in India: Incidence, Causes, and Policies', *World Development*, Vol. 31, No. 3, pp. 491–511.

Meier, G.M. 1995. *Leading Issues in Economic Development*, Oxford University Press, Delhi.

Milanovic, B. 1997. 'A Simple Way to Calculate the Ginni Coefficient and Some Implications', *Economic Letters*, Vol. 56, pp. 45–49.

Pyatt, G., C.N. Chen, and J. Fei 1980. 'The Distribution of Income by Factor Components', *Quarterly Journal of Economics,* Nov., pp. 451–473.

Stiglitz, J. 2002a. 'Ethics, Economic Development and Policy', a paper presented at International Meeting on Ethics and Development, in *Inter-American Development Bank*, Dec. 6–7.

——— 2002b. *Globalization and Its Discontents*, W.W. Norton, New York.

Vaidyanathan, A. 1986. 'Labour Use in Rural India: A Study of Spatial and Temporal Variations', *Economic and Political Weekly*, Vol. 21, No. 52.

25

Human Development and its Correlates in Nagaland

SUDHANSHU K. MISHRA AND PURUSOTTAM NAYAK

INTRODUCTION

Nagaland, which attained statehood in December 1963, is situated in the far north-eastern corner of India, located between 25°6'N –27°4'N and between 93°20'E–95°15'E, bound on the east by Arunachal Pradesh and Myanmar, on the north, north-west and west by Assam, and on the south by Manipur. It has a total geographical area of 16,579 sq km, and as per Census 2001, had a population of 19.9 million persons. It has a temperate climate ranging between 16°C–31°C in the winters and 4°C–24°C in the summers. Nagaland has a largely monsoon climate with high humidity levels. Annual rainfall averages around 70–100 inches, concentrated in the months of May to September.

Nagaland is largely a mountainous state. The Naga hills rise from the Brahmaputra Valley in Assam to about 2,000 feet, and rise further to the south-east, as high as 6,000 feet. Mount Saramati, at an elevation of 12,552 feet, is the state's highest peak and this is where the Naga Hills merge with the Patkai Range in Myanmar. Rivers such as the Doyang and Dhiku to the north, the Barak River in the south-west and the Chindwin river of Myanmar in the south-east, dissect the entire state. The entire state is earthquake prone (seismic zone-V). The earthquake activity in this region is due to the Indian plate diving (thrusting) beneath the Eurasian plate. This process can trigger some really hefty shocks. The state is mainly mountainous and underlain by several thrusts. Most significant are the Main Boundary Thrust, the Main Central Thrust, the Himalayan Frontal Thrust, and the Naga Thrust. The main boundary thrust forms the south-south-east trending Lohit thrust in the region of Nagaland and neighbouring parts of south-eastern Arunachal Pradesh. Earthquakes in the state are generally shallow but some intermediate focus events have also occurred in the past.

About 20 per cent of the total geographical area of Nagaland is still covered by tropical and sub-tropical evergreen forests—including palms, bamboo and *rattan*, as well as timber and mahogany forests. While some forest areas have been cleared for shifting cultivation, many scrub forests, high grass, and reeds still cover a substantial part of the land. Intermittently are located, 1,317 villages and nine towns inhabited by 16.36 million and 3.53 million people, respectively. The population belongs to numerous different Naga tribes. Nagas speak 60 different dialects, belonging to the Sino-Tibetan family of languages. Nagamese, a variant language form of Assamese and local dialects, is the most widely spoken market language. Every tribe has their own mother tongue language but communicate with each other in Nagamese. As such, Nagamese is not a mother tongue of any of the tribes, and, nor is it a written language. English, the official state language is widely spoken in the towns of Nagaland.

The state's population is 1.988 million, of which 90.02 per cent are Christians. The Census of 2001 recorded the state's Christian population at 1,790,349, making it one of the three Christian majority states in India. The state has a very high church attendance rate in both urban and rural areas. The largest of Asia's churches dominate the skylines of Kohima, Dimapur, and Mokokchung. Among Christians, Baptists are the predominant group, constituting more than 75 per cent of the state's population. Nagaland is known as 'the most populated Baptist state in the world'. About 75 per cent of the state's population professes the Baptist faith, thus, making it more Baptist than Mississippi. Catholics, Revivalists, and Pentecostals are the other Christian denomination numbers. Catholics are found in significant numbers in parts of Wokha district, as also in the urban areas of Kohima and Dimapur. Hinduism and Islam are minority religions in the state, at 7.7 per cent and 1.8 per cent of the population, respectively. A small minority, less than 0.3 per cent, still practice the traditional religions and are mainly concentrated in Peren and the eastern districts (Wikipedia).

ADMINISTRATIVE DIVISIONS OF NAGALAND

Presently, Nagaland is administratively divided into 11 districts, though initially it had only eight districts (Table 25.1).

Table 25.1: District-wise Area, Population, Number of Settlements
in Nagaland

District/ State	Area (sq. km)	Popn. (Persons)	District	Area (sq. km)	Popn. (Persons)	District/ State	Area (sq. km)	Popn. (Persons)
DMP	927	308382	Mon	1786	259604	KPR	1137	106136
KHM	1711	314366	PHK	2026	148245	WKH	1628	161098
PRN	2330	12882	TNS	2206	414801	ZBT	1255	154909
MKK	1615	227230	LNG	885	158300	Nagaland	17506	1858104

Note: These figures are compiled from different sources and may not be accurate up to 6 per cent either side; for example, Basic Statistics of NER 2002 reports area and population of Nagaland as 16579 sq km and 1988636 persons. Nagaland State Development Report 2004 data also are inconsistent.
KHM—Kohima, DMP—Dimapur, MKK—Mokokchung, TNS—Tuensang, ZBT—Zunheboto, WKH—Wokha, PHK—Phek, PRN—Peren, LNG—Longleng, KPR—Kiphire, T—Total

Dimapur is one of the districts of Nagaland with its headquarters located at Dimapur town. The district was a sub-division of the erstwhile district of Kohima and was carved out in December 1997. It is bound by Kohima district on the south and east, Karbi Anglong district of Assam on the West. Dimapur town is the commercial hub of the state, besides being referred to as the gateway to Nagaland and Manipur. A majority of the population of Dimapur is Naga tribes. Kohima is the most important district of Nagaland, as the state capital is located here. It is the centrally located district of the state, bound by the state of Assam on the west, Wokha district on the north, Zunheboto and Phek districts on the east, and Manipur state in the south. Kohima town, the administrative seat of the district, as well as of the state, is situated at an altitude of 1,444 m above sea level and is the political and cultural heart of the state. Kohima has the distinction of having the biggest Police Headquarters in the North East. Peren district came into existence as a result of the bifurcation of Kohima district. The district shares common boundaries with Assam and Dimapur district in the west and north-western part, respectively, with Kohima district in the east and Manipur state in the south. The administrative seat is situated at Peren town. Tening town is the other important town located in the district. Most of the inhabitants of this district are Zeliang and Kuki tribes. Mokokchung has its headquarters located at Mokokchung town. It is bound by the state of Assam to its north, district of Wokha to its west, Tuensang to its east, and Zunheboto to its south. The physiographic of the district consists of six distinct hill ranges.

Mokokchung district is home to the Ao Naga tribe. Kiphrie became a district as a result of the bifurcation of Tuensang district. The administrative seat is located at Kiphrie town. Longleng became a district as a result of the bifurcation of the undivided Tuensang district. The district shares common boundaries with Mon district to the north, Mokokchung district to the west and Tuensang district to the south. The district's administrative seat is at Longleng, which is situated at an altitude of about 1,066 m above sea level. Mon has its headquarters located at Mon town. The district is bound on the north by Sibsagar district of Assam, on the south by Tuensang district of Nagaland and Myanmar (Burma), on the east by Myanmar (Burma) and on the west by Tuensang and Mokokchung districts of Nagaland. On her northeast lies the Tirap district of Arunachal Pradesh. The topography of the district is hilly with steep slopes. The district can be divided into two regions, namely the upper region, comprising Longching, Chen, Mopong, and Tobu areas and the lower region comprising of Mon, Tizit, and Naginimora area. The foothills lie adjacent to the plains of Assam. Most of the people of this district live in villages and agriculture is their main occupation. They also largely depend on forests for their livelihood. Phek district is situated in the south-eastern part of the state with headquarters at Phek town. The district shares a common boundary with Myanmar in the east, Zunheboto and Tuensang districts in the north, Manipur state in the south and Kohima district in the west. Phek gets its name from the word *Phekrekedze* meaning watch tower. Earlier, it was a part of Kohima district. Most of the areas of the district are under high hills and deep forests with rich flora and fauna. Tuensang is bordered by Myanmar all along its eastern side.

On the north lies Mon district. Tuensang touches Assam on its north at a narrow strip between Mon on the east, and Mokokchung in the west. On the south of Tuensang lies Phek District and on the west are Zunheboto and Mokokchung districts. The district has approximately 180 km of international border with Myanmar. The district headquarter is located at Tuensang town. Most areas of the district are covered with hills, high ridges, deep gorges, and narrow valleys. The indigenous inhabitants of this district have mongoloid features as other Nagas. Wokha, an administrative district of Nagaland, is the home to the ancient Lothas. The district headquarters is located at Wokha town. The district is situated in the mid-western part of the Nagaland state, adjacent to the Sibsagar plains of the Assam state. It is bound by Mokokchung district in the north, Kohima district in the south, Zunheboto district in the east, and Assam in the west. The topography of the district is more or less similar to Tuensang district with hills and ridges. Zunheboto district is located in the heart of Nagaland state with headquarters at Zunheboto town. The district is bound by Mokokchung district in the East and Wokha district in the West. The topography of Zunheboto is defined by high hills spread over many areas of the district. Zunheboto is the home of the Semas.

THE ECONOMY OF NAGALAND

The economy of Nagaland is primarily forest-based and agricultural. It has very rich forest resources. Nagaland is also rich in mineral resources including coal, limestone, iron, nickel, cobalt, chromium, and marble. The approximate reserve of limestone is 1,000 million tonnes and substantial reserves of marble and decorative stone, petroleum and natural gas, nickel, cobalt, and chromium are available in the state. But these mineral resources are yet to be explored and exploited.

At present, Nagaland has an agrarian economy. About 68 per cent of the total working population of the state depends on cultivation (Table 25.2).

The main crops grown in the state include rice, millet, maize, and pulses. Cash crops, like sugarcane and potato, are also grown in some parts. Coffee, cardamom, and tea come under plantation crops, which are grown in hilly areas. A majority of the population is involved in the cultivation of rice as it is the main staple diet of the people. More than 80 per cent of the gross cropped area is under rice cultivation. A sizeable population of the state grows oilseeds, which include rapeseed, mustard, etc. There are two methods of cultivation which exist in Nagaland. The Naga tribes practice both *jhum* (shifting) and terrace cultivation. The area under jhum cultivation is about 87,339 hectares and under terraced cultivation is about 62,091 hectares. Although a majority of population is engaged in cultivation, still Nagaland depends on the import of food supplies from other states. This is due to low availability of foodgrains in the state, as the area under cultivation is low. Nagaland has achieved remarkable progress in small and medium scale industries. Today, the state has 30 industrial units, and over 300 small scale industries. The Nagaland Sugar Mill at Dimapur has an installed capacity of 1,000 tons per day. Nagas make beautiful decorative materials. Cottage industries such as weaving, woodwork, and pottery are also an important source of revenue. Tourism is

Table 25.2: Distribution of Worker Population (Census 2001)

Category	Person	Male	Female
Total Population	19,88,636	10,41,686	9,46,950
Cultivators	5,44,433	2,71,608	2,72,825
Agricultural Laborers	33,825	18,141	15,711
Total Non-workers	11,38,654	5,53,919	5,84,735
Main Workers	7,08,455	4,24,236	2,84,219
Marginal Workers	1,41,527	63,531	77,996
Workers in household Industries	18,072	6529	8,49,982
Other Workers	8,49,982	8,49,982	62,136
Total Workers	8,49,982	4,87,767	3,62,215

Source: Government of Nagaland (2007).

Table 25.3: Trends in NSDP at Factor Cost: Current and Constant (2003–04) Prices

(Rs Crore)

Year	CP	KP	Year	CP	KP	Year	CP	KP	Year	CP	KP
1980	105	372	1986	268	605	1992	811	1002	1998	2184	1605
1981	131	442	1987	349	680	1993	1251	1251	1999	2330	1614
1982	160	506	1988	424	733	1994	1457	1348	2000	3427	2230
1983	185	517	1989	477	761	1995	1656	1445	2001	3864	2385
1984	215	535	1990	579	843	1996	1849	1547	2002	4458	2641
1985	240	545	1991	691	878	1997	2137	1684	2003	4698	2785

Note: CP – Current prices, KP– Constant prices.
Source: Government of Nagaland (2007).

important, but largely limited owing to the state's geographic isolation and political instability in recent years. The major possibilities of industrial development of the state lies in food processing, bio-tech industries, tourism, floriculture, agro-forest-based industries, handloom and handicrafts, mineral-based industries, electronics and IT, sericulture, and petrochemicals.

State Domestic Product and Its Composition

In Table 25.3, we present the trends in the Net Domestic Product of the State (NDPS) for over 20 years. Except the brief period during 1997–99, when there were strong signs of stagnation, mostly due to unfavourable weather conditions, the NSDP of Nagaland has been rising continuously with added vigour. About 33 per cent of the NSDP is contributed by the primary sector and another 53 percent is due to the tertiary sector.

The secondary sector contributes only 13 per cent to the NSDP (Table 25.4).

Table 25.4: NSDP at Current price of Industry of Origin from 1999–2000 to 2003–04

Industry	1999–2000	2000–01	2001–02	2002–03	2003–04
Primary Sector	77,239	1,06,202	1,28,784	1,48,669	1,57,148
Secondary Sector	32,046	39,909	49,047	60,246	62,231
Tertiary Sector	1,46,333	1,82,491	2,09,599	2,29,274	2,50,496
Total	2,55,618	3,28,602	3,87,430	4,38,189	4,69,875
Per capita Income (Rs)	13,819	16,903	18,961	20,407	20,821

Source: Government of Nagaland (2007).

The secondary sector mainly comprises construction activities. Manufacturing makes up only a tiny sector of the economy. It contributes only 1.3 per cent to the NSDP. There are no large manufacturing units in the state. Small-scale and household industries are the only manufacturing activities. Table 25.5 presents the number of units and employment in the SSI sector.

DEMOGRAPHIC AND HEALTH ASPECTS

Growth of population in Nagaland accelerated in the 1950s and since then the population of the state is growing exponentially (Table 25.6). It appears that the population of Nagaland will surpass that of Manipur and Meghalaya in the coming decades.

Table 25.5: Small Scale Industry (No. of Units and Employment)

District	Unit/ Employees	2000–01	2001–02	2002–03	2003–04	2004–05	2005–06
Kohima including Peren	No. of SSI	49	35	39	20	24	25
	No. of Employees	335	556	512	280	161	278
Dimapur	No. of SSI	125	114	129	299	350	255
	No. of Employees	1,793	1,565	1,202	2,749	4,096	2,345
Phek	No. of SSI	6	7	2	2	25	12
	No. of Employees	35	54	16	24	264	142
Mokokchung	No. of SSI	42	66	73	44	26	17
	No. of Employees	415	678	623	509	282	204
Wokha	No. of SSI	14	11	25	12	17	13
	No. of Employees	118	117	161	135	172	178
Zunheboto	No. of SSI	38	56	60	132	84	35
	No. of Employees	441	567	380	1,252	733	312
Tuensang + Longleng + Kiphire	No. of SSI	15	12	26	57	40	51
	No. of Employees	173	132	171	427	563	452
Mon	No. of SSI	13	14	8	7	3	8
	No. of Employees	144	358	153	21	47	44

Source: Government of Nagaland (2007).

Table 25.6: Trends in Population Growth

Year	ARP*	ASM	MAN	MEG	MIZ	NAG	SKM	TRP	NER	India
1901	58	3,290	284	341	82	102	53	173	4.38	238
1911	78	3,849	346	394	91	149	63	230	5.2	252
1921	104	4,637	384	422	98	159	75	304	6.18	251
1931	139	5,560	446	481	124	179	90	382	7.4	279
1941	187	6,695	512	556	153	190	108	513	8.91	319
1951	251	8,029	578	606	196	213	129	639	10.64	361
1961	337	10,837	780	769	266	369	183	1,142	14.68	439
1971	468	14,625	1,073	1,012	332	516	247	1,556	19.83	548
1981	632	18,041	1,421	1,336	494	775	316	2,053	25.07	683
1991	865	22,414	1,837	1,775	690	1,210	406	2,757	31.95	846
2001	1,091	26,638	2,389	2,306	891	1,989	540	3,191	39.04	1,027

Notes: (1) Population figures for Arunachal Pradesh (1901–51) and Sikkim (1901–71) estimated by the authors. Population figures of the constituent States are in thousands. Population figures for NER and India are in million rounded off (and may not accurately sum up to total).
(2): ARP—Arunachal Pradesh, ASM—Assam, MAN—Manipur, MEG—Meghalaya, MIZ—Mizoram, NAG—Nagaland, SKM—Sikkim, TRP—Tripura, NER—N.E. Region.
Source: NEC (2000).

The existing and growth of health facilities (Table 25.7 and Table 25.8) in Nagaland have encouraged more and more people to take advantage of the same. Other particulars of health facilities in the state are presented in Tables 25.9 through 25.14. The data do not clearly show up any meaningful pattern.

EDUCATIONAL FACILITIES

Nagaland has a progressive educational infrastructure, both at the school as well as college level. The details are provided in Tables 25.15 through 25.22. Literacy in the state has increased very fast since 1951. Taking 1951 literacy as the base, the growth of literacy in Nagaland has been faster than any other state in the North East (Table 25.18). Growth of the educational system has also prompted private managed colleges to come up and operate profitably. As it has been mentioned earlier, Nagaland is known as the most populated Baptist state in the world. Other Christian denominations are also quite strong. Attendance in churches is very high. This is also reflected in the theological colleges thriving in the state.

Table 25.7: Number of Hospital, Dispensaries, PHC, CHC, SHC, Sub-centres, and other Health Facilities

PAR	KHM	DMP	MKK	TNS	ZBT	WKH	PHK	PHK	PRN	LNG	KPR	T
DH	1	1	1	1	1	1	1	1	1	1	1	11
CHC	3	2	3	2	2	1	3	2	1	–	1	20
PHC	12	6	11	8	9	8	17	8	4	2	–	85
SHC	2	1	–	3	3	4	2	6	4	1	1	27
DIS	–	2	5	1	1	1	3	1	–	–	1	15
TBH	1	–	1	–	–	–	–	–	–	–	–	2
MH	1	–	–	–	–	–	–	–	–	–	–	1
SC	39	47	51	39	46	37	44	50	16	9	19	397
STDC	1	1	1	1	1	1	1	1	1	1	1	11
DTC	1	–	1	1	1	1	–	1	–	–	–	6
PMC	1	1	1	1	–	–	–	–	–	–	–	4
T	62	61	75	57	64	54	71	70	27	14	24	579

Note: (1) DH—District hospital, CHC—Community health centre, PHC—Primary health centre, SHC—Subsediary health centre, DIS—Dispensaries, TBH—TB hospital, MH—Mental hospital, SC—Sub centre, STDC—STD centre, PMC—Post mortem centre.
(2) PAR—Particulars, KHM—Kohima, DMP—Dimapur, MKK—Mokokchung, TNS—Tuensang, ZBT—Zunheboto, WKH—Wokha, PHK—Phek, PRN—Peren, LNG—Longleng, KPR—Kiphire, T—Total
Source: Government of Nagaland (2007).

Table 25.8: Number of Hospital, Dispensaries, PHCs, CHC, SHC,
Sub-centres, and other Health Facilities (2005)

PAR	KHM	DMP	MKK	TNS	ZBT	WKH	PHK	PHK	PRN	LNG	KPR	T
2001												
Doctor	121	58	49	38	26	26	28	20	–	–	–	366
Pharm	68	35	63	99	54	49	60	69	–	–	–	497
Nurse	255	165	243	166	103	84	65	35	–	–	–	1,116
2002												
Doctor	121	59	49	38	26	26	28	20	–	–	–	367
Pharm	69	35	63	99	53	49	60	69	–	–	–	497
Nurse	282	120	203	205	123	100	134	111	–	–	–	1,278
2003												
Doctor	122	59	51	38	26	26	28	20	–	–	–	370
Pharm	69	35	63	102	55	49	61	71	–	–	–	505
Nurse	269	134	205	218	109	95	113	89	–	–	–	1,232
2004												
Doctor	122	60	51	38	26	26	29	20	–	–	–	372
Pharm	60	39	62	47	39	48	38	40	–	–	–	373
Nurse	277	130	206	196	114	98	110	94	–	–	–	1,225
2005												
Doctor	120	46	51	41	26	26	26	29	13	3	3	384
Pharm	69	43	61	47	39	47	39	67	20	9	16	457
Nurse	252	149	222	184	123	113	141	114	42	20	33	1,393

Note: Pharm—Pharmacist, PAR—Particulars, KHM—Kohima, DMP—Dimapur, MKK—
Mokokchung, TNS—Tuensang, ZBT—Zunheboto, WKH—Wokha, PHK—Phek, PRN—
Peren, LNG—Longleng, KPR—Kiphire, T—Total
Source: Government of Nagaland (2007).

Table 25.9: Number of Beds in Hospital, PHC, CHC, SHC, Dispensaries,
Mental, and TB Hospital (2005)

	KHM	DMP	MKK	TNS	ZBT	WKH	PHK	PHK	PRN	LNG	KPR	T
DH	250	150	150	100	50	50	75	50	50	50	50	1,025
CHC	90	60	90	60	60	30	90	60	30	30	-	600
PHC	72	36	84	72	84	66	144	60	30	12	12	642
SHC	12	2	-	10	6	8	4	12	-	-	-	54
DIS	-	4	10	4	2	2	6	2	-	-	-	30
TBH	50	-	50	-	-	-	-	-	-	-	-	100
MH	25	-	-	-	-	-	-	-	-	-	-	25
LW	-	-	-	20	-	-	-	20	-	-	-	40
T	499	252	384	266	202	156	289	204	110	92	62	2,516

Note: DH—District hospital, CHC—Community health centre, PHC—Primary health
centre, SHC—Subsediary health centre, DIS—Dispensaries, TBH—TB hospital, MH—
Mental hospital, LW—Leprosy ward, T—Total
Source: Government of Nagaland (2007).

Table 25.10: Patients Treated in Hospitals and Dispensaries

Particulars	KHM	DMP	MKK	TNS	ZBT	WKH	PHK	Mon	T
Year 2001									
Indoor	18,215	18,355	12,793	13,826	6,730	6,695	5,588	5,948	88,150
Outdoor	93,907	96,954	67,555	21,996	50,096	41,565	26,656	33,480	6,26,209
Year 2002									
Indoor	24,765	25,032	14,464	16,158	7,413	8,834	6,746	6,326	1,09,738
Outdoor	1,36,345	1,50,106	97,064	77,804	48,802	47,964	29,892	35,641	6,23,618
Year 2003									
Indoor	26,616	25,549	12,960	15,446	7,825	8,345	6,902	6,561	1,10,204
Outdoor	1,61,903	15,998	97,250	74,438	48,265	48,632	19,013	36,576	6,40,075
Year 2004									
Indoor	26,624	25,716	13,972	15,614	8,114	8,706	7,126	6,909	1,12,781
Outdoor	1,49,836	1,52,385	97,324	74,749	48,559	5,009	29,001	36,845	5,93,708
Year 2005									
Indoor	25,802	27,704	20,375	17,721	11,667	14,462	9,459	12,144	1,39,334
Outdoor	1,16,628	1,16,245	86,047	84,753	60,577	55,553	48,698	47,382	6,15,888

Note: KHM—Kohima, DMP—Dimapur, MKK—Mokokchung, TNS—Tuensang, ZBT—Zunheboto, WKH—Wokha, PHK—Phek, PRN—Peren, LNG—Longleng, KPR—Kiphire, T—Total

Source: Government of Nagaland (2007).

Table 25.11: District-wise Distribution of Doctors with Designations (2005)

Particulars	KHM	DMP	MKK	TNS	ZBT	WKH	PHK	Mon	PRN	LNG	KPR	T
MS	2	1	2	1	1	1	1	1	–	–	–	10
CS	1	1	1	1	1	1	1	1	1	1	1	11
ACS	1	–	1	1	–	–	–	–	–	–	–	3
SMO	–	–	–	–	–	–	–	–	1	1	1	3
SPL	35	16	4	–	1	2	1	1	–	–	–	60
AS	52	21	36	33	20	20	22	22	12	2	2	242
DS	5	3	3	1	1	1	1	1	1	–	–	17
ZLO	1	1	–	1	–	–	–	1	–	–	–	4
DTBO	1	–	1	1	1	–	–	1	–	–	–	5
ZMO	1	–	1	1	1	–	–	1	–	–	–	5
LMO	1	1	1	–	–	–	–	–	–	–	–	3
DIO	1	–	1	1	1	1	–	1	–	–	–	6
SDMO(H)	1	1	–	–	1	1	1	1	–	–	–	6
GEN	14	–	–	–	–	–	–	–	–	–	–	14
Total	116	45	51	41	28	27	27	31	15	4	4	389

Note (1): KHM—Kohima, DMP—Dimapur, MKK—Mokokchung, TNS—Tuensang, ZBT—Zunheboto, WKH—Wokha, PHK—Phek, PRN—Peren, LNG—Longleng, KPR—Kiphire, T—Total

(2): MS—Medical Superintendent, CS—Civil Surgeon, ACS—Asstt. Civil Surgeon, Sub-divisional Medical Officer, SPL—Specialist, AS—Asst. Surgeon, DS—Dental Surgeon, ZLO—Zonal Leprosy Officer, DTBO—Dist. T.B. Officer, ZMO—Zonal Malaria Officer, LMO—Leprosy Medical Officer, District Immunization Officer, GEN—Generalist in Directorate.

Source: Government of Nagaland (2007).

Table 25.12: Registration of Births and Deaths (2005)

Particular	Rural	Urban	Total
(i) Live Births Registered, 2005:			
Persons	24,595	22,684	47,279
Males	12,960	10,922	23,882
Females	11,635	11,762	23,397
(ii) Death Registered, 2005:			
Persons	3,383	2,966	6,349
Males	2,091	1,575	3,666
Females	1,292	1,391	2,683
(iii) Infant Death Registered, 2005	66	43	109
(iv) Maternal Deaths Registered, 2005	43	31	74

Source: Government of Nagaland (2007).

HUMAN DEVELOPMENT IN NAGALAND

In Tables 25.23(A) and 25.23(B), we present the indicators of human development and the Human Development Index (HDI) of Nagaland for the year 2001. These figures have been obtained from the State Government of Nagaland 2004, published by the Government of Nagaland. However, the indicators and the HDI index relate to the Year 2001.

The figures on HDI in Table 25.23(B) indicate that Dimapur leads, while Mon lags behind all other districts. Except Zunheboto, Tuensang, and Mon, all other districts score higher than the state average. Kohima has the 4th rank, although the state capital is located there.

Gender-related Development Indicators (GDRI) are presented in Tables 24(A) and 24(B). The GDI Index for Kohima, Table 24(B), is the highest, followed by Dimapur, Mokukchung, and Phek. Mon ranks the last in GRDI ranking. Tuensang and Zunheboto are a little better but below the state average.

Relationship Between Human Poverty and Human Development Indices

In Table 25.25, we present the Human Poverty Index (HPI) for different districts of Nagaland.

These figures are obtained from the SHDR (2004) published by the Government of Nagaland. We find that Mon and Tuensang are the two districts with very high HPI indices. Phek also is higher than the state average. Mokokchung has the lowest human poverty index,

Table 25.13: Vital Rates (per 1000 Persons) by Districts

District/State	Live Birth Rate					Live Death Rate					Infant Death Rate				
	2001	2002	2003	2004	2005	2001	2002	2003	2004	2005	2001	2002	2003	2004	2005
KHM	30.2	34.2	24.2	30.4	35.3	2.3	3.3	2.3	3.2	3.7	1.9	1.6	1.9	1.8	1.6
DMP	25.6	30.5	25.3	29.1	26.5	3.8	4.9	3.8	4.6	4.2	2.5	2.4	3.2	2.9	2.7
MKK	14.3	20.1	17.9	20.8	17.6	1.9	3.3	2.8	3.1	2.6	3.4	1.5	2.9	2.9	2.4
TNS	11.5	13.8	10.4	12.1	21.3	1.6	2.0	1.3	1.7	2.9	4.9	2.7	2.3	2.4	1.8
PHK	26.8	37.1	22.3	29.5	21.9	5.5	6.3	3.4	4.4	3.3	5.2	3.2	3.2	3.3	2.8
WKH	24.7	26.2	21.0	26.3	21.0	3.1	4.5	2.7	3.3	2.7	3.5	2.4	1.8	2.0	1.5
ZBT	16.1	25.5	20.2	28.2	21.4	3.6	4.0	2.4	3.3	2.8	5.9	2.9	2.0	2.3	1.2
Mon	18.7	24.7	14.7	18.2	14.0	2.7	3.6	1.8	2.5	1.9	4.1	3.6	2.8	3.1	1.4
PRN	–	–	–	–	4.1	–	–	–	–	0.4	–	–	–	–	8.8
LNG	–	–	–	–	2.9	–	–	–	–	0.3	–	–	–	–	13.9
KPR	–	–	–	–	3.2	–	–	–	–	0.3	–	–	–	–	20.3
NAG	20.5	25.2	18.8	23.3	19.47	–	–	–	–	2.6					

Note: KHM—Kohima, DMP—Dimapur, MKK—Mokokchung, TNS—Tuensang, ZBT—Zunheboto, WKH—Wokha, PHK—Phek, PRN—Peren, LNG—Longleng, KPR—Kiphire, T—Total, NAG—Nagaland

Source: Government of Nagaland (2007).

Table 25.14: Progress of Family Welfare Programme

Sl. No.	Description	2002–03	2003–04	2004–05	2005–06
1.	Family Planning Method				
	(i) Sterilisation	1,152	1,148	754	1,195
	(ii) I.U.D. Insertion	6,792	3,654	1,749	2,180
	C.C. Users	22,551	21,476	22,525	48,739
	Oral Pills Users	37,456	15,166	10,052	7,928
2.	M.C.H. Activities				
	(i) Tetanus immunisation for expectant Mother	22,143	20,817	21,504	26,363
	(ii) D.P.T. Immunisation for Children	11,954	17,239	16,827	20,872
	(iii) Polio	14,812	18,331	18,845	22,576
	(iv) B.C.G. Achievement	16,476	17,442	17,741	23,971
3.	M.C.H. Activities				
	(i) Measles Vaccination Programme	10,615	11,255	13,126	18,964

Source: Government of Nagaland (2007).

followed by Zunheboto and Wokha. Dimaur and Kohima have HPI lower than the state average, but not far lower.

The robust Campbell type-II (see Campbell 1980, Mishra 2008) correlation coefficient (not affected by outliers) between HPI and HDI is –0.70 and that between HPI and GDI is –0.72, both negative and statistically significant. This relationship indicates that human poverty is negatively correlated with HDI and GDI. It may be noted that Campbell's correlation matrix is a multivariate measure and not a bivariate measure (like Karl Pearson's correlation).

We have computed bivariate Karl Pearson and some other correlation matrices (Mishra 2008, Shevlyakov 1997) from the data presented in Table 25.26. Some points are worth noting.

First, the life expectancy has a negative correlation with all other variables including PCI, HDI, and GDI, irrespective of the formula used for computing the correlation coefficient (Table 25.27). What type of conclusion may follow from this and what policy implication can follow? Or, can we say that all measures of correlation are inconsequential and irrelevant? Secondly, PCI, HDI, and GDI are only poorly correlated with the health indicators such as IMR, IMRM, and IMRF. Only the measures of educational attainment are appreciably correlated with PCI, HDI, and GDI. But are the measures of educational attainment really correlated with the economic efficiency and performance of the economy? Do they go along with the measures of health attainment of the population?

Table 25.15: District-wise Number of Schools (2006)

District	Higher Secondary Schools			High Schools			Middle Schools			Primary Schools		
	Govt.	Pvt.	Total	Govt.	Pvt.	Total	Govt.	Pvt.	Total	Govt.	Pvt.	Total
Kohima	1	8	9	21	64	85	36	40	76	196	40	236
Dimapur	1	9	10	11	56	67	23	25	48	190	36	226
Phek	1	1	2	18	13	31	31	33	64	109	32	131
Wokha	1	1	2	8	15	23	17	17	34	102	10	112
Zunheboto	1	3	4	12	15	27	29	25	54	158	12	170
Mokokchung	2	3	5	15	24	39	37	27	64	171	16	187
Tuensang	1	-	1	22	17	39	55	36	91	268	36	304
Mon	1	-	1	9	12	21	38	15	53	125	18	143
Total	9	25	34	116	216	332	266	218	484	1,319	190	1,509

Source: Government of Nagaland (2007).

Table 25.16: Number of Teachers in Different Types of Schools

Institutions	2002–2003			2003–2004			2004–2005			2005–2006		
	M	F	P	M	F	P	M	F	P	M	F	P
PS	5,188	3,001	8,189	4,896	2,578	7,474	5,159	2,968	8,127	4,985	2,963	7,948
MS	3,076	2,163	5,239	3,775	1,590	5,365	3,921	2,375	6,296	3,871	2,361	6,232
HS	3,895	2,333	6,228	3,962	2,321	6,283	3,904	2,523	6,427	3,905	2,556	6,461
HSS	642	665	1,307	752	767	1,519	856	901	1,757	1,014	1,039	2,053
Total	12,801	8,162	20,963	13,385	7,256	20,641	13,840	8,767	22,607	13,775	8,919	22,694

Note: M—Male, F—Female, P—Person, PS—Primary School, MS—Middle School, HS—High School, HSS—Higher Secondary School
Source: Government of Nagaland (2007).

Table 25.17: State Government Expenditure on Different
Types of School (Rs Lakh)

Institutions	2001–02	2002–03	2003–04	2004–05	2005–06
PS	6,174.96	6,546.96	6,938.00	8,868.09	9,667.40
MS	4,723.17	52,138.70	6,154.23	6,616.48	7,033.10
HS	3,480.96	3,708.89	3,930.53	4,026.82	4,163.77
HSS	895.92	9,021.21	912.51	1,814.17	1,902.65

Note: PS—Primary School, MS—Middle School, HS—High School, HSS—Higher
Secondary School
Source: Government of Nagaland (2007).

Table 25.18: Trends in State-Wise Literacy Rates
(Percent) in North-Eastern States

State	1951*	1961*	1971*	1981*	1991*	2001*
SKM	–	–	17.74	34.05	56.94	68.81
ARP	NA	7.13	11.29	25.55	41.59	54.34
NAG	10.52	21.95	33.78	50.28	61.65	66.59
MAN	12.57	36.04	38.47	49.66	59.89	70.53
MIZ	31.14	44.01	53.8	59.88	82.26	88.8
TRP	NA	20.24	30.98	50.1	60.44	73.19
MEG	NA	26.92	29.49	42.05	49.1	62.56
ASM	18.53	32.95	33.94	–	52.89	63.25
INDIA	18.33	28.3	34.45	43.57	52.21	64.84

Note: * = for population 5+ years; ** for population 7+ years
Source: http://indiabudget.nic.in/es2005-06/chapt2006/tab94.pdf

Table 25.19: Gender-wise Literacy Rates in the States of
North-Eastern Region

	Male			Female				Male			Female		
State	1981	1991	2001	1981	1991	2001	State	1981	1991	2001	1981	1991	2001
ARP	35.1	51.5	52.7	14.0	29.7	35.8	MAN	64.2	71.6	67.6	34.7	47.6	51.9
MEG	46.7	53.1	53.0	37.2	44.9	48.2	MIZ	79.4	85.6	76.5	68.6	78.6	72.2
NAG	58.6	67.6	62.0	40.4	54.7	52.9	SKM	53.0	65.7	–	27.4	46.7	–
TRP	61.5	70.7	70.7	38.0	49.6	56.6	India	56.5	64.2	64.0	29.9	39.2	45.7

Sources: (1) http://www.education.nic.in/cd50years/g/Z/7G/0Z7G0501.htm
(2) NEC (2002).

Table 25.20: Number of Institutions of Higher Education

Educational Institutions	2000–01			2001–02			2002–03			2003–04		
	Govt.	Pvt.	Total	Govt.	Pvt.	Total	Govt.	Pvt.	Total	Govt.	Pvt.	Total
University	1	–	1	1	–	1	1	–	1	1	–	1
College of Gen. Education	8	27	35	8	28	36	8	28	36	8	30	38
Nagaland College of Teachers Education	1	–	1	1	–	1	1	–	1	1	–	1
Agriculture College	1	–	1	1	–	1	1	–	1	1	–	1
Theology	–	13	13	–	14	14	–	14	14	–	14	14
Polytechnics	2	–	2	2	–	2	2	–	2	2	–	2
Institution of Communication and Information Technology	–	–	–	–	–	–	–	–	–	1	–	1
Law College	–	3	3	–	3	3	–	3	3	–	3	3
Total	13	43	56	13	45	58	13	45	58	14	47	61

Source: Economic Survey 2003–04 of Nagaland.

Table 25.21: Details of the Institutions of Higher Education

Sl. No	Classification of Colleges	Number	Teachers/Lectrs	Students	Streams
A.	Government Colleges and Polytechnics	11	315	3577	
B.	Privately Managed Colleges (Govt. Aided/Not-Aided)	31	554	17731	
C.	Theological Colleges	24	NA	NA	
D.	Law Colleges	3	16	322	

Source: Government of Nagaland (2007).

Table 25.22: Growth of Enrolment in the Institutions of Higher Education (General)

Classification of Colleges (General Education)	Total Number of Students. (1999–2004)					Growth rate	
	1999–2000	2000–01	2001–02	2002–03	2003–04	Student per year	Annual Average
Government Colleges	3879	4136	3340	3178	3543	–84	–1.73
Private Management Colleges	14,004	13,683	14,251	15,263	16,776	+693	+3.96

Source: Jamir (2006).

Table 25.23 (A): Indicators of Human Development (2001)

District	PCGDP	IMR	IIMR	LE	ILE	LR	IL	ER	IE
DMP	16,837	37.5	0.781	73.4	0.78	78.15	0.78	0.8	0.80
MKK	12,305	35.05	0.821	72.3	0.743	84.27	0.84	0.627	0.88
WKH	13,647	47.42	0.657	68.6	0.619	80.56	0.8	0.545	0.87
KHM	11,906	37.9	0.776	73.2	0.772	74.28	0.74	0.852	0.80
PHK	9,880	29.22	0.885	74.2	0.807	71.35	0.71	0.783	0.75
ZBT	8,372	31.53	0.856	73.6	0.786	69.73	0.7	0.731	0.72
TNS	8,149	41.3	0.734	70.8	0.693	51.3	0.51	0.396	0.54
Mon	4,500	27.1	0.911	75	0.833	42.25	0.42	0.491	0.48
NAG	11,119	40	0.75	73.4	0.779	67.11	0.7	0.636	0.64

Notes: (1) KHM—Kohima, DMP—Dimapur, MKK—Mokokchung, TNS—Tuensang, ZBT—Zunheboto, WKH—Wokha, PHK—Phek, PRN—Peren, LNG—Longleng, KPR—Kiphire, NAG—Nagaland

(2) PCGDP—Per Capita GDP, IIMR—Index of IMR, LE—Life Expectancy, Index of Life Expectancy, LR—Literacy rate, IL—Index of Literacy, ER—Enrollment rate, IE—Index of Enrollment

Source: Government of Nagaland (2004).

Table 25.23 (B): Human Development Index (2001)

District	Index for Per Capita GDP	Combined Index for Educational Attainment	Combined Index for Health Attainment	Human Development Index
DMP	0.624	0.793	0.781	0.733
MKK	0.483	0.866	0.767	0.705
WKH	0.530	0.846	0.632	0.669
KHM	0.468	0.779	0.773	0.673
PHK	0.384	0.736	0.834	0.651
ZBT	0.310	0.713	0.811	0.611
TNS	0.298	0.530	0.708	0.512
Mon	0.031	0.459	0.861	0.450
NAG	0.438	0.661	0.769	0.623

Note (1): KHM—Kohima, DMP—Dimapur, MKK—Mokokchung, TNS—Tuensang, ZBT—Zunheboto, WKH—Wokha, PHK—Phek, PRN—Peren, LNG—Longleng, KPR—Kiphire, NAG—Nagaland
Source: Government of Nagaland (2004).

CONCLUSION

Discussing on the relevance of income as a representative measure of development, Simon Kuznets observed that the reliability of data reported by a socio-economic system is dependent on the level of development of the system. Underdeveloped socio-economic systems report highly unreliable data. This is not only regarding the figures of income, but also true of the figures on measures of attainment in matters of health and education. Official data on these variables are thrown up by a system that is administratively motivated and unsupervised with regard to their economic and developmental meaning. Use of such data, whether it pertains to income or any other measure of development, is not dependable for policy decisions meaningful to fostering development.

Table 25.24 (A): Indicators of Gender Related Development (2001)

District/State	FML	FMW	FYY	MYY	AY	AGDP	LEM	LEF	ERM	ERF	LM	LF
DMP	0.23	0.89	0.17	0.83	0.30	5,038.83	0.875	0.733	0.813	0.785	0.822	0.733
MKK	0.70	0.95	0.40	0.60	0.48	5,957.76	0.788	0.792	0.651	0.603	0.861	0.822
WKH	0.74	0.89	0.40	0.60	0.48	6,596.53	0.750	0.703	0.557	0.532	0.857	0.765
KHM	0.69	0.82	0.36	0.64	0.47	5,555.59	0.875	0.733	0.919	0.787	0.814	0.666
PHK	0.86	0.80	0.41	0.59	0.49	4,801.92	0.850	0.792	0.804	0.761	0.790	0.631
ZBT	0.84	0.90	0.43	0.57	0.49	4,115.95	0.875	0.743	0.715	0.749	0.734	0.658
TNS	0.82	0.82	0.40	0.60	0.49	3,954.42	0.875	0.645	0.355	0.442	0.560	0.461
Mon	0.71	0.79	0.36	0.64	0.47	2,114.72	0.875	0.792	0.491	0.490	0.467	0.371
NAG	0.67	0.86	0.37	0.63	0.47	5,203.00	0.863	0.738	0.641	0.630	0.718	0.619

Notes: FML=Ratio of female workers to male workers; FMW=Ratio of female wage rate to male wage rate; FYY=Share of female in total earned income; MYY=Share of male in total earned income; AY=Correction factor for adjusted income; AGDP=Adjusted GDP; LEM=Index of Male Life Expectancy; LEF=Index of Female Life Expectancy; ERM=Index of Male Enrollment Ratio; ERF=Index of Female Enrollment Ratio; LM=Male Literacy Index; LF=Female Literacy Index.

Source: Government of Nagaland (2004).

Table 25.24 (B): Components of Gender Related Development and GDI Index (2001)

District/ State	Adjusted Per Capita GDP	Combined Literacy Index	Combined Enrollment Index	Combined Education Index	Combined Life Expectancy	Combined Health Index	Gender Related Development Index
DMP	0.091	0.778	0.800	0.792	0.803	0.52	0.472
MKK	0.175	0.842	0.627	0.702	0.790	0.51	0.460
WKH	0.226	0.810	0.545	0.637	0.727	0.47	0.448
KHM	0.140	0.737	0.852	0.811	0.802	0.80	0.580
PHK	0.067	0.705	0.783	0.755	0.821	0.53	0.450
ZBT	−0.010	0.695	0.731	0.718	0.806	0.52	0.414
TNS	−0.030	0.508	0.392	0.432	0.748	0.49	0.299
Mon	−0.343	0.417	0.491	0.465	0.834	0.54	0.220
NAG	0.107	0.664	0.633	0.644	0.796	0.52	0.420

Source: Government of Nagaland (2004).

Table 25.25: Components of Human Poverty and the Human Poverty
Index (2001)

District	ED1	ED2	P2	P31	P32	P33	P34	P3	HPI
DMP	0.22	0.20	20.70	0.029	0.645	0.373	0.335	34.536	29.252
MKK	0.16	0.12	13.40	0.067	0.617	0.230	0.034	23.721	19.897
WKH	0.20	0.13	15.45	0.064	0.634	0.220	0.402	32.990	27.052
KHM	0.26	0.20	22.10	0.101	0.499	0.501	0.479	39.500	33.084
PHK	0.29	0.25	26.40	0.066	0.729	0.548	0.620	49.081	40.880
ZBT	0.30	0.28	28.70	0.092	0.095	0.428	0.133	18.725	24.718
TNS	0.49	0.46	47.05	0.077	0.954	0.451	0.549	50.766	48.979
Mon	0.58	0.52	54.10	0.071	0.040	0.780	0.820	42.778	49.092
NAG	0.30	0.36	33.90	0.071	0.547	0.437	0.430	37.119	35.583

Notes: P1: Health Deprivation Index (data not available); P2: Combined Educational Deprivation Index; ED1: Illiteracy rate; ED2: Proportion in 2001 not enrolled in schools P31: Proportion of people below poverty line.
Source: DES; P32: Proportion of children denied basic medical facilities at birth. Proxied by immunization measured as DPT (1st shot); P33: Proportion of people with kutcha houses. Source: DES Survey, 2003; P34: Proportion of population without own toilet. Source: DES Survey, 2003; HPI=Human Poverty Index.

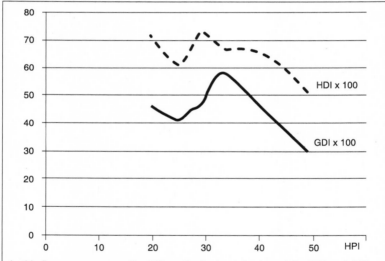

In this figure we measure the HPI on the horizontal axis and the HDI and GDI on the vertical scale. The vertical axis is scaled up by a factor of 100. We do not obtain any clear relationship between human poverty index (HPI) and human development index (HDI) or GDI. The Karl Pearson correlation coefficient between HPI and HDI is −0.797 and that between HPI and GDI is −0.666 although only weakly significant.

Figure 25.1: Relationship of HDI and GDI with Human Poverty Index

Table 25.26: Some Major Indicators of Development

	PCY	HDI	GDI	IMR	IMRM	IMRF	LIT	MLIT	FLIT	LEXP
DMP	16,837	0.733	0.472	37.7	28.0	48.5	78.15	82.15	73.34	73.4
MKK	12,305	0.705	0.460	35.05	40.8	28.0	84.27	86.14	82.2	72.5
WKH	13,647	0.669	0.448	47.42	48.0	46.8	81.28	85.69	76.46	68.5
KHM	11,905	0.674	0.49	37.9	28.0	48.5	74.28	81.44	66.64	73.2
PHK	9,880	0.652	0.46	29.22	29.6	28.8	71.35	78.97	63.08	74.2
ZBT	8,372	0.611	0.41	31.53	25.6	37.8	69.73	73.43	65.8	73.6
TNS	8,149	0.512	0.30	41.3	25.5	58.5	51.3	55.97	46.12	70.8
Mon	4,500	0.450	0.23	27.1	25.6	28.8	42.25	46.70	37.12	75.0

Note: PCY—Per Capita Income; IMR—Infant Mortality; IMRM—IMR Male; IMRF—IMR Female; LIT—Literacy Rate; MLIT—Literacy Rate Male; FLIT—Literacy Rate Female; LEXP—Life Expectancy.
Source: Government of Nagaland (2004).

Table 25.27: Types of Correlation among Major Indicators of Development and Life Expectancy

Correlation Type	PCI	HDI	GDI	IMR	IMRM	IMRF	LITR	MLIT	FLIT
Pearson	−0.370	−0.183	−0.159	−0.930	−0.701	−0.568	−0.321	−0.299	−0.341
Spearman	−0.452	−0.333	−0.190	−0.929	−0.357	−0.452	−0.548	−0.548	−0.571
Shevlyakov	−0.749	−0.109	−0.286	−0.864	−0.175	−0.694	−0.174	−0.484	−0.143

Notes: PCI—Per Capita Income; HDI—Human Development Index; GDI—Gender Related Development Index; IMR—Infant Mortality Rate; IMRM—IMR for Male; IMRF—IMR for Female; LITR—Literacy Rate; MLIT—Literacy Rate for Male; FLIT—Literacy Rate for Female.

REFERENCES

Campbell, N.A. 1980. 'Robust Procedures in Multivariate Analysis I: Robust Covariance Estimation', *Applied Statistics*, Vol. 29, No. 3, pp. 231–37.

Government of Nagaland, 2004. *Nagaland State Human Development Report 2004*, Department of Planning and Coordination, Government of Nagaland, Kohima.

——— 2007. *Statistical Handbook of Nagaland 2006*, Department of Economics and Statistics, Government of Nagaland, Kohima.

Jamir, Temjenzulu 2006. *Economics of Higher Education: Micro Analysis of Private Colleges in Nagaland*, unpublished Ph.D. Dissertation, Department of Economics, NEHU, Shillong.

Literacy Rates for States and Union Territories. http://www.education.nic.in/ cd50years/g/Z/7G/0Z7G0501.htm

Mehta, A.C. 2005. 'Dropout Rate at Primary Level: A Note based on DISE 2003–04 and 2004–05 Data', National Institute of Educational Planning and Administration, New Delhi. http:// educationforallinindia.com/Dropoutrates 2003–04&2004–05.pdf

Mishra, S. K. 2008. 'On Construction of Robust Composite Indices by Linear Aggregation', SSRN, http://ssrn.com/abstract=1147964

Mitra, A. and P. Singh 2007. 'Trends in Literacy Rates and Schooling among the Scheduled Tribe Women in India', http://www.ou.edu/ cas/econ/wppdf/trendsinliteracyper cent20am.pdf

North-Eastern Council (NEC) 2000 and 2002. *Basic Statistics of North-Eastern Region*, Ministry of Home Affairs, Government of India, Shillong.

Shevlyakov, G.L. 1997. 'On Robust Estimation of a Correlation Coefficient', *Journal of Mathematical Sciences*, Vol. 83, No. 3, pp. 434–38.

Selected Educational Statistics 2003–04. http://education.nic.in/stats/ detail/18.pdf

State-wise Literacy Rates, 1951–2001. S-114. at http://indiabudget.nic.in/ es2005–06/chapt2006/tab94.pdf

Contributors

KINGSHUK ADHIKARI, Faculty Member, Department of Commerce, Cachar College, Silchar, Assam. adhikari_lecturer@rediffmail.com

A.K. AGARWAL, Professor, Department of Economics, Mizoram University, Aizawl, Mizoram. akg_49@yahoo.co.in

ARINDAM BANIK, Professor, International Management Institute, New Delhi. arindambanik@imi.edu

APURBA K. BARUAH, Professor and Head, Department of Political Science, North-Eastern Hill University, Shillong, Meghalaya. akbaruah2000@yahoo.com

M.P. BEZBARUAH, Professor, Department of Economics, Gauhati University, Guwahati, Assam. ranab1@sancharnet.in

PRADIP K. BHAUMIK, Professor, International Management Institute, New Delhi. pkbhaumik@imi.edu

SAUNDARJYA BORBORA, Associate Professor, Department of Humanities and Social Sciences, IIT, Guwahati, Assam. sborbora@iitg.ernet.in

P.K. CHAUBEY, Professor, Indian Institute of Public Administration, New Delhi. pkchaubey@yahoo.com

ASHUTOSH DASH, Assistant Professor, Rajiv Gandhi Indian Institute of Management, Shillong, Meghalaya. Email: reachdashu@gmail.com

R. GOPINATH, Project Associate, Food Security Studies, M.S. Swaminathan Research Foundation, Chennai, Tamil Nadu. gopidina@gmail.com

PAOHULEN KIPGEN, Research Scholar, Department of Economics, North-Eastern Hill University, Shillong, Meghalaya.

BHABAGRAHI MISHRA, Assistant Professor, Department of Economics, Sambalpur University, Sambalpur, Orissa. bhabagrahi_mishra@yahoo.co.in

BISWAMBHARA MISHRA, Professor and Head, Department of Economics, North-Eastern Hill University, Shillong, Meghalaya. bmishra_nehu@hotmail.com

SUDHANSHU K. MISHRA, Professor, Department of Economics, North-Eastern Hill University, Shillong, Meghalaya. mishrasknehu@gmail.com

PURUSOTTAM NAYAK, Professor of Economics and Dean, School of Economics Management and Information Sciences, North-Eastern Hill University, Shillong, Meghalaya. nehu_pnayak@yahoo.co.in

DEBASIS NEOGI, Assistant Professor, NIT, Agartala, Tripura. dneogi70@yahoo.co.in

BHAGIRATHI PANDA, Reader, Department of Economics, North-Eastern Hill University, Shillong, Meghalaya. bhagirathi2@yahoo.co.in

BISWAMBHAR PANDA, Reader, Department of Sociology, North-Eastern Hill University, Shillong, Meghalaya. bpanda@iitk.ac.in

A.P. PATI, Reader, Department of Commerce, North-Eastern Hill University, Shillong, Meghalaya. apatiau@yahoo.com

KISHOR SINGH RAJPUT, Faculty Member, Department of Economics, St. Anthony's College, Shillong, Meghalaya. ks_rajput@yahoo.co.in

SANTANU RAY, Research Scholar, Department of Economics, North-Eastern Hill University, Shillong, Meghalaya. santanurayeco@rediffmail.com

HIRANMOY ROY, Faculty Member, Department of Economics, Karimganj College, Karimganj, Assam. hroy_au@yahoo.com

E. BIJOYKUMAR SINGH, Professor, Department of Economics, Manipur University, Imphal, Manipur. elangbambksingh@yahoo.co.in

NIRANKAR SRIVASTAV, Professor, Department of Economics, North-Eastern Hill University, Shillong, Meghalaya. nirankarsrivastav@yahoo.com

P.S. SURESH, Reader, Department of Economics, North-Eastern Hill University, Shillong, Meghalaya. sureshps03@yahoo.co.in

P.K. TRIPATHY, Professor, Department of Economics, Sambalpur University, Jyoti Vihar, Sambalpur, Orissa. pktripathy55@yahoo.co.in